COSMIC CHRIST WORLD LIGHT SHIELD

WILLIAM E. CAMILLERI

Order this book online at www.trafford.com
or email orders@trafford.com

Most Trafford titles are also available at major online book retailers.

First published in 2010
© Copyright 2022 William E. Camilleri.

Print information available on the last page.

ISBN: 978-1-4907-8484-7 (sc)
ISBN: 978-1-4907-8483-0 (e)

Trafford rev. 06/24/2022

 www.trafford.com

North America & international
toll-free: 844-688-6899 (USA & Canada)
fax: 812 355 4082

DEDICATION

**This work is dedicated to
the Cosmic Christ Jesus,
Son of the Living God, Light of all Ages.**

Cosmic Christ World Light Shield

Table of Contents

COSMIC CHRIST WORLD LIGHT SHIELD
CHAPTER 1

I had a beginning. The world had a beginning. The Truth is the beginning of seeing the Light. The Light created the world. I was created by the Light. The Truth gave me the pathway to it and to seeing how the world was created cosmically in this way.

The Light is the living power in the universe that makes my being and all mankind a part of it. It is first like a seed that grows in the ground in the darkness of the night and then shines like a golden rose glistening in the morning sunrise. This rose of Light outshines the darkness and its rays reach every human heart and every living being in the world. [Verse 1] [1]

The Light is the cause of all causes. Its effect is in the individual who follows the Truth. It reaches the Soul of man when a man opens his heart to it. Then the rays of Light will reach his Soul. John the Baptist was such a man. He spoke of the Light to come to the world. He asked the world to believe in this Light. I now see that I also can see that I am speaking of this Ultimate Light as the source of my Light in this life. I also see that the source of it is not me as before I can reach this Ultimate Light I need to have the Ultimate Truth in what I live. I need to know how to live my Truth in the Light. This Ultimate Light I saw coming to the world when I looked to it to guide me to know the Truth of the world. I see now with the Eyes of this Light I can see the Ultimate Truth and my Truth.
[Verse 2] [2]

The world was created by the Light. Mankind was created by the Light. Yet man does not see the Light as man does not live his Truth without living what he says is true.

However there are those who looked to the Light, lived their Truth and found the Truth. I, the author of this work, have found the Truth. I, like they that I speak of in this work, became part of the Light. They found the Truth and lived it. They made the moral choice to unconditionally love it as they knew that they could unconditionally trust it. They have become initiated into the Ultimate Light. [Verse 3] [3]

[1] John 1: 1-5,

[2] John 1: 6-8,
[3] John 1: 9-13,

COSMIC CHRIST WORLD LIGHT BIBLE

The Light became human. It became one person; a human being. This person walked the face of the earth. He was the Ultimate Truth; the Son of the Living God, the Light of all Ages. [Verse 4] [4]

John the Baptist declared to all mankind the presence of the Ultimate Light in this one individual human being. He said, "This is the Ultimate Light of the world, before man was the Light." His Light now shines with its rays to light up the whole universe. It is as bright as the rays of the sun. He is the Spiritual Sunlight of our world. Moses received the Laws of God. Now we have the Christ Being, Son of God, before us who is the Ultimate Truth and the Ultimate Light of all existence; the Christ Being. The Light came to the world and man does now see it. The Christ Being came to give Light to the world so that man can see it and live by it and so that mankind can reach God so that man can know God and His Light. [Verse 5] [5]

When John the Baptist was confronted by the priests of the Jews from Jerusalem to find out about his true identity and his background as a

Teacher of the Light, they asked him, "What do you call yourself? What do you really do as a Teacher of the Light?" He replied, "I am not the Light. I am not the Christ Being."

Then they said, "Then are you an incarnation of the Light? Are you the incarnation of Elijah?" He replied, "No." Then they said, "If you are not the incarnation of the Light and neither are you the Prophet the scriptures speak of that is coming into the world to give Light to it, then what really are you?"

He then said, "I am the human voice of the Light. I declare to the world the Truth of the Light and that the Ultimate Light has entered one human being in the Christ. As the Prophet Isaiah said, 'Create the right pathway to this Ultimate Light who speaks of its presence among you and mankind today.' I am a fulfillment of the scripture in what Isaiah said to our race and to mankind. This is who I truly am; John the Baptist, Teacher of the Light of the Father and now His Son, the Christ Being."

The priests who had been sent to John were coming from the

---

[4] John 1: 14,
[5] John 1: 15-18.

Pharisees. They asked him, "Why are you baptizing people when you are not the Christ nor Elijah nor the Prophet?" Then John said to them, "I am a Teacher of the Light and baptize with the power of the Light with water of the earth. In your presence is the Living Christ but you do not see him. He came after me but he is the Christ Being, Son of the Living God, Light of all Ages. He is the Living Light. I prepared the way for him but I am but a signpost for the Light. This Light was before man. The Christ Being Light is the Light I follow for all time and all life times to come. This is the Living Light of all Ages. The Eyes of the Light see the vision of John the Baptist as he speaks to the world." [Verse 6] [6]

When Jesus, the Christ Being, walked towards John the next day John declared, "You are the Son of God. You are the Saviour of mankind. You have the power to take away all darkness from the earth and from every human Soul. You are able to heal the sick and cure the blind so that they can see. You are the Source of all Light on this planet. You are the Redeemer of the world. You have come to the world to bring it Light and to take away darkness from the hearts of men. You are the Light. You are the Christ.

He is ever before me as I have spoken of him to you. He has the absolute power of the Light in this age and in all ages to come. I am a Teacher of the Light and I baptize with water so that I can prepare the Soul so it will be pure for the Light to enter it and so that I can create the vessel in the human being that will truly accept the Light into its Spirit as truly this is my task and the fulfillment of my dream to bring Souls to the Light of Christ as I bring my Soul to this Being. I also ask Israel to receive him so that his Light can bring salvation to its Soul and from it salvation for all of mankind. This is truly my will to the Light. [Verse 7] [7]

I, John the Baptist, say this now with all of my heart and with all the Light in my Soul. I see it now as I saw it happen before my eyes and before the Eyes of Light. I saw the Spiritual Being become one with the body of Jesus. I saw it descend from Heaven and enter into this person. I could see his Being merge into one Being of Light. Then this Light was transformed into a dove that descended upon

---

[6] John 1: 19-28,

[7] John 1: 29-31.

3

him. It remained motionless above his person like a living energy of Light was suspending it in the air. This Light I know now came from the Holy Spirit while the Spiritual Being came from God as the Being had the form of a man but with the image and movements of the Living Light of Heaven. Its majesty and beauty were incomparable to what I had ever experienced in my life. It was like Heaven had opened up with its glory in the sky and its Light descended into a human being. It was three complete forces of Light that merged into one living person.

The Christ Being image glowed like the sun and the dove above pierced the Heavens with a magic white Light that encircled this Being. Behind all of this was this other force that created this whole process in the beginning. This force was like a presence of a living energy that engulfed me and my whole being with this image that I could see in front of me. I was becoming part of what I could feel was this presence and it manifested itself only in the way it entered the Spirit of the person, Jesus, when I first saw him step into the river Jordan waiting for him to be baptized. This is truly what still lives in me; this vision of the Ultimate Light.

Then a voice spoke from this presence that had entered the Christ Being. This voice came from this Holy Spirit near the dove. The voice spoke out with such power so that the very earth moved with the sound and the hearts of all nearby trembled with fear and awe. It said, 'This is My Son, the Son of the Living God. He I have sent to you. I ask you now to listen to him as he is the Christ Being.'"

So John the Baptist said when he was next to two of his followers, "Here you have the Living Christ. He is the Living Light of the world. He has been sent by the Father to give Light to the world. His Cosmic journey ends here. He is the earthly and Cosmic Light of all beings." When he was saying this a radiant aura could be seen around Jesus by all those who could see the Light in his Spirit. [Verse 8] [8]

When John's followers heard him speak of Jesus the Light reached their hearts and then their Souls could see his Spirit speaking to them as if their eyes were able to see for the first time. The Eyes of Light

---

[8] John 1: 32-34.

had pierced their beings. Then Jesus looked at them and said, "What is in your hearts? Do you seek power, money or happiness above all things in your life?" They replied, "We seek Truth and the pathway of knowing how to live our Truth as this is what John taught us."

Then Jesus asked them again, "Do you seek the love of the Truth and its source, the Ultimate Light, above all things even above having a pathway or having earthly love if God asks it of you?" Then one replied, " I seek the Light that created this Truth." Then the Christ Being replied, "Then you have come to the Teacher of the Ultimate Light as I am the Light itself. Come and see where I live. There I will begin to show you this pathway that will lead you to become men with love in your hearts for mankind and with the Eyes of the Light to see its Spirit and the spiritual world." They both followed him to the place he lived and became his Apostles. [Verse 9] [9]

On the following day the other one that heard John speak, Andrew by name, who was Simon Peter's brother, went to his brother and told him, "I

have found the Ultimate Light in one man. He is the Living Christ. He is the one the prophets have spoken of. When he speaks we can hear his voice in our Souls. He is at the Doorway to the Light of all mankind. John the Baptist declared that he is the Light of the World. Come and meet him as from him you will have what we have been seeking all our lives; the Master of the Light that guides the pathways to Heaven and to our Father, God, Himself." [Verse 10] [10]

When Jesus met Peter he looked at him and said, "Peter, you are to be a leader of men as the Father has seen that you have walked on the pathway to Him. Now you have come to the Light as it is the Will of the Light that you walk on this pathway to me as I am the Christ Being, Son of God, Light of all Ages. What do you say to this, Peter, son of John?"

Then Peter replied, "I, Peter, accept this pathway with all of my heart and all of my whole Soul as I love the Living God and His Light and as I see in your Spirit the Eyes of the Light. This is what now speaks in my Soul. I have worked on this pathway to

---

[9] John 1: 35-39,

[10] John 1: 40,

find you all of my life. I see now that the Father has given me this gift of Light so that now I have the Cosmic consciousness to see with Eyes that have Light in them and to see with Eyes that see the Christ Being; my Lord and my God. This is truly my absolute will to you; the Living Light of the World." [Verse 11] [11]

On the following day Jesus went to Galilee. There he met Philip. He looked at him and said, "Come take on the pathway to the Ultimate Light of the Universe. See it and believe it and experience it. Understand it and know that I call upon you to live it in your life and to live your Truth by following My Light. This is I, the Christ Being, who speaks to you in the living flesh from the Father in Heaven; I, the Christ Being, Son of the Living God, Light of all Ages." [Verse 12] [12]

Philip's home was in Beth-sa'ida. Also Peter and Andrew came from this city. Philip, once he had met the Christ and joined the other two, decided to go and tell Nathan'a-el, his friend, about Jesus as he now had his heart filled with the Light. He said

to him, "The Living Christ has appeared to me and to John and Andrew. Come and meet him. They call him Jesus of Nazareth. We know now that he is the Messiah that has been prophesied by Moses and the law of our race. He is not only the Messiah of the Jews but the Messiah of the world. When you speak to him, he will give you the Eyes of the Light to see his Spirit. He has a Cosmic Light that shines from his being in living flesh. He is the Christ Being."

Nathan'a-el replied, " How can a human be God? How do you know the Truth of what you have just said? What proof have you of this Truth you speak of? How can a man come from Nazareth, a little town, and proclaim that he is the Ultimate Light with the Cosmic intelligence of all Ages? How did you get this Light in your heart? What magnificent experience brought such a glow of Light to your being? Please tell me how I can do this so that I can find this wonderful Light like you have now, Andrew, My friend?"

Andrew replied, "My friend, the living experience of the Eyes of the Light you can see

---

[11] John 1: 41-42,
[12] John 1: 43.

in my very Soul as my eyes have Light that now penetrates my being and my very body and Spirit. My psyche is overwhelmed by this aura of Light that permeates my whole existence. I tell you that this is my proof. As for the way to arrive at having the Eyes of the Light in my being, I can only tell you of this truly wonderful experience. I cannot tell you what is the experience as no words can describe what the heart truly sees in the realm of this Heavenly Light. I ask you to come and see for yourself as you truly will see what I see as you have Light in your heart or you would not have seen the love that I have now in mine for all of mankind as I can see that the Saviour has come. I can see that he will not only save the Jews but all races for all time to come. This is what makes my heart so glad and so rich in the poetry of my words when I speak of this Light I have seen in my mind and heart. Come and see for yourself and experience the Living Light of the World in your own being."
[Verse 13] [13]

Then Jesus saw Nathan'a-el walking towards him and looked at him with the Eyes of Light so that the Spirit of his

Being entered him. It was as if a bodily Spirit of Light walked out of Jesus and into Nathan'a-el. Then all of a sudden there was a great movement of Living Light in Nathan'a-el's Soul. His whole being was as though transformed into this experience. The experience was like seeing the Light of consciousness for the first time in his life then seeing the living Being of Light in the human form in Jesus Christ before his very body there in front of his physical eyes.

This was the moment that Nathan'a-el had dreamt about all of his life long; the moment he knew one day would come even though all in his world had told him that this was but something of wishful thinking and that this was his illusion of the real Truth of life. Hence he had swayed from his intellect to the Truth of his life. He was not sure which one was the Ultimate Light.

Now he could see that there was no more doubt in his whole being that this was the Living Christ Being, the Son of the Living God, in living flesh before his eyes. This was his ultimate destiny. His pathway had born fruit even though so many had said to

---

[13] John 1: 44-46.

him that nobody knows the whole Truth.

He knew that he was certain that the Truth can be found and that the Truth can only be in a person's heart when they will it in their minds and that the Truth is not above the Light. Hence then mankind has to live its Truth with the Truth of God; this being to love the Light and let it come to him freely of its own will. Hence then it is unconditional. "This," Nathan'a-el said, "is the pathway of the Light of all Ages for mankind and for me; I, Nathan'a-el, an individual human being, a lover of the Light of God and of man." [Verse 14]

Then Jesus came closer to Nathan'a-el and said to him and to all around him, "You are a person who has always loved the Truth and lived it. You have tried to live what you said in your Truth. You have found in the past no way to truly know the Truth. You have spoken of the Ultimate Light but really did not have it as a way to change your life and your being as you saw that others around you also struggled with your Soul to make clear your pathway to the Light of God. You have doubted even your race as it spoke of being the chosen

people as you can see all men that look to the Light are the chosen ones of the Light as you can see all human beings are equal in the Eyes of God. You can see that you have now been vindicated. You are no longer the fool looking for the illusion of Ultimate Truth. You have found it as you have a will to the Light in your heart. You have also accepted that to will morally the Light is to live one's Truth first without having the Light come to you first as there can be no Light when there is no Truth or when there is half – Truth. Only the whole Truth will create Light in a person's Soul. I am the Living Light of the Universe. I am the Son of the Living God. I am the Light of the World. I am the Messiah of the Light. When you come to Me I give you the Eyes of the Light that you have now. Hence you can now see Me; you, Nathan'a-el, My new Apostle of My Light."

Then Nathan'a-el replied, "Master, you are the Ultimate Teacher of the Light. Your heart shines through with this Light to all mankind. I see in you the Living Light as it walks upon our earth and transforms it so that it too will grow in this Light of God. It too will house man so that his personality can become God – like. I see now that I have the experience of the Eyes of the Light in my Soul. I see that I have found the Ultimate Truth and the Ultimate Teacher of the Truth of life. I see that now I have the beginning of my pathway and its ultimate destination before me; before my very eyes.

I ask you now, Oh, Christ Being, to show me the way to walk on this pathway so that I can discover truly the right Moral Will to the Light of God Himself and so that I can live my Truth and do what is right for my being and my Light and, yes, do what is right for the Light of the world. This is truly what is my will to you, Oh, Christ Being, Son of the Living God." [Verse 15]

Jesus then looked at him and loved him with the Spiritual Light coming from his Soul and Spirit. It was as if a living energy field of Light began to emanate from the Being of the Christ. All the Apostles were connecting with this Spiritual Light. It was as though a ring of Light surrounded their beings and was created by this Being of Light; the Christ.

Jesus then spoke and said, "Look into your Souls now with the Eyes of the Light that I have given you. Meditate upon the Light of My Being. Let your hearts be opened to the Spiritual Light of the Universe. Let the voices of the Hierarchies of the Angels of the Light speak to your Soul. Look to your Soul with the Eyes of the Light of My Father. Look now and you will see My Angels ascending and descending on the stairs of Heavenly golden shining Light. See this Doorway to the Light opened and you will see the Gates of Heaven opened before your very eyes. You see now a picture of Heaven as it comes to you as you are beginning to see with Christ – like Eyes for this you will have when you enter Heaven before My Father and all of His Hierarchies of Angels.

You will see now the Glory of Heaven and you will see then the Glory of My Father; the Living God, the Source of all of My Light and Love of all things, the cosmic centre of the Light of your universe.

This is the Light of Heaven in your Souls. This is the Heaven that exists for those who want to walk up the stairs to it and who do this with every lifetime as one step until all the lifetimes are completed to evolve to the Ultimate Light. This is the Heaven that exists for those who do not look down but up as those who do not go up the stairs will never see the Light. This is the Will of the Father who lives in Heaven. This is truly Heaven as we can see it on earth. This is the destination of all the Beings of the Light. This is the ultimate experience of the Light for all of mankind. This is what has been willed by the Father in the beginning of time.

Now those who will the Light will be a part of this Light and glory. This is truly My Word

to you, My friends and My Apostles; My fellow human beings. Join with Me now on this journey to Heaven.

Follow Me and never lose faith that the Truth and the Light is above all on earth and that real love will lead one to the pathway to find this Ultimate Truth and Ultimate Light. This is truly the pathway of the Light of all Ages. This is My Light; I, the Christ Being." [Verse 16] [14]

---

[14] John 1: 47-51.

10

CHAPTER 2

Jesus Christ and his mother with all of his Apostles were invited to a wedding feast at Cana, a town in Galilee. At the marriage celebration the supply of wine ran out. This was noticed by Mary, the mother of Jesus. So she went to her son and said, "My son they need more wine and it is their wedding day. Can you help them for me as I see that you could give them something that they need at the moment in the material world as I know your Spiritual Light touches the world now as well as the world to come out of it? I know that in your Being lies a brilliant power that will spread to all men. Today, however, they who have joined together in your Father's name and who have begun on their journey to the Light and need to learn how to love in the Light, need to win some of the Light of their world as ours is forever in the Ultimate Light.

What do you say, my son? Will you help them fulfil their pledge to the Light before all men in the presence of your Being, to honor the Truth, the pathway, the love, first to their Truth and to the Ultimate Truth until they part to the next world to come to your Father? Is this not what it is when couples say, 'I will be with you in sickness, in health, in misfortune and in wealth until death do us part?' My son will you help them see your Light for me?" [Verse 1] [1]

The Christ Being looked at her and loved her for her love of the union of two people that loved the Light through loving each other. He then said, "Mother I am not ready to begin my work to bring Light to the world. I need to see when the right time comes that is right for mankind to see the wonders of Heaven and its Light for all men. It is true I am available to all men, waiting for them to speak to Me; to come to My Being. Yet to come to man has been my destiny as it was willed by My Father. I became flesh for this reason. So I now change the earth and make it a part of the spiritual world of the Light.

Yes, I will do this for you and for those that today celebrate the Light in their living bodies and Souls and honor Me with their love together unconditionally for all time till they meet My Father and once again be joined into the one Being of the Ultimate incarnation Light to come

---

[1] John 2: 1-4.

when the earth will be complete with a universal union of Light in all of mankind for all time." [Verse 2]

Mary then turned to the servants of the marriage feast and told them, "My son can solve your problem of the shortage you have of wine. Can you just go and speak to him and ask him what he can do for you and for the hosts of this feast?"

The servants went over to Jesus and were expecting him to come up with the information about a source of wine that they could acquire and thought that he would show it to them as soon as possible as the problem was becoming apparent to all the guests at the party.

At that moment the servants felt a Spirit around Jesus and saw that there was an aura of Light around him. Although it was faint and somewhat elusive they could feel that there was a compelling look upon this man's face when he said to them, "Now I will ask you to follow My instructions and to let Me take responsibility for anything that happens from the request I have from you. I want you to take it on My Word and that of My mother that you will just follow these instructions and then you will see an immediate result."

The servants looked at him and they had no power to speak. It was as if they were commanded by a Spirit around Jesus to not disobey the Will of the Master. So they listened and said nothing but waited for his instructions.

At that moment Jesus walked over to the six stone jars used for purification Jewish rites which had a capacity of twenty to thirty gallons and said, "Fill all of these jars to the brim with water now and wait for the signal from Me to taste this water after all have been completely filled." The servants acted as if seized by an urgent order given by a secret commander that controlled their very beings and all of their body movements as when they completed what was asked of them they once again looked at Jesus for further instructions to carry out the next step, so to speak, of this man's will. [Verse 3] [2]

Then Jesus said, "Take six cups from the table and fill them from every jar

_____

[2] John 2: 5-6.

accordingly; one cup for each jar and so on. Once you have done this I want you to take all of the cups on a tray to the master of ceremonies of this feast. I want you to ask him to taste all of the cups so that it can be confirmed that what I have willed has taken place and that what you have now is six stone jars of the finest of wine."

When he said this the servants began to laugh and really woke up as if out of a dream. They looked at Jesus and for that moment thought him to be a magician with hypnotic powers as they could now realise that he had got them to do something that made no rational sense for them. So one of the servants took the cups and did what he asked and said to Jesus, "You are either a fool or a magician as no one can turn water into wine. So I will see if what you say is true for if it is I will certainly never doubt that God can reach out and help man when he asks him for what he needs."

Jesus replied, "I can see that you want to believe but find it hard to accept My Words. I ask you now; do as I ask. Then your lips can give you the taste of the Truth that I seek you to drink from as this is also why I am doing this to show you and the world that the Light created all things including the wine of the world and man's daily bread. Now this is what often a man wants above all things as he needs it to stay physically alive. Yet he does not see that truly what he needs above this is the Light in his Soul as if his body dies he can have another life to come. However if his Soul dies all of his lives to come will be not worth living. Hence I say to you, put the Light to the test and see that truly it is what I have willed today; to show the world the Light in this simple act of celebration of making water into wine." [Verse 4]

Then this servant did as he was told and brought the six cups of wine to the master of ceremonies and told him, "Look here we have six jars of wine that I want you to taste as we have more than we need now to give to all the guests." The master of ceremonies looked at him astonished at the news. He had no idea that Jesus had just used a Special Key of Light that created wine from water. He had not the slightest suspicion that a Heavenly power had just been used to transform matter into another form of matter. He just tasted the wine and with each cup that he tasted the wine got better and better. He was overwhelmed with this pure fruit taste that began to run through his veins. So he went over to the bridegroom and said to him, "Every man usually at a feast presents the good wine in the beginning of it so that people can enjoy it when they are the most sober. Now with you half way through this feast when all have drunken their fair share of wine there is an amazing difference to all other feasts I have attended. You have here left the finest wine I have ever tasted in my life for the end of your feast. I just cannot see why you would do such a thing and not inform me of such a plan. It seems as if you have left the best for the last of the festivities."

The Apostles of the Christ Being also tasted the wine and knew what had happened from Mary and from the servant who doubted Jesus. They then looked into their own Spirit and could see that the Light had touched the wedding feast. This Light they could see with their Eyes of Light as they could speak to the Angels that moved the servants to pour the water into the stone jars as this was for them the living proof of the living power of the Light of the Christ Being. [Verse 5] [3]

The Christ Being then left this place and went to Caper'naum. His mother and his Apostles followed him with his brothers. Following this Jesus decided to go to Jerusalem as the Passover was to be celebrated by the Jews.

When Jesus went to the temple he saw that all around there was a market set up to sell goods and to exchange money. There were shopkeepers who had set up temporary shop fronts to capitalize from the coming event of the Passover season by being near the temple; the centre of all political and religious activity in the city. He could see that oxen, pigeons and sheep were being sold and moneylenders were also visibly doing good business that day. There was a constant rush of people going and coming into the market place as if they actually blocked any entrance to the temple. The crowd was constantly growing and getting noisier by the minute so that it became almost annoying to feel this energy that was transforming itself to an irritating spirit that could almost be called dark in spirit.

Then the Christ Being looked

---

[3] John 2: 7-11.

at all the people who were possessed with their trade of making money and he called upon his Angels to give him a pathway to the temple to move all the traders who were selling animals away from the temple. As he walked through the market place all the traders were as if under a spell and could see a giant with a whip made out of cord coming after them. The fear of this giant gripped their very Souls so that they tipped their shop fronts and tables so that you could hear even the money of the changers clang onto the stone floor beneath them. They were in such a hurry to escape this fiend that they had demolished the whole market of fifty traders to a huge mess of tables and livestock everywhere by running away from the temple for they too became frightened of this mystical fiendish giant.

Then the Christ Being appeared at the doorway to the temple and said to the traders, "I tell you all that make money above My Father, God, put the love of money above the Truth. The Truth is above all forms of love. The Light is above the Truth. God created the Light so that man could see the Truth. So I say to you, you cannot make the House of My Father your

house when you put your will to make money above your will to the Light. Awaken the giant of darkness and you will lose your Truth and your Light. What you saw was your own shadow coming for you when you walked away from the Light. So I ask you now to see your Truth and let God have his Truth." He did this with the gesture of pointing to the temple.

Then his Apostles followed him and one of them said to the populace, "Belief in money and the will to get it at all costs is to put God and what every human being needs to be happy in his life below the Truth as what a man wants is not always what he needs. So that the House of God is above all the houses created for man." [Verse 6]

Then a trader looked at Jesus and went up to him and said, "Who are you and what do you want with us? How can we live unless we make enough money to pay our daily bread and our lodgings? What right have you to say what you have said and how do we know if you are not the giant of darkness you speak of? How can we be certain of the Truth here? Speak, tell us the Truth of who you are? The vision that we have all seen has made us fear you and your

God but this does not tell us if you are His Son. It tells us that you have magical powers and no more unless you have something to say that will prove who you are to everyone as this we truly need and want to know."

Then the Christ Being spoke out to all so that all could hear his Words, "I tell you this, I have the power to change the future of worlds and the cosmos and, yes, mankind itself. I can destroy such a temple and recreate it. I can say for your world that I can recreate the same temple in three days. This would, I am sure, be proof enough for you as then you would have truly what you want to know. You would have proof of who I am but My Father has willed that I tell you these things but do no more than His Will. I will not be provoked to demonstrate this power of the Light of which I speak. I will only use it when it is the Will of My Father in Heaven as the Ultimate Truth and the Ultimate Light can only be seen by those who have the Eyes of the Light. To will with your intellect to have this Light is to put the intellect above the Light. This is the wrong pathway as the intellect is the effect of the Light of the Soul. The Soul is the mirror of My Being in mankind. The Soul is the source of your being. The mind is the house of the intellect and it reflects the Light of the Soul and My Being.

So I tell you what you have seen today in the vision of the giant was the proof enough for you as to see more would only give you false eyes of a false Light as he who does not have a Moral Will to the Light will lose his Light to darkness. So I say to you, I will create a new temple in three days when all has to be transformed as it is the Will of the Father. After it is destroyed remember My Words as then you will see the true meaning of what has happened today. Before this is to come I can say no more to you as your minds are closed to what you have willed to know. When you should ask for the Truth, then you will find what you need. This is the pathway to the Light."

Then one of the Jews said to him, "You may be a powerful magician who has cast a spell on us and made us believe through your hypnotic suggestion that you have supernatural powers but in Truth it took forty – six years to build this temple and when you say you can build it back in three days this means that you are a false prophet as no one can do what you said. Therefore be honest and say this is so as you have been found out in that no one can do this."

Suddenly Jesus disappeared and the man speaking to him became very angry as everyone started laughing at him as he did not notice for a long time that Jesus was not there anymore in front of the temple. Also the trader became incensed as it was as though he was having a discussion with a ghost and no one else could see Jesus except this trader. [Verse 7]

Then the Apostles could see that the power of the Light once again took over the power of darkness and that the secret of the Light lay in another dimension of existence and that those who truly believed in matter above God could not see this dimension of existence. They did not have the Eyes of this Light to see the spiritual world.

Also when they saw all of this happening they consulted their own Doorway to the Light in the form of concepts given to them from the Father. Hence after this day they began to prepare themselves

for the change to come of the future that the Christ Being was speaking of. They could see that even though they had no real knowledge of the exact timing of the future or all of its contents they had the Light of the future in living flesh with them. So with this and the Eyes of the Light he had given them they could see that truly they were on their chosen pathway of aligning their Truth to the Ultimate Truth. Hence to the enlightenment of themselves and the world as the living Light was going to physically die and go to the spiritual world and return to the earth in three days. This they knew now and knew that they lived in a parallel world of the material and the spiritual.

In this spiritual world the opposite of the Light lived for now and would be overcome with the Light once the Christ Being went to the two worlds and resurrected in the material world. In the same way he was speaking of creating a new temple in three days. Hence he was speaking of creating a new dimension of existence in his Being as he had done when he entered material space and became a human being. He was going to leave material space and return to it as a Being of Light to redeem all of mankind and to redeem them. This consciousness the Apostles now had in their beings. The Light had reached their Souls and hearts. Their mind's eye was now changed so as to perceive and their eyes were transformed with the Light so that they could see. Hence they had Christ Consciousness from then on. [Verse 8] [4]

After all this occurred many of the Jews wanted to proclaim the Christ Being as the Messiah but Jesus knew that this was not what His Father had willed for him as he needed no accreditation as a Master of the Light. He did not need it from the Jews nor mankind. He had come to the world to give it Light in all its kingdoms of existence, mankind being one of these kingdoms, and he belonging to the Ultimate Kingdom of the Godhead had decided to become a human being. He had done this as His Father had chosen this and had chosen mankind to become a part of the Spiritual Light of His Being. So cosmically in the parallel worlds of spiritual and material existence the Christ Being could see what was in men's lives and what

was in the Souls of men before and after it happened to them. [Verse 9]

What he did not decide to see is what they would do with their free will at any given time except the times willed by His Father as His Father had given free will to all men. However with His Son He had given them free will to see his Being but not to act against him until the appointed time to fulfil the fate of the Light on the earth.

So the Christ Being could not be seen by the Jews anymore after he entered the temple and after the way in which he left it as he did not need to trust the blind faith of the Jews nor their free will to decide to act for him or against him. He trusted in His Father's Will to complete the mission he had come to earth to accomplish in this one incarnation upon the earth for this period of three years before he would leave it. This was why he followed the pathway of giving to the Jews what they could handle for a time knowing full well that ultimately there would be those who would embrace the Light and those who would act against him as this was

---

[4] John 2: 12-22.

inevitable and the reason as to why he had come to the earth

to give Light to all men unconditionally and everlastingly. [Verse 10] [5]

---

[5] John 2: 23-25.

CHAPTER 3

There was a man whose name was Nicode'mus who was one of the leaders of the Pharisees. He met the Christ Being at night as he wanted to keep his conversations with Jesus private and out of the public eye as he was well aware of the negative political implications if it was known he was meeting the perceived arch enemy of Phariseeism.

Now in one of his conversations with Jesus he asked him, "Rabbi, you are truly a Teacher of the Light of God. This has been proven as no person can create visions in men's minds of another living reality other than material or heal others, through this other world of another dimension, unless he has the power of God within his being. No one can say that you do not have this power of the Light as you have transformed matter into spirit and spirit into matter. This has been seen by the way you speak and create energy fields that change the future in one's consciousness and world conceptions. It is clear that you have powers over earth and spirit. You have supernatural powers.

The source of your power must be the other world where God lives. Yes, the source of your power must be the ultimate power in this universe. It must come from God, the Living God, as God is with you; with your whole being and Spirit. This I can see as I can see the aura of man and can read his Spirit. As leader of a group that follows a spiritual path I am also a teacher of initiates towards the Light. Therefore I know a person who has Light. I see that you have a unique, universal Light in your whole Spirit. Yes, you have the Spirit of the Living God in your being."

The Christ Being then looked at him and replied, "I say to you a person needs to first unconditionally love with his heart the dream of the right pathway to the Light. Once he has done this, a pathway is revealed to him or her who seeks the Ultimate Truth of life and his world. Following this a person needs to see how to define his pathway and needs to see if it leads to the Ultimate Truth or the Truth of the world that he is in. He needs to see if the pathway he has works for the world or works for him or her as a human being first in his life. He needs to see that if he has it in his heart to love and trust unconditionally in the Light that it will lead him to the Ultimate Truth as once he has the Truth he will have the Eyes of Light to see the Ultimate Light. This is the only way a person can be born again with this Light in his Soul.

We are always born two times in this world. We are born once for our bodies to live and we are born secondly for our Souls to live. To truly live then one must have been born twice. The third time a person is born is when he dies as then when he leaves the earth he is born again as a Spirit before the Light till he returns to earth to follow the same cycle again until the day he stands before My Father who will give him his Ultimate Will. So every time a person renews the Light he is born again to live and to die for the Light of Heaven and earth so that ultimately he will become from the many spirits into one Spirit. Then he will become a spiritual being. Then he will create the eternal Light of My Being or he will die alternatively and never be

born again. This is the quest that is given to humankind.

To speak to God and to live one's Truth is to follow the Light of what can be seen from the Eyes of the Light. This is what it is to be born again; to use the Eyes of the Light to create Light for one's life, one's Soul and the world. When a man can do this he gives Light to the universe and to all creation. He gives back to God the Light that was given to him to create out of his Moral free will to the Light. This is the Light of God meeting the Light of man. This is being born again with the Light of God. This is becoming a being of Light. This is what is born out of the Light of all Ages. To see the Kingdom of God with the Eyes of the Light one's Soul has to be reborn again like one's body with every new life.

This is the pathway of the Light to the Soul as the Kingdom of God belongs to all men who follow the pathway to the Ultimate Truth of life, who live in the Light of what they say and who tell the Truth of the Light of their lives. They become one with the Light in the Kingdom of My Father in Heaven for all Souls come from this

Kingdom and are meant to return in the Light to it. However this still belongs to the Moral free will to the Light, to live the eternal life in the Light or in darkness. To choose the Light is to be born again in the Kingdom of My Father; the Father of all Light in this universe, the Father of all universes. His Kingdom is My Kingdom. It is your Kingdom when you choose the Light." [Verse 1] [1]

Nicode'mus then said to Jesus, "How can I be born again in the way you say? You are saying that I must look to the Light. I must be born again physically and spiritually. You say that I have to also make a choice with every lifetime as to look to the Light or to look to darkness. Now how can I change the pathway I live now? I do look to the Light. So what are you saying about how I can possibly do all this again? I cannot go back to my mother's womb as much as I cannot see how my pathway to Phariseeism is the wrong pathway to the Light. What is it that I need to do then to achieve the Ultimate Light and the Ultimate Truth of your Father, the God of all universes? What can I possibly do to find the right pathway to the Light as you say? How can I now in my situation choose by my Moral free will the Light of this world, yes, to this universe with my life? How can I live my Truth and follow the Light of the Father in Heaven? Regardless of my age and my pathway now, what is it that I need to do to fulfil this pathway to the Ultimate Light?"

The Christ Being looked at him and said, "A person needs to be born again in both worlds to truly discover his Light and to find the Ultimate Light. To do this a person needs to know first what he loves. Then he needs to see that the Truth is above love and that to find the Truth a person has to have a pathway to the Light. Of this you are clear. However you are still not clear of how to find the Truth and of how to live your Truth. If a man lives his Truth he aligns what he lives with the Light. He can see the two worlds of matter and spirit. He can see that he needs both to fulfil his pathway to the Ultimate Truth. So unless a person is born in both worlds anew he cannot enter the

---

[1] John 3: 1-3.

Kingdom of Heaven. He cannot enter the Kingdom of God.

John the Baptist said that I baptize with water and there will be one that will baptize with the Spirit of the Light. He was speaking of My Being as I am this one that brings Light to the initiands who seek it. You as a spiritual leader do this for your initiates. However you can see you would not be talking to Me if you were certain of your pathway and if you could reach the Ultimate Light.

So I give birth to the Light in both worlds to My initiands. I do this simultaneously. I baptize with water and the Spirit of the Light. 'How do I do this?' you ask. Observe and you will see this Light. I show a person first how he needs to learn how to gain his pathway to reach the place in his Soul where he can use the Eyes of the Light. This is what you need, Nicode'mus, to see how you can be born again in both worlds.

A baby comes to the world out of the womb and is born and people say that it was the father and the mother who created the seed for this life.

This is true but before this happened on the earth in the spirit world the baby was also born first for this individual was first on a journey to come back to earth from the spirit world. He had to be born again there before he could be born again on earth. Now the question is, how does this all happen? What is the spiritual world? What is it that a person does in the other world, the other dimension, that gives him this spiritual identity at a point in time where there is no time measured by hours or days and nights. This is the mystery of the ages. To know what happens between death and birth is to know what the Light is physically and spiritually.

So, we have established what is born out of the material world is parallel to what is born out of the spiritual world. The spiritual world is parallel to the material world in evolution and development of its history and ultimate destiny. The cosmos is the composite world of spirit and matter. Now man can forever interpret this parallel and lose himself in this interpretation or he can decide to fathom its pattern and decipher the Truth of the pathway of the world and its universe.

For a man to become an initiand of the Light and to acquire the Eyes of the Light he needs the Moral Will to the Ultimate Light. This Moral Will to the Ultimate Light needs to have the development of a moral conscience along with a Doorway to the spiritual world as a human being can only see his spirit and travel in the pathway to becoming a spiritual being when he can see his pathway with the Eyes of the Light. This is what I mean by being born twice in both worlds as then physical birth and spiritual birth become parallel in the body of the spirit of a being. The person who lives his Truth and aligns to the Light achieves this pathway in his Soul and in his body simultaneously so that his psyche can see his Light and the Light of Heaven.

The Spirit of Heaven descends upon the earth and reaches the Souls that look up to it and look to the Light of Heaven. It reaches their Soul. The Light pierces their whole being. The Will of My Father makes this choice. It is not only what the Soul wills to the Light but also what My Father wills for the Soul as this is ultimately what leads the Soul to become an initiand of the Light. [Verse 2]

You, Nicode'mus, can see and hear Me now as you seek the Eyes of Light. It is your moral choice if you take up this pathway to the Ultimate Light. You had to first be shown the pathway so that by defining it you can explain it to yourself when you asked Me the questions you have asked Me today. However you are now asking yourself, 'What is the source of the Light in this man? Yes, I know that he comes from the Father of all universes. I know he has the Ultimate Light in his being but I cannot control whether the Father has chosen my Soul to become an initiand of the Light. How can I truly know this? How can any man know this for certain? Also what distinguished one man from another as to why he is chosen to have these Eyes of Light? How can I truly know now how to apply this Truth of the universe you speak of, Master of the Light?'"

The Christ Being then said, "He who is humble enough to wait for the Father to touch his Soul will receive the Light that will open the pathway to the Doorway of the Eyes of the Light of the Soul. He who accepts that he can only be led to the Ultimate Light and be initiated to this Ultimate Light not from his will but from My Father's Will, will reach this Ultimate Light. Such a person accepts that he is not truly certain of all that he needs to do to fulfil this pathway. He can never have the whole Truth of what truly the whole pathway is to the Light. Such a person knows he has part of the Truth and that he is part of the Light.

He also knows when people ask him about his Truth and say to him, 'You cannot be one hundred percent certain that all that you follow will lead you to the ultimate enlightenment of life. So how can you be certain? Do tell us as this is what all men who looked to the Light have searched for throughout the ages from the beginning of the consciousness of the Light on this planet.' Such a person of whom I am speaking will then reply, 'I am certain of my will to this Truth and to this Light.' This is the Moral Will to the Ultimate Light, Nicode'mus. This certainty can only be in the whole heart and Soul of a human being when he has been born twice

in both worlds simultaneously in Spirit and in body.

Hence initiands of My Light have My Father's Light. This is the certainty of the pathway but not of who My Father is as to the knowledge of His Being. However that to be certain the destiny of mankind is My Being, I, the Christ Being, is being certain of the will to find this Light and it is to be certain of the Truth of life. To know Me is to know My Father as I am the Ultimate Light of this planet now. I have come in living flesh to show the world how to find the Ultimate Light.

My Father gives you your Moral Will to the Light. I am its destination. To know My Father is to know all the knowledge of the universe in its entirety. One cannot know all of this unless He is God. However each person becomes a part of God, My Father, when he begins to will the Truth in his life and to live it. Then when he begins to align it with the Light of his life he will find Me; I, the Christ. So to be born again in the Light of the earth and the Light of the Spirit, you need to follow the pathway I have outlined

25

now to receive your Eyes of Light." [Verse 3] [2]

Nicode'mus then replied, "I cannot see all that you have said would give me the enlightenment that every man seeks who follows a spiritual pathway. I am a spiritual leader. I know that what you have said has been said before and does not give me the knowledge I seek to get to the Ultimate Light. So can you get to the point? How can I follow you, Master, when I already have a pathway to the Light which I have followed all of my life long? How can I justify doing this to myself and to followers in spiritual and political life? I am a leader of Israel. Do give me reason to then make this moral decision so that it is based on sound judgment and not just rhetoric about being initiated into the Ultimate Light?"

Then the Christ Being said, "You are a teacher of the Light but you cannot follow the Light. This is because you are not living your Truth in alignment with it. Hence you are putting the intellect above the Light. When you do this you will lose your Light and ultimately your Truth as you have listened to the Light and refuse to see it. You have identified with the way the world works for you now. The world possesses your identity. You say that you have already a spiritual pathway to the Light but you cannot change it as this would upset those who follow you and who identify with your standing and take you on as a role model as an initiator of the Light. You say that in the material and temporal world you are also a political leader of the Jews and that you have to maintain a political face that will remain credible with the populace.

All that you have said has said nothing about your Soul and your Truth. You have but sold your being to the world. You have put your identity of what you are in your community and your working life above who you really are as a human being. You teach brotherhood to men but you have lost your true brotherhood to Me. When I have shown you and described for you the ultimate pathway to the Light of Heaven, you have identified with God. You have lost your identity to this concept and not seen that by doing this you

_____

[2] John 3: 4-8.

have not followed the Truth. A man has Light only when he lives his Truth and follows the Truth. You know the Truth but do not follow your Truth. Hence you will lose your Light.

You say that you know all that I have said and have heard this rhetoric before. You say that the Eyes of the Light are no more than a perception of the Truth but not the Ultimate Truth as the Doorway to the Ultimate Light. So what is happening to you is that you hear the Light. You see the Light but you have closed your eyes and your ears to it. You choose to speak of it and to proclaim it. You choose to say you have seen it but you do not choose to live it. Hence you do not live what you say. You do not follow what is right for you and your Truth as a person first in your life.

To do this you would need to make the moral decision to walk away from power and accept the ultimate power of the Light. To do this you would need to take away the layers of tradition and heritage of the Light and accept that this is conventional Light. A record of the Truth of mankind is not the living Truth of it. I am the

Living Truth. I am the Living Light. I am the Son of the Living God. [Verse 4]

I have tried to show you the parallel with how the material and spirit dimensions exist. I have spoken to you in such a way as you know aligns with all the truths that you have learned in your advanced age and all the wisdom that you have tells you that I am aware of all that you know of life. Yet you still find it not possible to look to the Ultimate Light. So how can I truly ask you to see the Living Light before you as I am the Living Light and the Christ Being?

You cannot see this unless you have the Eyes of the Light; the Eyes to see Heaven and earth at the same moment and to know that the Doorway to both comes from the Soul but first from your will to find your being is the Doorway to the spiritual world I am speaking of. Through this Doorway the Father chooses to reach your being when he sends Light to your Soul. It is your choice, Nicode'mus. You have a Moral free will to choose the Light standing before you in physical form.

I could not speak of such things unless I was a part of

Heaven and I was the Light. I have come as it is the Will of My Father to give you this Light to your Soul. This is My Mission to baptize the world; to give it Light. I will light up the whole globe. My journey from the distant galaxies of the Light of the Spiritual Hierarchies has been to give Light to all the kingdoms of the earth but first to mankind's kingdom.

This is why I have come to the earth. I have come to the earth to speak to you, to give you this message from Heaven, to come in person to show you that the Father unconditionally loves you and all men. I have come to show you that that time for the salvation of the world and mankind has come. When I speak to you thus the Father is choosing you to look to the Light. This is My Pathway. This is My Work. This is My Ultimate Truth. This is Me. I am the Light. I give the Eyes of the Light to the initiands of the Light. They will carry on My Work when I am no longer in this physical form. This is My Destiny and mankind's destiny. I am the Son of the Living God; the Christ Being. [Verse 5] [3]

Moses walked in the desert with his people and saw the shadow of darkness come over the world. He walked away from the power of the Pharaoh to put Light above darkness. To do this he had to become a leader of men led by My Father in Heaven. In a parallel way the Son of the Father has to show the world its darkness and what is the source of this darkness. Then he needs to show the source of the Light of the world. To walk with mankind and to take it to the Ultimate Light is My Mission; I, the Christ Being, Son of the Living God, Light of all Ages. [Verse 6] [4]

Those who follow this Light know the Truth of My Father and ever evolve His Living Spirit in their whole lives. They know that they have to be humble enough to let the Father lead them to the Ultimate Light of all Ages. Of this they are certain. Of this Truth I am certain. The part of mankind that chooses the Light of the Christ Being is certain of this Truth eternally. My Father loves mankind unconditionally. He trusts in mankind unconditionally. He breathes His Spirit of Living Light into the Soul of

---

[3] John 3: 9-13,

[4] John 3: 14-15.

mankind and into the Soul of this planet. He saw that for mankind to survive the darkness He had to give mankind His Being unconditionally. He did this when He sent a complete Light Being to earth to become a human being. He sent His Son, the Christ Being. He did this to show His Love for all men and women who have ever breathed the air of the earth. He did this as when He created mankind and gave mankind the breath of life the Father let him evolve with a parallel spiritual and material evolution universally. First He gave Moral free will to Spiritual Beings and then to human beings.

He did this not in some ordered sequence of time but in a Heavenly evolutionary scale of it; this depending on the universal cosmic evolutionary spiritual process independently working of Him and controlling the same process materially. It had to be independent of Him or free will for the Light or for darkness would not exist.

Now with this free will given to every being ever created by God came the creation in the human Spirit of Moral Will to the Light or to its opposite. Hence the parallel also now exists in the part of the spiritual world connected to mankind in its present evolutionary scale of existence. Spiritual Beings that relate to mankind have already made the choice ultimately between Light and darkness while mankind is in this process of choosing with each lifetime given on the earth. So as the incarnation of the earth ever evolves it comes closer to becoming a part of the spiritual world. This is its ultimate destiny. [Verse 7]

Now as for the Father as He created mankind and gave it free will, He gave it also an ultimate destiny to the Ultimate Light when He sent Me to the earth to become a human being. He did this now as this is when mankind was ready to receive Me. Hence the Light of the World is here to fulfil the promise from the Father to mankind, to take responsibility for its destiny to the Light, to give it the power of the Light and to ask every human being who loves the Light to acquire the Eyes of the Light to see Him and to know that He has sent His very Son to become a human being.

To know this is to know that the living power of the Light of the whole universe will sustain mankind on its journey to the spiritual world. The spiritual world where Heaven exists is where that part of mankind that will ultimately choose the Light, will be eternally. In the material world those of mankind who experience the Light have a Doorway already to it and can walk in Heaven with their Souls, step by step, until they have evolved out of their earthly lives to live eternally in the Heavenly life. This is the destiny of those of mankind who choose the Light forevermore." [Verse 8] [5]

The Father willed Light into the world and created a universe. The galaxies of Light house the Hierarchies of the Light. He gave free will to the Hierarchies that created darkness. He gave them this so as to create an independent world of universes outside His realm of Heaven. He did this so that mankind and other beings belonging to other universes could evolve in a unique way and separate from God. Yet He also gave each being a Light and at the birth of each Soul He gave His Light when He breathed the breath of life into it.

Now the darkness came to also evolve so that it chose to command its own destiny with the Father. This was permitted only in so far as all Souls in the universe were given free will to act for or against Heaven. This was done so that whatever was created was let to flower, blossom and bloom through the creative forces of the powers of the Spiritual Hierarchies of the Light. Mankind is a product of this creative power of the Ultimate Light. The Hierarchies of darkness also gave man an alternative pathway and an alternative destination. This was so, as from the beginning of the creation of Souls, the Father in Heaven gave free will to all Spiritual Beings in Heaven to work with His creation or to leave Heaven and work for an existence out of it.

When the Father sent His Son to earth He did this to show His Free Will to act upon the evolution of the world. Until then He had not acted directly upon the fate of man and the Ultimate Light. He had given

---

[5] John 3: 16.

30

His Light to mankind through different individuals who had the Eyes of the Light in their being. These individuals gave Light to mankind and prepared the way for the Christ Being to enter the human world. They prepared world consciousness for it. They did this by creating a pathway for mankind in what they lived and in the legacies they left behind. Although different cultures and continents apart received this Light this way the world consciousness was being awakened with this evolution of the consciousness of the Light.

Gautama Buddha was such a being who existed five hundred years before the Christ Being was on earth and who ended his life by transforming into Light. He was able to transform his whole being from human being to Spiritual Light Being. He did this as he was able to surpass all incarnations on earth. His Light power contributed to the Christ Light as he prepared a part of mankind to have Eyes of the Light of what is to come when the Ultimate Light from Heaven would enter physical space on earth as an individual human being. He

spoke of the right pathway to the Light and like no other human being that ever incarnated on the earth he had a Light that was closest to the Christ Being with the difference that he was a human being originally who was given the breath of life by the Father, while the Christ Being is the Son of the Father who became a human being.

The Father gave human life to the human Christ Being when He gave him his incarnation on the earth. Then for thirty years He prepared the body and Soul of Jesus and initiated it with His Light to become the Cosmic Being for the next three years of His life on earth. Therefore Jesus left the earth when John the Baptist baptized Jesus and the Cosmic Christ Being entered into his body. From that moment mankind became one with the Ultimate Light. From that moment mankind was touched by the Father and given Light and the second birth of all of mankind and his planet and all of its kingdoms of creation were celebrated. All of the history of the human universe was at that moment incarnated in the celebration of this Light power which came from Heaven to give Light to the world. Hence it is so that the Father sent His Son to save the world from the darkness and to give it Light for all time and for all ages to come. [Verse 9]

So with every human evolution and with every incarnation a person has in his life on the earth his task is to celebrate the Light and be born first physically as the earth was physically born when it was created by the Father and then to be born again spiritually through the interception of the Christ Light when a person receives his Eyes of the Light that let his Soul see the Ultimate Light.

Hence a human being like human civilisation on the earth as it evolved looked to the Light. This is the way of Buddha. Then the human being found the Ultimate Light. This is the way of the Christ Being. Therefore he who lives his Truth follows the pathway of Gautama Buddha. He who lives his Truth and aligns with the Light of the Christ Being, lives his Truth with the pathway to the Ultimate Light. So to live one's Truth and to follow the Truth of life is to have the Eyes of the Light. Hence then one has Light.

To follow the material world by putting it above the spiritual world and then to will power over it by putting the intellect above the Light is to close the Eyes of the Light and let in the darkness.

He who knows the world knows what I speak of and knows that to let man see the Light of God He sent His Son to speak the Words of Light. This is a record of this conversation with the Light of God. So he who speaks with the Words of Light creates Light and lives his Truth by looking first to the Light and then aligning it with his being and his whole life. His life is the living picture of this Light as when he speaks the Truth he creates this pathway for all of mankind and its Truth. Also mankind's Truth is lived when man loves the Christ Being as man loves this Being as He is the Eternal and Ultimate Truth of all Universes. He is the Light of the World.
[Verse 10] [6]

The Christ Being and his Apostles decided to do their work of baptizing those who were seeking the Light in Judea. John the Baptist was doing this in Ae'non in the

---

[6] John 3: 17-21.

32

vicinity of Salim. In this area there were many water pools that really suited his work of preaching and then baptizing. He however could see also that he was becoming a fugitive from the justice system as he was not only a rebel spiritually and to society of the time itself but had also preached against Herod, the King of Judea.

He did this as he had to make the symbolic recognition of what amorality Herod was following when it came to showing the counterpoint of what Materialism put above God had done to a leader of their race. He did this also to show the power of evil and how it had overtaken the Jewish society by its identification with Roman power paralleled to what Herod, a Jewish King, was doing as a Roman puppet politically who followed the Roman empire's moral code in his personal life. He also did this knowing full well that ultimately Herod would hear of his rebellion and would retaliate with death or prison. When he spoke to the people his aim was to speak the Truth regardless that he did not have the power to take away the darkness materially.

He had chosen this incarnation to purify his whole being before the Light of God. He wanted to make an example of his being that with no material power he was defying the greatest empire in the world which ruled his country not with political proclamations of dissent nor physical violence but with completely moral ones. It was his way of fulfilling his Moral karma to be materially powerless but absolutely dedicated to the Light first above all things in his life. In this way he was chosen to show the Light Pathway to the world and to speak of the Living Light in the flesh in the Christ Being when he appeared before him in the river Jordan. So he gave his whole being to the Light in physical form as he put Light above his life.

In the beginning he was living in the desert to escape the darkness of his society and also to fulfil the Spirit that was calling him to preach to mankind out of the position outlined in the remote wilderness of Palestine. He then evolved a pattern of life sustaining himself on locusts and honey with no material possessions. Following this he began to evolve his preaching as a Spirit was calling him and getting stronger and stronger to give to the Light and God above anything his body or well – being needed or wanted. He did this and lived out in the wild praying and developing his Eyes of Light in his being.

Through these Eyes he also saw that he had a karmic debt to pay the Light as when he was revered as a living 'God – King' in a past incarnation thousands of years before, he had put the Light above life by making this into a law for millions of people. He saw now that this is the reason he left himself open for the opponent of the Light in the spiritual world to seize this opportunity to blind him to give Light to mankind with no protection of the Light to his own person. So John the Baptist had come to this realisation after he had met the Christ Being and saw that with this Light of Christ Consciousness he could see his ultimate death at the hands of Herod as he made public knowledge Herod's evil in an era where to say words against a king meant your death.

Once this realisation had come to John he did not recriminate against the Light but welcomed his coming death as a proof that he had lived with a certainty of a Moral Will to it. He had no regrets that he could have avoided Herod as he saw that he wanted to pay this karmic debt to the Light. This is so as the Light had given him the Eyes of the Light to see Heaven on earth in his daily life every time he gave a new person a pathway to take one more step to the Light as this he knew was his mission in life and his task to fulfil the dream to see the Light before it transfigured upon the globe eternally, physically and spiritually as this dream was born in that world lost to the Light when he ruled through a golden throne symbolized by the rays of the 'Sun God' giving him Light from the centre of the universe.
[Verse 11] [7]

Now John the Baptist was confronted by a number of those whom he was baptizing and they said to him, "You are a Teacher of the Light and you are losing your following. You will soon have no disciples. We thought that your way was

---

[7] John 3: 22-24.

superior and a way to the Ultimate Light of this universe. Now we see that you are failing as people are not coming to be baptized by you anymore. Soon all will go to the Christ Being. What has happened to your teachings? Where do you stand now? He whom you baptized yourself has now Apostles that are doing your work many times over. They speak of the Ultimate Light and when they speak it is as if this Master of the Light speaks through them and they become as though radiant with a Light aura around them. This Light aura we can see comes from this man, Jesus. What have you to say then, John, of your Truth and the Truth of life?"

Then John spoke up and said, "The Ultimate Light has come from Heaven and is with you in living flesh. He is the Christ Being. God, the Father, has given His Son to mankind this day. He who has a part of Heaven in his heart sees the Eyes of the Light as I do and as you are beginning to do. Jesus Christ is the Son of the Living God and he is the Light of all Ages. His way leads one to the Ultimate Truth and Light of this universe.

When in the past you asked me if I am the Messiah I made it clear to you that I am a messenger of the Living Light and that the Christ Being is the Living Light of the World. You know that these were my words then and now they are the same. I am a Teacher of the Light but I am not the Light. The Light is the Christ Being.

My mission was to speak of him and to prepare seekers of the Light for his coming. He has come now and those who see him will be able to create the Eyes of the Light in their being if they ask for his Light to come to them. That is the reason I began to baptize before Jesus came to do the work that His Father has sent him to do. My work is coming to an end as this is the Will of God. His Will is the Will of the Light. So the Light is above the Truth as the Light created the Truth of life.

This is so as I spoke the Truth of the universe and prepared the way for the Ultimate Light to come. This is now before you as it faces you to live your Truth and to align it with this Ultimate Light as living one's Truth leads one to the Truth.

However the Truth leads one to the Light of the Christ Being as ultimately he is the Ultimate Pathway. So he who loves him first loves the pathway of the Truth that leads to the Ultimate Light as the Ultimate Light now lives as a living proof that the Almighty God is giving Light back to mankind for mankind's Moral Will to the Truth of His Being. So he who puts Light above the Truth and the Truth above love, loves unconditionally mankind. As he knows he loves one person unconditionally, he loves the Light unconditionally. Is this not then the love I spoke of? Can you not then say that I do not live what I say? Can you not say then I am living my Truth and following the Truth and the Ultimate Light?
[Verse 12] [8]

The Christ Being is the Son of the Living God. He is the centre of this universe spiritually and materially. He stands before your eyes and you do not see him as your mind is still ruling your heart. Look at what I have said in the past. I have shown you a pathway to follow the signs that lead one to the Ultimate Truth and then the Ultimate Light of this universe.
[Verse 13] [9]

Now there are those who make a union of intellect and Spirit and speak of the Light being above their whole lives and go about preaching the words of the Ultimate Truth but have never reached the Ultimate Light. Why is this so? This has happened to them as they have not evolved as yet enough to reach it. They have seen that when they had put their ties to love and blood above the Light they could not reach it. Then they saw when they put the power of their mentor, be it a wise man or a great initiand of the Light, above the Light they also did not find the Ultimate Light as they had not reached the point of putting the Light above life. This means that they could not live their Truth aligned to the Ultimate Truth but aligned only to an intellectual, spiritual truth. They did what was right for their intellectual truth but did not do what was right for them first as human beings aligned with the Ultimate Light. Had they done this they would have seen that the ultimate evolution of all religions is the religion of the

---

[8] John 3: 25-29.

[9] John 3: 30.

Ultimate Individual of a Spiritual Being in the human flesh; the Christ Being.
[Verse 14]

So, yes, I am a great mentor of the Light. I have great supernatural powers as you have seen. Yet I tell you my powers are only mine as he has given them to Me from His Father. His Father sent Me before him to prepare the wedding feast. I was the master of ceremonies but the feast is over. The bride is now with the bridegroom. The Father of all the Light in the universe was the uniting Light of mankind with the Christ Being. Then mankind was being merged with the Christ Being. So when I hear the people of the earth follow the Christ Being and into the decades of centuries ahead when mankind will walk in the Light of the Christ Being, I see my own being filled with this Light.

I see that I am one individual human being who has evolved with so many life times and with so many life times to come to reach the fulfillment of the Light in my heart. Hence I am with the Christ Being with my whole Soul and

being. So when you tell Me that all of my followers are following him then I can let the evolution of the world of Light reach every human being in the universe parallel my own journey to the Light of the Christ Being. So when your pathway parallels what I have said then you know your ultimate pathway to the Light is the Christ Being."
[Verse 15]

To see the centre of the whole universe in the person of the Christ Being and then to see the rays of Light from his Being reach all life on earth is to have Eyes of the Light. To see the equivalent centre in the earth and to see that the source of all his Light is the earth is to have eyes of darkness. The Light is above the darkness as if it were not no one could see in the dark. One could see his earth without the Light of the sun. Therefore Heaven is the Sun of the Universe. Man lives on earth as a part of a material and spiritual journey to take him to Heaven, to take him to the Light and to take him to the Living Christ God.

When a man has the Eyes of the Light his being lives

already in the spiritual world and simultaneously in the material one. He develops out of both worlds. He does this by living in both worlds and fashioning his pathway according to the directions to the Ultimate Light. Those who can see with their Eyes of the Light can speak of it from their heart as they have the power of the Light in their words so that they learn to speak in both worlds. This way their Souls become on a parallel journey with the body when the ego communicates with the Light of the Living Christ Being. Those whose bodies and Souls run at different evolutionary journeys have a split ego that speaks about making Truth relative.

An individual human being who reaches this union of the Light in his being has a credible pathway to the Ultimate Truth of life as he has the proof of his own life and its own individual Light having its source in the Christ Light. Having this superior Ultimate Light perception a human being has the Truth by following his Truth in life. He then has the Ultimate Truth which is followed by the Ultimate Light when the Father wills the Light into his

Soul as once a person has this he speaks with the words of God and sees with the Eyes of the Light of God. He sees the Father giving Light unconditionally to His Son, the Living Christ. He sees that the Christ Being is the measure of all things in his life and that the Father has given Him the ultimate power of loving mankind in the Light and of giving mankind unconditionally the Light of Heaven. [Verse 16]

So when mankind follows the light of the sun it gives light to mankind and his earth as the Light of Heaven shines upon the sun so that its sources of light can be sustained for eternity. As the galaxies of stars are sustained with their worlds so will the individual be sustained with the eternal Light of the Christ through all life times until the sun becomes a part of Heaven. Then all who have followed the Christ Being will have one eternal life in the Light forevermore.

Those of mankind who walk away from the Light will be like a man who turns his back to the sun and says it does not exist as he cannot see it. This kind of man will lose his Eyes of the Light and will not see

38

the Light. He will die in many life times and ultimately one death will close his eyes to the sun as when it merges with Heaven he will have no more life on earth as the earth will no longer be separate from God. Then the Father will take back the unconditional Light He gave this man's Soul and he will have to disappear from the sight of the Light for eternity as this is the Eternal Will of the Father who created Heaven and earth.

[Verse 17] [10]

---

[10] John 3: 31-36.

CHAPTER 4

The Father directed the Spirit Body of the Christ Being. He was the Eyes of his Heavenly Light. He could see the future but had given man free will to decide between good and evil. He did not prevent man from choosing evil but he did not ever give up His own Free Will to act on behalf of His Son or to change world or daily events if He saw that His Spiritual Hierarchies of the Light could counteract the Hierarchies of darkness that tried to seduce man into choosing evil as they were whispering evil thoughts into the minds of the Pharisees that the Christ Being was an evil magician and that he was creating a following of initiates that would rival theirs and ultimately he would become a political, religious power taking their moral power away from them that they had enjoyed for generations over the Jews.

The Pharisees could see that the Christ Being had Apostles that baptized people as John did even though he himself did not baptize anyone. They could also see that he was becoming a force to be reckoned with and one that out of nowhere was succeeding in showing the populace a pathway to a Truth of life that they did not have except intellectually. They had spoken of the things that this man had spoken of again and again but there was no response from the people. John the Baptist had awakened the consciousness of people with a Spiritual Fire demanding redemption and directing them to the Christ Being as their Redeemer. With this endorsement he was becoming a perceived political threat. So knowing their minds the Father directed the Christ Being to leave the inevitable problem of the Pharisees in Judea and to go to Galilee. [Verse 1] [1]

On his journey he had to travel through Samar'ia or the city of Sy'char. Near this city there was a field Joseph had received from his father, Jacob. Now there was a well next to this field known as Jacob's well. Jesus was quite tired from walking and decided to sit down near this well. It was also late afternoon about six o'clock when he had been thinking about his

---

[1] John 4: 1-3.

journey and where it would lead him now. He had sent his Apostles to buy food in Sy'char. Then suddenly he noticed a woman who had come to Jacob's well to draw water. The woman was a Samaritan.

Then the Christ Being looked at this woman and said, "Will you please give Me some water to drink?" The woman replied, "Why do you ask me to give you a drink? Are you not aware of who I am and who you are? A Jew does not have anything to do with a Samaritan. This is the law of your race and my race. Is this not the right way to preserve our cultures? What is it that you really want from me as after all I try to follow the law that it may be my guide to the truth of life? What say you to that, Jew man? What is your answer to this Samaritan woman?"

The Christ Being said, "God gives the gift of life to man. I give you also this gift unconditionally to see who I am. I am he who was sent by the Father to unite mankind beyond race and culture, to give him the Spiritual Light of loving his fellow man unconditionally and eternally and to then unite his Spirit to

have everlasting Eyes of Light so that he could see the Living Light in the centre of this universe.

I am coming to you from this centre in the universe as I am the Ultimate Light of your planet. Yes, I walk in your world as a man with human body and heart, yet I am the Son of the Living God. All ages of Light have waited for Me. Now you see with your physical eyes My Being which was evolved for you to see Me in the flesh at this very moment in the history of the cosmos. This moment also in the history of the spiritual world where I come from was created with parallel evolution. Spiritual Hierarchies of the Light prepared mankind's Souls for this very moment to exist in time so that the material and spiritual worlds were ready at the same moment in time. Your being and My Being are now in this moment.

I am asking you for a drink of water in the material world. You are seeing that who I am is both material and spiritual. Who I am will be the ultimate evolution of all human beings in the whole universe no matter what dimension they are in or receive Me in. In this

41

dimension on your earth I am now asking you to see who I am and to listen to My request as had you known all that I have outlined to you in Truth you would realise that I have the power to give you a well with water and when a man drinks from it he will have eternal life. This is what the Living Spiritual Light of the world can do for you and for all of mankind. So look carefully at the living power of the Ultimate Light before you. This Ultimate Light is the ultimate goal of all men who seek eternal Truth and who seek to quench their thirst for the Light that is above all in this universe. So had you known all of what I have just said to you, you would surely give Me the water I need from you now." [Verse 2]

The woman then replied, "How can I quench my thirst for this ultimate knowledge of the universe and its meaning in the Living Light you speak of? What is the pathway I need to walk on to know how to do this? You speak of a living well of eternal Light and Truth yet you have to see that you have to show me how I can draw this Light from this well. You have to show me the pathway that I need to follow to fulfil this in my life. I do not see you with your hands create this Light. I do not see what tools you use in the material world to achieve this. I see this Spiritual Light but I need a way to draw from it. I see then truly I will be able to nourish my being with this Ultimate Light of God.

I live in the material world and I need a way or a tool with the way to change the pattern of my material life as if I cannot do this the material world will stop me from reaching my goal to the Light. I see everywhere the material world winning for those who do not look to the Light. Now I see your Spiritual Light but it will not ultimately help me unless I can have the power independently of you to solve my daily material problems besides the one of drawing water everyday from this well.

So I ask you what possible tool could change the world so that it would look to the Light? Also our spiritual father is Jacob and he is the spirit guide of our race. Is your Spiritual Light above his? As I said I draw from this well the water that lets me survive in this life physically. Jacob and all of his generations have done the same. Jacob has also represented for my race my whole spiritual identity with my being. I have no way of changing who I am and the race to which I belong. So what is the pathway now that you speak of? How can I relate to it so that I can drink from your Spiritual Light?"

The Christ Being replied, "I am the Living Light of this universe and of your planet. I have come to give men a pathway to eternal love by following a pathway to the Ultimate Truth of life and by showing mankind that this Ultimate Truth has its ultimate source in the Light of My Being.

This Light can be reached by any individual human being who seeks the Truth of life with the Eyes of Light that can be given to any initiand of the Light of the Christ Being who loves the Moral Will to it. This Moral Will is the tool the person has to have to acquire the Eyes of the Light. It is the tool that can only be used with the freedom of using free will to choose the Light. To have living Light is to have the living water of life. Like water Light needs to be drawn from a well. The well from which the Light is drawn comes from

the Ultimate Light of this universe; the Living Christ Being, Myself.

I have come to show the world a new pathway that is superior to mankind's fate and speaks of his ultimate spiritual fate. This fate is based on spiritual love. This is the highest form of evolution in this universe. So he who sees that there is any greater task than to fulfil the incarnation of a whole universe sees not the Light. To accomplish this task the individual human being needs to learn how to draw from this spiritual well of living Light that can sustain a person for eternity. A person does this by learning how to speak to My Being; I, the Christ Being.

You will be able to do this when you look to the Light and then let My Light reach your being. When this happens you will have the power of the Light to let your Eyes of Light be opened so you can see into the spiritual world. Then with this power you will have the living spiritual water of Living Light pour into your Soul and your living body. This power will let you live forever in the

Light of God, the Almighty Father; My Father in Heaven." [Verse 3] [2]

Then the Christ Being said to this woman, "Ask your husband to come here as I need to talk to him to tell him about the Light and the future of the Truth of life and that he has a woman who has learned how to put the Truth above a relationship. He has a wife who has learned to love in the Light unconditionally and he is to take responsibility for the love given by her."

Then the woman looked at Jesus and said to him, "I am not married but I have given my word to one man to love forever with my whole heart. We are united in this love and we have Light."

The Christ Being then replied, "The Truth is that you have been married five times and each time you loved unconditionally. Each time you lost your Light as you gave your Truth to the wrong person. Now you have found the Light as this love has been returned to you unconditionally. Hence by putting the Truth above all relationships and living your Truth in relationship, regardless of whether or not you received love back, you ultimately were given the Ultimate Light in relationship as you put the Truth above relationship even though each time each person whom you loved did not take responsibility for the love you gave. So by taking the right Moral Steps you walked away each time from each relationship when it was not in the Light. Hence you suffered greatly until you had the Truth in your life in loving another person. So thus you fulfilled your Moral karma. This is the reason now you have the moral power to change the pattern of your life. This is the reason you can speak to My Being, the Christ Being, about the Truth of marriage as marriage is a symbol that is legally and spiritually recognised by mankind as the ultimate expression of the Truth in relationship.

Every person who loves in the Light has been married twice in their lives to the same person. They have done this by first being married or by first consciously deciding to give their whole being to the

---

[2] John 4: 4-15.

other person by putting the Truth above the love they have for them. This means that a person is married for others and a person is married for himself with this other person he loves unconditionally with a life commitment. He does this as this way he gives his word for life. However again today so many embrace the marriage for the people without being married for themselves. To truly love in the Light a word between two people is enough. However for a person who seeks to fulfil the pathway for the future of his children marriage legally gives Light to the community as a whole. Hence symbolically both are necessary for the spiritual needs of the human being to truly live his Truth in the Light." [Verse 4] [3]

The woman then said, "You have truly spoken of what is in my heart. You have said what I have needed to say all my life long about loving unconditionally a person who loves you in the same way and putting this above the society you are in. That is, putting this type of marriage of Truth between two people above the community and its rules. Then

to try to fulfil what society asks of you for the sake of your children and future generations."

The Christ Being then replied, "To do this and in this way know how to put Truth above love, one then wins the future of his being and his happiness in relationship when one follows the pathway of accepting that he does not know the future of what another person will do in the relationship. However he is certain of his trust in that person. He is certain that this trust will win over the world and what it can do to stop the Truth in that love.

So you have truly the pathway to love another person in the Light of the Christ Being as I have come to all men so that they can love the Truth and live it. The Light creates for mankind the healing Light of all relationship problems as without this Light the Truth alone will never prevail. As truly I say to you he who has love in his heart for the Light has My Being in his Soul. So only love another being when the other loves in the Light. So woman that the man you love now is not your husband tells

---

[3] John 4: 16-18.

Me that as you love in the Light you have Truth in your heart."

The Samaritan woman turned to speak to the Christ Being with warmth of the love she had in her heart for the Light and said, "You are truly the Christ Being as your words are full of Truth and tell the story of a life of one who can see behind the veil of material existence in the spiritual world. Hence you are not just a prophet who tells of the future of this planet but you are a Spiritual Being with supernatural powers as you can see the future of what is in a man's heart as what is in a man's heart is what is in a man's life. His heart is his future. Your heart is made of pure, golden Light. Yes, you are the Prophet of the Light.

The spiritual guides of our race in past generations gave us the Light of their beings on this mountain. This Light still is in my heart and Soul. I see that your pathway is to be the Spiritual Light Being of the whole world. So you say that Jerusalem is the City of the Light and that this is where the Saviour of mankind will sit on His throne to give Light to all of mankind. The guides of the past were all pointing to this evolution of the Light of your Father's Being."
[Verse 5]

The Christ Being then stood up and said, "Woman be aware that the universe needs to be redeemed to follow the Ultimate Light of My Being. The Ultimate Truth of life stands before you. If a man worships in Jerusalem or on the top of this mountain unless he speaks from his heart he will lose his Light as when one opens the Doorway to the Light he has to be worthy of the Light. So it is his pathway that will make him worthy of his will to follow the Truth above all things in his life to find the Light. What makes him unworthy is when his pathway is false and he does not live his Truth even though he may acknowledge the Light. Even if he acknowledges the Light of My Being it can be worse for him when he does not live his own Truth as this contradiction the evil one will exploit to get the person to believe in the lie that God is a lie. So know this; a person needs to know his pathway on how he aligns his Truth to the Light. He needs to know how to align also the Light with his Truth. So this way he truly worships in the Light.

The Jews have been chosen to receive Me in their race. I have chosen with the Father to follow their pathway and be a Jew. However now I see that I am trying to speak to you so that you can see how your race with the Jews needs salvation in the form of following the Ultimate Light of My Being. [Verse 6]

When mankind has evolved to the point when the world will come closer in the next epoch to the end of time on earth, when all of mankind will acknowledge the Living Light of God, the Father, then this is when mankind will know how to make Light above all things in the universe. This is when the Father, My Being and the Holy Spirit will become one with mankind on an earth that will belong to Heaven.

Then those who have given their Souls to the Light of the Father will be at one with My Being and they will shine before the universal cosmos of beings for eternity in the Spiritual World in the Light. It is then that the Spirit of the earth will be part of the Spiritual Light of God and matter will be merged with Spirit as this will be the end of the material existence of the earth. This is the Ultimate

Truth of your planet. This is its fate and the fate of those who follow the Light of My Being and who honor My Father and give Light back to Him for those who do this worship the Eternal Light of all Universes. They worship My Father, the Living God of the Light." [Verse 7]

The woman then looked at Jesus and said to him, "The Messiah is coming. He will reveal the eternal Truth of the cosmos and of the Light of Heaven. You speak the words of the Messiah of mankind. Are you not he then when you have brought Light to my heart and made a picture of my Soul with your words to me today? Do you see in men's hearts and Souls and do you see truly the Truth of the world as you are he, are you not, the Messiah of the Light of the world?"

Then Jesus looked at her being and said, "I am the Living Christ Being, Son of the Living God. I am the Light of all Ages. I have come to speak to you today as you have spoken to Me every time you walk in the Light with living your Truth. You honor the Truth of life. Hence you have won the Light of My Father who has sent Me to you as you

47

have loved in the Light. So now God and His very Being loves you for he who loves the Light loves God and loves My Being and mankind as when a man can love unconditionally one person in the Light and it is returned the Light of God is with this union. This is so as this union is aligned with Heaven and its Light shines upon the Souls and bodies of those who honor the pledge to love with one's whole heart and with one's whole Soul in the Light." [Verse 8] [4]

Soon after this Jesus' Apostles came back from their shopping and saw him speaking to this woman. They wondered what truly he was doing as this person was intensely interested in the same Light they could see in the Christ Being. They observed that when he spoke a radiance was about him and in his presence there was an energy field that permeated an aura of majesty. Yet with his white flowing garments and his face that had a shining quality to it that had eyes that were full of Light, a person could not help fall under a magic spell of this being that radiated this white Light all around him.

The woman was beautiful in a special way. Her hidden type of beauty was not only her body but was within her eyes and in the way she spoke to Jesus. She had a Light like they did. This they knew. What this Light was now was obvious to them and its ultimate source was their Teacher; their mentor, their Light. So they could not interrupt him talking to the lady although they knew he was hungry as they with him had not eaten all day.

They were too busy traveling and talking while they were being instructed about how they had to take the right initiation steps to secure how the Eyes of Light in their Souls would grow and be able to see into the spiritual world as they were already beginning to see into it when they heard the Christ Being speak about His Father or about his mission. It was like a veil was lifted over the sense world and they could see behind the material world into the spiritual world.

When this happened around Jesus this Light appeared around him and around them. In the beginning this was not

---

[4] John 4: 19-26.

48

so strong but appeared now and then when he would speak but now they saw that the more the instructions became clear the closer they came to speaking out of their Souls and into the spiritual world and back to the material world. They began to see the Angels around Jesus in the spiritual world and they could see that he would talk to them even when he was talking to his Apostles. They could even see glimpses of this Heaven he spoke of as if a Doorway to Heaven was right next to Jesus when his thoughts centred on teaching them about his journey to redeem mankind. [Verse 9]

Once the woman saw that Jesus was being prepared a meal by his followers she decided to leave the jar of water next to the well and go into the town to bring her husband in name to Jesus as she knew she had found the Messiah; the Christ. When she met her husband in name she explained to him what had happened at the well when she met Jesus. She told him about how he knew how to make a picture of her Soul and how he also knew about her Moral Will to the Ultimate Light of the Universe. Then she made it quite clear that

she met one man who spoke in the same way as they had both lived. That is, to love unconditionally in the Light and that the Truth is above love and that the Light is above the Truth. Knowing this she knew she had also all her life with her previous husbands followed the pathway of her parents and gave love unconditionally to the wrong individuals.

However when she met her real love in her husband in name she had created a real pathway to the Truth of life. Hence the Truth of life can only be fulfilled when a person loves in the Light of the Ultimate Truth of the World; this being God's Light as He is the Ultimate Truth.

When she said all of this her husband could see that there was confirmation for him and his life commitment to his real wife in name of what unconditional love is when it is aligned with the Light of Heaven. This meaning that the Light of the world and the Light of mankind comes from the Light of God as He loves mankind unconditionally. Therefore when a man puts Him first in his life his Soul grows up and is initiated into the Spiritual Light of the spiritual world. He could see that he can trust in God unconditionally and that when he gives back Light to God as he and this woman had then God lights up his life. He knew that as truly mankind has a Principle of Light and a Principle of Truth that unless it first works between husband and wife then the cosmos itself cannot breathe or live and be nourished in the Light as man's body was evolved out of the spiritual world and made material with a parallel evolution to the elements in his material world.

He knew that this parallel evolution of the earth and mankind had a beginning. Its ultimate destination is God and at the end of time on earth man must have another home in Heaven with God. The Messiah is the Christ Being who shows mankind in the flesh this cosmic evolution and how it evolved into humankind. This Principle has to have as its centre, love. As a human being needs love to live as it is above even his want for food to survive so the food of the Soul is love and the food of the body is what he needs to sustain it materially. Hence the riddle of the universe could only be

answered when a person could speak of the Truth of love and how it works between man and woman as this is truly the ultimate expression of God in man's heart. His love for man is shown in this man; the Christ Being. The only way a person was going to see the Light of the Universe was for him to speak to the Living Light in the flesh at some time on earth in one of his life times. He was privileged now to have the experience of the Light in his love of the Truth in his relationship and how he could see from what his partner in life had said to him that finally the world had been given with mankind the living embodiment of God in one person. This was truly the ultimate love of God to mankind and to himself and the person he loved most in his whole life; the person he loved with his whole heart and Soul and body. Hence this was now clear to him that the pathway to Ultimate Light is unconditional love of the Light.

Once this was clear in his heart this man wanted others to share in this realisation of the Ultimate Truth knowing full well that only those who truly loved the Light would listen to him. So he was sure to advise his wife in name to speak only of what Jesus had told and not of what she knew of him as the Messiah. He advised her that she should let others make up their minds not from their understanding of what she alone experienced but also from their experience of this being. He told her that not all she would speak to would respond to the Light as this was quite obvious to him now as he had not as yet been able to marry for the community and had to marry only in his heart the one he loved. So he had to be aware of being able to be speaking the Truth and living it when he spoke of the Truth of life. Therefore he cautioned his partner to say all that was in her heart but only from the standpoint of letting the person involved have the experience of the Christ Being before having his reality in their life and the life of their world.

So his wife in name began to tell all her friends of what was in her heart and what it was like to see the Eyes of the Light in another human being. This being gave this Light directly from his being and not only had these Eyes filled with the Light but could see with these Eyes into the very Soul of any man and into the secrets of his heart and speak of the future of mankind with words that outlined a pathway to an ultimate destiny for it, where the Light would shine upon the face of every person in the universe who looked towards it. [Verse 10]

Then this woman once again approached Jesus and said to him, "I know that the Ultimate and Eternal Father in Heaven has given us the consciousness in every epoch, in every life time, to see the evolution of the Light upon the earth. I also see that this Light comes from an infinite, universal and Cosmic source that has traveled to the earth through Celestial time. This time is engineered by the Heavenly Hierarchies of the Light of the Messiah to come. So that I am a living being, living in Cosmic time with an ultimate destiny to the Ultimate Light of the Universe and all Universes.

When I speak to the Messiah called the Christ Being I am able to know who I am as a human being and as a Cosmic being. This meaning that I will have all the knowledge I need to fulfil my pathway on this journey to the Ultimate Light.

The Ultimate Truth of unconditional love of the Light is my Truth and the Truth of life. The Light of the Christ Being is this Ultimate Light."

Then Jesus looked at her and could see that the Eyes of the Light had revealed to her his Being of Light. He then said, "I am the Christ Being. I am the Living Light. He who sees Me sees the Light. He who follows Me follows the Ultimate Light." [Verse 11]

After this Jesus could see many had come to hear him speak as this woman had spread the message of Light to all she met. She told her friends, "If you want to know what is in your Soul and have your Truth revealed to you out of a pure heart of golden Light the Christ Being had arrived on the planet earth." She told them that the Messiah of the planet had come to redeem mankind with a Philosophy of Light and behind the Philosophy was a living power that one could see in living flesh in one man.

In his words one could have an everlasting source of nourishment for his whole being as she said the picture of her Soul that Jesus gave her

was a living **Light Shield**. This Shield was now imprinted upon her very heart. Her Soul could now speak with an absolute Moral Will to the Living Truth of the Light and truly the Living Light was the Living Light Shield for the world as it gave the Shield mankind needed to begin to see with the Eyes of the Light the picture of the Light in its being. This way mankind could see its being. So it created the Spirit of Light in this Shield of Light around the whole self as then a person became a self of Light. His higher self became a part of this universal Light when he could see into his Soul with this Light Shield as the Christ Being is this Light Shield in living form.

His words which compose this Light Shield create this consciousness for the individual to have these Eyes of Light so that the Eyes can see what one has lived and what one has to live to change his pattern of life on earth this time and so that the past lives lived in the past on earth can ultimately come to one being in one life in Heaven. To do this a person has to have the guiding Light of the Christ Being as then he truly walks in the Light and avoids the darkness. Then truly he knows that he needs the Light to shield him from the darkness.

The Christ Being is the Ultimate Light that will ultimately make the ultimate darkness leave the planet earth at the end of physical time on earth. The Cosmic Light clock of the universe has been created by the Father so as to give mankind his universal and ultimate free will to choose His Son, the Christ Being, who will give Light to the planet so that it will live with a living Light that will propel it to the Spiritual Heaven of Light where all the universes that have chosen Light will be in the sphere of the Hierarchies of Light. So that all mankind will live in a Spiritual Light made up of planets of Light with Light Beings.

All of these things this woman spoke of to her friends so that they could see what the Eyes of the Light that she had acquired from the Christ Being had revealed to her. He had given her a Cosmic map of her Soul and that of mankind and his earth as it is placed in the galaxy around it at its

stage of evolution towards the Light and the Father of all Universes of Light. [Verse 12] [5]

After this Jesus' Apostles asked him to have something to eat as he had not had anything all day long. He then replied to their request by saying, "The food that I eat is the Heavenly bread of My Father. He places it before Me everyday so that I can nourish My Being. When I eat it I am in communion with the Light of the Universe. His presence fills My Soul with His eternal love. It gives Me this great love of all beings and the power to share this Light with you that I have come to earth for. So I tell you I am well fed already with this Heavenly Light."

The Apostles still had not at this stage of seeing with the Eyes of Light been able to see that Jesus was actually in the other dimension at the same time as he was with them on earth. So they said to themselves, "Who has given him something to eat today?" They looked at each other in amazement as he was with them the whole day from sunrise.

---

[5] John 4: 27-30.

53

The Christ Being then looked at their incomprehension of his words and continued to say, "My Being is being nourished by the Father. He is telling Me that the world is receiving the food of Light from it. He is saying that My task is the dream of the world to fulfil its pathway. This pathway will lead it ultimately to a goal where it will evolve into this Spiritual Light in a cosmos of Light. Each human being will become an organism of living Light on his planet. Like nature his evolution will be perfected to completion so that at the end of physical time on earth his body will not need any more physical food but will need only the nourishing Light of His Being and My Being. This is the moment when mankind will become one with the pathway of the Holy Spirit as His Being now circles the universe to create the pathway to this ultimate goal of one body and one Spirit in the whole cosmos of being. This is when a human being will have a complete body of Light.

The universe is evolving in a cycle of evolution and development. Each man with every moral act he undertakes propels the movement of the universe forward or pushes the evolution in its opposite direction with immoral acts. The Light pattern of the universe is the macrocosm and the Light pattern of every individual Soul is the microcosm.

When a person can cosmically time this process of how the microcosm relates to the macrocosm in his own individual life then he can see demographically where he is in the Cosmic Light map of the universe. He can see his journey to the Ultimate Light. He can know that his task is to become a part of those who will see that nature works in cycles. This cycle works in man. The cycle of Light in the cosmos shows man that he has to have the tools to relate in the right way to the cycle. The tools are the methods used to harvest the fields of work that enhance mankind's consciousness of the Light of his universe.

He who uses the right tools to enhance this consciousness of Light on earth bears the fruit of God as this fruit comes from the labor of his whole being as when a human being walks in the Light of My Being he labors in the Light. His work changes a world. His will propels the universe to its ultimate journey of the home of eternal love. Hence his eternal home is the place where his Soul lives at times until the completion of this journey on the earth.

He sees this home of the Light through the Eyes of the Light so that when he looks up to Heaven he is looking to the Light. He sees that his participation of creating this pathway to the Light that he is walking on gathers and harnesses this eternal power of the Light of all Ages. So that the Living Light of God becomes part of his Soul. Hence he becomes perfected in the love and Light of God. He becomes complete. He becomes a person standing before God with a whole being of living Light. This is the Ultimate Will of My Father in Heaven for all men; to join in the work of redemption and to accept that to be saved is to evolve to the ultimate potential of evolving into a Being of Light.

This is why I have come to the earth, to show you the pathway that has been given to you by the Father; the Father of all Universes. Being saved by the Saviour of the Light means being saved to be redeemed to follow this pathway away from its opposite which only devolves the world into darkness. This Light in the darkness comes to every human heart when the person labors for this love of the Light which means when a person sees that as he has created this pathway with the Eyes of the Light God is creating His parallel pathway in the cosmos so that the ultimate meeting will bind this eternal pathway into the pathway of eternal Light in Heaven as this is the work of redemption.

Hence this is why I have come to the world; to make all mankind have a share in the work of My Father. Before this there was no ultimate pathway to Him; this being a pathway to My Being. All religions spoke of Me from the beginning of time. Now I have come; I, the Christ Being, Son of the Living God, the Living Light of all epochs and the Eternal Light and Life of this World." [Verse 13] [6]

Many of the Samaritan woman's friends came to Jesus after he had spoken to her. They listened to him and

---

[6] John 4: 31-38.

55

his Spirit walked among them when he spoke to them about the eternal Light of the fruit of God. It was as if there were more than one of him as each person was speaking to him individually with their Souls in the other dimension of their physical existence which they perceived radiated around him like a Spiritual Heaven, while physically he was giving a sermon to them all.

A piece of Heaven had descended in their midst. The echo of Heavenly music could be heard when he spoke with the golden tones of the Orator from Heaven. He said, "Be holy. Find the true pathway to the Truth. Put the Light above all things. Let your Soul evolve so that it can have Eyes that can see the Heavenly Light come to it. Be a whole human being. Face the world but do not become a part of it. Become a part of its Light. Shed its darkness away from your being. Let this part of it devolve with those who seek it. Let the law of the Light rule your heart. Speak the Truth of your life then make the choice to love in freedom. Make the choice to love in freedom. Make the choice to love in the Light. Let your hearts open to its Truth. Then let the eternal Light speak to it so that it will

follow its pathway. Walk in the Light of God and know the Truth.

Do not forsake the Truth for power, money or love as all this a man needs to be a part of the world. However know the world for what it is. Real love lives in the heart and not only in the body. Money and power are there to create a material home for mankind and not a prison of wealth where the jailers hypnotize their prisoners with it. False wealth creates a false Light. Its beauty shines until its darkness is revealed. This is evidenced by the relationship those have to others who have sacrificed their Souls to power. Their motive is always to be the most important people of the world. Hence their falsehood is shown by their putting this above the Light.

The first point of this revelation comes from the suppression of doing what is in a person's heart and in doing what is in a person's mind. Hence the intellect is put above the Light. This is the way to the power of darkness. So the right pathway is when a person understands the power of the Light. When he knows this he

56

knows My Being. He knows that all that he does in his life propels a whole world towards the Light of Heaven or the darkness of hell and that in his hands he has the power of the destiny of the world.

I, the Christ Being, have come to save the world and not to speak of its darkness or of the evil one who would devolve it for his own kingdom. My Kingdom belongs to those who want to be saved and are willing to live their Truth to save their being. That is, those who also know that unless they can align their beings with the Light of the ultimate Light of the universe they will not have protection from this dark power against the Truth of the world. This is now My Truth. This is now what I have come to you today to say to show you how to bring your Souls to see with the Eyes of the Light."

After this one of the Samaritan woman's friends turned to her and said, "We have been redeemed by the Christ Being, the Saviour of the World. His Soul has touched ours and now we can see into it and can speak from it ourselves. We no longer need you to tell us about the Truth of this being. We have experienced this being in our whole spirit. He is the Light of the World. He is the Christ." [Verse 14] [7]

Following this Jesus decided to go to Galilee. At one point before he came to Cana in Galilee he began to speak to some Galileans and he said to them, "You have heard Me speak to the Samaritans but you do not really believe in My Words. You have come to know Me but not who I am. I tell you above all things a person is who he is no matter what the world measures him to be. You are measuring Me by My background. You are not making the measure of what I have said or done for mankind but what was My origin according to your society. You have made the measure of man your rules about him when you should be making the measure of man the ultimate Truth of life.

You say that the law is the truth but this is traditional Light. I say to you that until your traditional Light touches the Light in your Soul there will be no Ultimate Light in your life. So make the

---

[7] John 4: 39-42.

measure of all things first your Truth in relation to the Ultimate Truth. This way you will learn to honor the one who brings Light to the whole world; the one who is speaking to you now. I am the Christ Being; he who brings Light to the whole world. Open your eyes and you will see the Source of the Light of the Universe. Honor then the Light above the Truth as to know the Truth is to know the pathway to the Ultimate Light; the Christ Being."
[Verse 15] [8]

Following this Jesus went to Cana where he had first showed the Special Keys of Christ by turning the water into wine at the wedding feast. Then later he went on to Caper'na-um. Here he was approached by an official who was looking for him as his son was seriously ill.

This man had been told that Jesus had left Judea to come to Galilee. When he met Jesus he said to him, "Master have pity on my son for he is about to leave this world. I love him with all of my heart. I love him more than life itself. I ask you to look with compassion at me and my real love for my son.

Please use your powers so that he may live as I have heard it said that you have this power to give life to those who ask you for it; to those who ask you with a pure heart. I am asking you with all of my heart and Soul. Master please look at me and help me in my desperate hour of need. Let me see the sun shine again in my life as death has cast a shadow upon my life and my whole being. I cannot live without my son as he has made the sun shine in my life as I love him and this gives me the Light you speak of and the one that I also seek in my life to align my whole being with. Please, I beg you, help me Master and save my son."

Jesus then looked away from him and said, "He who loves another unconditionally and with Truth in his heart has Light in his life. However when it is returned only then does the Ultimate Light become a part of that union of Light and love. Only then is there truly Spiritual Light in that person's being. I say to you, those who only believe because they get ultimately what they want do not really ever receive what they need to be happy in their life as they

---

[8] John 4: 43-45.

have only loved when they know there was no real giving from them. There was only a form of receiving as the material world took over the spiritual one in their hearts. So you have those who want to have physical proof first to prove to them that they can only trust another person when they have all the rational facts before their eyes. Truly this is the basis of a materialistic scientific mind that believes only in what it can see with its eyes and its intellect. Hence what you have is the identification with love above the Truth or of success above the Truth. So once again this is transferred on to all human levels of relationship.

So truly only when a person loves truly unconditionally in the Light and aligns this to the Ultimate Light does he learn that the Light is above the Truth and the Truth is above success in getting what one wants as the Truth belongs to receiving what one needs from the Light of his being. So truly a man can believe in only what he sees or he can create in his being the Eyes of the Light that not only see what is in his life but what created his life and what can

take it away. So death and life have a different meaning as he can see their ultimate goal in the Light of the Universal Truth of God." [Verse 16] [9]

Then this man said, "I love my son unconditionally. I know that the Ultimate Light in your being, Master, gives him life. I also know that my son will die unless you decide to give him this life. I ask this in my name and on the point that I love the Light unconditionally. I know also that this is the Will of God if my son dies. I ask you as the Son of God to see that I have seen who you are with the Eyes of the Light in my Soul. Please now let your power set free the Light upon my son's Soul so that he shall live."

At that moment Jesus, the Christ Being, looked directly at this man and one could see that he loved him for his faith in his words. He said to the man, "I have already been speaking to My Father in Heaven who has asked the Holy Spirit to take your son's Soul back into his body. He will live as the love you have for your son has shown the Father that you love in the Light. So now go to your son.

---

[9] John 4: 46-48,

59

He will be well now and his illness will leave him. Be aware that as you have aligned your Soul with a pure heart and followed the Light with your own Eyes of the Light you have been able to let this Cosmic Light reach out and change physical energy fields around your son's being. I, the Christ Being, have used a Special Key of the Ultimate Light to fulfil My Father's Will as this Spiritual Cosmic Light comes to those who follow their Truth and the Truth of the Ultimate Love of God for mankind and his world. Your son is saved as the Light is above death."

Then this man knew in his heart that this energy coming from the Living Light Being before him in the flesh had transmitted the power of the Light and transformed imminent death into life. So he thanked Jesus for his compassion and his love of humanity and began to run back to his home anticipating the well – being of his son on his journey to it. [Verse 17] [10]

In the middle of the street close to his house one of his servants who knew where he had gone stopped him and grabbed him by the shoulders and shouted out with all the power of his voice, "Master, master, your son is well again. He lives and he speaks like he did before he was ill. He laughs and he talks full of life and there is Light in his heart. Please come and see for yourself. I had to run and come and tell you as soon as I saw you coming down the road and as I am certain of the Truth. Before my very eyes as I have seen what I just told you."

When the servant said this he could see a strange look in his master's eyes of calmness and found it hard to believe with his own eyes that his master was not overwhelmed with happiness at this news as he knew very well how much this man loved his son. Before he could speak and say what was on his mind his master asked him, "Tell me now when did my son heal? When did the illness leave him? Do you know the time that it happened? Did it happen suddenly or do you recall a specific hour? Please tell me as this is very important to me."

Then his servant said, "It all

---

[10] John 4: 49-50.

60

happened suddenly at seven o'clock yesterday evening. He just got up from his bed and began to speak coherently and with a light heart. The fever had gone out of him in a flash. At first we thought he was going to just relapse and drop back to bed from sleepwalking or something like that but he kept speaking on and on. We could not believe our eyes. I must say, master, as I think I love your son almost as much as you love him, tears were beginning to flow so it took me a while to compose myself to speak and to verify for myself that he was really free from this cursed fever. However he was and we have been waiting for your return with such eagerness to tell you such good news. A million tons have been lifted from my head." He could see then that his master was smiling and tears were in his eyes with this truly wonderful news.

The servant's master then felt this great joy not only because his son was saved but also because his own Eyes of Light had revealed to him the touch of God's love upon his Soul. He had met the Son of the Living God; the Christ Being.

He had met him at this hour in the evening the day before. The words came back to his being; "The Light is above death." Then he said to his servant, "Truly I have learnt today that from now on I need to put the Ultimate Light above life. This is truly now what is my Moral Will to this Light."

He then came to his house and embraced his son who was filled with the magic of the love of his father whom he knew in his heart had saved him. The sun was shining in his life again. Then the father spoke of Jesus. "I tell you all I have found the Ultimate Light of the World amongst us. I spoke to him yesterday evening and he told me that my son will live as the Light is above life or death. I now also see that with the Eyes of the Light in my being I have been able to find the Light of all Ages in the flesh in one human being. He has given back to us my son."
[Verse 18] [11]

The Christ Being had now begun to use the Special Keys of Light to change the future of mankind. This was now the

---

[11] John 4: 51-53,

61

second Special Key of Light

used since he had left Judea to travel in Galilee. [Verse 19] [12]

---

[12] **John 4: 54.**

CHAPTER 5

Jesus was now in Jerusalem when there was a festival celebrating a Jewish holiday. He was walking among a crowd of people near the place where there was a pool of water covered by a roof of stone with Roman columns holding it up with walls in between them. In this place, which was called Beth-za'tha, a group of handicapped people used to gather as the belief was that a Spirit would stir the water and whoever would enter the water first would be healed.

There were all types of people seeking this healing power from the lame to the blind and the paralyzed. One who was there had come to the pool for thirty – eight years to find this healing power. He had now done what he always did; wait for the water to stir and then hope that at the same time someone would put him in the water as he could not walk.

He had been an invalid for most of his life. Yet every time he hoped that God would give him this chance to be cured of his handicap he never lost sight of the Light. He would ask God to let him walk again just once before he would die as he had already accepted his fate of never walking again in his lifetime. Yet at the same time he willed that the Eyes of the Light would show him his real fate to come when he would die. He had prayed everyday that his Soul would walk in Heaven with a Body of Light.

Those around him who got to the pool every time it stirred always disregarded him and ignored his pleas for help to get to the pool as he could not walk fast enough unaided. So the Angel of the Lord seeing what they were doing would not cure them. Then they would curse the water and blame him for disturbing the Spirit from performing the healing miracle they were asking for.

So seeing all this the Christ Being came closer to the edge of the pool and looked across to this old man and his eyes met his. In that instant this old man knew that Light had come to his being. He knew that his prayers were now being materialised as now the Light had come to him. He had always dreamed that he would be the one going to the Light in death. Around the Christ Being there appeared to his eyes a golden Light that emanated from his being and his garments. This Light could only be seen by this man. However everyone could see that Jesus was a being who commanded an authority that could only be explained as a living magnet of energy in white garments that gave him an aura of Light and brightness in the sunlight of that day. [Verse 1] [1]

Then Jesus said, "You have been asking for the Ultimate Light to heal your being and your body as you know your being was healed long ago as you have had Spiritual Light in your very Soul for many decades. However now you are asking for your body to be healed so that you can walk in Heaven. So you want the Healing Light of Heaven to reach your physical person so that you can be worthy to walk in the streets of the Kingdom of Heaven. I tell you the Healing Light is already reaching your limbs as the Father and I have willed it long ago. You will now see that you are already being healed by your work on your being now and by your absolute faith in the Light. So I say to you, what is truly in your heart; to live or to die and to go to Heaven? What is truly your dream now of life?"

The man then said to Jesus, "I truly love the Light and the Truth of life. I know that my Eyes of Light can see that you are the Living Light before mankind's eyes come to save it for eternity. So it makes no difference to me what is truly the Will of God as I have lived my Truth and aligned it with the Ultimate Wisdom of God. I have trusted in His decision to let me wait for your coming for thirty – eight years. I see that I have now been rewarded as I have the privilege to speak to you about my plight. I would have liked, of course, that my fellow man would have given me some Light so as to justify my unconditional love of mankind. Yet I see now that as I have truly loved myself and my being unconditionally, I have truly loved the Light in the same way as I can say truly that I have lived what I have said about life. Hence I have put the Truth above my ailment. I have put the Light above it. Now I say then I have been put second to all those who could get to the pool before me. The Eyes of the Light have revealed to me the Angel that stirs the water but does not let the Healing Spirit heal such people, has today put me first as I am speaking to the Light behind the Angels of all the universe. So this is my answer to you, Oh, Christ Being."

---

[1] John 5: 1-5.

Then Jesus said to him, "You will now begin to walk and start a new life with the Eyes of the Light as they will not only show you your Truth but will give you the living power to live it. You will be able to change the pattern of your life with the living power of the Eyes you created with the Light in your Soul. You did this by your Moral Will to My Light. You put the Light above your life. Hence now you are healed. So I, the Christ Being, say to you; you will walk in My Kingdom now in your Spirit and you will walk in body on the earth as you have become a living example of one who lives in the Light. So walk in the Light of My Being.

You are cured as you first healed your Soul and your psyche before asking that your body be healed. So now you have transformed your being as you waited for the right moment to let the Light germinate in it. Hence you now walk in the Light of the Christ Being. You could have reprimanded God for making you wait for all these years and you could have this way identified with making Truth relative by saying that simply this is what I am suffering and no one can say I deserve this. Hence you would have talked only of the effect and not of the cause of your illness. This

way Truth would have been lost to the materialistic conceptualizations of your world. Yet you put the Truth above your whole being and this way the Light put you above your world; your spiritual world first and now your material world.

So I say to you, your Moral Will to the Light has to be the shining example of the man who puts this first above all things in his life. His karma or his environment come second. Surely one could see that by saying to you that you are paying for your past misdeed in a past life or that it is your lot and luck in life that your world does not have a remedy for your sickness are the words of the proponents of those who want to sell Intellectual Materialism [1b] as their view of the cosmos. They want to speak about what affects one's being but not of what is the cause of such effects unless they are collective generalisations where individual moral responsibility is but simply an attitude in a person instead of

---

[1b] The ideology of Intellectual Materialism is discussed in the second volume of *The Collected Works of The Science of Spiritual Talking* and is related to the work done by the Inner Light Society of the Cosmic Christ.

a real moral value, meaning that a person who has no moral value speaks always first about the reasons for his problems but never speaks about his Truth concerning them. Once a person depersonalises Truth then he objectifies the Light and darkness enters and the Light then cannot take away the power of the creator of darkness.

However when the Moral Will is there a person begins to heal his very Soul and his personality regardless of the gravity of the darkness creating the problems faced in life. So truly your Truth has given you your Moral Will when you chose to carry on waiting for the day to walk physically in the Light of the Ultimate Truth. This is the Truth. So go and walk now as the Truth has made you free for this life time and those to come in the Light." This took place on the Sabbath, the weekly Jewish holiday. [Verse 2] [2]

Then a Jew approached the old man who now was cured and could walk and said to him, "You have no right to walk around as you do on the Sabbath proclaiming that you have been cured by God. This is false as you cannot say that God has done this or you will be just speaking for Him. You have no right to do this. God has to speak for Himself. When you read the book of our laws you hear Him speak. He does tell you that only by following His law will you be saved. So obviously something else has cured you but it was not from God as if this were so it would not be against His law and you would not be pretending as you are that God cured you when you have obviously not observed the Law of God.

The Law of God states that the Sabbath must be observed and that work cannot be done on this day. Since you have broken this law what has happened to you does not come from God, meaning you are saying things that come from your head and this is not being objective about what happened as anyone can say anything and believe in what he wants to believe but it does not change the truth in our law as our law is fundamentally the words of God. He is in the words of the law.

---

[2] John 5: 6-9.

No other religion of our earth can claim that the living personality of God is in the words of their law but we can claim this. This is the reason He has chosen us to save the world with the Messiah to come. So the Spirit of God cannot be with you as if it were you would not have compromised the law and your identity would be free of all other ideas or voices of conscience as no voice of conscience can take away the voice of the eternal law of God as He is my conscience and the conscience of the Jewish race.

So, old man, you have obviously done something wrong. So I ask you, who helped you with this magic? Was it coming from some occult power that works with miracles of darkness? Come clean now. Tell me and all of us, what is it that you did to accomplish this transformation in your body? Who did this for you? Tell us and you will begin to redeem yourself in the eyes of the Law of God."

Then this man replied, "I am not going against the Law of God when I am following my own conscience and the Spirit of the Law of God. I also accepted that the person who gave me the Light power to walk is a living being that has come to this planet to save it; to redeem it to the Light. Only when a person loves the Light with his whole heart will he observe truly the Law of God is the law of love.

You speak of the law of rules and conditions. Your love of the law is conditional and one-sided. You have lost your Light when you speak in this way. You do not look to the Light. You look to a shortcut to getting its power through rhetoric about what the Law of God says. You are hiding your conscience behind the written law. A conscience that is free is based on the free will of the Light. The Light of God has given this free will to man and that is why mankind was created to ultimately become a being with the Ultimate Light of God in his Soul which will ultimately choose freely to be in God's World of Light. Your conscience is in a straight – jacket that wants to have a highway to the spiritual world without any moral responsibility to the way you live your Truth.

Look here, man, you have accused me of breaking the law when truly it is you who have not followed the Light of God. So why do you not go and speak to the man whom you have defamed by saying that he uses darkness to cure human beings when in fact his occult Light has given me the Light power to see his being? He is the Living Light of this World. I know as I have been waiting to talk to him for thirty – eight years. You have just decided that it is not written that one should cure on the Sabbath. Your intellectual neutralisation of the Light of consciousness is fooling you with false pride. To say that you know the law because you can quote it and interpret it accordingly to what you live and others live is a delusion as the Truth is that one can do all of that and still be evil in his heart as the true measure of Truth comes when a person lives the Light in what he says and does.

I say to you clearly that the evidence is that this man who gave me these Eyes of the Light does all of this as he is the Source of the Light of this world. So to the contrary I have every right to walk around claiming that I have found the Light of my life as the Light is above the Law of God as the Law of God as it is written is based on the will of the Light in the human race. It also needs to respect the Free Will of God to act and to create in man the power to evolve the Law of God so that it meets the challenges of its every evolutionary stage of existence. So I say to you, follow the Truth first before you speak of the Law of God or you will be guilty of losing your identity and moral responsibility to the Law of God by intellectual materialistic interpretations of the religion of our race." [Verse 3] [3]

The Christ Being was present when the old man was approached by the Jewish fundamentalist, in the other dimension of the spiritual world. This had given the old man the Spiritual Light power to speak from the Eyes of the Light in such a way that his words were the voice of Christ in his Soul.

Then when he was walking away from everyone he saw Jesus suddenly next to him. Jesus then said to him, "You have been healed and your Soul and body are now filled with My Light. Follow the new pathway that I have revealed to you and you will meet Me

---

[3] John 5: 10-12.

again in the Spiritual Heaven that you have dreamed of all these decades when you have been speaking of Me and searching for Me as when you were doing this you were really not fully seeing that I was next to you and giving you the Light you needed to live on; to have faith in the Light, to love its pathway and to love ultimately My Being and My Father.

So now as you let your heart receive this Light you have been rewarded with the gift of My living presence in your being. So now follow the Ultimate Truth and you will have the Ultimate Light. The Ultimate Light is the Christ Being. This is I, the Living Christ of the World.

My Father created the Law of your race. He sent Me to create the Law of your world and its universe. You know now the Law of the Light as you can read its Scripture in your very Soul with the Eyes of the Light you have now gained from the Moral Will to meditate on My Being regardless of the pain or the suffering in your human life. This is now your fate to overcome sin and to surpass its power over your life as its power paralyzes first a man's

Spirit and then owns his Soul. From there the other realms of existence are affected and the aftermath is the karma to be lived and evolved from to the Light or devolved into darkness. Hence you have now your chosen Moral Will in the journey described before you in the Eyes of the Light. It is the parallel journey of all human beings who walk in the Light of the Christ Being, Son of the Eternal Light." [Verse 4] [4]

This man then went and told all the people in the place where he had for so long meditated on the Light of God that he had been healed by the faith he had had all along. He told them that the Christ Being had arrived on the planet earth and that he is the Son of the Father in Heaven, for who else could grant him his greatest desire after thirty – eight years of suffering? Who else had the power over life except God Himself? He was met with amazement and disbelief. So there was a negative reaction from some of the crowd who were getting closer to the old man so that they could hear what he had to say. One man said to him. "It is unlawful to work on the Sabbath. This healer has gone against our sacred laws. There

[4] John 5: 13-14.

69

must be something wrong with him and with what he did for you. It must be some kind of dark magic as it does not follow the Law of God which is a clear sign that there is another power here that is not from God as God does not break His own laws."

The man replied, "How can you say such a thing when he has cured me of an illness I have had for thirty – eight years? What in the world is God's Law but the Law of Truth above one's opinion of what is written in the Holy Scriptures? No one can deny that I have lived my Truth and lived what I have said all of my life long. Hence I speak now the Truth of what I have lived.

You, sir, are only speaking of what you have read in the law about the Sabbath. I have read it too. God did not break His own law when he healed me but to the contrary He gave Light to it, as the law is not above the Light. The Light of God comes from His unconditional love of mankind. He showed His love today.

If He chose the Sabbath then does He not have the Free Will you have to act out of mercy and compassion when a person has been asking Him for decades upon decades to give him Light to heal his body? So I say to you, sir, you are mistaken. You have made yourself qualified to speak about our religion but you are not qualified as you are obviously not living its Truth as its Truth has never denied that the Moral Will of the individual and its freedom to be used to fulfil the law and evolve the law is above just reading from it and saying that this is it. Who so ever does not follow it literally has no Light. To not have a living Truth then is not to live your Truth.

Sir, what right have you to say to me that I have participated in sin by not following the letter of the law? Who are you to make such an accusation? You have no more right than a person who remembers passages of the scripture and then purports to live his Truth by The Bible of God and then gives up his responsibility to question each passage accordingly to what he lives. Such a person does not relate his living experiences to the knowledge of the scriptures but relates what conveniently intellectually he can say to justify his own standpoint. Such a person, sir, has what I call a manufactured conscience and not one born of the Truth of what one lives in his being and in his life; just one born out of Intellectual Materialism.

I tell you what has been proven today is not only for us here in this time on earth but for the whole world evolution. It has shown mankind that not only what the Law of God says is the whole Truth when it is taken from the scriptures exclusively but it must also align to the type of eyes a person has in his Soul. If they are the Eyes of the Light then he will see what I have seen. He will hear what I have heard. He will experience the living Truth of what I am living in my heart and in my Soul and in my body. Truly this is living proof of the Fire of this Light."

While he was saying this the Christ Being was in his Spirit. It was as if he had spoken the words but the Spirit and the very Being in living form was the Being of Christ in his personality. Christ was next to him in this parallel invisible world; in this other dimension. [Verse 5] [5]

While Jesus was walking away from this place where he had talked to the old man about how to relate to his cure with the Light Power of God in his

being as the Christ Being, a Pharisee came up to him and said to Jesus, "You are following the wrong path and you have magical powers but they are from darkness as you put yourself equal to God and then use the powers of a black magician to make yourself look like a superior being. Be sure he who works with darkness will meet an evil end. I say this to you as I am a teacher of the law. I can be certain that what you are doing is fooling the gullible with your fantastic stories about another world. So what makes you truly one with God? How could anyone really tell if you are not just masquerading as the Almighty? What proof can you show me, a mere, mortal man?"

The Christ Being replied, "I the Christ Being, see that you have darkness in your heart. A true religion of which you are a teacher does not speak of condemnation of human beings. You have labeled Me as working with falsehood. You have said that I am working against the Law of God and then you say that Satan is My master. I say to you My Father is the Living God of this Universe. I am the Eternal Light of this World as

---

[5] John 5: 15.

71

I am His Son. I am the Living Light of all Ages.

You are a person who has chosen darkness for this is what you have incarnated again and again with to defy the Light of My Being. If you ask for redemption, I am saying to you that you are unredeemable as in your heart there is no real love of God. If there were you would not put the lie above the Truth. You are evil as you are asking others to believe that you are good and that they truly are responsible for following the Laws of God as written in the scriptures above their own Light of conscience.

Your eyes are those of the eyes of darkness. You have lost your Light and now want to defy Me with the power of the dark spirit. This is why you have come to attack My Being. You can kill My body as this is the ultimate aim of the dark spirit but you cannot take away more than this as this is the Will of My Father who is in Heaven. The Eternal Kingdom of Light will not have your kind there as in this Kingdom you will not be able to breathe its air as its air will be for the new human Spirit of the Light Beings to come. Yours will be for a spirit that will have lost its humanity to a pre-evolutionary stage of development. As you are working with evil this will give you the fruits of evil which will manifest even before the end of physical time on your planet.

So I say to you, turn away from the pathway of darkness. Repent. Stop working with the wrong doorway to self power and work with the Doorway to the Light that will lead you to the Eyes of the Light that the old man I have cured has spoken about. Be aware that I can see what is totally in your heart and Soul. So be aware also that your words and your evil intent to kill Me will only cover your Spirit with darkness. As My time has not yet come I will leave you now to continue My Ministry." As soon as the Christ Being said this he disappeared from physical sight.

The Pharisee was enraged and started shouting obscenities. Then all of a sudden he heard a voice. The voice said, "Follow darkness and you will fall into the abyss of hell." Then such a great fear gripped this man that his face turned a sickly white and he went to talk to his colleagues waiting for him as he was plotting with them to kill Jesus.

Then he looked up to God in his mind's eye and he saw an

image of the Christ Being crushing a huge serpent that had a face like his own. This so terrified him that he said to his followers, "Today, I have truly seen evil at work. This man, Jesus, was hypnotizing me to believe that he is a god. He falsifies the Prophets and blasphemes. He must die." [Verse 6]

Then the Christ Being met with this man he had cured again and told him, "Be aware when you work on yourself with the Meditation of the Light and align this to the Eyes of the Light that you acquired upon meeting the Christ, you will have the power to stop the darkness taking away your new consciousness of the true Religion of the planet earth.

This is the evolution of God in mankind working on a world Light creation in the future cosmos of Light to come. The Christ is the living proof of the work of His Father to take away evil from mankind. The Eyes of the Light created in man a direct consciousness of the Light of God. Ultimately when darkness has lost its battle with the Light it will be banished for all time from this universe. When this day comes man will have no more

nights and the Light of God will make the Light of His Son at one in every human being who has walked in His Light.

This is what I am working for now with My Father to accomplish this pathway for mankind and all Spiritual Beings of Light. This is the subject matter of the work I do on Myself and My Being. This is what I do for mankind. I ask you now to follow on with this Light and do the same for others; to work on yourself to evolve this Light for mankind with My Being and My Father who eternally loves all men and who asks all men to accept Me as I am His Son. I am the Son of the Living God; the Christ Being." [Verse 7] [6]

Then the Christ Being began to speak to those around them and said, "I am the Light – Giver of the World. I walk in My Father's footsteps as He and I are one Being. I have come into the flesh as a human being to become a part of you and the planet earth and its spirit. I came to the earth to give Light to all its kingdoms and to bring the Kingdom of God to it. Before I came the Light was dim on this planet. Yet now it grows and grows until it will

[6] John 5: 16-18.

73

envelope the whole being of this globe and man.

When My Light has reached all beings who morally will Light in this universe then My Mission will be accomplished as this is truly the plan worked out in Heaven by My Father for Me and the cosmos. Everything I do is a mirror of His Being. Yet as I have become flesh I have also now become a part of the creation of the material world so that I can give to this evolutionary stage of this world the power of the Light it needs to give it the consciousness of a Being of Light as this is what I have come for; to give Light to the world specifically at this moment in Cosmic history as I am the Initiator of all initiands. I am in living flesh what they seek as they seek the Ultimate Incarnation of Light on this planet earth.

I am he as My Father has willed that I come to create for mankind a vessel of Light in His Being. This vessel is the pathway to the Eyes of the Light that can see My Father and My Being in living form as the Living Light of this World. So I walk in the Light of My Father as it is He who loved mankind first. It is I who love mankind now eternally as human beings as well as the future spiritual beings as I have done this by becoming a human being Myself. I have done what no other Spiritual Being can do which is to become a person who walks the surface of the earth as the Living God in human form living his Truth. This is truly My world now.

This is truly My Will to prepare this world for the final evolutionary stage when it will enter its ultimate evolution as a World of Light. This is the future of this cosmos and the ultimate future of all of those in mankind who walk in My Light. This is the ultimate future of this cosmos now. This moment in time was prepared at the beginning of time. Its significance will be born out at the end of time on this earth. Then My Father with My Being and the Holy Spirit will complete this evolution of the Godhead of Light.

So I say to you that I, the Christ Being, Son of the Living God, the Father, who is in Heaven will create a World of Living Light to live in with mankind as the ultimate love of the Father is to create a world where Ultimate Light is in every heart of every human being as it is in the heart of the Christ Being. This ultimate love for one human

74

being, His Son, is His love of mankind as now creation ever evolves on this planet so it will evolve further at the end of physical time on this planet. Then the Father will create a new Universe of Light where love between all human beings and love between all Spiritual Beings will reign supreme for eternity so that in the future universe creating Light will be eternal and all of the universe will become Light. This is the Gift of Light from My Father to My Being. This shows His love eternally to My Being in His Light. [Verse 8] [7]

My Father creates life for all beings. He gave life to every single human being who ever lived. He decides when each evolutionary stage of birth and death occur in every being in all his lifetimes materially and spiritually. He gives free will to all beings to act for Him or against Him. He also acts with this power accordingly unconditionally and eternally.

He has in this way allowed those who oppose His Being to gain power and to have their own kingdom of darkness. He has done this as His love of giving all beings He creates freedom to love Him has no

limit. However He has decided to act upon life and death in such a way that each individual being regardless of his stage of evolution can only decide against Him or for Him ultimately with one limitation. This being that a person can only live forever in His Light providing at the end of time that this is what is in his heart as no matter who kills who or how many lives a man lives in the Light or lives in the darkness he ultimately can only live or die according to what God, the Father, has created to be his Cosmic fate.

So evil men will ultimately choose the evil kingdom of their own free will at the end of time. Accordingly good men will choose the Kingdom of My Being, I, the Christ Being, who has power over life and death and the creation of the Cosmic Light to heal mankind from the darkness as the darkness is attracted to the Light.

So I say to you all who can see the Eyes of the Light in My Being, you have the power of life and death. When you choose Light it is life and when you see others choose darkness you can pronounce them dead as they have become, out of their own free will, blind to the Light of My

[7] John 5: 19-20.

Father; the Giver of Eternal Living Light. [Verse 9] [8]

I, the Christ Being then have come to the earth to create the **Cosmic Christ World Light Shield** that shields the good from evil. I have done this by the Power of the Light of My Father. Hence I have done this so that those who have lost heart about the progress of Intellectual Materialism on earth which has sold to billions of people that the intellect really is My Father and that Truth is just a moral idealism will once again see the Light.

In the twenty – first century man needs to know who he is and needs to face his Truth. He needs to know that the Truth is not relative. My Being is not relative. I stand only for the good of mankind. I bring Light to the open hearts that seek Ultimate Light and Ultimate Truth. I know those who make the Truth relative say that good and evil are but unscientific words and that really the intellect controls forms of opinion in a person. I say that one has to make a judgment of what is the Truth of life. One has to put the Truth above all things in his life. The proof that a man does this is not what he says the Truth is, but if he lives what he says.

This is the final judgment of life. This is My judgment of those who mouth My name but have never lived what I have said to live. They will lose their Light and their Truth as they have made their Truth relative. They have lost the Truth in their judgments of the cosmos and of My Being; the Living Light. This is the meaning of unconditional love of the Light; when a man puts Me first in his heart and he judges the Truth first in My Light as the Light is above the Truth. So My Father gave Me this power to judge all men in His Light.

So this is why I am the Son of the Living God as I have come to the world to give it the Light of My Father; to create for mankind a pathway to the Light. This pathway has an ultimate destination which is My Being, meaning those who follow the Light know in their hearts who I am. Those who see Me have Eyes of the Light. They call Me the Christ for this reason as I am the Saviour of the world and He who brings Light to the cosmos.

---

[8] John 5: 21,

So he who worships My Being as the Living God worships My Father in Me as those who walk in the streets of Heaven can see My Being and My Father in this Heavenly Light. I am worshipped in Heaven and on earth as I am the Creator of the Light in all worlds. So he who looks up to the universe to see the Cosmic Light of My Being holds in reverence My Being and My Father. Hence he is one of whom it can be said, 'He looks to the Light.' [Verse 10] [9]

Judgment is for those who have chosen to look to darkness. They have lost not only their pathway but the Truth and the Light as when the heart becomes hard the Light leaves it. I say to you, those who fight the battle of good and evil in their Souls and in their lives will not always be tempted by the tempter. There will come a time when their Souls will have the choice to choose bodies that will have transcended the temptation of evil while the others who have chosen the race of evil will be open to this temptation to power and glory with the one with the false Light.

I have come now to give the power of the true Light to those who seek it. They are the future generations of the cosmos that will create a race of Light as this is truly what is the Will of My Father to test the individual and his world spiritually, psychologically and physically and to then let the evolution take its course as the Spiritual World of Light will be peopled only by the race of Light. This race will be an evolved human race that will separate its evolutionary Spirit and psyche in a visibly physical manner from the unevolved human race. This unevolved human race in future epochs will stop evolving and devolve back into matter in a similar form for example as brother animal is now on the earth as the real death of this type of mankind is to come. So is the real life of the human race of Light to come once this Light power takes away from mankind what it spiritually cannot ultimately live with, the closer it comes to fulfilling its spiritual destiny at the end of time on earth as it is now physically.

Hence truly those who love

---

[9] John 5: 22-24.

My Father love Me. They seek the Light in their Souls. This Light will manifest in their living bodies in future incarnations to come first on earth and then in the World of Light to come.

However the opposite of this development will also occur and this will rid the human race of the need to fight the battle of good and evil with his fellow man in the same way as his fellow beings will then no longer have the need to be tempted by evil to prove their identities as beings with Souls of Light. This will mean that their karma will already show demographically that the human race of Light will be free of conflict of conscience but will know clearly its enemy in a sub – race which will ultimately no longer be a part of the human race as human beings but a part of an inferior race of subhuman beings as the Soul in its darkness in these beings will no longer look to the Light for all ages to come. This is the legacy of the Light of Christ and the legacy of those who love My Father as they love Me, or those who turn away from the Light. The judgment of the Light is to live in it. To turn away from it is to die in one's Soul.

Spiritual Light lives now in the world through My Being; the Christ. Ask for My Light to be sent to the darkness and the darkness will not reach you. Encircle yourself in the ring of Light and let Me protect you. Do not fight evil without the tools of the Light or you will lose to the tempter. Give up your power to My Light. Let Me pour Light into your hearts. Let the Christ Being judge the evil and put this outside the Circle of Light. Say, 'I ask the Christ Being to send His Light to the darkness and its source.' Do this; I will let the Light fill your being with the power of God, My Father, in Heaven. [Verse 11] [10]

I, the Christ Being say this to you, that the cosmos of Light and the cosmos of darkness are filled with Souls that are incarnating and finding new bodies in different races and in different epochs to fulfil their Moral karma. In the spiritual world time and space are of no consequence unless it relates to a living epoch currently in physical time. When this is the case the Souls of past ages need to fulfil their task consecutively in this world, for example, and in the ages to come as they evolve on the earth in various

---

[10] John 5: 25.

stages of the incarnation of the earth.

This is the moment in the universe when I, the Christ Being, have incarnated on the earth this one time to speak to all of mankind and its Soul as all who have died in all epochs will now listen to My Voice. Those who choose to hear it and act upon it will awaken from the dead and transform their beings in their Souls and see that I am the History of the World. I am the Giver of Life. So as they arise from the dead they will see the morning sunrise of My Light upon the horizon and will have life.

Like a flower that responds to the rays of the light of the sun they will bloom like a rose with a golden shine. They will blossom so that they will become the golden flower of Light which has the sun's light beaming in its very being. They will, with this Light, put out the darkness with the unfolding of their Souls which fills the world with the rays of this God – Light. This is the Living Light of God. This is My Living Light as I am the Son of God. I am the Eternal, God Soul of Light. [Verse 12] [11]

My Father created this universe and all of its beings as He is the Giver of Life. His Life has no end or beginning. His Life is eternal. He created beings to create time so that Souls could be evolved to His Light. Hence He created epochs of time which would evolve in the freedom of beings who were given free will to challenge the darkness or put the Light first in their lives.

He also gave His Son, the Cosmic Christ, supreme power over life as He shares His Light with My Being. With this power He, the Father, has also given Me the power to change the evolution of the universe and its worlds so that they may know how to relate to the Light. This is why I have come to the planet earth; to do this and to give Light and the power of the Light to those who hear the Voice of God in Me as I have also come to protect the Light of My Father in this very moment in Cosmic time as it parallels the history of the earth. I am doing this when I not only ask all human beings to live their Truth and to follow the Truth but also to align it with the Light of My Being. When they do this they will align with My

---

[11] John 5: 26.

Father and His creation as He has given His Son to mankind so as to save mankind for the Light World to come. So I am the Son of man. I am the Son of the Eternal Light.

Those who hear My Voice and do not imprint it in their Souls but let their Souls sleep out the storm to come of the struggle of the Spirit in man to come will not awaken from their self – made coffins. While those who hear the voice of My Being and let their Souls awaken to its Light will arise out of all of their cemeteries from all ages and walk with Me in the Light. They will all stand at the end of time for Me and My Being. They will look up to the Christ at this moment and see him in his Living Glory in the Golden Temple in Heaven. All the Angels of God will surround this eternal moment in the cosmos. At this moment those who have Eyes of Light in their Souls will pledge to the Christ Being the living Light in their Souls. This will be counted by the Angels of God so as to put those who have chosen My Father as the Living Light, separate from those who have chosen the living darkness and its beings.

This will be done by the leadership of the Four Archangels of God. Each will have a Cosmic Sword that will have the power of the Light of Heaven and at that moment will touch the fire of hell at its boundary with Heaven. At this moment the Cosmic Light of Heaven will open up and will encircle all of the Beings of Light so that the darkness will be shut out forevermore. At this moment you all will walk with Me, in the streets of Heaven, who have walked with Me in the Light on earth. [Verse 13] [12]

I, the Christ Being, follow My Father. It is He who has created this universe. It is I who have chosen to become a human being so that I can save mankind from losing its Light and its Truth as the Truth is that I also follow My Father as I have come to ask you to follow Him as He is the Living Light of this Universe. He and I are one. So when I speak of Him I am speaking of My Soul. When I speak of My Being I am speaking of the Living Spirit in the flesh before you on this very day on earth as My Light comes from the Eternal God Soul of Light. So everything I do is an

---

[12] John 5: 27.

80

expression of My Soul. It is an expression of who My Father is.

I decided to become a human being as it was My Father's Will to fulfil His unconditional love of all beings. As He loves Me eternally I wanted to show this love to mankind. In becoming human I have completed this first step to fulfilling My Moral karma which is to do the Will of My Father; the Living God in Heaven. I have come at a specific time in the history of mankind so as to fulfil a Cosmic destiny. I do not know truly all of the future of mankind or of My Pathway when I look with the eyes of a human being upon My fate but I unconditionally love the Light of My Father. I unconditionally trust in His judgment which was for Me to become a human being as He saw that this is the only way mankind could be saved from the darkness as mankind needed a Saviour in living flesh to relate to, or its evolution would stop evolving on the right pathway to the Light World to come. Only by fulfilling My Moral karma of being human could I give back to My Father the Power of the Light He needed to save mankind as in the beginning of time on this universe He

gave freedom to all beings to challenge His Creation by letting Spiritual beings of darkness create an opposing world, and even life forms, to the Light.

So by creating the Ultimate Form of Life in My Being, the Christ Being, My Father also exercised His Free Will to will to change the future of human terms for human beings and spiritual terms for Spiritual Beings. So this is why My proclamation as the Living Light of the World could only be based on unconditional love when I took on the power of a mortal human being with limitations of consciousness and being but with a Soul of the Eternal God, My Father.

So really by My coming to earth My Father made a choice to act upon the evolution of the planet so as to correct its course so that it will follow the Ultimate Light as what I say is belonging to the Eternal Truth. What My Father says is belonging to the Eternal Light. So the Light is above the Truth. So I follow My Father as He wills now that you listen to Me and make My Words into a Philosophy of Light. Make My Pathway your pathway to the Truth of life. Then use this Truth to live your Truth as human beings as I am living My Truth before you in living flesh upon the earth.

So by doing this I truly show My unconditional love of your beings as I am doing what I am asking you to do; to align with My Father's Light as this way your pathway in this life time will be a credible one based on honouring the Light above your lives as this is truly also what I will show you when My living flesh will be given up to the Light in My death to come. This is the Will of the Eternal Truth and the Eternal Light of God, the Father. [Verse 14] [13]

I, the Christ Being say to you today, you went to ask John the Baptist if I were the Living Truth or but another Prophet foretelling the coming of the Messiah. He told you that to follow Me is to follow the Eternal Light. He fulfilled his Moral karma as he renounced all wealth and all material power so as to grace My Presence in living form. He did this as his Soul spoke of echoes of a living Religion of Light from past ages. This Soul testified to the living legacy of Light made flesh in My Being as John out of all men in the universe spoke of Me first among all human

beings. He spoke of Me as the Living Christ.

Human recognition of the Christ Being is not what I speak of. What I truly speak of today is that John also saw the right Pathway to the Light. He lived his Truth for this day to see Me coming into the earth to bring it the Living Truth as he received the Eyes of the Light in his Soul from Me. So those who receive this Light Doorway to their Souls will show the rest of mankind the steps it needs to take to fulfil its Moral karma and its Moral task to recognise the pathway to salvation and redemption.

John the Baptist was like a golden rose that bloomed in the sunlight of the sunrise that I spoke of earlier as this is what it was. In the darkness before the sunrise he waited and then he rose to life from the rays of the sun upon his Soul. This 'Rose of Light' radiated the Light to you all and you basked in it as you would from the rays of the sun. This sunlight lit up your Souls for a time and overwhelmed the darkness that was there in it. I am the Creator of the sunrise upon your planet. I gave the golden 'Rose of Light', life. I ask you now to see John in this symbol

---

[13] John 5: 28-32.

of Eternal Light and to align your Souls with it so that you can follow in his footsteps to meet your ultimate destiny with the Ultimate Light which is My Being; the Christ.

The Keys of Light I have demonstrated to you change spiritual and material spheres of existence. They are the Works of My Father in Heaven. He gives this Light power to change the destiny of a universe. He also fulfils in Me His unconditional love of all mankind. He does this through His Keys of Light. The Keys of Light can be used only by Me for those who choose the Light as this way darkness has its free will to roam and devastate the world equally with its spells of darkness. However with the difference that the Light will always overpower the darkness when the choice has been made by the individual human being to fulfil his Moral karma and task. This is also the Will of the Father; the Almighty God.

So I now stand for the Ultimate Truth and the proof that I have the Ultimate Light in My very Being and that I am the Christ Being is that I have overcome the darkness in living My Truth as a human being as being the Ultimate Spiritual Being in the whole universe. This is the fulfillment of My Father's plan for Me and my fate on earth now. This is My Truth. [Verse 15] [14]

In My Living Soul My Father speaks to Me as He is My Being as a Spiritual Being of Eternal Light. I unconditionally trust in His Will for My Being. His Words created a universe. He is the Words of the Light. I am he who speaks these Words.

You try to see Him by not looking at Me. You seek him out in many different philosophies of life which you observe but do not fulfil or live. You seek Him out in visible manifestations of nature upon the earth but you find yourself lacking in believing in Him and say it is but a phenomenon of nature. Then you try to find His Words in scripture but you get caught in interpreting a version of the truth of what it says as your eyes are filled with a darkness that stops you from seeing the Light. So this has happened to you as you have not lived your Truth. You want to speak of the Truth and

[14] John 5: 33-37,

83

say you live it but proof that you are not doing this is that you do not truly see Me as the Son of the Living God whom you seek.

So in Truth you have lost your pathway and need direction as to who you really are and what is your ultimate destiny as human beings. You have to see that mouthing Holy Scripture in and of My Father's name a million times will not change what is in your heart. The mouth has to speak what is coming from the heart. You should truly see that without living your Truth your heart will harden and it will lose its Light and will be blind to the Living Light standing in living flesh in human form in front of you. You need to truly become conscious of the Light to truly see that without Cosmic Christ Consciousness there can be no Ultimate Light in your Souls as only by choosing this Light can one live eternally in all the incarnations to come.

You then will succeed to the level of evolution where the need for the battle between good and evil will be surpassed. This will be for

every individual who puts the Light above his material life and who chooses My Being above his being; who chooses to ask Me to save him in the Light of My Father. This is the destiny of mankind in this universe now. [Verse 16] [15]

I, the Christ Being am a Spiritual Being that is not separate from a human being and is a human being. I, the Christ Being, am the Son of the Living God. At the same time I am now an individual human being. So regardless My human form has the male sex and historically My name is Jesus. The Father chose that by exercising His Free Will He would counteract the forces of darkness by sending the Ultimate Light to the planet earth. So now I am before you a product of the final evolution of time on your planet as a single person with the Ultimate Light in his Soul. Hence this is your destiny to ultimately become a part of this Universal Light eternally at the final moment of evolution. So My Mission is to show mankind the pathway to the world of the Eternal Spiritual universe of Light. Yet I can only show this pathway to those who have Light in their hearts.

---

[15] John 5: 38-41.

My Father has given My name, the Christ Being, as in the beginning of time He created all the stars and the planets as homes for the Spiritual Beings and He then gave each being the pathway to the Ultimate Source of Light. So I, the Christ Being, have come to all stages of evolution with different beings at the human being stage in all levels of material and spiritual existence where the human being stage existed as well as in different dimensions of existence. So I was the Christ Being of all the Hierarchies of Light in the spiritual world at their human being stage until they became a part of their Spiritual Hierarchy of Light in the spiritual world although they, of course, did not start their evolution at the same stage as the present human being on earth. So it is My Father who chose this for Me, to step into the creation of your world at this specific moment in time.

I see that today you do not accept the reality of My Being and cannot see that life on other planets in the cosmos belongs to the Spiritual Hierarchies and that they parallel the life of your planet. I have come to your planet at this stage of evolution to redeem mankind as I have come in the past to redeem other beings at the human being stage in a different dimension on your planet and elsewhere. Hence I am the Christ Being of the Angels and the Archangels and the Hierarchies of Light.

The opposite Hierarchies have chosen what you are choosing today to ask for a proof of what I am saying to be true. So in doing this you show what is truly in your heart and you see you become a part of the beings of darkness I speak of now that rejected My Light in their human being stage of existence in other dimensions of existence. You see that your identification with Intellectual Materialism today is making you choose the Lord of darkness unwittingly believing it is higher intelligence when all you are doing is putting the intellect above the Light and above the Ultimate Light in My Being.

So now you unconsciously follow a pathway to darkness by making laws that support economic rationalism, putting it above the human Light of the Ages. You do this by your total identification with what is mathematically right financially regardless of whether it is right for a human being. This has happened to you as you have not yet learned how to become a total individual human being living in the Light of the Christ Being. You lose your identity to materialistic conclusions about the origin of your being and Word of God. You speak of the Word of God like reading a manual about the scriptures instead of relating the scriptures to your living Soul as those who wrote the scriptures related to the Ultimate Light of this Universe in their Spirit. I am the Ultimate Light. I am the Christ. The Christ Light is the Ultimate Light of your planet. [Verse 17]

I am worshipped by those who love the Light and know that their ultimate destiny is the spiritual world. I am dismissed by those who worship material power and wealth as they have chosen the glory of the world that will never spiritualize; the world that will hold beings that will ultimately hold soulless entities of former human beings that did not progress to being Spiritual Beings of the Light. So to spiritualize one's being and to become a living Spiritual Being of Light in the spiritual world is the destiny of all human beings who have put the Light first.

Those who love the Light love God who is My Father. They will ultimately evolve the Light in their beings to the point where in future incarnations to come in the following epochs they will have the power to spiritualize their evolution to the level of Spiritual Beings of Light as this Light power comes from the love they have of the Living God of Light.

My Father is the Ultimate Being. He created all creatures and the stars in the Heavens. The planets He made the home of beings like yourself, now like Myself in part, as I have come to give My Father, the Living God, a place in the human family of men.

You do not accept My Being. You do not listen to the Living Light of the World. You prefer to neutralise your beings and to look the other way. You do this as you cannot accept the Living Truth as you do not live your own Truth. Hence your consciousness is blocked. It has not the level of consciousness to comprehend Me. This happened to you as you have already begun to devolve from deciding to not face the Truth of your lives. So you have neutralised your consciousness.

Instead of going to the higher development of consciousness that your evolution meant you to go to you have stopped it and now there is no progress in your incarnations to the point that they even exist. This has happened to you as you have lost sight of the living Light in your Souls. So you cannot see the Living Light which is My Being. This is proven by the evidence that you deny anything that is not based on the ideological foundations of your creed. You will not see the Light as you have chosen to deny who I am. I am the Light.

You accept instead anyone who sells the false Light and promises eternal power. You do this as you are dragged down by a force that bears no name other than the Prince of darkness as this being is a force of dark power that challenges My Father and My Being. He is the corrupter of conscience. He defames My Being. So those who honor mankind above God have lost their Light as they have no pathway to it as to find the Light one needs a pathway to My Being. Those who have lost this pathway have not the knowledge to experience the God of Light; My Father. To know the Truth of My Father is to know how God lives His Truth. [Verse 18] [16]

Be aware that I, the Christ Being, will not condemn you to My Father because you have lost your pathway to the Light. However your pathway has been the law of Moses as you can see it is he who wrote of My coming. However you do not read his words but put your faith in your belief in your interpretation of the law instead of into living your Truth and aligning to the Spirit Light of God. So when you read the words of Moses you intellectualize their meaning instead of seeing the Truth in your own Spirit of his words in written form.

So My Words you will not listen to as what you really seek is a formula for truth in logical form. This way you can love the thought of your being with the Light and you do not have to live in the Light in its total reality. This way you can give pride to your conceit. The real Truth comes to a person who lives it and then it becomes a living Truth.

I am the Living Truth as what I am saying to you are the Words of My Father; the Words of Light. He who follows them is redeemed and has the Ultimate Light.

---

[16] John 5: 42-44.

The Ultimate Light created the planets of this solar system. My Father's Light created Spiritual Beings that created beings such as yourselves on this world. Your evolution on this planet was created by a specific design and the right balance had to be reached before your form became that of a human being.

Intellectual Materialism has said that your origin is that of the animal and that the universe was created by accident of masses of material configuring into galaxies of stars with solar systems like the one to which this world belongs. Yet it does not answer that simple, logical scientific mother of all questions about the fact of who created this original matter in the universe. It also does not answer who created man's Soul nor where it comes from and why it has a free will to act for the evil or good of its being. It does not answer who created Light. This is the ultimate question of existence.

I say to you, I, the Christ Being, that only by seeing the Light in the Universe can man see with his inner eyes its ultimate origin being the Ultimate Light which is My Father. He created all things.

Intellectual Materialism says that the brain created all things and not the Soul of God. This is the ultimate lie that lets darkness enter into one's Spirit as once a person loses his Light he does this on the basis that the intellectual conclusion in his head is above it. This happens to a man when he loves not the Light in the Living God and when he has put his mind above the Truth and he has neutralised his consciousness to see only the effect of existence but not its cause. My Father is the Cause of all Light in this universe. With this Light the Soul of the universe lives. With My Light the Souls of the universe now have a Principle of Light to live forevermore. This is I, the Christ Being; the Light of all Ages.

The Soul of the universe is filled with Cosmic Light when man puts the love of the Light above all things in his life as then he is working with the Cosmic Light Principle of My Being. He is letting in the rays of the Light of Heaven into his Soul as the Spiritual Sun in Heaven shines so brightly that it creates a cosmos of Light which bathes the streets of Heaven that lead to a community of Beings that

have ultimate, eternal love of this Light in their hearts. This

is truly the Brotherhood; the Brotherhood of the Light of the Christ Being." [Verse 19][17]

---

[17] John 5: 45-47.

CHAPTER 6

After this lecture to this group of people the Christ Being decided to go to another side of the Sea of Galilee called the Sea of Tibe'ri-as. Hundreds of people were following him as there was an energy propelling the crowd to bring to Jesus so many who needed to be healed. It was like they were being drawn by this magnet sending messages to their Souls telling them that the source of their lives and its meaning was about to give them a Living Light before their very eyes. Yes, it was a Spirit walking among them speaking to each individual conscience the Words of Light.

Now the Words of the Light were spoken to each and every Soul like a vibe of energy filled with Cosmic power which appeared in living flesh sitting down on a rock in the hills of Palestine. Here was Christ Jesus now again beginning to speak to a vast group of people who could hear his every word as when he spoke the sound of his words needed no amplification as the Soul of each person there could hear the sounds of the Living Great Soul of Light.

They could hear him speak and feel his Light as he began to say in the midst of his Apostles, "Now, I say to you that the bread of life is eaten so as to sustain the living body. There is, though, a greater need and that is how to feed the living Soul. I have come to do this for mankind. I feed the Soul with Light. It is the time of the Passover. In this time you feast as it is the custom of your race. I tell you, you who have come to hear Me and have shown today that you concern yourself not about feeding the body but feeding your Souls as otherwise you would not have followed Me into such a remote place as this today. Do not fear. The Light will provide us with what we need to eat to satisfy our bodily forms." [Verse 1] [1]

Then the crowd began to murmur as it was in the late afternoon and everyone was getting hungry. There were many women and children. The men began to look at a way to work out what they would do as it was a couple of hours walk to the next town. Also they felt quite amazed at themselves for not thinking of

---

[1] John 6: 1-3.

90

this earlier considering that now the problem would soon be acute to do something for their families so that they would have something to eat.

Jesus, of course, could read what was in their very Souls as he could see the picture of everyone's Soul at any time as it was he who had spoken to their Souls to come to see him speak. This he did by giving Light to the good – hearted Souls before him when he spoke to their conscience through his Heavenly powers.

So now Jesus stood up and looked up to the sky with hands outstretched and said, "What is to be now our fate out here in the wilderness? Shall we find a way to feed our bodies or our Souls? Which of you knows the answer to this?" Then as he knew no one would answer as he already could foresee his actions, he said to the Apostle Phillip, "How can we afford to buy so much food for such a large group of people? What shall we do? Do you have any ideas?" He said this to Phillip as he was experienced in accountancy as he had worked as a tax collector and knew the importance of making calculations for the Christ Apostles. He also said this to him to see how Phillip would

react considering that mathematically the fact was that there was no way they would have money to feed a few thousand people no matter what calculations he made. Also he wanted to show Phillip that the pathway to knowledge of the Light comes from putting the Light above the Truth. Now as he was the Living Light he could easily do this.

So then upon saying this Phillip looked at him and replied, "Master, we have two hundred denarii' and with this money we could not buy a piece of bread for everyone here let alone any kind of meal. Look, there are up to five thousand people here. What you ask for is an impossibility."

Then Andrew, another Apostle who was Peter's brother, said to Jesus, "Look here, we have a young man who has a basket of food. He has five loaves and a couple of fish. Now this would not feed too many of us." He said this half amused at his own discovery at what he was proposing as some kind of solution to the dilemma he found he was facing.

Then Jesus took hold of the basket of food and held it in

his raised hands. Looking up to Heaven he said, "I, the Living Christ, ask the Ultimate Light of My Father to give the food of life to His people." Then he began to meditate on surrounding the five thousand people with a ring of Cosmic Light. In his Meditation he opened a Doorway to the spiritual world so that the Light could enter from Heaven and into the material world where he was asking His Father to bless the loaves and fish for the people to eat. Then all of a sudden everyone could see that they had loaves and fish before their very eyes in baskets all over the field. They could no longer trace what happened. Only the image of Jesus walking about and giving baskets out to different people was all that each person could recall in their mind's eye.

However all could see that they were eating the bread with the fish heartily. Also they could see that they had more than they needed to satisfy their hunger. They had in fact too much food at the end of this Spiritual Feast of Light and Bread as they all knew that a miracle of Light had touched their bodies and Souls. They could feel this although they could not

explain it. They were graced by a Special Key of Christ. [Verse 2] [2]

Then the Christ Being said to his Apostles, "I would like you now to put together all the baskets of food left over as we would like to be certain that all is eaten and if there is any left we can save it this way." The Apostles did as they were asked and gathered twelve full baskets of bread pieces and half eaten fish.

Once the total of the number of baskets was made public to the thousands seated before the Apostles and Jesus there was a great roar from the crowd of such great joy that one could feel the magic of the Light in every person's eyes as he or she clapped their hands in praise and thanks for what was given to them as a gift from this Heavenly Being. There was at that moment a choir of Angels singing in the background of the Christ Being. The air was filled with a fragrance of a sea of flowers coming from the presence of the Christ Being.

The Christ Being then said, "I, the Christ Being, now have spoken of the Heavenly food of My Father as it is He who has today given Me this Light

_____
[2] John 6: 4-11.

92

to give to you so that you may see with your very eyes the evolution of the Living Light on your planet. As it evolves it nourishes your bodies and Souls.

So I say to you, live your Truth. Align your Truth to the Living Light. Do this by putting the Light above the Truth as the Source of the Ultimate Truth is the Ultimate Light. The love of My Father for your beings created what was given to you today. He now gives Me the Special Light powers to open with a Golden Key the Doorway to Heaven. I am the Doorway to the Light of the World. Come to Me and you will find eternal peace and eternal Light. Follow My Father and you will have everlasting life. This is the living miracle of Light power before you; to eat at a banquet created by the Living God. To eat with Him is to eat with the Ultimate Being of Light. Share in His Light and you share with Me Light everlasting; Light eternal.

Become then complete human beings. Behold the Light in the Heavens from the Angels of God carried the very baskets of food for you so that you could witness this Heavenly Feast. So now you

have listened to the Son of God and shared in the living power of the Light of God." [Verse 3]

Then one man looked up to the sky thanking God for His Son saying, "This is the Christ Being. He is beyond the Prophet of all Prophets as it is he who tells of the future of the universe and shows us the way to our salvation. It is he who now lays the foundation for mankind to evolve with a Heavenly identity. It is he who gives us all citizenship in this universal family to come in the World of Light to come."

This man then looked at Jesus and Jesus responded by saying, "Blessed is he who sees the Light as it is he who will find the right pathway to it. It is he who will then know his path and will receive the Light power he needs to fulfil his task in his life as the Light will come to those who seek it. It will be given to those who love it from My Angels that stand before the Living God; the Light." [Verse 4] [3]

The Christ Being then walked away from the crowd as if he disappeared. He then spoke to all of his Apostles or to their Souls as he was no longer with them physically as he

---

[3] John 6: 12-14.

93

stayed in the parallel dimension to the very dimension they were in, in the material world, so to speak. He did this as he did not want the people who saw the miracle Light Key from Heaven to want to adulate him other than in their own Souls. He could see that this would be of no value for this pathway now at this present stage of his cosmic karma on earth. He saw that man's material self was quite fragile and could not take Heaven for too long and that it needed to come back to earth. So by making his bodily Being disappear it made all the crowd disperse and go back home. Also it gave the Apostles a way to leave and to say to everyone that they had to carry on to go with their Master without answering any more questions as they could see that the dawn was coming soon.

Furthermore the Christ Being did not want to be made a king in the material world. This would have gone against the evolution of his mission on earth as a Heavenly King has no need of a material fate. It was of little interest for his Being other than that Jesus Christ was also human. However by the time of the occurrence of this event the Christ Being, the Living Son of God, was living in the Jesus body. This meant that the body of Jesus when John baptized him was not the same as before he was baptized as at that moment the man, Jesus, died as a human being. Then the Christ Being took over this body that was prepared for him by the Jesus Being who walked the face of the earth for thirty years. In this time he had evolved with many initiation processes the evolutionary stage of the Buddha Being; a Being that had incarnated before in evolved human beings throughout the ages to prepare the Pathway for the Christ Being as the Gautama Buddha also incarnated again as Jesus. This is what he knew his Moral karma was and hence the reason he traveled to the east to become initiated into this pathway to fulfil his task in his incarnation.

[Verse 5]

So truly the Christ Being then having a human body and using it as a vessel of the Ultimate Being wanted to live his Truth first and then the Truth of his life, meaning that he as much as possible wanted to abstract his being from public power as this way the powers he had would only be

used for the purpose of saving the Soul of the world. This was his mission as the distraction of earthly power would only stop his real fate. He could see that man, at his present stage of evolution on that part of the globe, then needed first a spiritual identity as he needs now in the twenty – first century as the parallel situation on earth now two thousand years later is that while man then was dominated by the material identity of the Roman citizen, today man is dominated by the material identity of the culture of the money being. So likewise man needs to know how to take this away from his being so that he can put it in its right perspective. Hence the challenge for every human being to live not only for the material world but for his Truth; to live to align this Truth to the Ultimate Light and to do this in the Light of the Christ Being.

Hence to be a king in earthly life then or a money being now above being a human being with the Light of Christ is to forfeit the eternal Light in all life times to come till the time when the Light will be no more and the person would lose his Soul. Hence this is the greatest hell of all to know that a person will lose his Soul and devolve into a sub – being ultimately for all time. Hence this is truly why the Christ Being found earthly power simply something to identify but not to relate to unless it was a secondary part of the journey of the Light of Heaven for him and all of mankind. So you have now comments from the one who works with the Light and with the Eyes of the Light about the Creator of all Light for all time to come; the Christ. [Verse 6] [4]

After this dispersion of the people who had seen this miracle of Light the Apostles decided to go to Caper'na-um by boat. The skies were darkening as it was almost dawn and the clouds were being moved by a strong wind that was reflecting a sea that was beginning to brew into a storm. The Christ Jesus was not as yet with them as they had set sail without him anticipating that he would appear among them from this other world that they were getting glimpses of, when he used the Special Keys of God or the miracles of Light.

Then suddenly a storm erupted and the boat the

---

[4] John 6: 15.

Apostles were in almost seemed unsafe. They were now two or three miles out at sea and the waves were tossing their boat so that they quickly folded the sails and tried to steer it with their rows. This was only partly successful as the waves were getting more and more powerful and the sea was showing an angry face so that they feared for their lives.

It was at this moment of terrible panic that out on the sea appeared Jesus walking calmly on the waves but with a slow and steady even pace towards the boat. His Being was shining and the waves seemed to part where he walked. He looked at them and they were truly afraid for they could not believe what was before their very eyes. Then Jesus said to them, "I am the Christ Being. Do not fear what you see as I walk on the waters of the sea of your world to show you that the Son of Man is also the Son of God. Be aware that you can hear Me and see Me in the turmoil of the world's elements. Do not fear the wrath of God when you have Light in your hearts." Then he suddenly got on board and the sea was calm. All the Apostles were so glad to see him with

them. In the next instant they were docking at Caper'na-um. Not only had they seen the Christ Being walk on water but also he had calmed the sea and not only gone back to his dimension of existence and came back accordingly but also had this time transported them into a future time in their own dimension. They reasoned amongst themselves that this would be bringing them back on the right time when after all he had so many times now changed the future with the Special Keys of Light. Of course they also reasoned that there was no sense of the same type of physical time on earth as in this other dimension that the Christ Being slipped in and out of around them daily. One of them asked Jesus, "Could you see us rocking in the boat lost at sea from the world you were in before you walked on the water to us?" Then Jesus said, "The Father sees all things and gives Light to those who seek it." [Verse 7] [5]

The following day many in the groups of people who were listening to Christ had observed that he had disappeared. They were also aware that his disciples had set sail without their Master. Hence they suspected that he

---

[5] John 6: 16-21.

had gone elsewhere which intrigued them. So one group out of all the other groups decided to find Jesus as they felt surely where he walked the Light would follow him. They knew perceptually that this person was other than human for there was such a magical Light upon his personality when he spoke and they felt such radiance upon their Souls when they were in his presence.

Now this group of people was a part of those people who had witnessed the miracle of Light when the Christ Being spoke to His Father and fed the five thousand through the power of the Cosmic Keys of Light. Near the place where this occurred there was also a mooring site for boats that sailed from Tibe'ri-as. So when this group decided to find Jesus after looking for him all over in the immediate area they concluded that Jesus must have gone to Caper'na-um in some unknown way. So they took a boat and sailed to this city in search of this bringer of Light.

When they got to Caper'na-um they were astonished at their own discovery of finding Jesus among his Apostles as they could quite easily work out from the timing that he could not have arrived at the place where he was with any other alternative route. So the spokesman for this group asked Jesus, "Master, how did you get here when you did not sail across the sea like we all had to, to be here now? How could you be here when no human being can travel at such speed without a vehicle that would transport him from place to place like a bird at will? Can you tell us as we are seeking the Truth of who you are and the source of your magical powers? Can you please tell us the answer?"

Then the Christ Being replied, "I, the Christ Being, say this to you. You have seen the Special Keys of Christ change energy fields in the material world. You have experienced their power by the very bread you eat when My Father multiplied the loaves of bread to feed His people. Now you seek the source of My powers but truly you are still identified with Intellectual Materialism as you have put the intellect above the Light. You have done this as you do not ask what is the Ultimate Cause of this Ultimate Light but you have concentrated on the effect, meaning you want to know the source of what you call the magic but not who created this magical Light. So you are creating eyes that see only through the intellect and not through your Souls. You have elevated your thinking process as the property of your brain. You have not seen that in your thinking process there is the ultimate source of all thoughts, human and cosmic, being in your Souls. You feed your brain but not your Soul. So you do not see with your Soul the Truth of life.

You seek a pathway to the Light. This gives you a superior consciousness as you have tried to see the pathway I have travelled in order to arrive where I am now speaking to you. However I say to you that unless a person uses his superior consciousness and aligns it with the Ultimate Light he will not have the force of Cosmic Light he needs to fulfil his Moral karma. He will ever work on the pathway to find the right information as an answer to his questions but he will not have true knowledge of the Truth of life or of the cosmos as this is a Cosmic Law which is an expression of who My Father is as a Spiritual Being.

He gave free will to all beings when he created them. He also gave free will to the creators of Spiritual Beings that chose to oppose His Light as well as those who chose to fulfil His Light. There were ones who chose to change the evolution of the cosmos and to create their own kingdom of darkness. So the Father then used His own Free Will to counteract this measure without taking away the free will of any being in the universe. He did this by sending My Being, the Christ Being, as I am the Son of the Living God. I am the bringer of the Eternal Light as I am the Ultimate Light. He who puts Me above his life finds eternal existence in the succession of his incarnations before the Light of Heaven. He sees with the Eyes of the Light, My Being. He sees that the Souls of Light were created in the beginning from Spirit by the Father. Now because of the evolution of the cosmos and the granting of the free will by the Father to all beings, a force of Light had to be created to take away the Prince of darkness and his King as those who do not know Me will ultimately lose their Souls to this power opposing the Father. This is an eternal Cosmic Law.

So the Father has in His Infinite Wisdom created steps for each lifetime for every human being to follow so that through his or her free will they can choose to put My Ultimate Light above their earthly life. This is the evolution of the cosmos. The stages are sealed by the power of My Father in the way that He who walks in darkness will see only material conclusions for the origin of the earth and his being. He who walks in My Light will see that My Father created the cosmos for the Beings of Light.

So I say to you, ask Me to send My Light to the darkness and you will see your Truth and the Truth of your Souls.

Follow your own will and you will be trapped in the future planet to come of the King of darkness as this is the promise of My Father to mankind. A man who knows this Cosmic fact participates in the Divine power of God and His creation as he creates a pathway to the Ultimate Light which is creating now in the Higher Worlds of Light; in the World of Light to come. At the end of mankind's physical existence when his being will astralise into the Universal Cosmic Light with the planet of Light to come, which is the ultimate destination of all human beings who have Souls of Light." [Verse 8] [6]

Then another in the group hearing all of what Jesus said

asked, "Master and true Teacher of the Light, you are saying that there needs to be a matching force of Light to counteract the power of darkness. You are saying that he who does not follow you will not have this power as he has not seen the Will of the Father. Now how then can a mortal human being relate to such spiritual forces and create these Eyes of Light in his Soul so that he does not lose the battle between good and evil you speak of? What must he do so that he walks then in the Light and wins his incarnation by fulfilling his task in it? How can he have the power of the Light to achieve this?"

The Christ Being replied, "I, the Christ Being, have said to you that I am the Son of the Living God. So follow Me and you will know My Father and I will initiate you into creating the Eyes of the Light you need to win all incarnations and to fulfil your tasks in them. Make the Moral Step to put the Light above your lives."

Then the spokesperson intervened and said to Jesus, "You ask us to believe in you and to put our lives below your being. You ask us to base all that you have said on the

---

[6] John 6: 22-27.

presumption that we will be saved ultimately at the end of time on this planet providing we dedicate our whole Souls to your being. True, you have shown some fantastic powers but to say that you are the Son of the Living God and that you can see two evolutionary processes at work on the earth and that there are Spiritual Beings that the Father has created which have a division in their Hierarchies for the good and for the evil of mankind in that those Spiritual Beings who side with your being will win over the dark beings: now look here, what proof have we that what you say will ultimately come true? What living evidence in the material world can you provide us with, after all who can believe in such a world of Spiritual Beings creating planets and the human race? This, you say, is what happened at the beginning of time in our universe. You purport that this is the explanation as to the source of the universe. You have in fact given us a Cosmic story about creation and told us that unless we make a moral decision to follow you we will devolve in this creation into darkness; to a kingdom ruled by a Monarch of darkness.

I say to you that there is no real proof that what you say is ultimately completely true as we know that when our race was in the desert for forty years seeking a homeland the Father gave us the Light to find our country. He also sustained us with food from Heaven in the course of this journey. Now our scriptures say quite clearly that we are the chosen people and that the Messiah will come to liberate us in our earthly existence. Your powers seem to me only to speak of the evolutionary process of epochs to come where man has to have many lifetimes to create a Moral Light that will create for him a pathway to the Ultimate Light in you.

So I say to you, on behalf of those around me, use your magical powers to show us all the Ultimate Light as in reality the Jewish race is controlled by Rome. The chosen people of God have to follow the political and financial power of the absolute intellectual materialists that rule a whole planet. So how come this man who proclaims himself to be the Son of God does not have a solution to this problem? After all the King of darkness surely protects Caesar who decides whether we live or die. Is this not the most important point to settle first then, Master, to change the present evil in our world or is it just following a Truth that is to come a hundred thousand years from now? I tell you, Master, prove to us your theory of knowledge saying that you have the power to take away the evil one. Show us so that we may believe in you. Is this then not a living example of what you can really do to redeem all men for the Father, Rabbi?"

The Christ Being then said to this man and his group, "You say that Moses led you to your homeland. You say that he was a true Monarch of the Light as he gave you identity in the human world and saved you to create a race of chosen people to prepare for the Messiah sent by the Father to redeem a whole world to the Light. I say to you this is true but again you are still putting the intellect above the Light as you want to enforce your will above God's Will as God, the Father, gave the power to Moses in the wilderness to lead a race of men to the Light. He did this so that you could evolve your beings to the stage of meeting the Living Son of God in the flesh.

As for the question of changing the earthly power of Caesar to prove that I can take away the King of darkness from the planet earth, this is asking for a way to take away the ideology of this planet which is Intellectual Materialism through the power of the Cosmic Motivational Science. You are asking for a proof of the power of the Light so that I can become a Messiah of My people. This would give you living proof of who I am. I say to you, the Father has Free Will to act. He has given you free will to act. He has given Me this mission to save this planet for the Light. I walk among you to do this. I do not take away Caesar's power as this would be taking his free will to act and I would only be reacting to Intellectual Materialism and succumbing to the maxim of 'where there is a will there is a way' and not seeing that the end does not justify the means. The means is there to do what you ask but there is no justification for it as you are the chosen people only because you have by moral right asked for the Father to send His Son to redeem you as part of mankind to the Light. You are asking to be above mankind's karma. You refuse to look at the Cosmic karma of Spiritual Beings that put Caesar in his position for now in history. You want to have a material solution as proof that God will save His people.

I say to you that this is the challenge of mankind; to ask the Christ Being to send his Light to the Caesars of the world and not to send one's own Light. When you fight this ruler of the planet earth you identify with his weapons of evil. As he has stolen power and wealth from you and the races of the world you see that the only way to win over him is to destroy him and get back what is yours materially. This is right and just but what is not right and just is to ask for God to do it for you when you do not follow His Son, the Ultimate Light, as only when a man follows his Truth first can he have the Truth of life. Only when you, as a race, can follow your Truth in the family of humanity can you know its Truth. Caesar is a manifestation of the power of the evil one. His power will pass as will many who will come after him and have come before him. The day that a Caesar follows the Light is when mankind will begin to be redeemed as then Rome

will seek to live its Truth as now it seeks only falsehood and power over other races. So material power must be used to change this power. Spiritual power needs to be used to change the ultimate source of this power.

Hence the Moral Will of mankind would have to come into place before a Special Key of Christ can take away the power of Caesar. This will happen in ages to come when Caesar's race will devolve into darkness and will separate from the human family. This is the Ultimate Will of the Father as with the individual with his Moral Will to the Light.

My Being and the Father are one. If I use the Special Keys of Christ I can only use them when it is morally right for mankind and morally right for God. God gave free will to all beings. I have not come to change the Moral Will of mankind by force. I have come to proclaim the message of the Ultimate Light in living My Truth as a human being in the flesh as I have to save all mankind from the first born on the planet to the last born to come. So I have come to create a cosmos of Light with beings who choose to become gods with the divine power of their free will or choose to follow the evolution of existence to the Light.

So be aware, I say to you again, unless a man lives his Truth he does not really have free will as without the Truth of life one's free will belongs to the tyrants of the world. You say, 'How can this be when there is no political or financial freedom from Rome?' I say to you there is ultimate freedom for all lifetimes if you choose to put the Light of the Christ Being above your life. This is truly the Ultimate Truth of mankind." [Verse 9] [7]

Then another person in the group said to Jesus, "Today I have seen the Light. I have seen the Light of all Ages as truly the Truth lives in your words and in your heart. You have solved the riddle of the ages. You have shown me today that the individual human being becomes a divine being when he puts his Moral free will above his life. This is truly what makes him have this Cosmic identity that separates him from the evil race to come the predecessors of which, now can be seen, in the Roman empire.

The living Soul of a human being is above his body. His Soul is eternal. The Father in His eternal wisdom created beings who have to choose in freedom His Light above the opposing force of darkness. In many lifetimes a man has to make this choice until finally his Soul and his body become one Light Being. Truly this is what the Christ Being is in the flesh before us today; the Son of the Living God in the flesh. He is a person who has a body and Soul that is one being. This is the Ultimate Spiritual Being. This is the destiny of all human beings. Those who forfeit this destiny lose their Light for eternity.

I now choose to follow the race of Light to come. I choose to have a Soul that will stand in the sight of the Father and at the end of time I will glorify His Being with His Angels as I see now that the Eyes of the Light can see you, Oh, Christ Being, as they are the windows to the Soul of Heaven. You are my Saviour and my God. I ask you to bless us all and let our Souls live by your side in the eternal Light of Heaven. This is now my will to your Light, Master of the Light." [Verse 10] [8]

---

[7] John 6: 28-33,

[8] John 6: 34.

103

Then Jesus addressed all who were present and said, "I, the Christ Being, created Souls with the Father and created Spiritual Beings as I, with the Holy Spirit, wanted a Universe of Light to complement Heaven. This is the ultimate Will of God.

Bread feeds the body of the earth. In Heaven the Light of My Father feeds all beings. I am the Being of Light that feeds all of mankind with the Living Light. I am the Light of Life. Those who walk in My Light surpass the need to eat the bread that sustains the body. They do not need to drink water from the springs of the earth to take away their thirst as when they believe in My Being their Souls and their bodies ultimately become one being. As you have seen I am such a being but you still question and ask, 'Can it be true?' So you doubt the Living God.

My Father has given Me these powers and this Living Body Soul Being of Light to show in the flesh on earth the final evolutionary being to which all human beings with Light will evolve. Those who seek this superior evolutionary Light will ever evolve the Light of the Christ Being on earth and in this way the Doorway to Heaven and its Angels are open to his being and his Soul.

I have descended from Heaven to follow My Truth as this is the Will of the Father; the Ultimate Truth of the Cosmos. I have come to demonstrate to man that the flesh can never be lost when it is connected to the Soul of Light. I am the Living proof that a human being will, at the end of physical time on earth with the mother earth, become a part of the Ultimate Spiritual Heaven where the planet earth will exist in Ultimate Light. He will become a Soul Being of Light with a transformed body like I have now as the Living Christ Being.

So in Truth no man loses his body for his Soul as the flesh is recreated and only transformed from all the bodies from all incarnations so that the perfect Body of Light will be incarnated in Heaven for the final incarnation for eternity. So the Father willed that mankind follow these evolutionary stages until he would send His Son to change the future to create the race of Light. He willed that the Christ Being would redeem mankind and show him the Pathway to Heaven.

Every human being individually creates a piece of Heaven every time he puts the Light above his life as then he creates this pathway that gives him this Cosmic link with the chain of incarnations to the final incarnation in Heaven. Truly this is the destiny of all those who unconditionally trust in the Christ Being and put him first in their lives. This is truly the Will of the Father in Heaven for all men to fulfil this mission on earth to become one with the bodies and Souls in the Light. This is the Christ Light.

I, the Christ Being, am the Living Light. I send My Light from Heaven to mankind so that he can evolve his being to create the final evolution of the human being to become one with the Being of Eternal Light. Those who choose Me choose the Light." [Verse 11] [9]

Following this the crowd around Jesus began to question who he was. One man said to him, "Look here, man, your father was Joseph and your mother was Mary. You are a human being just like the rest of us but you say that you are the Christ Being and you send your Light from Heaven to us. Now can you

explain how this can be possible as, after all, how can a human being be God? It is incomprehensible to us how you can say what you say and be telling the Truth besides making sense."

Then the Christ Being said to them all, "I have come to save those who love My Father and give them the power of the Light to save themselves from the power of a world obsessed with Intellectual Materialism. I have come to show a pathway to the Ultimate Truth of Life and the Cosmos. He who follows the Christ Being knows that the Pathway of the Ultimate Truth leads to the Ultimate Light as what I have come for is to give the Eyes of the Light to the initiands of the Light. They are preparing for the race of Light to come that will evolve out of the humankind of today. I have come for this race of Light to come as they will be by My side at the end of time when the earth will complete its incarnation and the spiritual world of Light will become its permanent home.

Those who follow darkness will be a part of the race of darkness as their evolution will lead them to the planet of darkness in that part of the

---

[9] John 6: 35-40.

spiritual world of darkness reserved by the Father from the beginning of time for His opponents both in the material and spiritual realms.

The Prophets spoke of Me from the beginning of time. They all knew that I would come to reveal to the world the ultimate fate of the planet earth as willed by My Father. My Father willed that all beings would have free will to choose Him or to oppose Him.

He also did not relinquish His Free Will when He did this. He, at the beginning of time, gave each being a human being stage where he would meet the Christ Being. Mankind is meeting the Christ Being now. It is speaking to the Father through Me. He who can see Me has the Eyes of the Light. He who can see the Father in Me knows God.

My Father can be seen by those who have the Eyes of the Light as they are fulfilling their task and their Moral karma. They have aligned their Truth with the Ultimate Light. In this way they fulfil the Will of the Father eternally.

Eternal life is the gift given to those who have the Ultimate Light in their Souls. At the end of time the Soul with Ultimate Light surpasses its evolution as human being and becomes a Spiritual Being able to live in a World of Light while those who deny the Father deny the Ultimate Light and will devolve back into the material realm in a reversed evolution.

I, the Christ Being, am the Ultimate Evolutionary Being who gives life to a whole world of humanity. With My Being the planet earth has a future with the Light. He who follows the Light of My Being never dies. You still follow the light of your forefathers and they died as you will die. Only when you follow the Ultimate Light of the Christ Being will you live forever in My Father's House in Heaven.

I, the Christ Being, am the Living Light. I bring My Being to every individual who has ever lived and ever will live on this planet. I was there at the beginning of time and I will be there at its end. He who sees My Light becomes complete in his psyche and in his Soul and then ultimately in his body as at the end of time the Ultimate Body of Light will be given to everyone who has walked in the Light of Christ. This body will be a vehicle of Light that will live on eternally in the Golden Mansions of My Father.

He who forsakes Intellectual Materialism for the sake of My absolute and Ultimate Light may lose his body in many incarnations but his Soul and his psyche will ever evolve into the Light until he or she has purified it with the Light. Hence once this is done the purification is translated to an evolutionary process of making the flesh part of the Living Light.

So this is why I have come now to show you the Living Light in the flesh as this is what you will be when you give your Moral Will to the Light and stand before the Ultimate Light beyond birth and death when you look to the Light and live the Light in your Souls and in your Truth. This is the Truth. This is why those who have the Truth in their lives have the Christ Eyes to see the Living God work in their Souls. The future of the Light will be when the Soul will become a Body of Light in Heaven living with My Being and My Father; the Eternal Light. [Verse 12] [10]

Now Jesus walked into a synagogue in Caper'na-um. Then he went before all that were gathered before the priests as they had come to hear him as it was already

clear that he was a Prophet and in the lineage of the Teachers of the Light.

The Christ Being said, "I, the Christ Being say to you, you ask how I can have the Body of Light when I have not come at the end of time on your planet. You ask how you can have My Light when you have as yet not known this Ultimate Light of the Christ Being.

So I say to you, walk in the Light of My Being and you live your Truth and do what is right for you as human beings. This means you align with the Ultimate Truth of life and hence with its Ultimate Light. You do this every time you work on living your Truth and aligning it to your Moral Will to the Light. You do this symbolically when you purify your beings at the synagogue and ask your Father in Heaven to make you worthy to enter the Kingdom of God at the end of time.

I say to you, the Kingdom of God has come to you on your planet today. It is in living flesh before you. I am the Body of Light in the flesh. When you have Eyes of the Light you can see this Body of Light. I have come to give it to you. I have come to show you

[10] John 6: 41-51.

this Pathway to the Ultimate Light. I have come so that you can learn to communicate with the Spiritual Light of Heaven. In your Souls you have this Doorway to the Light of Heaven if you open your eyes and your hearts to the Christ Light. I ask you to open them now and to meditate on what I say. I ask you to place Me in the centre of the ring of Light around your whole beings and around this synagogue and I ask you to expel all that is dark from your Souls. Then I ask you to look up to Heaven to the Light of My Father and to see the Angel of God that comes to make a Pathway of Light across the Circle of Light with a Mighty Golden Sword from the Fire of the Heavenly stars. You can ask that the Christ Light be sent to the body of darkness of spirit trying to take away your Circle of Light. Then you will see what I see now in your Souls."
[Verse 13]

Once the Christ Being spoke in this way he slipped into the spiritual world and walked into each Soul in the gathering and each that received him had a vision of eating his flesh and drinking his Blood in the Golden Mansion of His Father in Heaven. In this image that was implanted in their Souls

as time stood still in the synagogue on that day in that very moment in time, they could see the Christ Being with all his glory and his Angels giving hosts of bread as symbols of the Body of Christ as this is what they were told by the Angels of God and perceived they were eating the Body of Christ into their Souls.

Hence at the end of this vision they all woke up as if from a trance and the Christ Being once again appeared as the Prophet before them in living flesh. Then the Christ Being said, "He who eats in My Father's House has tasted the nourishment of the Eternal Light as it feeds the Soul and the body. He who has experienced this has seen in this meditation of the Light, My true Being. When an individual human being aligns with My Light and lives his Truth in all incarnations until the end of all life times he will become worthy to live in My Father's House in Heaven as his Body of Light will be able to breathe in the Spiritual Heaven.

Those who cannot eat of this flesh of Light now cannot eat it at the end of their time on this planet which will come when all life times have been lived as to fulfil the eternal

108

justice of My Father to give to every human being every experience in the universe as equal to every other experience to every other human being. This experience may be of the Light. Those who have chosen to have the experiences of the dark beings will also eat of their flesh of darkness and will nourish their Souls with this dark bread of death.

So I say to you I am the Christ Being. I am the Living Light in the flesh. Follow Me and you nourish your being with My Light as those of you who have seen in the Meditation of the Light, My Ultimate Being, see that My physical death will bring life to the whole planet as truly I will never die. I die only as a human being but this is what I have come for; to die for the sake of the eternal life of the evolution of all human beings who follow the Light of My Father and to replenish the Light in all the kingdoms of life on this planet. Once I die My Blood which is filled with the Light of Heaven will give the Eternal Spiritual Light to your planet. It will give it the Light of Life as it is giving you when you see it with your Eyes of the Light.

So I tell you all who have this

Light now, drink it into your Souls; the Blood of the Ultimate Light Being of your planet. Eat of the flesh of the Light Being of your planet. Do this when you meditate on the Circle of Light as I have shown you today and from it when you awaken from the visions of this Light in this meditation do as I have shown you and you will reach My Body of Light when I am in Heaven. You will extend this Circle of Light to reach the Heavenly Bodies of Light where the Spiritual Hierarchies of Light live. They will also then participate as you saw in the visions in your mind just before to help you evolve your Body of Light in every life time until you have My Body and My Light.

Then you have fulfilled the evolution of the Light on your planet as this is truly why I have come to show you how to nourish your Souls that will become the Bodies of Light at the end of the incarnation of your planet so that as you knew how to talk to My Father in prayer and meditation from the scriptures now I show you how to talk to My Being, the Ultimate Light of your planet, so that you may prepare for the last life on it when you will have the Body of Light. This is when your body and your Soul will become like the Christ Body of Light. This is I, the Christ Being, Son of the Living God and the Light of all Ages; the Son of Heaven." [Verse 14] [11]

Once Jesus completed this lecture upon the ultimate evolution of the earth and its description from the point of view of how the Spiritual Hierarchies of Light transform the Light in all human beings through the Christ Being, he then waited for the gathering to disperse and for the Apostles to express their views on what he had said about the cosmological future of the Light.

One of the disciples then turned to him and said, "You speak as though only those beings who know of you and follow you will be saved and the rest will be damned to hell and that in all life times a person is on trial and he has to resolve more and more conflicts. Is this not a living hell now, living under the Roman powers and making us bow to their Intellectual Materialism? So how can man be so damned and how can he have to suffer so much in so many life times? What is this, a cruel joke from the Father

that He should send His Son to die for us? Well, I for one, did not ask the Father to do this. How come I do not get a say in all of this? I thought that I heard that the Father gave free will to all of us. What do you say to this as after all you are saying I have to wait thousands of years to purify My Body of Light? Who knows? You could be wrong! What about the Truth of all this? Who can prove it? So can you be more precise and tell me how you can prove what you say as after all, what is the difference with believing in Intellectual Materialism which I can see and have to fight every day, or believing in a story about a future a million years from now?"

Then Jesus saw that those who did not receive him into their Souls were seized by an ill spirit. This man who was speaking to him had taken many away from his gathering and many who said they would never follow him again.

Then the Christ Being said to this man, "Your eyes are shut to the Light as your point of reference of the truth comes from your intellect. You do not look into your Soul and hence you have blocked your being from hearing My Father's

---

[11] John 6: 52-59.

110

Words. You have chosen to make only what you see with your physical senses to be the Ultimate Truth. Hence your tools of mind and Soul belong to an inferior intelligence and to an intelligence that only accepts a cold intellectual rule that has no real person living that rule but only a mind without a body or Soul.

This is a mind that says that my intellect and my will, will get me what I want as a human being. It says that ultimate intelligence is putting myself as the most important person in the world and that putting myself as number one in my life and in the life of this whole planet is real intelligence. It says that thinking of what is my origin or my ultimate destiny stops me from living in the here and now and weakens my Motivational Science to win my present life and get what I want. It says that truth is relative and that a man believes in what he wants to believe in. Hence you mock the Eternal Truth and My Father. So in doing this you have now eyes of darkness. You cannot see the Truth as you are a man who does not live his Truth. So you have now lost your Light. So go away from Me as you do not look to the Light.

You ask Me to take away your responsibility for who you are as an individual human being with the free will to choose good or evil. You tell Me to put the body above the eternal Soul. You put matter above Spirit. You put darkness above Light but I tell you the darkness is attracted to the Light and I attract the opposite of the Light. So be gone now from My presence as you have chosen the Devil as your master.

I say this as I am the Christ; the Master of all human beings and Spiritual Beings. The Devil is subordinate to My Being. He who follows My Light and asks Me to send My Light to the Devil will put him away from his life. This is My pledge and promise to those who follow the Light."

Then Jesus said, "I chose all twelve Apostles to create the Movement of Light on the earth so that the Circle of Light will be around the planet earth and all will be expelled from it who seek the darkness. I say to you: one among you will be expelled from the twelve as it will be at the end of time. Those who walk in the darkness of evil will descend into the evil planet.

So also the one who will betray Me will symbolize this event to come upon the earth at the time when it is about to ascend into the spiritual world of Heavenly Light as at this moment all who have chosen the Father will see Him as the Living God and the Light of Heaven. They will then be free for eternity from darkness as their Bodies of Light will transport them out of its range forevermore. This is the Word of Christ." [Verse 15] [12]

On the completion of this answer to this man who had evil in his heart many walked away from Jesus as many were tricked into believing this man who had the force of spiritual darkness speaking to their Souls. The dark spirit was saying to their beings that Jesus was guilty of fabricating the real Truth about the material facts of life as it was a mathematical impossibility to talk of measuring time in the way it was explained.

The Christ could also see that the dark spirit was trying to speak to the chosen twelve Apostles who had not walked away but one of them, Judas the Iscariot, said to Jesus, "What clock do you use to measure such a time scale to explain scientifically the world's origin and the origin of mankind?"

The Christ looked at him and said, "Judas, look carefully at the world and how it is ordered so that man can have the right amount of sunshine and the right amount of air to live on his planet. Look carefully and see that the forces of Spiritual Beings created time and created this present balance on your world. So to truly know how to measure this time you need a Cosmic clock that measures time and how this measurement can be seen evolving actively in different epochs evolving the Light of the universe. This is controlled by the Spiritual Hierarchies of the Light for the Cosmic Father of the Light. I say the Light as the measurements made of the other force are only of value ultimately in the material world. This is so as those human beings who do not walk in the Light of Christ will ultimately join the spiritual beings that have chosen his enemy."

Then the Christ Being turned to the Apostles and continued by saying, "Of course, it is clear that at the end of time

---

[12] John 6: 60-65.

when you all will have a Body of Light you will take your place in the Spiritual Hierarchies of the Light. Then your evolution with the work with My Heavenly Father will flourish as your Light will have reached the very streets of Heaven.

I say to you all now, do you see the Ultimate Truth before you? Can you see with your Eyes of the Light, the Body of Light of your planet or do you choose to walk away into the oblivion of the crowd which heard about its ultimate destiny and chose to deny its Truth? This is so as its intellect mathematically discounted the Truth as it did not align with the material facts of the ideology of Intellectual Materialism on this planet now as its intellect refused to truly accept Ultimate Light as the ultimate power. The intellect that does this has made an ideology of God in the scriptures. This intellect only lives on this intellectual power. Hence it is doomed to the neutralisation of the Truth of life and in this case the life of this planet."
[Verse 16]

Then the chosen leader of the Apostles, Simon Peter, replied for all of the twelve as he perceived what was in their hearts and said, "You are the Son of the Father in Heaven. When we can see you live in this other world of Eternal Light we know who you are. We know that with the Eyes of the Light we do not need to believe in you but can say we have experience of who you really are. We understand that those who have not these Eyes that can see into the spiritual world, can only believe, but cannot know as we know.

We see now that you have come to the earth to shed Light upon the darkness in the whole cosmos. We can see that your Pathway is that of the Living God. We also know now that the unconditional love of your Father gave your Being to us from His Free Will to save mankind for the World of Light to come. We can see that you have shown us how to love your Father as we love you as you have in your heart that Spiritual Love of all human beings eternally.

So I say to you that I, with my Eyes of the Light, can see that you are the Living Christ of this World. You have come to redeem all men. With your Body of Light you can walk in the material and spiritual world simultaneously; hence in this way can see how time travels through the cosmos. You can see past, present and its future at will. However as you have shown us it is the Will of the Father to give us free will to choose you or the darkness. This choice you have given us makes us eternal beings and makes us a part of God eternally as with this power to choose the Light over evil a man evolves to become a Spiritual Being of Light at the end of time. This gift of eternal life is given by your Father. So, Oh, Christ, I pledge my whole being to fulfil my task and my dream in this incarnation to serve you and your Father for all life times to come. I also pledge as the leader of your Spiritual Light Group to stand with them before the Father for the Christ Being at the end of time; to say, as I am saying now, at the end of time on this planet that I am a man who has the Body of the Christ Light. I am a man who will walk in the streets of Heaven as my Light has been able to reach it only because the Christ Being created this Body of Light for me." [Verse 17]

Then the Christ Being turned to Judas the Iscariot and said to him, "You still have time to be redeemed as in your heart you are not really with us. Look into your Soul and seek

the Light as the evil one is tricking you into doubting in it. Be aware that your pathway is being lost as you are putting the intellect above the Truth.

I say to you do not be alarmed at the weapons of the evil masses who flock to the guardian of material power. Be aware that the Truth is above life and that the Light is above the Truth. Here stands before you the Living Truth of all the cosmos. You are fighting Intellectual Materialism with the intellect and you are losing as you do not see your true opponent; this being the leader of the dark spirits. You do not see that he will betray you as he wants you to sell your Soul to Intellectual Materialism. You do not see that you need a superior weapon of Light that transcends life and the material world. Hence you lose sight then of the meaning of this one life as its meaning is the reason for your Moral karma. Fulfil it and you will join Me in the walk that takes you to the Golden Pathways of Heaven. Deny its existence and you will lose this life time to fulfil the dream of your incarnation which is to make

the ultimate choice of putting the Light above your life. This

**is truly what your Moral Will should be to the Light."
[Verse 18]** [13]

---

[13] John 6: 66-71.

CHAPTER 7

Christ then decided to go to Galilee as he knew that there were many now in Judea that were plotting to kill him. He was aware of this as he could see that his popularity was growing and the dark forces were mounting in the spiritual world to influence evil hearts as darkness is always attracted to the Light.

He knew that ultimately this darkness would engulf his physical existence as this was the pathway he had chosen to challenge the status quo of the order in the Jewish state with his Light power. This he did knowing full well that it would be falsely interpreted as a political threat to the religious power the Pharisees had over the Jews.

A Pharisee came up to Jesus and said to him, "Master, it is the feast of the Tabernacles. Surely you will come to speak at the synagogue as this would give the public in Judea a way to know of you in person as you know you already have a following by many who have never met you there. After all you have miraculous powers and you say you have come to give Light to the world. Well, this is your door to the world if you would only come and teach in the synagogue about your spiritual powers. After all if you are the world teacher you say you are, you have to present your powers to the world so that you can leave it up to the world to judge the truth of what you say."

The Christ said to this man, "I have to save men's Souls and to show them the Pathway to the Ultimate Light. I know that each person who follows this pathway will find the Ultimate Truth and gain the Eyes of the Light. I have not come to address the world and mankind upon a platform to be viewed as a guru of Light. I have come to show man a way to independently live up to the power of the Moral free will to choose good over evil; to have a Cosmic identity aligned with a human one. This Cosmic identity would give every individual human being an eternal destiny with the Light of God in a World of Light to come. This is an identity that will transcend worlds and life times so that ultimately the fusion of one Soul from all life times will create this complete Being with a Body of Light that can live in its home in the Spiritual Heaven of My Father.

So when you say to Me that I should teach in the synagogue so that the world will know of

Me I say to you only those who have gained the Eyes of the Light can have a Doorway to My Being as others can only speak of Me as you do and name Me a teacher or a guru. However they cannot know Me as when they would know Me they would know that I have come to change the life pattern of a world and to do that I have to first reach the picture of the Soul in the whole of mankind so I first started by giving to the Soul an inner Light; a Light that will shine out into the personality of an individual person. I will do this by speaking to the heart of the man who seeks this Light. I do not speak only to the mind as you ask Me to as obviously you still work too consciously with selling your intellectual materialistic religion of your cult while I have chosen to reach first the unconscious of the human being by asking him to create the Eyes of the Light first which guides an individual to live his Truth first before he speaks of the Ultimate Truth.

So, yes, it is clear that when a person truly lives his Truth and does what is right for him as a human being first in all things in his life he has real authority to speak of the Truth and its ultimate

foundation in the Ultimate Light of God. Truly as I do this now I know that I will wait for the right time to act so that I cannot only live My Truth in living My life by aligning it with the Light of My Father but I will also fulfil My Moral karma at the moment ordained by the Hierarchies of Light that created the universe and this planet as truly they and their Light activate all things on your planet with My Light.

Hence now the Hierarchies of darkness are speaking and whispering in the ears of the populace that have identified with Intellectual Materialism that I am a demon and that I need to be killed and that really the good that I have done must have an evil source. This is so as it is the fate of the Hierarchies of darkness to try to rule this planet by the force of spiritual darkness.

I say to you that evil always tries to discredit the Light by telling it that it is guilty of the very sin it perpetuates upon the life of mankind. It says that it is superior and truly natural and truly belongs to the planet earth. It wants to speak to the senses of man and to cut out the supersensible as this is its way to put the intellect above the Light. This is its key to win over the planet earth for the Prince of darkness.

I say to you, learn not to give this darkness your Light. Ask that the Light of the Ultimate Being of Light send His Light to this darkness. Ask it that you may be aware that you do not accept the lie that you are guilty of the evil in the world and that the source is you and not the Hierarchies of darkness in the spiritual world. Be aware of this false perception. You will live your Truth in the World of Light and ultimately in the Light to come. This is why I have come to win this for mankind from all epochs past, present and to come."

With this reply given Jesus walked away from this man and said to him with hands raised up, "You are one of those who seek power over matter so go to your feast as this is the place where you will lose your Truth and your Light as Rome has made you identify with its power that its evil is really the evil of the world while in Truth its Negative Motivational Science has given it an army that rules the world by force. It purports like you that it is justified in doing so as it has superior weapons of war and therefore superior moral power over the earth. So truly this is the falsehood of evil that tries to tell the victim that it is guilty of its very offense. So be aware that those who lose their Light like you identify their personalities with the dark Hierarchies that protect the ruthless evil powers that rule by force.

Hence I say to you, be aware to put the Truth above this lie or you will ultimately lose your Soul to the real evil of the world. This is truly the Truth that you lose your Light when you do not live your Truth and then as you can see, you can never truly speak the Truth as one who does this puts his own personal perception of Truth of life above the Truth. I am the Ultimate Truth of Life. I am its Ultimate Light; I, the Christ Being." [Verse 1] [1]

Later on Jesus decided to go to Judea without any set plan to speak at the synagogue but to just mingle in the crowd to see what he could do among those who were seeing his Light. He could see that many were talking about him and it was apparent that the Pharisees were trying to tell small groups of people everywhere

---

[1] John 7: 1-9.

that Jesus was a false Prophet. Many he saw listening to the Pharisees who would not truly say what was in their hearts. As he made himself invisible among the crowds he could see that they feared speaking up in front of the Pharisees. So this way the Christ could see who it was that truly saw the Light and was prepared to be initiated into the Circle of the Christ Light and who was turning away from his being. [Verse 2]

Then when he had walked among the people in both the spiritual and physical worlds intercepting each Soul with his Being and choosing ones who were given the Light originally by His Father he began to address those chosen by the Light and the others at the temple. He began by saying, "I have come today to give Light to the Scriptures of God. I am the Word. The Word and I are one. My Father is the Word. He who knows the Father knows Me. He who knows Me does not speak of the universe and this planet without knowledge of the Ultimate Truth. He sees that My Father is the Cause of all existence and I am the Christ, its effect, here before you today.

The Holy Spirit is the Being that relates between the Father and My Being. This Being guides Me today to speak about the Father and His Will for the cosmos. His Being is the Living Spirit in mankind that shows it the Pathway to look to the Light.

I am the Living Light. He shows the Pathway to My Being while the Father created the Beings of Light to create this Universe of Light. I am the Living Light of your planet. I embody all these Beings in one Being. I am the Christ Being, Son of the Living God." [Verse 3] [2]

Suddenly there was a hush in the crowd as a prominent teacher of the Pharisees came up beside Jesus and said to him, "I have listened to your lecture and cannot see truly the source of your education or learning. Where did you study? It is said that you have traveled abroad in the Asian and barbarian lands and met with many prophets of darkness who showed you the magical powers you have.

Now I put it to you to explain to the people of Judea before you how you can speak about sacred scripture when you

---

[2] John 7: 10-14.

have never truly trained to read it and interpret it. I have spent a life time of study at the academy of religious learning of all of Israel. So please, I ask you, it is well known that your education is no more than that of the background of a craftsman, a carpenter, I understand. Well, no carpenter could ever speak like you and articulate with such eloquence the mysteries of the world.

Speak, professed Prophet of Israel, and tell my people and myself where you really come from. What is the group to which you really belong? What purpose do you have in spreading controversial political and spiritual concepts to the chosen people of God? By what authority do you do this as after all I hold with my office the combined learned and respected men of the whole nation and we recognise that you are a Prophet who is misguiding the people as if it were not so then where is your document that speaks of your teachings and what is its source that you could stand before the nation of the chosen people of God and proclaim that your Light is above it and the Ultimate Light? Please tell us who you really are?"

The Christ Being replied by saying, "I am the Christ Being. You ask Me to tell you what is the source of My Being. I tell you that this is a false question. You should be asking, 'What is the source of My Light?' Once again you have put the intellect above the Truth when you say to Me, 'What have you studied to truly know the origin of ultimate existence upon your planet?' It is true that I have traveled the world to seek Initiation of the Light among many people and among many Prophets who looked to the Light. I have done this deliberately to know My world. I have done this so that I could create a vessel for the Light to enter My Being. I became an Initiand of the Light through first knowing about the spiritual world through the work on My Being and not only My intellect. I did this by following different pathways to the Light and at every turn of My life education I put My studies of the sacred books of the world never above living My Truth. I could see that the Prophets of darkness had also many documents outlining the law of their god which they never lived. So I chose only the Prophets who followed the Initiation Pathways to the Living Light.

So I say to you, sir, as you are the high priest of the law of the Pharisees, are you living your Truth? If not then you are not doing what is right for your following or your people as I follow My Truth first as a human being in all things in My life. I align all the knowledge I have gained through the actual practice of My Spiritual Powers of the Light. I put My opinion of the scriptures by putting Myself as a person first in all that I live in relation to what the scriptures say. I also put the Truth above any man who says that I am the supreme authority on who God is. I also say to you that if I followed the Prophets of darkness, how is it that what I live and say are identical to the Light? How is it then that My Truth is aligned to the Ultimate Truth? This has been proven in all the healing work I have done and in all the sermons I have given to this whole nation and to those nations abroad that were ready to receive the Light of My Father.

So I say to you, sir, what is education when it sells intellectual Spiritism and when it wants to interpret the sacred scriptures and sells Intellectual Materialism when it talks of changing the ruling political and military force of Israel? I say to you it is an education of a man who has no real life education and who assumes authority over the Soul of a people first without first purifying his own Soul. If this were not so you would not have begun to interpret Me but what I have done as he who interprets others loses his Truth. He who interprets what they do speaks the Truth. I speak the Truth and tell you now that you are speaking from the real motivation of self-interest to put Phariseeism above the Truth. If this were not so then you would allow every human being before you to speak of his own Truth in the way he interprets the scripture in accordance to what he has lived and not only what his education is. Also when you assume moral authority and say that your source is credible and that mine is dubious, I say to you I am the Source of the Light as I am the Ultimate Light in the flesh. I have come to your planet to bring Light to it so that its evolution will change and it will create the right Pathway to the Will of the Light.

The Moral Will to the Light of this World has to change. This is why I have come to the earth; to pour Light into the Souls who seek ultimate initiation by the Supreme

Light in the Living Body of My Being as I have said that I have come to teach mankind the pathway to the Ultimate Light and its Ultimate Truth which is the Light. This Will to the Light is in the hearts of those who seek Me. The Ultimate Source of My Spiritual Powers is the Father. His Will is My Will. So with this power I can take away the Prince of darkness from the planet earth and banish him to where, at the end of time, he will be imprisoned for all eternity. I do this every time I use a Special Spiritual Key of Light to heal a part of mankind's Soul by healing one Soul. Then I heal the body or the psyche of man.

So you see that the magical powers you speak of are the magic of the Light. I use these Keys not for the purpose of gaining material or political power but to gain ground in the consciousness of mankind so that there will be a seed that will grow in it where the golden flower will bloom in the Sunlight of the Gods of Creation which are the Hierarchies of the Light. These Hierarchies are the special Angels of God that are creating universes of human beings who will evolve to being Higher Beings of Light when they learn to love the Son of God unconditionally and as unconditionally as the Father loved them. It was He who loved them first in giving them the Living Light in their Souls and in giving them the free will to choose His Being or darkness and also in using His Free Will to send Me to your planet to redeem all of mankind.

So I say to you all today, be aware that I have not come to create a kingdom based on gold and armies to conquer the oppressors of the Jewish race or the oppressors of any other nation. I have come to create a new evolutionary process that will transcend many life times for all of you. I have come to show you that your Souls will create many civilisations based on this Light power of which I speak.

However I have come also to tell you that all ultimately are preparing for the final stage when Jerusalem will become a City of Heaven that will shine with such golden Light that the whole universe with all its stars will pale next to it. I have come to tell you that this is the Will of the Father who has sent Me. So truly what I say to you has its ultimate source in the Ultimate Spirit of God, Almighty, who is My Father and who has written your scriptures through the Prophets of the Light for you.

I am the Ultimate Prophet of Truth and the Ultimate Light of all Prophets as I am what all the Prophets spoke of in living flesh. In Me there is no darkness. He who says there is speaks for the destruction of the dream of the world; the dream to save its Soul and to be in the community of the Jerusalem of the Golden Light of Heaven. This is My dream for mankind. I ask you to participate in this dream in your very Souls and let the Eyes of the Light see Me; the Living Light of Heaven and earth. I am the Christ.

Moses gave you the Ten Commandments so that you could know the Laws of My Father. He also asked you to wait for the coming of the Ultimate Light in the scriptures and to align it with living your Truth."

The Christ Being looked towards the Pharisee and concluded by saying, "You have done neither, sir. You defame My Being and want to have Me killed as I am now a threat to your moral authority over the people of this nation." [Verse 4] [3]

The Pharisee then outstretched his arms and declared, "I find this man

_____
[3] John 7: 15-20.

possessed of evil spirits. He is an evil hypnotist. He consorts with all kinds of people. He is known to be in the company of thieves and rebels of Israel. He is also being investigated by the legal system of our country for his opinions about how we, the leaders of the people, should exercise our powers that are the guardians of the laws of the land. All that he has said today is a fantastic sales trick as the very Devil speaks through him. I say to you, follow him and you will end up in hell – fire as it is his false dreams of madness that will bring the Romans to destroy our very nation as it stands with some measure of freedom to worship our God. So I say to you all, let us get rid of such a threat to the national security of our people.

I say to you, Jesus of Nazareth, your days are numbered as the people can see that you have an evil heart and you need to be condemned before the whole world. When you say that only those who are evil would seek to kill you, I say this is your trickery as you are obviously aware that you have angered the good Souls of a chosen people of God to speak of God as your Father when you are but a person like the rest of us with grandiose ideas that you are the Messiah. I say to you that you are the Messiah of darkness and deserve to be killed!"

The Christ Being replied, "I, the Christ Being, say to you that you have shown your truth to all men that you are speaking of the evil in your own Soul as a man who is evil speaks of evil filled with darkness but has a will to evil as if it belonged to the man he accuses. He who accuses another only accuses himself when his heart is not only evil but has a will to darkness.

You can see, all of you who have walked with Me in the market places where I healed the sick and the lame, where I gave sight to those who could not see from birth, where I cast out demons from the afflicted minds in the people all over the country, to all of you I say I have never done anything that has taken away anything from the law. To the contrary I have come to give it life.

You, sir, have lost all of your Light. You have identified for a whole people what the law says, for example, that without circumcision a man cannot follow God. You have put this law, for example,

which is but a cultural law, above the law of Truth. Now I say to you, likewise you have put your opinions of who I am above the Truth. You are blinded by your abstract judgments of the Ultimate Truth of your world and its origin by Intellectual Materialism.

Also, as I have pointed out earlier, you are blinded by intellectual Spiritism when you speak of interpreting the law. You are like a man who says, 'I am in fine clothes so this proves that you can judge me for my fine qualities of character.' We have seen throughout the ages different civilisations that have spawned various evil tyrants that you certainly could not judge by the fine clothes they wore. To the contrary if we judged them by the way they appeared to the physical eye from a distant star with no human comprehension of the history of mankind one would say that these kings were the finest specimens in humanity when in Truth they were often aided by the Prince of darkness to enslave whole nations for centuries.

So I say to you, Moses surpassed the powers of a Pharaoh as he wore the Crown of the Light upon his Soul. I say to you that this Crown of

Light belongs to the King of Kings of the Light as I am the King of the Light. Judge the Ultimate Light with the Eyes of the Light and you will see that Spiritual Light shines eternally in the heart of My Father and My Being. My Light ever shines through the cosmos so that the stars can build suns for the Spiritual Hierarchies of Light. They in turn create worlds for beings at the humankind stage of evolution. So you can say that you are the products of the thoughts of these Light Beings while these Spiritual Hierarchies are the products of the thoughts of My Father in Heaven.

This is the ultimate Cosmic conception of what is Cosmic Light. This Cosmic Light reaches all of mankind and is expressed by every individual human being when he lives his Truth for the sake of aligning with the Ultimate Light of God. So to love God is to have a will to the Light of the Christ Being; the bringer of the Eternal Light in your Souls. So walk in the Light with My Being. Speak to My Being in your Soul. See Me with the Eyes of the Light. Then you will face the Ultimate Truth in the countenance of My Being. You will face the Living God Light of all Ages.

So, I, the Christ Being, say to you again to look at the law of the Truth. The Truth is above one's individual Truth. The individual Truth of the Jewish nation which is composed of individual human beings is that circumcision is an obligation of the religion of the chosen people of God. However the law of Truth is above this cultural law as you yourself have shown this to be so by your actions. You have circumcisions on the Sabbath although this is a holy day and one should not work on this day according to Jewish law. Then you accuse Me of healing on the Sabbath those who have been ill for decades with no cure in their whole life times in sight. Tell Me, are you not also following the law of Truth? So truly I say to you that the Prince of darkness deludes you into accusing Me of your own misconceptions of Truth for in Truth it is his evil that now is the enemy of mankind and its ultimate evolution to the Light. He makes you believe that the guilt for sin and evil is within My Being when it is truly in him as he is the dark spirit and whoever follows him also becomes like him.

So I say to you, align with the Ultimate Light and walk away from evil. Try to live your Truth with evil and you will fall into a pit of demons in hell as the evil one knows that he is the ultimate lie in everyone's Soul in that they are really responsible for the evil in the world and really everyone who is mentally healthy knows that evil is but a part of the organism of the human creature. Yet I tell you that this lie lives in your hearts now when you condemn Me as I am showing you how to judge by not only looking with the physical eyes where you have seen Me use the Cosmic Light to heal mankind's body and Soul but also to use your will to the Light to learn how to open the Eyes of the Light in your Souls so that you can see the Pathway to the Light.

When you know how to walk in it you will reach the level of consciousness that will give you the Christ Light power to make the right judgments of loving all men unconditionally and giving Light to the whole world with your whole heart and your whole being as well as giving your livings Souls to the Light of God so that in all ages and in all incarnations to come until the end of time your Moral Will to the Light will live so that ultimately it will become a part of the World of Light to come. You will at the same time love the goodness of mankind and

have compassion for every single human being who walks the face of the earth. You will do all this and be aware that only when we do this with complete free will can we accept the law of the Truth.

He who chooses darkness and its way to power over the Light has made a choice to align with the Prince of darkness. Hence one cannot give Light to this being. One has to believe in the redemption of all men but one has, at the same time, to know that all men will not choose to be redeemed but will choose another pathway. These men and women can only be helped and given Light when they take responsibility for their evil. If they choose not to do this then they cannot be trusted with the law of the Truth.

So I say to you, teacher of the Jews, that you have asked me to consider your arguments about my person and I have given you my reply. My judgement is based on the physical and spiritual evidence outlined. Yours is based on your opinions of the law. The law of Truth is My Pathway. Yours is the law of the land as you interpret it now as your pathway. I let the legacy of My Being upon this planet make the final judgment of My Light." [Verse 5] [4]

Once Jesus spoke as he did the populace began to cheer loudly and there was a great sense of jubilation and joy. So many looked up to the Christ and knew in their hearts that this man was the Messiah. The crowd was very enthusiastic about the way Christ lectured the Pharisees as no one had ever stood up to them with such clarity and Truth as their hypocrisy was hated by everyone regardless of their political alignment.

The Jews were divided as to the question of how to relate to Jesus. Was he a political or a religious Messiah? The Pharisees wanted a political leader but branded anyone who came near taking over their roles as supreme leaders and teachers who were not following their will as evil. So Jesus was really beginning to become a threat to their moral and political power and hence they interpreted ultimately their economic power as they knew very well that the Romans wanted them as leaders of the people morally regardless of the battalions stationed in Israel as it was clear to the Romans that to truly rule you have to first conquer physically but then morally to win a people's Soul. Hence they knew economic power rested upon this formula to gain power over the whole material world. This intellectual materialistic philosophy was what Phariseeism was being tainted with. Hence you had leaders in the Pharisee movement collaborating with the Romans to get financial power. So the Prince of darkness was now manipulating some of the top leaders of the Pharisees and he was whispering to them that this man would become their new Jewish Caesar. This was what brought on the evil intent to kill Jesus by such men who had already long ago identified with the power of Rome and who craved its world position as well as supported it morally in the community in disguise to maintain a very good material life.

Hence they would speak to the people with the attitude that the Messiah would ultimately save them against the Roman empire and that they would help this Messiah achieve this goal. The translation of this would be that Israel would become a world power like

---

[4] John 7: 21-24.

Rome. This they sold to the people by aligning scripture with the popular ideology of telling all the Jews, as they were the chosen people, then surely the material world must pay their respects ultimately to a spiritually superior race. This delusion, of course, is what these hidden collaborators fostered so that they could wield power that brought them financial gain from the Romans who knew that if you corrupt morally a race you win over the will to the Light of the race. Hence they became masters of the material world with a philosophy based on force and diplomacy like never seen on earth before as they were the first to evolve the ideology of Intellectual Materialism and to sell it to those they had invaded and conquered as the moral truth of a whole world. Hence they also saw Jesus as a potential troublemaker who needed to be put away or stopped. However, of course, in their cunning of the right philosophy to rule, they were going to get his own people to do this work for them. Hence Jesus in speaking out in Jerusalem that day proclaimed who he was and exposed his being to ultimate certain death.

However as he knew his Pathway in both worlds of the spirit and matter, after the lecture to the people he once again disappeared temporarily. He walked among the Jews and the Romans and their leaders to hear their talk and to choose those who were ready to see him with the Eyes of the Light. He also saw that there were many that day who had chosen darkness for the sake of power over the Light as the Pharisees had a hidden agenda and it was to kill Jesus at all costs as soon as they could lay their hands on him. However also their plan was to prosecute him first as they now had a body of evidence that he was going against the law and the Romans would support them in their plan as they had the same political interests at stake. [Verse 6]

So before appearing again to speak to the people Jesus could see that many had made the choice that the Christ Light was the one in their hearts and this truly pleased Jesus. He walked into the being of each person. He became a part of their Souls and their Spirits. Therefore they could see him with the Eyes of the Light.

When one had seen this in his being he said to one of the Pharisees, "This is surely the Christ Being and the Messiah we have all been waiting for as how is it that he was saying what he was before the whole nation and not one of you nor the Romans have stopped him from speaking out about the Light? Surely you must see that this is the man the Father, our God, has sent us."

The Pharisee said to this man, "Look here, you are truly going to get into trouble unless you watch your words. This man is singled out by the Roman guards already in Jerusalem. He is the one they have already planned to be killed, once apprehended. It is well known that this man is a rebel against the Jewish state."

Then the man said to the Pharisee, "I have seen with my own eyes and heard with my own ears what Jesus said and I can see that for you there is no Christ. Caesar for you is the Christ." Once this happened this man ran off so that the Pharisee could not reply and could not threaten him any further with his accusations and lies.

Also the Christ Being created a mist in the eyes of the Pharisee so that he could not see for a couple of minutes and could not point to the Roman guards as to who the man was. So in this way the Christ from the spiritual world stretched out his Hands of the Light to change the material energies around this man's being. This was a Special Key of Christ directly intercepting from the spiritual to the material world.
[Verse 7] [5]

Then the Pharisee, overcome with rage, began to cry out to the populace to listen to him and to what he had to say about the false Prophet, Jesus. He said, "I know and you know that Jesus of Nazareth is but a carpenter's son. He has achieved nothing of note in his whole life. He has become a preacher and a black magician. He can cure the sick and speak to demons because his energy comes from this power of evil. I say to you, people of Israel, let us find this man and make him pay for his blasphemy of our sacred scriptures. Let the law make its choice about his false testimony to be the Living Christ. When the Messiah appears on the earth he will be coming from Heaven on a golden carriage and he will

[5] John 7: 25-27.

bless his chosen people with the powers to create a nation that will be fulfilling the prophecies of our fathers who told us that the Christ would redeem our situation for the whole world to see.

Is this Jesus of Nazareth, a mere carpenter's son, going to achieve this with his strange and fantastic stories about what the future of mankind is and about a cosmos that no one has seen and no one with any sound training in intellectual judgment of the facts of life could ever accept? I tell you, take away Jesus from our midst and the Romans themselves will agree to let us ultimately deal with him as they do not want a rebel troublemaker putting himself above Caesar."

Then Jesus suddenly appeared in the Temple again speaking to the people before him. The Pharisee who had just spoken now found that his whole body and mouth were frozen and immobilized. The Archangel Michael was standing in front of him and fear completely gripped this man as no one could see the Archangel except him. The Archangel had a golden, diamond studded silver Sword that gleamed in the sunlight. From it Fire was being unleashed and the heat of this Fire was singeing the Pharisee's hairs. The Archangel just stood there in front of him with the Sword in a threatening posture ready to attack him with the target being the person's heart.

The Christ Being then replied by saying, "I, the Christ Being, have come to this planet to show you in the flesh the Living Light of the World. Yes, you know that I am a living, breathing human being just like all of you. However you also know that I have used the Powers of the Light to cast out demons and to heal the sick physically, psychologically and spiritually. You also know that no man can have such powers unless he has the Power of the Living God.

I say to you, I have come to show you that the Truth has come to the earth in a living person. The Truth is above your Truth. This is truly what you, mankind, has to learn. My Father in Heaven has willed My coming to you so that you can see the Body of Light and so you can see what is your ultimate destiny. I tell you that I bring to you the Eyes of the Light that can see the World of Light to come. This World of Light will have streets of solid gold and pathways in beautiful white jade where there will be completeness. This is where there will be completeness in everyone's heart and where the Prince of darkness will not be able to breathe the air of this World of Light. This is where the whole cosmos will have the same balance nature has now in every Soul Being of Light. This is where the fate of evil will be sealed for eternity and where My Father will finally complete his world creating powers for mankind. This is where He will then give mankind the Ultimate Body of Light and where the Soul will unite with the Living Light of God. This is truly the wonderful and beautiful destiny of the human race. When it joins the Spiritual Hierarchies of the Light this will be the day that mankind will ultimately become a race of Light living in a World of Light in the House of God, My Father, in Heaven.

As for the allegations against Me and My person and that I am a black magician, I say to you that the physical evidence shows that anyone I have cured has Light in his heart and in his personality. One only needs to look and he will see the Truth of My Words now as they are the Words of Light. I tell you My Father and I are one. I have come to earth as a human being with a life span and a human body. I have come also to you to show you that the Father and My Being have Free Will to act. You have free will to act; to listen to the Words of the Light or to be seduced by the Prince of darkness.

I also have come to you as a vulnerable human being who can die ultimately normally or can be killed like any other living person. I have done this so that you will accept that I have come to become one of you; to face My Truth as a living person and to also show you by example how to do this. This is why the Powers of the Light I have, have come from the Powers of My Father. They do not come from Me; Myself, being the living personality before you. I came to the earth to experience being a whole human being and not just a Spirit Being. The hour is coming when you all have to make a choice to follow the Christ or the Prince of darkness. This choice will be your moral choice and the Moral Step that will give you the ultimate experience of the Light power in your lives.

So I say to you, it was My Father who has willed that I walk among you as a normal person. However it is also My Father's Will that He gives you free will to act for or against Me. I say to you, all of

131

My Being is human completely but I am the Living Christ when I act for the sake of the Mission of My Incarnation; to bring to you the Living Light of the World and the World of Light to come." [Verse 8] [6]

Once the Christ Being had finished speaking the Archangel Michael disappeared from the vision of the Pharisee. At that same moment the Pharisee had a seizure of pain around his neck. He cried out, "Please, someone get help. I am being suffocated by this horrible feeling in my throat." He then fainted and was taken on a stretcher to a physician.

Also Jesus went into the spiritual world temporarily as he knew otherwise he would have been arrested by the Romans as His Father had told him to wait before he would let his being be exposed to the power of evil, as the moment in evolution of the Light of God on the earth had not yet come. This meaning that the Cosmic clock hands were not yet ready to strike until some time in Jesus' incarnation as Jesus and the Christ Being were with different Cosmic patterns. Jesus, as the incarnation of

Gautama Buddha, followed this pattern of the normal human being with the Eyes of the Light of the Buddha for the first thirty years of his life on earth while Jesus, the Christ Being, followed the Cosmic pattern of God, the Father, after the Almighty Spiritual Being incarnated into his body and Soul the day he met John the Baptist on the river Jordan at the baptism. So the Doorway to the Light of the Christ Being became the Eyes of the Light of the Father, the Ultimate God of Light, as Buddha had appeared at the birth of Jesus and became a part of his incarnation as human being and then left his body when the Father took it over as the Christ Being and continued on his own Cosmic journey to give Light to the next planetary system in the Heavens. [Verse 9]

Then the Christ Being once again looked upon the people of Israel from the spiritual world and walked among them to see truly what was in their hearts as his being could also be a part of human existence at the same moment physically. This happened in the time when he used his Eyes of the Light to see mankind's Moral Will to the

---

[6] John 7: 28-30.

evolution of the cosmos that His Father had created for it.

The Jews were divided. There were many who for fear of retribution agreed with the evil Pharisee who had previously spoken so as to collaborate with his Roman guardians as they were watching through their spies which were dissenters of the Jews, so as to mark them down for investigation. Many feared this as the Roman soldiers chose at will whom they would arrest if they in any way could make the claim that the individual or group was openly against the power of Rome.

However there was one man who with great courage spoke out knowing full well the consequences of what could happen to him. As he was a physician he knew the art of diplomacy and was prepared to present a political dilemma for the Romans. So he said to the group around him, "Ladies and gentlemen, I would like to say one thing if I may. I, as a physician of the body and spirit, have examined a number of cases this man, Jesus, cured with his spiritual powers who have had known physical illnesses. I have also examined psychotics who were speaking of darkness from hell for the last three or four decades in some cases who now follow the Jesus Religion of the Light. I have testimony from my colleagues that all I have said is true.

So I ask you, what do you do with a person who heals with wonderful powers that he says come from another world and at the same time asks us as a race to follow him to this other world in future incarnations to come? He has not said to change this world unless it is based on living one's Truth. We can only live our Truth as a nation when we accept our allegiance to the Roman Empire of which we are a part. We can align with our own religion as this is also Rome's will to allow this freedom of worship.

So I say to you, what do you do with a man like Jesus? He says that his world is not this one yet he heals the sick and dying and gives hope to mankind and tells it that it has a magnificent Cosmic future in the Light. I tell you all to ask yourselves, 'Is this not the Christ Being or is he just another would – be Messiah?' The ultimate judgment will be for the people of Israel. However

133

remember that in the future I hope mankind will judge you as a nation of the Light." [Verse 10] [7]

Once the chief priests were informed about what the physician said they went over to one Captain of the Roman soldiers who was sent to oversee the crowd in the square where Jesus had just spoken and said to him, "We would like you to arrest the man, Jesus, as he has blasphemed against our religion. Now we know that he has not broken any Roman law but we are just pointing out that after you arrest him you will see that we will want an audience with Pilate. This is because we have word that the people here will make him their leader. Also the Jews are seeking a Messiah to give them political freedom. As we know Rome is the master of the world, our allegiance is to it above Israel as we know what is good for it. As you can see we are not mad. We do not want to fight the power of Rome." After hearing this the Captain of the Guard sent his soldiers to look for Jesus amongst the crowd. [Verse 11] [8]

Then all of a sudden the Christ Being appeared again and the crowd was amazed as the people could not see from whence he had come. Then he said, "My Pathway now is to give those who are seekers of the Truth of life the power of the Light to change the pattern of your lives and that of your nation and to do this only with the Moral Will to live your Truth first and to align this to the Ultimate Light of God as well as to know clearly that no power on earth or in Heaven is above His almighty power as He created the cosmos and He created every Soul that passes through it in all ages.

I tell you that He has sent Me to redeem mankind. He has sent Me to give it Light. He has sent Me to create a revolution of Light so that a Movement of Light will take form in the minds of men and to then use this Light to create wisdom for all of mankind that will give it a Moral Will to live in harmony within itself regardless of creed, religion, race, nation, empire, kingdom, social status or financial power. I have come though to ask one thing only from all

---

[7] John 7: 31-32,
[8] John 7: 33.

mankind and this is the reason I have come to earth; to ask you all, as individual human beings, to love the Light.

I love My Father in Heaven as His Light shines through My Spirit and gives it life. He loves you all as His Heart is of Golden Light. I say to you, I need to go from the earth soon and be with My Father in Heaven. Then generations upon generations will seek My Being in all the cosmic worlds to come and they will see I have come in this very moment of Cosmic time on earth. They will see that I have come to you, seekers of the Ultimate Light.

Souls for thousands of years to come will seek the Light of the Christ Being and know that until they can ultimately incarnate in the Ultimate Body of Light they must follow the pathway My Father created for them in the cosmos. My Pathway is to be the Son of Man and to show mankind that man has the Ultimate Son of the Light, the Christ Being, who was born as human being to show in the flesh the Body of Light. This Body of Light will be the final incarnation for every human being in that every human

being will have his own Body of Light. Each human being who is a seeker of the Light will ultimately find it in his ultimate incarnation on the seventh cosmic world to come. I have come to show you the Cosmic Pathway to walk along to the Ultimate Light."
[Verse 12] [9]

Then a member of the audience to this speech given by Jesus said, "You are the Son of Man and this means that you are the Ultimate Being for this planet. The Cosmic clock of the cosmos predicted your coming and its hands can only be seen by those who have the Spiritual Eyes of the Light you speak of. Now tell me, how can I today see the evolution of the different cosmic worlds in relation to this cosmic world called the earth as apparently earth is only one of these worlds and in my measurement of time this would be thousands of years to come, to come to the seventh world?

You also say that this is the pathway of many incarnations before a person evolves to become a being with a Body of Light. So I ask you now, how can we and I know where Heaven is without physical

[9] John 7: 34.

135

eyes, or shall I rephrase this by saying, how can we see your Heaven as our fathers told us that we would ultimately be a world power and that we would be a superior race of enlightened people? We are the chosen people of God and yet you make no mention of this in this scheme of the eternal in every human Soul. Also how can we know that the darkness will not overtake the Light in epochs to come? What guarantee does anyone have that this will not happen as, after all, you say yourself that your time is coming and the hint is that you are going to leave the earth? Now, no one leaves this earth unless he dies. So I say to you, Jesus, Son of Man, how can I comprehend this seemingly incomprehensible philosophy of life of yours?"

The Christ Being replied by saying, "I, the Christ Being, see that you have comprehended with your head all that I have said today but you have not felt it in your heart. I say to you, first of all, the Body of Light which all human beings will receive will be at the end of physical time on this planet. This succession of cosmic worlds [9b] will

---

[9b] The names of these cosmic worlds are identical to the names given to them by Anthroposophists, Rosicrucians, Theosophists and members of the Inner Light Society of the Cosmic Christ. These are the Cosmic Worlds of Saturn, Sun, Moon and Earth: *See The Seven Cosmic Worlds. William E. Camilleri. Copyright, 2008.* In more detail these cosmic worlds refer to:

Cosmic World of Saturn: Saturn cosmic world existed some hundreds of billions of years before Earth cosmic world. In physical size this cosmic world was more than a million times the size of our earth planet. To the eye it resembled a globe of air and gas and its atmosphere was similar to that of a warm breeze. At times one could see light present 'flickering....flashing and darting.' Here time was created. So too was created the mineral kingdom and the blue-print of the sense organs within the individual human being spirit.

Cosmic World of Sun: Sun cosmic world was the incarnation of Saturn cosmic world. This cosmic world had a higher density of air and gas than that of Saturn cosmic world. Here was created space and limited movement. Here the evolution of the blue-print of the organs, specifically the glandular system, of the human being spirit continued. Also the manifestation of the power of smell and sound took place. In the human being spirit the beginning of the Ego ["I"] occurred.

Cosmic World of Moon: The cosmic world of Moon was the incarnation of Sun cosmic world and the ancestor of Earth cosmic world. Here a condensation of air to create a form of liquid comparable in condition to water took place. 'Water' bodies were permeated by air currents and warm effects and the beginnings of the plant-mineral kingdom to provide nutrients occurred.

Here took place the 'beginnings of the forefather of the complete human being' where the genesis of the head, figure and form of the human being spirit occurred as did the beginnings of the faculties of creative and destructive feelings, like, dislike and limited decision making.

Cosmic World of Earth: During the first stage of the incarnation of the cosmic world of Earth the origin of the Big Bang event, the solar system, oceans and land masses took place. The evolution of gas, air, warmth, light and fire was completed. The solar system and its planets were created from the mother cosmic world of Earth including the present sun in order to complete the evolution of the perfect planet of earth. During this stage the Milky Way ever evolved to create the next cosmic world of Jupiter; when the present Jupiter will become ultimately the next cosmic world after it has been spiritually transformed upon the material end of the earth planet at the end of the cosmic world of Earth.

Within this stage of the evolution of the cosmic world of Earth occurred the beginnings of the animal kingdom. Also all the scales of evolution of palaeontology occurred in relation to the origin of life in the oceans and onto land. The self-regulatory systems within the human being spirit were also here evolved specifically the circulatory, nervous and breathing systems whilst the head of the human being spirit continued to evolve. The creation of the faculties of a form of mental life, memory and taste took

number seven and with each one man will evolve closer to the Light of God.

Concerning the darkness overtaking the Light, God's Light is eternal and He gave free will to all men so that they can follow the darkness if they choose. The darkness in itself was not created by God. However God did allow it to create its own kingdom so as to give free will to love or to reject Him eternally. So the Creator is totally superior to any powers of evil from any being.

As for the seventh cosmic world being thousands of years from now this is true but it is also true that a moral act to align one's being with

place and the human being spirit was able to perceive sound and color in the process of becoming a 'definite form of being;' an in-duplicable being with a further evolving Ego ["I"].

Scales of parallel evolutionary processes as regards human evolution occurred from prehistoric times to the twenty-first century. The later stage of the evolution of Earth cosmic world included the evolution of races, epochs and historical figures pertinent to such epochs as the Atlantean epoch and post Atlantean epochs in connection to cosmic worlds to come. *See The Seven Cosmic Worlds. William E. Camilleri. Copyright, 2008.*

the Ultimate Light and to live one's Truth aligns a person to the eternity of time, meaning that upon death every person becomes a part of the Light until he returns to the earth. There is no physical time in the spiritual world. Yet there is an evolution of beings. Hence a person with every life that he completes shares in the destiny of the cosmos and he can see this evolution of beings and how it relates to physical time on earth in between life times so that this way a person then in the spiritual world with every life time returns to the birth place of his Soul and adds one more part to his Soul from the Spirit of every life time he has lived. In this way his Cosmic identity evolves as a Being of Light.

However, at the same time, every time a person enters this other world, called the birth place of all Souls, if he has lived a life aligned to darkness or to meaninglessness he then adds a spirit to his Soul which devalues the Soul so that it gives it a false blue – print to a Body of Light as the Light will be insufficient for the individual human being to live on the earth as a whole being. Hence you have the problem of seeing with the Spiritual Eyes of the Light when there is no Light in your heart, sir, as truly God, with all His mercy and wisdom, will give equal opportunity to every human being in the composite of all life times if not in one life time as otherwise you will have the king and the beggar ordained by God. This would be false as, yes, the king and the beggar have been each individually ordained by God to be in their position but, at the same time as you know, often evil overtakes the Light in one life time materially but never does it do this spiritually as a man's Moral Light lives on eternally. So the king must pay for his sins as well as the beggar but the difference is that the king has a greater debt as he has to answer to God for the responsibility he has taken for the power he has been given by his fate ordained by God.

Henceforth what you have is this then, that in the scheme of things, as you say, a person will by the end of time on this planet have had all the opportunity equal to every other human being that has ever lived to use his or her free will to choose the Light or darkness. So the question really is not how to see the Cosmic clock of the cosmos to estimate how many life times a person has to be redeemed but how to see the living moment in time which is now to follow the Light as when a person lives his Truth he is on time with the cosmos as he who lives his Truth will find the Truth. Then when a person aligns with the Light of the Christ Being he then is on time with the cosmos and its outlined progressive evolution to its ultimate destiny which is to be a part of the World of Light to come at the end of time.

So when I leave you soon and go back to where I have come from in the Spiritual Heaven of Light I have spoken of, I will leave behind for you My Doorway to the Light for those who choose to look with the Eyes of the Light. So My Philosophy of Light is the Cosmic Philosophy of the Living Love of the Light." [Verse 13] [10]

Finally the last lecture given by Jesus was presented to the populace. The Christ Being, on completing the answer to this person about his Cosmic Philosophy of the Light, went on and said, "I ask you, all who are seekers of the Light, to open your eyes and look with them to Heaven as the Doorway to Heaven will open and the Angels of God will descend to earth to give

counsel to mankind. See with your Eyes of the Light those who have Eyes of the Light, the Living Heaven. Listen to the music that is being played by the Angels of Heaven. See that for those who love with their whole heart, drink the living water of Heaven. This spiritual water is purifying the Souls of mankind and needs to be used to sustain the Body of Light that lives in the Souls of those who are looking to the Light of God.

I say to you, come to Me all you who have sought in every corner of your hearts and your world for the Truth of life for you can see with your eyes what the spiritual world is revealing to you now next to Me. I ask you all to pause and to reflect as you see the Spiritual River in Heaven flow out of My Being of Light."

At this moment all who had aligned with the Christ Being could see upon meditating on the Light, the Spiritual Heaven unfold before their Spiritual Eyes and then like a vision in front of them unfolded, a Doorway opened up in the sky around Jesus. They could see the Christ Being with white radiant Light around his whole body. Then they were conscious of Angels coming down from

---

[10] John 7: 35-36.

Heaven and the Christ Being Light was shining through them from his very heart. It was as though each Angel received a ray of Light and it was as though the Angels were being transported from Heaven on the current of this River that flowed beneath their feet as they glided upon it. Then the Christ Being opened up his arms and outstretched them and the vision disappeared. It was as though all who followed Jesus with their hearts knew what they saw but could not speak about it to each other until later as it was like a dream that came to them which was abruptly ended.

Then all of a sudden they saw Jesus being lifted up above them as high as a tree and then higher and higher until he disappeared into a cloud. The others listening to him experienced nothing and just said that he had gone but they did not know where he had gone. [Verse 14]

As soon as this occurred the Romans became suspicious and began to question several people as they could not believe that Jesus had gotten away from their sight. So they began to say to each other that this was the work of a black magician and they were very embarrassed as one of the

Pharisees said to the centurion, "That Captain of the Guards has lost him. We demand you act as we know of even the Romans who have paid for his magic with favors."

The centurion was very angry and replied, "I heard this man and I can only say one thing that you should examine your own conscience before you accuse Roman soldiers of not following their duty. As for their being tricked by this magician's magic, well, this may be so but the truth is his magic has cured people but as it seems it has not cured your condescending deceit towards Rome. However never mind my opinion of politics; you will have your request fulfilled as I can only be certain that security is put first. Pilate will have to be informed, nevertheless, once I bring him to you. Do you understand?"

They agreed and felt very uneasy about the centurion's attitude towards them and their credibility as they knew then that this Roman saw through their strategy to cry for national security for the sake of keeping their positions of power and favor and that their charges against Jesus were false. However they justified their actions to themselves by pointing out that only a madman would reject the power of Rome as Jesus knew their warped minds and did not mention that they were the chosen people of God in this lecture but said instead that he who follows the Light becomes chosen by God to live his Truth and to align with the Eyes of the Light of the Christ Being. [Verse 15] [11]

After this lecture and the Roman's interrogation of the people many began to speak to each other about what had happened to them. One person said to the other, "This person was the Christ Being. I saw this vision and the Light of Heaven spoke to my very eyes." Then the others listening to him replied and said, "No Prophet has been able to speak of the Light and have the power of it. This Prophet is also the Living Light. I saw his being and I know he is the Son of the Living God. I worship his being now in my heart and in my prayers as he has taught us to create a Circle of Light around us when we meditate upon the Light of God and to have him next to us and then to have the Angels of God next to us and him inside this Circle of Light.

Then he taught us to ask that his Ultimate Light be put against the darkness outside our being and outside this Circle. He sends his Light and not our Light. He does this for us as he has done now to save us from the Intellectual Materialism of the Romans and the Negative Motivational Science of the Pharisees who are now taking our Light away by telling us what to think and by siding with the Romans and pretending to be saving Israel when what they are really doing is selling Israel out for the positions of power they possess.

I tell you all has been revealed to me now. He who puts the intellect above the Light believes in money and power and will lose his being to darkness. This Prophet is the Christ Being and this man from Galilee is the human being born in Bethlehem who is the Christ Being. With his Body of Light he can give us the pathway to get to the Spiritual Heaven and to give us the Eyes of Light that will show us the way to walk on this Pathway to the Light." [Verse 16]

Another man said to the others, "This is all very well

---

[11] John 7: 37-39.

but where does this leave us? The Romans are running the real world and no one is going to make us into a world power unless he has money and superior leadership powers. I say to you that Jesus is a Prophet but at the same time he is no more than a very clever man. No one can change this world without physical power. No one can do it. I say to you, how can we solve the material problem now as it is this life that matters otherwise how can one believe in this Philosophy of Light?"

Then one man replied to this by saying, "No one can take away the power of Rome with military power. No one can do this now on earth. Yet even Caesar himself recognizes that the gods have power above man otherwise he would not try to become one in the eyes of his people. I say to you that the God of Light is speaking about the Religion of Light. To live your Truth, and for Israel to live its Truth, it needs to face up to its level of development politically and militarily. This is the wrong analysis. The meaning of we being the chosen people of God is that we are the spiritual leaders of mankind. We are the nation of initiates of the Light and this is the reason the Christ Being came to earth to us as a race. I say to rationalise that Israel will become a world power because it is of the chosen people is identification with Intellectual Spiritualistic Materialism and it is with this ideology of the Roman world that gets different races to fight its superior war machine so that in this way it can justify its domination of a race with its false Roman morality. I say to you the Truth is above all things. That the world has lost its Light to the power of Rome does not make Rome above the Truth. The Light is above the Truth. The Christ Being is the Ultimate Light." [Verse 17] [12]

Then this centurion went back to the chief priests and told them that he could not see what to charge Jesus with and that he wanted to know truly what his offense was. A chief priest said, "Be aware that I am saying to you that this man, Jesus, is trying to replace Roman power in Judea. He has already made it clear to those who listen to him that he is above the law of Rome and that he is the Son of God. Now I tell you he is claiming divinity when really he does not have any real

---

[12] John 7: 40-44.

material power. Yet he does have magical tricks that the people are fascinated about. So I say to you, arrest him or I will report you to Pilate."

The centurion then said to the priests, "Is there any just man among you who would give me cause to arrest this man for whatever reason?" Then Nicode'mus, a Pharisee who had consulted Jesus in secret about the Law of the Light said, "I say to you that we will judge him with our law and what he has said and what he has done as a subject of Israel which is a province of the Roman Empire. I see that only with a court of law can this man's innocence be judged. However as this man is a Prophet of the people it is wise to judge him with the standards of moral law first."

After he said this the chief priest protested, "You and the Roman have been hypnotized by this magician. He has got to you and you do not see it. I say to you that he is not a Prophet of the people and he is getting the people to believe in him so that he can rule over us. His prophesies are dangerous as he talks of a spiritual kingdom that rules the material world. Now obviously he means to make himself king; a spiritual king first and then a material king.

So I say to you only by following the laws of the land can we protect the national security of Israel. So I demand that this man be arrested for the good of the people as the people are being manipulated by his trickery. They will soon follow him above Rome. Be certain of this. He has already pointed out that ultimately the power of Rome will disappear on this planet. I tell you if Caesar were to hear that a rebel in one of its provinces speaks of being the Son of God and says that a king and a beggar are equal and that ultimately all will be equalled out with incarnations, then I tell you he would act and would direct his anger at those who let the rebel gain political power. After all this Prophet speaks of a world movement not just a movement in Israel. He is asking for all humanity to follow him. I perceive that he has secret ambitions to sit in Caesar's place. No one can talk like he does without an ambition to power."

The centurion replied, "Look here, we have gone through this before and we still have nothing to go on. The man is talking about a Spiritual Kingdom not a material one. Granted he speaks of the evil of any empire that is not based on equality and the love of every human being which is, of course, insinuating the situation in the country as to the Roman occupation, but my point is he has done nothing wrong and he is speaking about a Philosophy of Light for mankind. So I feel that you will have to have more than negative interpretations and accusations about a rival to your moral power in this country."

Then the chief priest said, "I will seek an audience with Pilate myself as I see that this man has stopped you from thinking clearly about the fate of this nation. We must get rid of this rebel before he becomes a real force to deal with politically. I will have to act now alone without your immediate support but I tell you, be certain that Pilate will listen to me as he will see the larger picture of what is going on here. No governor of any province can risk dissent like this from a charismatic leader just about to take control of the masses.

I have heard this man speak about this Philosophy of Light and I can only say that it is an ideology to get political power by his selling of his Cosmic identity persona as really the point is he has to go to safeguard the people of Israel from Rome's anger upon not being notified about such a potential rebellion."

So with this statement the centurion said, "I will bring this man to you but I will first inform Pilate of my concern and your views about Jesus." [Verse 18] [13]

---

[13] John 7: 45-52.

CHAPTER 8

Then Jesus spoke out once again and said, "I am the Living Christ Being. I am the Son of Man. I am here to live a human life as this way I can love as a human being. No man can love perfectly as no man is perfect. However the Father is perfect. The human being will be perfect at the end of time when the Father's work is complete.

The Light of the cosmos is in My Being. I am the Light of this Universe. I bring Light to the planet and I bring its new philosophy. It is the philosophy of the ages. Every human being who follows his heart knows that he follows the Light of God. I follow this Light. I also do all in My whole Being to be a whole person living My Truth. I am the whole Being and the complete Being of Light. So he who follows his Truth and walks in the Light of the Christ Being ultimately will become a being with a Soul of Light now and a Body of Light when the Son of Man rises before all of mankind as the Ultimate God of Light. This is the promise of what is to come when the World of Light will transform this world at the end of all seven epochs.

This is I, the Christ Being, incarnated as a human being before your eyes. I have come to give you the Ultimate Truth so you can see the Ultimate Being with your Eyes of Light." [Verse 1] [1]

Then a Pharisee said to him, "You are saying that you are the Living God in human flesh and that you incarnated into being a human being to experience the imperfections of a human life. What proof have you to say such things? Can you show us your powers so that we can believe in your declaration of being a part of the Godhead?"

The Christ Being replied by saying, "I, the Christ Being, see that you are asking Me for proof and for physical evidence of My statements as to who I am. I say to you I have already shown you this in what I have done for so many of your race. I will also ultimately present the ultimate proof once I leave this earth. However for now I say to you that you have not ever proven to Me that you are at all credible human beings who live their Truth or follow the Light. You are truly not genuine in your search for the

---

[1] John 8: 1-12.

Ultimate Truth let alone the Ultimate Light.

So I tell you as I tell every person who does not look to the Light and only seeks to deceive it that I will give you nothing as you have no basis for criticising negatively My Being other than saying that I am affecting the Jewish race with a false philosophy of Cosmic powers. I say to you that the cause of this delusion in you is that you seek not to truly find the Truth of My origin but you dismiss this and all the Special Keys of Light I have used on earth to heal thousands of people. You only talk about how you relate to the effect of what it is; this new Philosophy of Light in a negative sense. This is because you do not live your Truth. You live a lie. So then you ask to be unconditionally trusted.

I say to you anyone who cannot be trusted cannot be forgiven of his sins as he is never genuine. He asks to be heard so that he can slander and deceive. I say to you every human being has to follow the Truth. Anyone who does not follow it does not live his Truth. You follow falsehood but ask to be treated equally. I say to you evil cannot be taken away this way. It can only be taken away when a person

walks away from it for all time.

This is what I do to you now. I tell you to leave Me and to speak your lies to those who are willing to listen to you. Many will be seduced who try to live their Truth when they listen to you as they do not know who you are as they have not yet learned to follow the Light but I know who you are and hence I know what is your mission. You think you know My Mission but you do not. This is why you will ultimately fail on this planet and you will end up falling into the pit of darkness in all ages.

You make judgments about the universe and the Truth of mankind in relation to who God is as a Spiritual Being. I say to you that your judgements are false as they are based on Intellectual Materialism. Proof of this is that you want physical proof of who God is. You want to know where He comes from. Hence you rationalise the Light. You ask who was God before He became God. Then you say that only what you can feel and touch with your very hands and what you can see with your very eyes will you say that something exists. Well, let Me tell you, you see the Living Christ, the Son of the Living God, and you say that this is only a pretender to be the Messiah.

I say to you, My Father in Heaven hears you when you whisper to each other dark secrets that discredit Christ. I say to you that when you judge Me wrongly you are defying God, the Father, Himself as it is He who has sent Me to this planet to redeem mankind and to show it the way to walk on the Pathway to the Ultimate Light.

The law of your religion says that it knows the Ultimate Truth as it is based on the Words of the Living God, My Father. I say to you that I, the Christ Being, am the Ultimate Truth. You speak of knowing God intellectually and replacing your Souls with your intellectual material god. You identify with this world ideology as you have become identified with the powers of using rationalistic conclusions that suit your moneymaking schemes. Your political positions have made you lose your Moral Will to the Light. So you have abstractified morality to sell your worldview of keeping the status quo where you hold religious power and put it

above the Truth. Therefore I now have come to create a new pathway for mankind to see that all religion that does not follow the Light of My Father does not know the Ultimate Light.

I say to you as you have falsified this Light you denigrate My Being. My Father has sent Me to show the world the battle between good and evil and to tell of its ultimate outcome. He has sent Me to give the world recognition of its ultimate destiny and to show the world that human beings are first individual human beings who can live their Truth to fulfil their Moral karma. This is now the fate of the man who is cosmically on time in his universe and to, with this, also show mankind that every human being has a Cosmic identity that is related to the Christ Being, Son of God the Father. This identity gives each person who has ever lived and will live in future life times to come an eternal Light. This means that all human beings who love the Light and live their Truth will come to one last life time which will let them enter the World of Light to come in the Spiritual Heaven with a Body of Light." [Verse 2] [2]

---

[2] John 8: 13-18.

Then a Pharisee said to Jesus, "Can you give us an address where your Father lives as after all you look very human to me and this Spiritual Heaven of Light you speak of is just a fantasy? If your Father was God, the Father, why would He reveal Himself through a person who has no power financially or politically but is just a magician who sells hypnotic ideas about how the world is going to evolve and how redemption only comes through Him? Come on now, what can you say to this argument? What can you produce as a living proof that your Father is God, Himself? If you can do this I will even consider your Philosophy of Light."

Then the Christ Being said, "You are mocking the Ultimate Light of God. You will ultimately fall into the oblivion of hell – fire. Your knowledge of My Father is confused with the ideology of your scriptures. You make laws for the people which you, yourself, have never kept. Hence you have never lived your Truth. You accuse Me of fraud but in Truth your hearts are cold and seek revenge as I have taken your place among the people you have preached to till I came to them. You hate anyone who speaks the Truth and are blind now to its ultimate source. Your alignment is with intellectual materialistic power as you have replaced your Souls with this power. Hence you have become empty within your beings. Your inner darkness can be seen by all who experience your ideas of life.

I say to you, if you knew who My Father was you would fear your ultimate fate at the end of your incarnations of Light in this life. I say to you, ask not what is the address of My Father but ask what is the source of the evil in your heart. Your answer if it is honest, which is of course dubious in your case, would be the Prince of darkness. This is he who speaks through your mouth today, follower of the Devil." [Verse 3]

When Jesus said this to the Pharisee he was speaking from the centre of the temple. The populace heard him speak in stunned silence as the people were afraid to offend the Pharisee. However at the end of the talks and lectures Jesus disappeared into the spiritual world. The Pharisee then shouted out, "Guards, where are you? Jesus is here. Arrest him."

A Roman soldier came up to the Pharisee and asked him, "Where is this person, Jesus, as he must have left from here in front of your eyes? There must be a secret passageway." The Pharisee then replied, "This magician has given you the slip again. He is a sorcerer. That is the reason we did not see him leave. Find him and arrest him. He is blaspheming our God. Also he is a threat to national security. He is saying that Rome is evil with a false god, Caesar, ruling it. Find him or you will ultimately pay the consequences."

The Christ Being observed the evil Pharisee and after he had been speaking to the Romans the Pharisee had a seizure of panic. He shouted out, "The demons are coming for me." He became very ill and began to ask God to help him from this attack of the demons he was seeing around his being. No one else could see them but finally it was clear that the dark energy was being sent back to the Pharisee.

Hence the Light once again returned in that the Christ Being appeared for a short moment and said to the Pharisee, "Behold the Son of Man has a Cosmic Sword that will take away the darkness of hell. Fall into it or redeem yourself by walking away from it. See the Spiritual Fire as it bolts from Heaven like a sun full of diamonds towards the shadows of your being. I say to you to look into your Soul and you will see the many incarnations where you darkened the Light for others and where you falsified it and sold a false love. I say to you to face the Son of Man with your Truth and face the Christ Being with your Light. When you do this you will fulfil the universal karma from the first human being to the last human being on earth.

I say to you, listen not to those who seek power above the Light. Surrender to the Light of the Christ Being. Then you will find eternal peace in the love of your own eternal Light as this is why the Father gave you free will to act even against Me, His Son. So when you suffer the pain of persecution for the sake of the Light you live your Truth and you evolve My Being on your planet as your planet becomes a planet of Light when the human being will have the Body of Light.

I have come with the Body of Light to show you your

pathway and your ultimate evolution. Progress to this level of evolution and you will become a part of the Christ Being with a Christ Body which will be the body with which you will live in Heaven as a Spirit Body of Light. This is My Word to you that this will happen as this is the legacy of My Kingdom. I am here now. I am not here now."

Once the Christ Being said this he disappeared into the spiritual world. He did this as he knew that he had not fulfilled all that was willed by his Father as he could not be apprehended until the Cosmic time was fulfilled in a parallel sense to the human pathway in the dimension of physical time on earth. [Verse 4]

The Christ Being said to these people "I, the Christ Being, will leave this world and enter its spiritual atmosphere for all time until time itself will become one Light. This will happen as I have predicted in the seventh cosmic world. Some of you will not reach this world in the right form but will be burdened by your physical body of darkness. You will still be living in this cosmic world of Earth. You will travel to the other cosmic worlds but the Spiritual Beings of darkness will be your vehicle on this journey. This will result in your not being able to breathe the air or to drink the water of the World of Light to come as your bodies will shun the Light on this future planet. Then when the final death will come for the evil you have created for mankind you will die on this world and return to your state in the spiritual darkness eternally lost in the planet created for you by the Hierarchies of darkness as they will also have their death in this end of all ends of time.

You will then look up and see that I, the Christ Being, am the centre of this Universal Light that you can never reach as you have fallen like the fallen angels for the power of the Prince of darkness. So when you ask for redemption then My Father will speak to you as I will never be able to again as this is His Will. So I tell you, look up now before it is too late as your Intellectual Materialism darkness is making you destroy your hope of salvation. Your journey in the cosmos will be as I have outlined as it is He, My Father, who has willed this from the beginning."
[Verse 5] [3]

---

[3] John 8: 19-20.

Then once again the Jewish Rabbi stood up and said, "I am a teacher and a religious leader of my race. I have heard of your fantastic allegations and I tell you that I can only believe in what facts I can rationally put together. I know God exists. I do not need anyone to tell me that He does. I also am certain that no man can possibly be a god. So I am wondering if you are talking about some kind of self – destructive paranoia when it comes to what is going to happen to those who do not follow you. Obviously you are contemplating suicide as you are constantly talking about how your Father has sent you to save us.

Look here, my dear sir, nobody here asked you to come here to do this; to save the world. So I would say that you really are losing your mind as you say you are the Son of Man. Well, you have delusions of grandeur that all of mankind should be at your feet worshiping you.

I say this is one thing that one could put down to being a religious maniac obsessed with a will to power over the Jewish race but to say that you have the power of God Himself and that all are damned that do not follow you and that cosmically all will devolve into a subhuman race that does not is showing signs of being a pathological liar with dangerous attitudes towards society and societies worldwide as a whole. I say to you, Jesus of Nazareth, that you are a fraud and selling the fear of the Devil and hell to coerce the uneducated and the religiously gullible into following your cult."

Then Jesus answered this man in this way, "You, sir, have spoken of what is in your dark heart. No Light shines through it. You have insulted the Son of Man by saying that he does not live his Truth but is just doing what is wrong as a human being in his life. Well, I have lived among you all and you all can see that I have lived My Truth. I have spoken the Truth. I have not looked for accreditation for doing this in your eyes but I have looked for it in the Eye of My Father in Heaven. I have done all in this life time to live as a person first. I have done all that a human being can do. I have traveled the world to see many other cultures and many other races. I have seen that the Truth rests in every human being in what he lives. I saw that the wise men who were teachers of the Light that lived what they said I could follow. I came to earth to follow them first to see the pathway of the world. I did this until I came back to My country, Palestine.

I did this and then My Father showed Me how to use My Eyes of the Light to initiate My Being with His Cosmic Light. When this happened to Me on the river Jordan, when John the Baptist baptized Me, My whole Being and Personality was symbolically and spiritually transformed. I then became the Cosmic Christ Being. I then incarnated into the Body of Light I have. So in doing this I showed all of mankind from all ages that I am the Light of all Ages. I thus also, by doing this, showed the alignment every human being must make in the presence of his Heavenly Father or he cannot live his Truth and walk in the Light. I do not ask others to honor Me as a King of mankind but as a King of the spiritual world I come from. There is no proof that I have ever asked for any political power or financial control of anything other than that the people listen to Me when I speak of the Pathway to the Light.

At the same time I have also shown that there are two evolutions on this planet that are opposing each other. I am the focal point of these evolutions. I am the source of the Light and the source of this conflict on this planet as I have come to change the pattern of this evolution on this planet. I have come to do this not with force of a mighty empire with a military machine that kills people and robs them of their cultural and religious identity. Nor have I come with a spiritual force that will dominate every human being to submission so that they are compelled to love My Father or to die in hell – fire. I have come to give mankind his ultimate free will to choose the Light or its opposite and to know that he who chooses the Light will truly love the Truth and put it above all things in his life by living his Truth and aligning with the Christ Being eternally, while those who choose its opposite lose their Truth and never live what they say. They also follow the pathway to material and physical power above the Truth of life. Proof of this is that they will never align their Truth with the Light of God. They will align the Truth intellectually and say that they do this but they do not live this. Hence the Intellectual Materialism of this Rabbi. He not only says that God is the intellect but also says that everything comes from his head. He is heartless and has not Light. He makes his Soul into his brain. He confuses one for the other. The cause of personality is one's Soul. The intellect is not God. It did not create the Soul forces of mankind. So he who interprets Me as a megalomaniac is giving his negative psychological worldview as his philosophy of life. He is not looking at what I have lived and what I have done in this life time let alone what I have said. In doing this he has analyzed and concluded but he has not interpreted the Truth with the Truth but with his negative personal psychology.

I say to you all this Philosophy of Light I speak of is based on the Pathway to the Ultimate Light of My Father. It is based on the Living Truth of an individual human being's life who has a body of Light created from the Cosmic World of Light called Heaven. I am he who has shown the Keys of Light that activate special powers that have healed all disease on your earth. I am in living flesh the Christ Being. I am the Son of Man as human being. I am the Son of God as the Christ Being." [Verse 6] [4]

Then a Pharisee who heard this speech got up and said, "How can I and the people be certain that you are the Messiah; the Christ Being? After all we are human beings and in the world of human beings nothing is perfect. Our judgment is not perfect. So how can an imperfect being like myself speak to someone perfect and then be ultimately judged perfectly at the end of time? Surely God with all His power and mercy would save even the evil man at the end to time as after all no one is perfect like God? Can you answer this, Jesus of Nazareth?"

The Christ Being replied, "I am the Christ Being and I am the Ultimate Messiah of this planet. I have spoken of redemption. I have spoken of free will. I have spoken of how man will ultimately be divided into those who follow the Light and those who follow its opposite. Now when you say you are not perfect that is true as no human being is perfect. However when you say that your free will to act imperfectly has no moral basis then you are not living your Truth as a man who lives his Truth lives his life imperfectly and will never be

---

[4] John 8: 21-24.

balanced completely no matter how much he tries to be perfect.

However man has a higher identity than being a human being. Man also is a Cosmic being with an eternal Soul. That Soul has many life times on earth. Each life time a human being lives out his imperfections, so as to become more perfect until he creates a perfect Body of Light. He does this when he has chosen My Father above his Truth. He does this when he has put the Light above the Truth and when he has said, 'I am created by God, the Father. I am evolving my being with this journey to the Ultimate Light with the Holy Spirit of God.' When a person can say this he puts the Light above the Truth and above being a human being as then his Cosmic destiny through thousands of lives and worlds will give him equality with the Hierarchies of the Light as it is they that create with him the Body of Light that will give him the Light power to enter the Cosmic World of Light in Heaven. So, I, the Christ Being, say to you all the Light is above life.

I say to you, try to understand the Light through your minds and you will not feel its Truth in your hearts. I say to you I am the bringer of the Eternal Light of My Father. It is He who has sent Me on this journey into humankind so that I can show the world the Light and give this planet its new evolutionary course. I have come to turn the globe around with the Hand of My Father so that it will no longer be spinning towards a creation of human life submerged into physical matter.

Man is descending into matter as his Soul has been abstractified by Intellectual Materialism. It has become dormant and almost extinct. The eternal Soul will never die when it has Light. When it belongs to the Hierarchies of darkness it devolves into a reverse evolutionary process back into matter from spirit. Instead of progressing its spirit body of Light it creates a spirit body of darkness.

The reason the forces of darkness want man to devolve back into matter and to not proceed on the progressive evolution to acquire a Body of Light is because these Spiritual Beings of darkness have already long ago stopped evolving as they chose not to follow the Father but wanted their own path about the same Cosmic time when they faced their Truth at their human being stage of evolution. With this will – power these Spiritual Beings serve as the vehicles for that part of mankind that chooses being an individual human being above being a Cosmic being. They have put the material life above the Light. Their Truth is bound with the condition that they do not have to take the Moral Step to put the Light first in their lives. Hence they live without God and ultimately without His Light. Hence in this life time as in future life times such individuals choose completely of their own free will not to take any more incarnations where they have to take the Moral Steps but choose incarnations where they want to be in a position to get power over others and the material world.

I have come to gain no power over the material world and to not change the free will that My Father gave to all individuals and to all mankind at the beginning of conscious human being time on earth. I have come on this one incarnation to earth to give Light to it and to show that by living My Truth as a human being I become an individual Cosmic Light Being. This happens as when I do this,

living My Truth, I have a Pathway that simultaneously leads Me to the Ultimate Light. Hence I do this as My Living Soul belongs to My Father as My Spirit is the Holy Spirit of God. So on My journey to becoming a human being I took on the Pathway to use My tools of Light which are the Special Keys of Christ to change the future of this planet. I am doing this now when I fulfil what I have come to do which is to redeem mankind.

So I say to you all, look up to the Light of God. Live your Truth as human beings. Put the Light above the Truth and above life. Do this and you will have the Light shining in your hearts. This is the Truth of the ages; I, the Christ Being."
[Verse 7] [5]

Once this lecture was completed many Jews began to cry out in unison over and over again deep into the night, "You are the Messiah of the Light. You are the Living Christ come to save the world." Jesus responded by taking up his hands and looking up to the ceiling of the marble temple. Then he said, "Father, save My people and let them see Your Light. Let

[5] John 8: 25-30.

them stand before the Living God."

Then the Christ Being looked upon those who had Light in their hearts and he said, "I say to you, he who loves the Truth loves Me and loves what I labor for to create the Cosmic fabric of Light in mankind's Soul. He who knows Me knows that I am the Son of Man. I create a pathway in man's being so that he will see truly the Pathway to the Light. I do this when mankind speaks to Me from his or her heart. Mankind needs this Cosmic identity as no matter how much of a human being he is in his love of humanity he has been created by the Hand of the Light of My Father in Heaven. God, the Father, became a human being when He let Me become the Christ Being.

So I say to you, when you align with the Ultimate Light you align with Me. When you love your neighbor as a human being first, as a person first, you love the Son of Man first. When you put God first in your life you put the Christ Being first in your being. Then you begin to see with your Eyes of the Light and you become followers of the Christ Being. Then you walk with God in His Light. He who lives his Truth without guarantee that he will find the Truth of life has it already in his being. He who proclaims the Truth but does not live his Truth has already lost his being. So to know the Truth you must first know its source which is the Light. To know how to be free of darkness is to know that the Light is above the Truth as the Light created mankind's Truth.

He who seeks power over his Cosmic identity puts himself above God. This has already happened before physical time on earth where there was a War in the cosmos between the Hierarchies of the Light and the Hierarchies of darkness. There were Spiritual Beings at the human being stage of their evolution that chose not to follow My Father but to follow their own will.

I say to you, to live with the ultimate free will of a Cosmic identity is to ask for no guarantees from God as to this life and its riches. However to ask for the ultimate guarantee of asking to be aligned to God by putting your Moral Will to the Light as the ultimate value of life, meaning that the human being puts his identity with the Light above his life, this way he is free to evolve his being till the end of physical time on earth when

he becomes a Being with a Body of Christ Light."
[Verse 8]

Then a wealthy Jewish merchant listening to the Christ Being said to him, "My dear sir, you are talking about being aligned to God and that a human being can only be aligned when he exercises his free will to live out his thousands of life times doing God's will regardless of any reward except the person will ultimately get to Heaven and have this eternal Light. However I cannot see the logic in what you say according to scripture as truly we are the chosen people. We have chosen to follow our ultimate father, the father of our nation, who is Abraham. We have our identity as Jews from him. He was the closest to God for us. So when you say that we must follow you and take on what you say as being above what Abraham said you are trying to fool us into going against what our scriptures say. After all, can you explain to me really who you are as how can you say a person really has free will when he has so many life times to make this ultimate decision of the Truth of life? I cannot remember I have ever lived before and if I have, so what! I cannot change what happened and also, yes, granted it seems

likely we have lived before but we cannot do anything about it and there is no connection to this and what I have to do morally now in this life.

So on what grounds can you say that I, as a Jew, can put you above Abraham and in this way I can become the chosen follower of one greater than he and that this will give me a higher evolution providing I put what is to come at the end of time above what is happening now? I cannot see it. No one can be sure about such things as you talk about but I can be sure about my father, Abraham."

The Christ Being replied to this man by saying, "I say to you that you have not seen the Truth and have taken no responsibility for your eternal Soul. It goes on from one life to the other until it reaches its destination in the Ultimate Light. As for your reference to scripture and your alignment to your Truth of life, be aware that you are not living your Truth as you have not said how you are going to become an individual human being in the present following Abraham's laws. You only have said that you cannot see past him in your philosophy of life. This means you are neutralising your pathway and you lost your Light, as when you do not live your Truth you live your lie. This lie then becomes institutionalized. You become the lie. Hence you align with the wrong perceptions about the cosmos and you put your rationalistic Intellectual Materialism above the Truth. You do this when you say that your personal interpretation of life is aligned to the scriptures when you should be saying that you need to first see that the scriptures were created as the basis of a moral pathway to the Light. This moral pathway is above your theory of knowledge about the cosmos as you have selected the facts that justify your philosophy of darkness as the Truth is one can only see with his eyes but when you have darkness in your Soul your eyes are blinded and cannot see the Light. You have become a slave of material interpretations of your own scriptures as you do not connect your Truth with the Truth of life and the life of the Light.

So I say to you, your pathway will end in the material realm in future cosmic worlds that will not allow you to evolve past the levels of consciousness of where you are now while those who follow the Ultimate Light of

Christ will be free to evolve onwards to the Spiritual World of Light that created the material world in the first place through the power of God.

I, the Christ Being, bring you eternal freedom from the world of darkness so when you follow Me you have ultimate Cosmic free will. You will be like a flower of gold that will bloom at the sunrise and when it shines it will light up the whole world. So I say to you, he who has Light in his or her heart lights up the Soul of Heaven.

You who follow darkness say that you are belonging to the chosen people of Abraham and that this is above My Being, the Christ Being. You say that I am trying to take over your allegiance or your very Souls and that this is falsehood and that I deserve death for My wickedness. You say that My Word is that of evil. This is truly your identification with the ideology of your race that splits you off from God as you are denying Me, My Truth; I the Son of the Living God, My Father. You have accused Me of sin when it is your sin. So you place guilt on Me and in doing so you show your evil as evil ever tries to hide its sin in the clothes of innocence. It says that it is faultless and blames the other constantly to hide behind its delusion of the Truth. Hence your truth belongs to the Father of darkness." [Verse 9] [6]

Then another Jewish person spoke to Jesus. He was a prominent lawyer. He said, "You challenge the identity of the Jewish race. You have no real credentials to do this apart from explanation of your reality. Our reality is that Abraham is our father. Your reality is that anyone who does not follow you follows darkness. This shows me that a man believes in what he wants to believe in regardless of the Truth. You have your own ideology and we have ours. So in the end everyone has his own opinion and you are saying we are not entitled to ours. So what does your interpretation of your Philosophy of Light say to this argument?"

Jesus replied, "I say to you once again that your ideology has made you identify with darkness unconsciously and at times consciously. This has happened to you as you have made the Truth relative. This means you have put your opinion of what is in the

scriptures above the Will of God. This has happened to you as you have not lived your Truth. You have made a theory of your Truth, meaning you have not said that one's opinion is not above the Truth.

You have said that no one really knows the Truth but I tell you that this is the reason you have lost your Pathway to the Truth and the Light of life. So truly if you read the scriptures and see what Abraham said you will see that he spoke of Me but instead of seeing that I speak to God, the Father, and I have come to fulfil Abraham's dream of the Light you are plotting to have Me murdered. This shows Me that you are those of mankind who do not want to take the Moral Steps to evolve to being human beings and Cosmic Beings of Light. To the contrary you have sold your Soul to a world theory of knowledge which gives the power beast as your higher authority guiding your moral conscience. You have sold your Soul to the Archenemy of the Light." [Verse 10]

Then the Pharisee stood up and angrily said, "Who are you? How can you say God is your Father, after all no

---

[6] John 8: 31-38.

human being can be fathered by God? What madness is this? You speak from a sexual delusion about your origin. Your father was the man, Joseph, and you are faking this whole story of your Cosmic origin while the Jewish race and myself belong to the chosen people of God. This is our origin."

The Christ then spoke and said to this Pharisee. "He who loves Me puts the Truth above love as then he lives his Truth first before he asks to command knowledge of the laws of Truth. You are saying things that accuse Me of deception and illusion while in Truth I have clearly shown the Truth and its way for all of mankind. I have shown mankind God's way. I am His Son. So when you say I am falsifying My Truth when I speak of a false origin you show truly your evil intent. You create your own delusion as when you belittle the Supreme Being of the Universe you belittle your being eternally. You now put the lie you live above the Truth.

If you were with God in your Spirit you would be in His Light but you are truly not from God as when I came to this planet I could see your incarnations manifest in the cosmos and I could see that you came not to do the Will of God while I came to do His Will first. I put My Father above Me. Hence I became a human being. I did this as I loved the human race. I love mankind. I will not relate at the end of the universe to that part of mankind that seeks what is in your dark heart.

This is because you have sold your Soul to Satan. You have done this as you worship him as your god. He has the power to delude you and tells you that evil only exists in man's head and that it is but a thing man has that he acquires because of the struggle for survival in a material world. He tells you that God is really only an idea to make money with. He tells you that you are no different than any other man that deep down any woman will do to sleep with. He tells you that really this whole business of the concept of God is merely a phenomenon of the mind and that the mind controls all in the universe of existence. He tells you that truly the Soul is only a word and that the mind is really the Soul. He tells you that Truth is relative and that there can be no Truth of one man above another's and that Satan's truth is really supreme wisdom as after all there is a devil in everyone's

160

heart if one is really honest about his needs in life. He says that everyone really wants power but religion is really for the ones that do not make it financially and that really the real world is the one a person can see, touch and feel and the rest is a matter of selection of physical evidence otherwise it is a fantasy like the Moral Will as after all circumstances can change any Moral Will. So a person who controls his mind gets ultimately whatever he wants in life as he puts his mind above his emotions, above his Soul and above this idea of God. Then he truly sees that dark truth of life. The rest is an excuse to believe in a Light and that is delusion as there is only one Spirit that really rules the world and all ways will rule it. He tells you that this is the force of material power regardless of how it is achieved. This is a proven fact throughout history. He tells you that Cosmic religions are but answers for failures to comprehend the Truth of life and that destructive energy in the world is really what is ultimately the force that rules it. This he says is obvious. Look at the way civilisations come and go. Look at Rome. It rules with this ideology and will rule successfully for a thousand years.

So I say to you, look at what I have said. This is the philosophy of darkness. It is the lies of the Devil. It shows him as the Father of darkness. He has the power to make men worship him as the living god when they sell their Souls to him. He that is the Devil first infects the intellect and then the rest of one's being. His followers believe in him consciously and unconsciously. Cosmic Christ consciousness reveals his ugliness and shows now his philosophy of darkness is destroying the natural balance of nature upon the living earth. It shows that the real cause of this destruction comes from man's dark thoughts about his origin and his environment. These thoughts come from the Spiritual Beings that belong to the Hierarchies of darkness. They want man to devolve and to become total slaves of material power with the King of evil becoming their god. I say to you, interpret scripture with the eyes of this ideology of Cosmic darkness and you will deny the Ultimate Cosmic Light of My Being; I, the Christ Being, the Messiah of the Light." [Verse 11]

Then Christ said to them all, "I ask you who can face Me now and tell Me that I have come from evil? Who can come up to Me and say to Me that I follow evil? What man can truly say that in any action in the whole life that I have lived on this earth I have not followed the Light? With words you can accuse Me of evil but you have no real proof apart from your rhetoric of the evil in your minds coming from your eyes of darkness given to you by the Devil. You say that you accept that everyone has his opinion and is entitled to it but you are denying Me this basic right you proclaim. You hypocrites! You say you protect God's Word but in Truth you are protecting God's enemy for the sake of power.

I say to you the mind is closed to the Truth that listens to the voice of darkness. You cannot anymore hear God. You ask for physical proof as you need to see it in black and white before your very eyes. Yet at the same time you say that God is with you as you speak His Word from the scriptures while in Truth you write out a script in your very lives that is aligned to a lie. So you then ask Me to listen to your lies about My Father. I tell you I

speak the Ultimate Truth as it is I, the Christ Being, who has met the Father in Heaven and who speaks to the Father daily and is one with the Father in His Soul.

I say to you that you do not have a way to speak to Him as you are not of His Light. You have forsaken the right for His Light for the sake of your lie about Me. Hence you lose Him who sent Me now and will lose Him for eternity when you stand before Him at the end of time. You will not be able to pledge your Truth for My Being, the Son of the Living God. Then you will truly see the wrath of God, My Father, who will banish the Devil with you to the world of darkness which will be separated eternally from the World of Light to come. This is I, the Christ Being, Son of the Living God and the human being who is the Son of Man, the Living God of all human beings, for all their incarnations to come until the end of them and until the incarnation which will create the ultimate fusion of Light. This is the moment the Body of Light is born forevermore in the Christ Light."
[Verse 12] [7]

---

[7] John 8: 39-47.

Then a Pharisee with real anger got up from his place and said to Jesus, "No one can speak like you unless he has a devil in his heart. You are not a Jew but a true Samaritan; a person who has no allegiance to the ultimate law of our race. You are truly possessed. You have come to send darkness to us all. I tell you to leave us as you talk for the Prince of demons!"

The Christ Being then said to this man, "You, with those like you who have accused Me of evil, only show in your defence the very evil you have in your Souls as he who accuses another only shows the lie in his heart as you try to justify your allegiance to your idea of race above the Truth. Your hatred of Me shows My Father that the demon is controlling your thoughts as all thoughts are created by the Spiritual Hierarchies.

These thoughts are those created by Satan, your master and your friend. Your desires are to defame the Supreme Light of the World as your heart is now filled with the darkness coming from the mouth of the Devil.

I, the Christ Being, say to you that you look to evil and in this way try to use its power to force others to believe your lies.

I say to you that the power of the Light is above your powers. Your powers will ultimately disappear into a future of a world polarized into matter for eternity as this will be the home of you and those who can no longer evolve progressively into the Light but must devolve into this vortex of matter supported by the powers that are beyond matter and that created the material world originally with its Cosmic clock defining its scales of time where you will be in the end as there will be a static suspension of energy supported by the Spiritual Hierarchies eternally in the ultimate grave of the universe created for those who choose darkness above the Light. This is your fate.

I tell you all that I have come not to create fear nor to talk of demons but to create Light and to talk of the Angels of the Light that walk amongst you invisibly every day of your lives to counsel you and prepare your beings for the World of Light to come. I have come to do this and to also warn those who destroy the pathway of others that they do this with their proclamations of pathways to darkness.

These will be truly struck down by the Mighty Cosmic Sword of the Hierarchies of the Light. I say this not to put My Being above all human beings and to threaten retaliation for those who follow darkness but to make it clear that every human being has the right to passively resist attacks from evil only up to the point that evil wants to take away the Light as if an evil man takes everything from you to the extent of paralleling to the story of Job then he has taken nothing in comparison in that he did not take any of these things but managed to take your Light away as one has to protect his Light and his Truth. To do this one must fight for it with weapons of Light. If one fights with the weapons of Negative Motivational Science aligned to Intellectual Materialism then he uses the tools of the Devil. However if one truly uses the tools of the Light he uses the tools of the Christ Being. These are the Keys of the Light.

So I tell you now that to have the Christ Eyes of the Light you need to know how to live your Truth and to align with the Light consciously and unconsciously. You need to also ultimately align all the Light in all your past incarnations to take away the darkness of this incarnation you have now. Then you need to use the power and force of Light in your Souls to direct your whole beings to speak to My Father in Heaven as when you can do this you will have the Body of Light that you need to have to walk in the streets of Heaven as then truly will you have the Christ Body of Light and it is there that I will greet you with the Golden Light of the Living God.

I, the Christ Being, speak to you now to tell you of My Father's Word to you. When you surrender your whole being and Soul to Him you will have not only eternal life but an eternal Light. I tell you death is welcomed by those who have lived in the Light. I tell you all men must die so that they can live eternally in the Light. All men and women need to know how to love the Light. This they can only know when they love in the Light of their lives with each other and in sharing the Light of the Christ Being. They do this every time they love unconditionally their will to the Light. They prove this in living their Truth accordingly aligned to this Ultimate Truth.

He who follows Me will never truly die as death for him is

but a change of state of existence. In his being he will know that it is but walking into another Door that leads to the Ultimate Light. I tell you this is truly the promise of My Father. He who but dies physically lives forever in the Cosmic Light and never really dies as his Soul shines eternally ultimately in Heaven. I tell you this is why the Light is above death. The Light is above life. It is the ultimate expression of existence as the ultimate destiny of mankind is to live in a World of Light where death and life have passed from the cosmos and where Light will reign supreme as the source of every being's existence eternally and where My Being will be free of what is to come and the beginning of time and its end will have passed into God's Light."
[Verse 13] [8]

All of a sudden a harsh voice from the crowd cried out and said, "You are the Devil incarnate as you are possessed by the seven demons of hell. I tell you our father, Abraham, has never really died as he is in us all in our spirit, while you have the arrogance to proclaim yourself above the Prophets and above him. You say that

you will live forever and that those who follow you will do likewise. I say to you that you are truly the evil one in the flesh. I say to you, answer my challenge and say to us all what your origin is, in Truth. Where do you come from? What do you say truly is the source of your being?"

Then the Christ Being said, "I say to you all that he who defiles the Light of My Being will touch the boundaries of hell. I also make it clear to you that My Light is the Light of the world. I have come to cast out its demon. He is the Archenemy of Truth. The voice that has no face in this crowd spits out its vile words as it comes from the source of all darkness, meaning that I tell you all to be aware that your opponent in life is not your neighbor regardless of the degree of evil in his personality as he is but the agent of the invisible enemy of Satan.

I say to you those who say Light is darkness say that I am but the carrier of evil when in Truth I have come to overcome the darkness with the Mighty Cosmic Sword of Light.

I say to you then as the Light shines from the Spiritual

---

[8] John 8: 48-51.

Hierarchies of Light in the cosmos into our sun so will the darkness overshadow the planet of evil at the end of time. It is the day the Father will extend His Light so the sun will disappear as it will no longer be needed to give Light to mankind as at that moment I will stand next to Him with the Holy Spirit and He will glorify all the planets of the cosmos and the stars will surround Heaven as a crown of Light.

The planets of darkness will join the planet of evil and henceforth free will to the Light will have triumphed eternally for every living Soul that has Eyes of the Light. I say to you I, the Christ Being, see what I am and you will love the Light. I say to you that I walk with the Father in Heaven and I talk with you now. I am a Being of Light that lives in all the worlds at once. I come from Higher Worlds and now am in this world to raise it up to become a World of Light. I see a million miles away and I see in front of Me a meter away. I look now to the Light of Heaven. I can see it descend upon the sun so that it gives you Light. The Father in Heaven directs this Light to mankind.

He gave mankind a voice in My Being, the Christ Being. I speak now so that you will hear the Truth. I see that he who listens to darkness listens to its lies. I do not listen to it and so I speak the Truth of My Father as He is My Soul. He gives Me life. He and I are one. So when you say that I lie then you speak for Satan. He who can be counted as a human being, who follows his Truth first in life, follows My Father's Will. I do this. So I follow My Truth and align My whole Being with the Light of My Father. Hence I know His way will never fail Me as He is God.

Abraham could see the Light coming to the sun of the earth as he saw the source of all Light in the cosmos. It is from the Spiritual Beings of Light that Light shines to your sun that gives Light and warmth to your earth. He could see this with his vision of the future of mankind. He could see Me coming to earth from the sun as I rode upon the threads of Light that streamed to his Soul. I say to you that he worshipped My Father and thanked him for My coming to earth as he could see that the day I would come is the moment that earth would begin its spiritual material astralisation into becoming a globe of Light with Bodies of Light." [Verse 14] [9]

Then another voice spoke out against Jesus and said, "How can you possibly know what Abraham said when you have not even passed thirty years of age? Who do you think you are, speaking about a Cosmic future that no one can really prove exists? I can see that you are but a man in his thirties and that is it. I cannot see anything more. So enlighten all of us and myself. How do you know what Abraham said?"

The Christ Being responded by saying, "I, the Christ Being, say this to all of you and to you who charge Me with evil. I am the Living Light of this World. I have come to challenge Satan for this planet of the sun. His works are darkening its atmosphere and he seeks its union with his planet of evil to come.

I say that I am going to create from My Incarnation on your earth an ultimate planet of Light. I say to you that My Father who is the Living God created all incarnations including Abraham's who will reincarnate again upon your planet. I say to you that My years are but earth years.

When man had no eyes to see nor ears to hear the Light speaking, I was. I always was, as I am the Living God as human being. I am the Son of Man and the Cosmic Christ." [Verse 15]

Then a group organised by a clique in the Pharisees began to rush at Jesus with spears and swords with the intention of killing him. They began to cut into him with swords until a spear touched Jesus' clothing or so it seemed as at that moment he was no longer visible to his would – be murderers.

He had walked into the spiritual world as he had to wait for the right Cosmic hour before he could let his Being become one with physical time on earth. He knew that this was to come but he also knew that he had to complete a Mission for the Light of this earth. He could only do that while being the Christ Being and a human being and living in both worlds according to the Will of the Father.

So what occurred next was that all of the crowd could see Jesus leave the temple unharmed. He walked away from it and his would – be killers hid in the crowd so as

_____

[9] John 8: 52-56.

to disguise their true intentions as all the people began to cheer him and say "Blessed is the Christ! Blessed is the Christ! May he live eternally in our hearts; the hearts of Light!" The people sang and cheered with a beautiful harmony as the Angels of God were surrounding the Christ. They came to the people and appeared before their Souls.

Their leader, the Archangel Michael, held a Golden Sword studded with diamonds that had a blade of Fire that was emitting heat with a scorching Fire that was singeing Jesus'

would – be killers. The other Angels of God stood next to Jesus and created a Circle of Light around him so that no evil could come near him as there were many Roman soldiers there secretly ready to kill him. Then finally there was a Legion of Angels on white horses that surrounded this Circle of Light and they, with the Circle of Light, let the Christ Being walk back into earth time. This is when the Christ Being appeared once again out of the city with his Apostles to tell them of the Pathway that they would also have to travel to reach his Light. [Verse 16] [10]

---

[10] John 8: 57-59.

168

CHAPTER 9

The Christ Being was walking down the street and he saw a blind beggar with a bowl in his hand sitting on the ground. Then one of his Apostles, Luke, asked him, "Why is this man blind? Is he paying for his karmic debts for surely God is merciful? Is it a karmic debt for his karmic circle coming from his parents or his group Soul that is still a part of his Soul in this life? What is the reason that one man lives from birth in the house of a king while another begs all his life long to find his food to live? Why did God create such inequality in mankind's circumstances? Please tell us, Oh, Jesus, the Truth as this has been a riddle that has made me question life and the power of money in it. It is what has made me at times consider the perfect society which would not have such injustice in the daily lives of men? Then I look at this world and see that the unjust rule it with the invincible legions of Rome. Why does God then give a man such an affliction and the Jewish nation such an unjust fate?"

Jesus then replied, "I say to you, My trusted initiands of the Light of My Father in Heaven, that this man pays the karmic debt for mankind.

Every human being pays his karmic debt first to the Light in this universe. Then he pays his own personal karmic debts related to his past lives in general. Alongside with this he has his karmic credits for as you know only the Christ Being has no karma and has a complete Body of Light. This is your destiny at the end of the seventh cosmic world to come. You now see that your Eyes of the Light can see Me. You can see that what I am is the Truth. When a person comes to earth he comes to live and speak once again all his life all over again so that he may ever improve his journey to the Body of Light. If he damages his Soul then truly this Light will dim and every time he comes to earth his shape and form will change to adapt to this Light or to this dimness of it as ultimately there can be only an ascent or a descent of every human being to freely will his Pathway to the Light or to the darkness even though this may be disguised in a million ways that it is the Light.

As for this point the fact is that a person returns to his race or to his group in that race or culture with a renewed Soul from his previous past life until he evolves past that level of evolution and the

169

evolution of the circle he is in or he devolves below that circle to a lower karmic circle of existence. He then once again works on changing his principle of his being so that he can evolve to the Light of My Father or he reduces this principle to Intellectual Materialism which will bring himself and his Soul to the devolution of his being.

Now this is found and revealed to him by the way he lives his Truth and by the way he can align it in the material world and to the Spiritual Light which is the source and the origin of all things material in the universe. Once this is done by a person and, of course to various degrees this can only be done in the human condition, then a person faces the karma of his race. Whatever this karma has to offer him is an opportunity to evolve one step further towards the Light in Heaven.

Now following this there are those initiands who choose, like yourselves, to fulfil their own karma and that of their race and then follow the next step to follow the karma of the world. By doing this you have found the ultimate karmic credit of mankind which is Myself as I am the Living Christ. I have become a human being to prove to the whole spiritual and material world that My Being is the Ultimate Being in this universe as it is I who have come to you as a human being.

However as you can see the evil one from hell can only perform the trick to be a human, meaning he will appear in the Soul of another and convince another that he is God and above God's law. Then this person defies the power of God with the power of the sword to cut the flesh of mankind and spill its blood so that with killing the body he can say, 'I have won this person's Soul.' Rome has done this now and may do this for some centuries to come which is not a long time in the scheme of the cosmos.

Also as you can see Caesar is no god. He is but a man. He can pretend to be a god and to be all – powerful but all his power depends on God. His origin is human and he will have to return to earth to face a beggar's life as well without free choice as this way he will be giving back to God what God has given him regardless of his will as he has a karmic debt to the Light first and then to man. Hence the evil one tries to create the false perception in man of his origin and of his ultimate destiny. He tells those who

170

listen to him that there is no need to know why you are here or where you are going as this is simply a waste of intellectual effort on something no-one can know. He says this as he himself does not know it apart from the fact that he also reads the scriptures and falsifies it in men's hearts. He does this in its meaning and spirit by saying that it is not scientific to believe in something you cannot see, touch nor hear.

Well, I say to you, you can see Me, you can touch Me and you can hear Me; I, the Christ Being. So that you can do this now I will demonstrate for you the Ultimate Light and its power on your planet to transform matter into Spirit and Spirit into matter. This man with his karma has presented himself to live his Truth and to align it with My Father. Hence he has at this moment become a part of the Light as he has waited all his life to be given to the Light. Now the Light has come to him. I am the Light. I am the Living Light of the whole world. I am the Christ Being. So now I will give him the Christ Light and he will see again the Light of day as the Light of the sun gives you the Light of day that shines from the Spiritual Beings into your Souls.

So now I create this Light in this man's Soul to transform and change his being so that his being can begin to see in the material world as you can see now the Eyes of the Light let you see into the spiritual world and as initiands this gives you the special vision of My Being and the spiritual world that opens around Me when I show you My Cosmic Being as I will show you now to fulfil the Will of the Light in this man's heart and Soul as he chose to sacrifice his being to meet the Light in this incarnation. To touch historical and Cosmic fate he had to be the blind beggar from birth so he has paid his karmic debt but first he knew he wanted to pay his karmic debt to the Light which is My Being, the Christ Being. [Verse 1] [1]

You see the Father is the Source of all the Light of all the Spiritual Beings in the spiritual world. He is also the Source of the Light of all the sun stars in the universe which warm our world and give Light to our Souls. He has sent His Son to earth in flesh and blood to give His Light to humankind so that man can work on his being and with free will love Him eternally. Only with the Body of Light

---

[1] John 9: 1-3.

171

can man surpass the material world and enter the new World of Light to come. This is the Cosmic karma of the universe.

Satan's Cosmic karma is to prevent this evolution so that his kingdom will reign in the material world eternally as he has chosen to be evil eternally. He has chosen to defy God and to do this with the power of the material world. This will disintegrate into the spiritual world and he will become a part of this spiritual dark, evil planet which will be surrounded by the satellites of Cosmic debris peopled by the lost Souls who choose him for eternity. At the end of the seventh cosmic world mankind will be divided and the ones who have chosen him will go back to the physical level of unconsciousness of the Light forever. It will be a universe of darkness suspended by the Spiritual Hierarchies of the Light. This will entomb Satan and the Spiritual Hierarchies of darkness with their and his hell – fire forevermore. Hence the boundaries of hell will be sealed off by the Spiritual Fire from Heaven as the Cosmic karma of this universe at that moment will end. This is the Will of the Father, the Living God. [Verse 2] [2]

I came to earth to give it Light. The Father gave free will to all men. In His own Free Will He chose Me. The alternative would have been for mankind to have no way to change its pattern of Cosmic life. I gave life to the world. As I breathe the Spirit of the earth, the earth can breathe this breath of eternal life. If I had not come to give man Light, the shadow of darkness would have engulfed the earth and man would have been lost to the power of the opposing forces of Light.

When the War in the Court of Heaven split the Hierarchies of the Light from Lucifer's Hierarchy of darkness the Father was greatly saddened. He saw in His Eternal Wisdom the Cosmic plan unfold and he ordered the Archangel Michael to send Lucifer outside the boundary of Heaven. He also gave him a Cosmic Sword which had the Living God – Fire in it which could burn all darkness away from its taint on Heaven. In doing this the Father, at that moment, made a pledge that what had now been created was a Cosmic Free Will to create worlds and to create

---

[2] John 9: 4.

172

men who would people them who also had free will.

He also made it clear that He had Free Will too to decide on the fate of the universe and to let the contest begin for the fate of the earth. He could see that many would see this as an unjust contest based on rules that were inhuman and cruel. This was the perception in Heaven by many Beings that did not know which pathway to take after the War in Heaven. Yet they soon discovered that they were also lost to Heaven as they had not faced their Truth which was to make a choice to act for the Light. Hence now at this moment the Father with His Cosmic Free Will about this War between good and evil said, 'I will ultimately make the Light overcome the darkness the day the Light is loved in freedom by all beings, Spiritual and human.' " [Verse 3] ³

When the Christ Being was telling the Apostles all about the Cosmic drama that had occurred and was still unfolding he put his hand on the earth next to this man. He took some clay in it as it had been raining and spat into the clay so that the spit was mixed into the rainwater that had made it soft and watery. He then rubbed it between his hands and made it as soft as sand. Then he rubbed the clay into one right eye and then into the left eye of the blind beggar. While doing this a bright Light appeared around his hands.

The Apostles could see a Light pierce the man's eyes and the Christ Being was heard saying, "I, the Christ Being, send Light to your Soul. May you follow the Truth of life. May your heart be glad that the Father now speaks to your Soul and that He gives it Light from Heaven. You will join Him when you see Him with the Eyes of the Light. Let your eyes see His Son now."

Then the Christ Being looked deeply into this man's eyes as they opened up and a Light flashed into them as though a sparkle of a tear drop ran down his face. The man's countenance was radiant as he faced the Christ Being and said, "You are the Son of the Living God. I can see you. You are the Ultimate Light of the World. I ask you to redeem me as I seek to follow you as one of your initiands as I can see that I have my eyes back. Yet I also have new Eyes of the Light as I see that your aura of

---

³ John 9: 5,

Cosmic Light has also healed my Soul." He then went on his hands and knees and wanted to kiss the feet of the Christ Being." Christ then said to him, "You honor My Father as you have had faith in His Light. You will now first practice to live your Truth with the new physical eyes you have. Once you do this you can open once again the Eyes of the Light in your Soul. Then you can align with the Light of the Christ Being." [Verse 4] [4]

The man then went to wash at the pool of Silo'am as he wanted to make a statement to the world that he was healed. When he was putting his clothes on the people around him recognised that he was a blind beggar. Yet they were all very puzzled as this man, the man they knew was blind from birth, could see. Then a man was heard saying, "This could not be the beggar as this man can see. Something is very strange here." The woman next to him replied, "He just looks like him. There is no way this is the same man. It must be his double or twin brother."

Then this man said to this couple, "No, you are mistaken. I am the man you speak of. I was blind but I have been healed by the Messiah, Jesus of Nazareth." The lady then said, "Now I know that you are the same man but I just cannot believe that such a thing exists. You were blind from birth. What could any man do to heal such an affliction? Do you know what he did, this man, Jesus, so that your sight would return? Can you say how he did this?"

The man replied, "Well, let me see now. He took the clay from the ground next to him, rubbed it in his hands and then blessed my Soul. Then he said a lot of glorious and beautiful words and at the same time rubbed the clay on my eyes.

Soon after this I felt as if a bolt of lightning hit my head. Then a massive Light came to me and at first I could only see the brightness of the sunshine in my being or in the eyes of my being. Then slowly but surely I could see him greeting me with those eyes of his. They shone like living suns in my heart! At that moment I knew I could see a Living God in front of me. He smiled and said to me, 'Your heart now sees the Light that shines into the sun from Heaven.'" [Verse 5] [5]

---

[4] John 9: 6.

[5] John 9: 7-12,

174

The Pharisees heard about this miracle of Jesus restoring sight to the blind beggar from birth and were enraged as they feared such proof of the power of Christ. They summoned this man to the Temple offices to hold a form of tribunal to establish that Jesus was a fraud as evil was in their hearts.

This man then asked the head priest what the reason was for the summons as he wanted to know what the tribunal was for. The priest then said, "I know of this man, Jesus. I also know that there is, at the moment, a strong public opinion that supports the view that this man is evil and that he has the magical powers of a sorcerer. Also he does not respect the Jewish laws and will work on the Sabbath as he did when you saw him." Saying this he reconsidered his slip of the tongue and said, "...when you met him! Also this tribunal will establish the truth of what I am saying when you tell us how he used his black magic powers to make your eyes able to see again. So can you tell us what happened to you and why you can see now after you met this man, Jesus?"

This man replied, "I was blind from birth. I have been begging all of my life; some thirty – five years. I have not seen sunlight nor a man's face until only last week when this wonderful thing happened to me. When a person says to me that your Soul is now able to see the light from the sun as the Light comes from God, then I can see surely this is not from evil. If so how can it be that such an act of true mercy would be a work of darkness? Light is what gave me this way out of the darkness of all those years. Also my Soul is now with Light. I tell you I went to Silo'am to show my new self to the world. I am reborn in the Light. I can see. I can now see this Light I speak of." As he said this he turned his head towards the sky.

Then another Pharisee asked this man, "Do you say that this man is the Messiah?" The man replied, "I say that he sure looks like a man who creates Light and heals the body and Soul. Now if that is what the Messiah is going to do I say that it must be him as no man can heal a man, blind from birth, so that he can see unless it is God's Will."
[Verse 6] [6]

---

[6] John 9: 13-16.

175

Then one Pharisee who knew Jesus personally in secret said to the other priest who was now very embarrassed at his accusations in front of his colleagues, "I find that there is no truth to the allegations made against Jesus in the present case as I do not have any physical evidence that he is a black magician. To the contrary this man is a healer and a living Prophet."

Following this the head priest then became very angry with what he had looked forward to be an easy indictment of Jesus. He then said, "I summon the parents of this man before the tribunal to establish the identity of this man who says he was blind from birth."

His mother appeared before the priests and then said, "This is my son and he was blind from birth. I do not know how he has received his sight but I do know that he is truly my son and everyone who knows us here knows I am telling the truth. Furthermore I cannot see that I need to establish the identity of a thirty – five year old man before this tribunal when he can establish it himself to everyone here." [Verse 7] [7]

Once again the head priest summoned this man and said to him, "I demand that you truly now declare that God healed you and not Jesus. This phenomenon that you can see occurred as God willed it as we know Jesus works with dark magical powers and God would never work through him. You must look at the truth. You believe he healed you but in truth something else happened but you are not really telling us what it is as it just does not stand to reason that you can see because you were healed by Jesus. So I ask you again how can you know that it was Jesus and not God that cured you?"

Then this man replied, "I know that as God is my witness I did not see until I met Jesus. I also know that for thirty – five years I did not see but I can see now. If Jesus is a sorcerer why would he bother with me? I cannot see Light coming to the eyes of a blind beggar from birth from a sorcerer of darkness. I feel anyone who truly looks at what is happening here has no basis to say that Jesus is with darkness. He has taken out the darkness and given Light. That is what I see.

---

[7] John 9: 17-23,

You keep on asking me about his powers and what he did so that I could see and you say that only God has these powers. Well, I ask you then if that is so then this man has the power of God in his being. Then God's Light works through his hands as it was through them that I can see you now speak to me. I also see that you could know more if you asked him what he did to me, as after all you speak like those people who question skeptically everything and deny that a spiritual world exists and then use your spiritual authority to deny me my freedom of faith.

I say to you again ask Jesus, himself. I am sure that he will give you the knowledge you seek of what he did. I only know what I told you. I am not a learned man. I have been trapped blind in a black box all of my life. I now have a whole world to investigate and see because of this man who creates Light for this world and for me. I am the living proof of this Light before you now!" [Verse 8] [8]

The head priest then said to him, "We follow the Light of Moses. He gave Light to the world; God's Light. You follow a false Messiah and the

Jewish nation will vindicate my words in time to come. We also do not know the origin of Jesus; where he got his learning and his powers. We know that he has traveled abroad in the east and has been involved in many pagan religions. We also know that he is not above Moses so whatever you say about him does not change the truth that no man had Light like Moses for us. So you need to be aware that you are almost blaspheming when you say that Jesus is the Light – bringer of the world."

The man replied, "How is it that you are baffled by the origin of this man, Jesus? What man in this whole world could have cured me and given me sight? What man could heal with such a miracle unless it was a power beyond the material world; a power that is spiritual and filled with Spiritual Light? So I say to you, how can it be that you of all people cannot see where this man comes from nor, more to the point, where his being comes from as no man can use God's powers unless he comes from God? What man prays to God and asks for His help and then receives it unless God wills it? Does God give power to heal others from blindness who are evil? Tell

---

[8] John 9: 24-27.

me, do you know of any physician who can do this? No, you do not. Yet you keep on accusing this man who used no physical healing tools apart from his Spiritual Light to heal me, a blind man from birth. What is the reason that you are so against good works? What will the blind of the world see in their Souls when you speak as you speak now of how the Light reaches one's Soul. You seem to not want to see this Spiritual Light; the Spiritual Light that gave me my sight. What is the origin of your complaint about what he did as after all I have my life back and I can see yet you are saying that this was given to me by an evil man? Please explain your conclusions as we, all before you, want to hear what you have to say." [Verse 9]

Then another Pharisee spoke up and said, "Let it be known that no man can be sick from birth but one who has come to pay the sins of his forefathers. Also let it be known that as this man is cured it does not say that this man truly was cured in the Light as God relates to a person with Light. He does not relate to someone who is paying his karmic debts as this person known as the blind beggar from birth before us."

Then the man replied, "I tell you all that I am no less a human being than you though I was blind and could not see and could not earn a living. Also as for my karmic debt the only debt I have is to the Light of Jesus Christ, Son of the Living God as it is he who has saved me from delusion and a life of misery in darkness. It is he who has given me back my eyes. I now see him with Eyes of the Light. He is the Messiah of the Light of this planet.

I stand before you all and this tribunal to proclaim that I am a person who was blind and now I can see. I am also a person who now lives his Truth and is aligned to the Light of Christ. Hence I see the Light from Heaven stream into the stars and the sun to open the eyes of men so that they can see God's love for them. I dream that one day compassion and love will rule this planet. I ask that this be known that I will never deny the Truth about the Christ Being as he is my Saviour and the Son of the Living God."

Then the head priest said to him, "You are blaspheming and the ruling of this tribunal for this is that you will not be allowed to enter the synagogue until you confess the truth of what happened with Jesus. You will be shown

out of the temple now. Also if you ever return you will be charged with an offense of denigrating our laws."
[Verse 10] [9]

The Christ Being was present in the spiritual world when this was happening to this man. He was giving Light to his Eyes of the Light so he spoke with such eloquence and knowledge that the priests could but only accept his arguments regardless of the ruling. So once out of the Temple Christ appeared to this man as he did the first time when he gave him his sight.

The man then said to Jesus, "Are you the Son of Man and also the Cosmic Christ Messiah from Heaven?" Jesus replied, "I am the Christ Being who is cosmically the Christ human being. I have come to fulfill your karmic wish which was to serve the Light of My Father who sent me. You are now able to see My Light in Heaven and earth as you possess sight in both worlds. You will ultimately ascend to Higher Worlds of Light where you will create a Body of Light I will give you. You have taken the Moral Step to live your Truth before God and before man. So now the Light

rewards your vision with the Light of all Ages coming to you to tell you that when you walk in the Light of Christ you have Eyes of the Light and ultimately a Body of Light to be in, in the world to come.

Those who judge the Light and put it below the intellect can only see Intellectual Materialism. They are blind to the powers of the Soul. They cannot see Spiritual Light. They want to have a superior evolution and refuse to humble their being to the evolution that was given to them. Because of this they become blind to the Light. Their being becomes a part of the oblivion that will come at a time after Me in another Cosmic age on earth in the end of the next epoch to come. They will try to create a human being from the chemical compositions of the earth and to give him the power of the evil forces that come from the dark Spiritual Hierarchies that want earth's destiny to be theirs and want to abort earth's task to evolve to become a planet of Light.

This human being in the flesh will then have the power to destroy the Christ Light in the whole world as he will have the spiritual power of the evil one.

_____
[9] John 9: 28-34.

Yet this will be their delusion as even though all beings in the universe have free will only My Father can create life to a Soul. So they will create a being with spiritual powers to confront the Christ Light which will lose its Truth as this being will need to have the Father's Light to live as those who follow this dark path are identified with and will be then identified with Intellectual Materialism, and accordingly will believe that this humanly created body will have the powers of the Body of Light. This is the delusion as only those who know how to control the Soul forces by living their Truth can have this power of the Ultimate Body of Light.

Hence this mad dream is in their hearts now, yet thousands of years hence when they walk the face of the earth again they will seek this power over Me. They will fail and will fight a War with spiritual force and darkness which will be against those who follow the Eyes of the Light. Those who follow the Eyes of the Light will be the bearers of the Light of the Christ Being. They will be the ones you will choose to lead for Me as you have now seen that as you have lived your Truth in My Light all of your life you will be given a legion of Souls to lead into the War of the Light against the darkness in this future epoch I speak of now. I say to you now, live your Truth in the Light of Christ. Fulfil your dreams and your task now in this life time. Do this for Me, the Living Christ." [Verse 11]

Immediately after this a Pharisee, hearing this, said to Jesus, "You speak of a War between evil and good. Is this not the War to come between the white magicians and the black magicians? Is this not the ultimate War on this planet for the Soul of the earth as spiritual power is superior to any material power on earth? Is this not so, Master?"

Jesus then replied to him and said, "There is no white nor black magic that is really spiritual magic. There is a War between the Light and the darkness. This War is the one in your Soul now. What I spoke of and what is to come is of an age when man has evolved past this level of evolution in your world as it is now. However the Truth is that as you speak of this War, this way, this shows Me that you have not as yet seen the Truth. The reason darkness still has a hold of your vision and makes you feel guilty of not having been able to live your Truth in the Light is that you have not seen that the War is between the Christ Light and the darkness of the Anti – Christ. Truly this is the War now and forevermore till man evolves past his being into a Being of Light. Your being now wills to win this War. I tell you, you will come to earth to fight many wars in many life times as this is your incarnation pattern. When you come to this final War, the one I speak of, this is when you will enter a body with a Soul that seeks the Light of the Christ. I say to you, remember Me then and I will show you how to not fall under the spell of the magicians, white or black, but to disregard them and to use the Circle of the Christ Light that will surround the globe so that it will shine like a golden sun that has risen to spread its Light beyond the horizon of

time. Its Christ Cosmic Light power will burn away into the depths of darkness and the boundaries of its domain as willed by the Father to exist apart from Heaven for eternity. You will become part of this Light at this moment and hence you will pay your karmic debt for not seeing Me early enough in your life to walk with Me to the Light."

Once the Pharisee heard this he said, "I am guilty of the sin of unconsciousness and ask your forgiveness. I will meet you in this epoch to end all wars between Light and darkness. I will follow this man you have healed in this life to come. I pledge this as my will to you, Oh, Christ Being, Son of the Living God. This is my ultimate karmic wish to serve the Christ Cosmic Light." [Verse 12] [10]

---

[10] John 9: 35-41.

CHAPTER 10

"I, the Christ Being, say to you today that the Ultimate Light is available to all men good and evil when they make a choice to look to the Light. I say to you that he who cheats on life and tries to rob others of their proper evolution will lose his pathway. He who works for the purpose of furthering his own personality first in his whole life is obsessed with Negative Motivational Science. He wants to have a pathway which he does not have to take responsibility for. He wants others to take that responsibility but in turn he wants to steal their Light. So he who steals the Light will be forced to return at the end of the War with his karma. He will have to face the Hierarchies of the spiritual world and concede his Truth to them. If he chooses to follow the Hierarchies of the Light he will have another chance to change his pattern of life and to change his pathway so that it will ultimately lead to the Light.

However if he chooses to follow the hierarchies of darkness his pain will be nothing in intensity to a million piercing knives cutting human flesh as his whole being will burn into ashes and his Soul will suffocate with the smite of darkness. This will happen to him as the Spiritual Fire that has neither fuel nor material source for its energy comes out of the power of the Spirit of Heaven. God's Face is shielded from the darkness by this Spiritual Cosmic Fire. The man who falls to this fate becomes a dark being.

So those who truly follow an initiation to the Ultimate Light find the right Pathway to it as they live their Truth and take responsibility for their pathway. They do not try to force others to live their Truth. They win others over to the Light and its future which is to have Eyes of the Light that take you to the Doorway of the Light. This leads to the Christ Being. This leads to a person who becomes an initiand who leads mankind on his journey to evolve the Light. He will be the first to reach his evolution in his Body of Light as his body will have the Christ Light.
[Verse 1] [1]

When he comes to the Gateway of Heaven the Cosmic Light will let him enter the World of Light to

---

[1] John 10: 1-2.

come of which I have spoken. Initiands of the Light who travel from life to life and from body to body with their Souls upon the earth address their Cosmic karma and align it with the World Light karma. Because of this their pathway leads to the Ultimate Light; the Christ Light.

Their pathway others follow as it is a pathway that does not belong only to what is good for one year or one decade but to what is good for all centuries. Their pathway is marked by the personality which lives its Truth and knows the Truth of life. Every human being who follows the Christ Initiation will know how to create his or her pathway so that they will reach in each life time the ultimate Truth of how to love in the Light as when a man loves the Light the Christ Light is shining through his being.

So the Movement of Light that will create the Pathway to the initiands of the Christ Light will command the power over the Armies of God with the Angels of God against the foes of the Light in the War between the Christ warriors and Satan's magicians. So a person knows who he is when he knows how to live his Truth by walking in the Light of the Christ. He then knows how to follow the Son of Man in living his Truth and the Cosmic Christ Being in aligning his Light to the Ultimate Light of the Universe. [Verse 2] [2]

A false Prophet will prophesy that his pathway will lead to the Light but in his pathway he will not have any physical evidence that he has ever lived his Truth. He will live a lie. His science of the spirit will be tainted by half – lies and half – Truths. Those who hear him saying that he has a world system of knowledge that explains the origin of the cosmos and who man is with scientific certainty can only see the god of Intellectual Materialism speaking as such a Prophet of darkness and doom prophecies cataclysmic end without mention of God's Hand and His Spiritual Light prepared for that part of mankind that seeks union with His Being. He only speaks about the comets crashing down upon the surface of the earth and smashing civilisation into a hell – fire.

He does not see that the pathway of the Cosmic map

---

[2] John 10: 3-4,

has a direction which mankind needs to travel on with the Light of Christ and that he is the Guiding Light enlightening mankind to see its pathway to surpass material human evolution to the spiritual evolution to come." [Verse 3] [3]

When Jesus spoke in this way about the future of mankind and the Universal Doorway to the Light of Christ the Apostles did not know really how to respond to such a profound and complex mission that mankind was following unconsciously. Jesus was trying to make it conscious to their beings the way in which the earth would ultimately turn into a spiritual globe of Light preparing the Bodies of Light for the future World of Light to come. So when he saw this he asked them to open their Eyes of the Light and to see the Face of God. They saw a golden rose that was shining with such intense Light that it shone like the sun at its Cosmic sunrise at the beginning of time. Their Eyes of the Light could see that the Cosmic Christ then descended from this vision into the world around them to greet them. He said, "I have come to show you the Pathway to My Light and for you to walk with Me to My Father. This is the Ultimate Truth." [Verse 4] [4]

Then the Christ Being said to them, "I am the Universal Doorway to the Ultimate Light as I am He who created Light for mankind. I have come now to lead you to My Father in Heaven. I have come to show you that to reach the Golden Light of the Father you need to walk in the Pathway of Truth. You need to create a new mankind that in time to come will abolish Intellectual Materialism for God's Light and Negative Motivational Science for the Christ Light. This Light will create for you a Pathway that will lead you to spiritualise mankind with ultimate spiritual love. This is the way I now show mankind to love in the Universal Light.

I, the Christ, love you all as individual and as human kind. This is My Will to you; to offer My Cosmic Friendship and My Love for humanity. See it and you will touch Heaven in your heart as the Source of this Heaven is the Living Light of Christ.

I, the Christ Being, am the Spiritual, Cosmic Leader of

---

[3] John 10: 5,

[4] John 10: 6.

184

Mankind. No Prophet can surpass My Incarnation as I come but once to your planet to proclaim the Will of My Father in Heaven. Those who live their Truth and put Me above Negative Motivational Science in their lives will have a will to the Light. This will, will give them their Pathway to the Ultimate love of the Light. Those who align with the Light will put My Father above Intellectual Materialism in their lives and will have the Ultimate Truth as man in his development on earth needs to evolve out of these two levels of Intellectual Materialism and Negative Motivational Science so that he can love with a pure heart in the Light. When he can do this the redemption of his Soul will begin. When he does this he will begin to nourish his Soul with a pure heart as only then can the Light reach it and transform his personality so that when he speaks at the Doorway to the Light he can communicate with God. He can speak to the Light. He can see the Light.

Many will speak to the disguises of the Doorway to the Light and its shadows as they have not purified their hearts to let their Souls open up to God. They will simply unconsciously channel spiritual darkness. As My Father feeds the Soul with Light and I give Light to the heart so what is in the heart of man is what he will follow and what is in his Soul is what he will perceive. So with a pure heart and Soul a man has the vessel for redemption. With the Eyes of the Light he has its tools to speak at the Doorway to the Light of the Christ Being. This Doorway is the one I have shown you when I use the Special Keys of Light and when Heaven opens up as a vision to the initiands of the Light. [Verse 5] [5]

The leaders of men who sell Negative Motivational Science and Intellectual Materialism identify with the brain as the Soul and put the intellect above the Light. They see that the origin of man comes from a chemical composition of matter. They rationalise that spirit and matter are incomprehensible. Hence life is only comprehensible to them when no limit, like the concept of God, is put on their science of speculation about man's origin. To them truth is only relative and up to an opinion as intellectual reason is really what God is as God is

[5] John 10: 7-9.

185

in everyone and all men are God.

They do not want to show mankind anything that does not come from these formulae of reasoning. This protects their theory of knowledge which aligns with the physical needs of man. It however kills the Light in the Soul and disguises evil as a lack of Moral Will. Hence all who follow this pathway of knowledge speak not of the origin of mankind other than in these terms but cannot explain what is the cause of man and his world. They will speak about the effect of this cause logically, meaning they cannot say more than what happened at the beginning of existence other than with the eyes of the intellect. They will logically say that no one knows and no one will ever know as this was not meant to be known at our stage of evolution and development. So with this argument the logic is lost in the rationalising of the facts of existence.

However I, the Christ Being, say that everything comes from something. Ultimately that something has to be the cause; the Ultimate Source. This problem of not using the right tools to know what happened at the beginning of time is coming from this identification with Intellectual Materialism. It also comes from the problem of those who want to justify that Truth is relative. They do not want to live their Truth. They want to use Negative Motivational Science to get what they want in life above what they need. Hence they simply will not acknowledge that there is Ultimate Truth nor Ultimate Light as this would mean that the relativity of Truth would mean that this would make their perception of the world evolution relative. However those who follow the Ultimate Light that created this book, the **Cosmic Christ World Light Shield**, have a World System of Knowledge as they could not ever reach it perceptually unless the tools that they had to reach it were superior to the intellect.

Hence this tool is the Doorway to the Spiritual Light. Those who can use it will gain their Eyes of the Light to see what happened at the beginning of time. They will see that the real treasures of the Light of mankind are stolen by those who steal Light from their fellow man. They do this by not living their Truth. They do this by falsifying the Ultimate Truth. They do this when they live a lie and when they do not accept that a man needs to do what is right for him first as a person before he does what is right for his material well – being as when he puts the satisfaction of any one physical need above what he needs all round to be a human being first in his life he identifies with what he wants above the Truth. Yet no man is above the Truth nor the Light. Let a man walk in the Light and Heaven will be in his heart. Then he will find the treasures of Heaven are in his home and in those whom he loves in the Light. [Verse 6] [6]

I came to the world as the Ultimate Light of it. I am the Living Light and hold the superior knowledge of all the world and the worlds beyond this one as I am the Christ Being. I have come to create a Movement of Light upon this planet. This Movement will give the pathway to those who want mankind to evolve into the Living Cosmic Light so that mankind will be in itself a complete Body of Light globally and as individual beings and so that the earth will become a part of Heaven and its being will evolve into the Cosmic sunrise when God will join with mankind and matter will spiritualise into His Light.

I came to lead man into a new world where Light, love and Truth will rule it eternally. The pathway to it can only be walked by those who will journey with Me through the bridge between earth and Heaven from one life time to the next to where the Buddha Being lives in the spiritual world and to where I have been as human being on your earth before the Father entered My Soul with His Cosmic Light and gave Me His Light to transform the Son of Man into the Christ Being.

Buddha once again walked the face of the earth in the Being of Jesus. This Being reincarnated to once again experience the Light of My Father. I took his body and became the Christ Being when I was baptized by John. I did this as the Father willed this. My Will now is to live My Truth as the Buddha did but to add to this pathway the way of the Christ who is the Ultimate Leader of all men as he who follows Me cosmically becomes the Buddha in the Christ Being. As Gautama Buddha transcended all incarnations and hence left the planet in a Body of Light, so now will he who gains the

---

[6] John 10: 10.

Eyes of the Light gain Buddha's Light in his being which will give him the power to live his Truth and the power to walk in the Pathway of My Being; the Christ Being. He then becomes a person who can purify his Soul to enter the Doorway to the Light of Christ so that all the karma is transcended at the moment when the Light reaches his Soul. This is the moment that the initiand becomes a Christ initiand. This is the moment that man evolves again and again with each life time to prepare his Soul for the final union at the end of time of all cosmic worlds when the World of Light will be the home of mankind in the transformed planet of Christ Light where the Father will rule with the Holy Spirit and the Cosmic karma of mankind will come to its Cosmic end in the Light.

Hence I can die for mankind physically only because I will live forever in the spiritual world as I have lived in it before time was created by the Spiritual Hierarchies by the Will of My Father as I live in and out of it now when I am speaking to you as I am material and Spiritual. I am a supernatural Being of Light. I am the Ultimate Leader of Mankind as I have shown that I became a human being in the flesh. I have lived the Buddha Being's life form on your planet as Jesus. I have done this as I have loved mankind from the beginning as I love all beings that have been created by My Father. Yet no being in the universe have I loved as I have loved man as I have become a man; a human being.

So I say to you on My journey in the cosmos, be aware that mankind is the first of the beings I have chosen to lead into the Light. The Spiritual Hierarchies that I came to, I did not transform into flesh for but manifested into their world as their Living God. Know their world and you will know the next evolution of man to Spirit Being.

So I say to you, rise up all human beings and face your Cosmic Truth. Take up your destiny and will your Light to live forever among the stars in Heaven as the stars you see are but like grains of sand to the Heavenly stars that shine at the Court of God when His Glory is manifested before his Angels and Hierarchies of Light." [Verse 7] [7]

---

[7] John 10: 11.

The Christ Being then said to the people, "I have talked about the Truth of life. I have given Eyes of Light to My initiands. I have shown you and the world the Living Light of the World. I have physically healed the sick and given sight to the blind. I have walked among you and followed a Pathway that puts the Truth above all things, material and spiritual. I am the Living Light as I created the Cosmic dimensions of your planet's existence. I am the Son of the Living God. Darkness belongs to those who try to discredit My Being.

I say to you, why does a man say that he hates the Light and loves the darkness? He does this as he follows falsehood. Hence the serpents of evil are hissing and spitting their venom at Me through the mouths of those Pharisees who say that I am speaking with darkness. Yet I create Light and give it to all mankind as it is I who am the Living Light in the living flesh. I am the human Light of the World in a Cosmic Being. I am the Christ Being." [Verse 8] [8]

The Christ Being then surrounded himself with a Cosmic sheath of Light so that

the Pharisees who were stirring up the people against him could no longer see him. He then walked away from them into the other dimension so that he could speak to his initiands once again about their Pathway and his Mission.

Following this he suddenly appeared in the temple near the portico of Solomon. It was a grey winter day and was almost beginning to rain, as huge dark clouds were accumulating in the sky. Jesus was really personifying the mood of the situation with what was about to happen to him with the spiritual darkness approaching and its ultimate threat.

His Hierarchies of Angels created this Cosmic sheath so that the dark angels of Satan could only squirm at the Light when they came near his Being. He had come to change the world and to change the spiritual dimensions of its existence. His Mission was for the cosmological transformation of matter and spirit on earth and in the whole universe.

So his Archangel Michael used his Cosmic Sword to send the Flaming Fire of

[8] John 10: 12-21.

Heaven to spiritually burn beings that challenged the Being of Christ. His millions of Legions of Angels created a Circle of Light around Jesus wherever he went and opened it for his Being to enter the human realm at his will. He did this so that he would decide on the moment in Cosmic time when he would become part of human time. Hence he lived in both worlds simultaneously as the business of administering Heaven with his Father was part of his eternal, celestial existence. So when the opportunity in time presented itself, he would appear to preach the Cosmic Gospel of Light. Hence mankind had then its Pathway from his Word; the Pathway of the Word of Light.

The Christ Being came to the world to give man a choice to put his Being first and to give man a choice to choose the ultimate destiny to become a Body of Light [and had to do this on human dimensions]. Hence he became a human being and an historical being for mankind's sake so that mankind would be able to relate to him also in the material realm, meaning being able to see him there and identify him as the Ultimate human being [as this is where so many would be blocked by the darkness].

The Eyes of the Spiritual Light could not be opened until the vision of the Cosmic Christ could be seen by human beings as only the supreme initiands of the Light could find ultimately the Christ Being in their Souls. For most of the others it would take thousands of years to see his Cosmic Being as this Light can only reach the Soul when the Soul has evolved to it while this speaking of the historical Christ will be the beginning of the Initiation Process for mankind to see ultimately the Cosmic Christ.

Therefore what was about to happen was inevitable as the Pharisees saw him as a threat to their authority; a threat for the future of their power base with their Roman rulers. Hence when they saw Jesus on that day they wanted to find a way to discredit him publicly so that they could defame him and his character in some way as they knew he had special powers and really felt intimidated that they could only talk about healing miracles while this person could perform them and call them liars and hypocrites as the populace knew well that he had Special Keys of Light.

190

These were healing powers that far surpassed their temporary healing or treatments. This created great jealousy.

So with this evil intent they went up to Jesus and tried to trick him to say he was against the values of their religion; the religion of the chosen people of God and the religion that acknowledged the ultimate truth of mankind only through their interpretation. So interpretations of his identity were what they started with that day as there they could see he was vulnerable. To their minds he was a religious fanatic who had a messianic psychosis and they were saving the people from this imposter who was stopping them from living the lie they lived and demanding that they live their Truth.

Also they knew that when he talked about the world in that it was not living its Truth this is where they thought they could get Jesus to proclaim something against Rome. This would be ideal to arrest him for sedition and blasphemy and charge him with treason and devil – worship. This would give them back the power that they were losing to Jesus. The populace would forget him and they would resume their position of moral authority. [Verse 9]

So one legal advisor for the Pharisees said to Jesus, "Tell us truly who you are? You speak of being the Messiah but you hold us in suspense and never truly proclaim yourself the Teacher of the Light and the Spiritual King of the earth and that you have come to save mankind. Tell us truly that you are superior to any power on earth and any monarch. We look forward to you truly giving us a pathway to the truth that is above Rome and above our own religion. Surely you can say something that can clarify this for us!"

The Christ Being replied by saying, "I, the Christ Being, tell you that as you speak darkness pours out of your Soul as you do not ask Me who I am but you are telling Me by insinuating that I am lying to the whole world. You do not follow the Truth or the physical evidence of the Spiritual Keys of Light. You simply mock Me and the Truth I have given to you and to the whole world. Israel bows down before you and asks you to morally overthrow Rome but instead you are aligning with its power and dominance of the world. You have decided that material

191

power represented by the gold in the synagogues is above spiritual power and that Rome holds the reigns of this power on earth and that morality can be compromised for the good of the survival of the nation and the lifestyle that it supports financially for you. I tell you, you do not follow the Light. You are not living your Truth nor the Truth of Israel. If you were you would recognise that the King of the Light that I profess to be does not challenge Rome or its power on this earth nor does it challenge the religion of the Jews.

I tell you the truth lives only for you when you count the gold coins and come up with the number that will give the power you crave for. You pretend to be initiands of the Light but in Truth you are initiands of darkness as you love power and material gain. So all I have said here has been evidenced by the very patronising question that was asked by your legal advisors.

Look now into the darkness of your hearts and you will find no Light to speak from. Walk away from this darkness and embrace the Light I speak of and then you can redeem your beings or fall into the abyss of your delusions and be gone into the oblivion of doom.

I, the Christ Being, have come with the power of My Father in Heaven. He guides My thoughts and My Soul. I ever evolve on this planet with His Light and I speak with His Spirit. I ask you to see that when the Light comes to the Soul you can see it in your being, and in your heart of hearts the Light shines. Here is the beginning of the seed of the Light. Here the human being begins to face and relate to the Being of Christ as I am in all men who seek the Light. I am the Cosmic seed of Light in all beginnings in the universe. Hence those who walk in the Light create with My Father who created the world and all human beings. Those whom the Father has chosen speak the Truth of the Light and can see Me. Those who deny the Father deny Me as I am the Light. This Light now comes to this planet with the Cosmic force of the ages when it enters the initiands of the Light.

In thousands of years to come men will speak of these initiands as the first born of the Light of Christ. They will see that centuries of evolution and incarnations were necessary for mankind to see the Light. So to be an initiand is to be a human being who has a Cosmic future; a Cosmic power that sees the future of all ages.

So I say to you, the Father has chosen such initiands as they are the leaders of Light of mankind. I am a Teacher of the Light. I have come to claim the Cosmic birth – right of every living individual on this planet and every individual in all spheres and dimensions of existence. I have also come to set the boundary of Heaven and that of hell for mankind. I have done this so that mankind can learn how to worship the Light and ever evolve out of the darkness for all eternity as to have eternity is to have the Christ Light. To have eternity is to have eternal life. What sustains this eternal life is the Eternal Light of My Father in Heaven.

I hold this Light in My hand and with this Light I rule the universe so as to give it the life it needs to transform itself to reach Heaven. This is truly what Heaven is built on; the Light power that never ends and has no beginning and no end. This is the Light power that is measureless and is filled with the Spirit of eternity; the Spirit that rules the spiritual world and rules eternally in the Light.

This Spirit combines and unifies all the initiands of the Light in the universe of Light to come. They need neither air nor food to evolve their beings or their bodies as they have the Body of Light in their Spirits. They create from this body a Light power which transforms their beings into Light and changes all forms of energy fields on this planet and in the universe. The initiands have this Spirit in their Souls and with their Eyes of the Light they see the Christ and the Holy Father in Heaven. They see that I, the Christ Being, have created what the Father is creating in the universe. They see that in My hands is the power of the Father. They see that this Cosmic Light power can transform matter into spirit and spirit into matter. This is the Christ Truth of life. This is the Truth of the world. There is no greater power in the universe other than the power to create life and time in which to live it. This is the Cosmic power of the Father. No greater power exists in existence. No other power can change the pattern of the evolution of the planets in the universe or their cosmic worlds.

I say to you, this power ever

abstracts the darkness from the universe and puts it back to its hell development. It puts it back to its retrograding evolution as well as to its backward development of life and its regression of time. There is only one Pathway and that is the Pathway of the Christ Being. This Being of Light shows you that the origin of all things is the Father of the Light. His Being speaks to Me daily and gives Me Eternal Light."
[Verse 10] [9]

After the Christ Being said this there were some Jews who were prepared by the Roman soldiers and their collaborators, the Pharisees, to call for a riot to kill Jesus. One man said, "He has blasphemed and profaned the truth of the Jewish race. Kill him! The Devil is inside him!" This man took up a rock in his hand and threw it at Jesus and this missile was followed by another ten to twenty stones meant to stone Jesus to death. What happened then can only be described as truly amazing and bizarre for the people listening to the Christ speak. The stones disappeared as soon as they were thrown. The Christ Being kept on talking to the stone throwers and to the people around them. He said, "I have shown you the golden Pathway to the creation of the Body of Light. I have spoken to you of the eternal destiny for the Souls that leave their race to evolve into the race of Light. I have explained to you that in the future of mankind the evil will be seen not only by those of who have the Eyes of the Light but by the physical eye. The initiands of today will have this as a part of their physical makeup and Soul – being while you, who have wanted to murder Me, will not be able to see the Light. You will only defy My Being and My Father's Being and you will mistake the Light for darkness. Hence you are blind to your ultimate fate as is the evil one that commands you to destroy Me.

I ask you, what evil have I done to you for you to want to destroy he who has created your Soul, your body and your world? Tell Me what it is that the evil one has said so that I can show you that what you are doing is killing the life – force of the universe? Why do you want to kill Me? What is it that you do this for? Tell Me why your stones disappear for can you not see the Light

---

[9] John 10: 22-30.

194

comes to your world?"
[Verse 11] [10]

Then the leader of the stone – throwers said to Jesus, "You are not God. You are a man with black magic tricks. You are an evil magician. We want to kill you for this evil in your being. No man is above God. Blasphemy is punishable by death. You deserve death for your evil. All of what you do is based on these tricks so you deserve to die as darkness is coming to the Jewish race by your proclamation that you are a superior Soul. I hate a liar and I am doing God's work when I kill a criminal like you!"

The Christ Being replied, "I say to you, even you with the evil in your heart can be saved when you look to the Light and when you see that you are a being who has a mission on the earth to evolve his being and to recognise the Truth of life. I say to you, see with your own eyes as the stones you throw at Me turn into air. See with your own eyes the Truth of My Light power. Follow up the physical evidence and then your charge of black magic will be false as no man can do what I do unless one sees that it is above changing energy fields at a distance. It is changing actual matter into the spiritual substance that propels the life – force of the universe.

I say to you, this life – force of the universe is in My Body of Light. I am the living force of the universe. Killing My physical body will not change anything other than that you have followed the evil one. See the Truth of My Words. The Special Keys that I used to transform matter into the spiritual world healed your sick and cured your crippled. These Special Keys turned water into wine and took the dark spirits from the infected human beings who suffered a life time of agony. I have healed the body and the psyche and the spirit in all human beings who asked to be healed. They are the victims who now are healed. You are the perpetrators and I ask even you to follow the Truth before you fall into the pit of oblivion.

I ask you to face this Truth. I am not a black magician but the Ultimate Source of all Light and Truth on this planet. I am not only a magician of Light as this would say that I can make white magic but I am the Source of all the Light that the

---

[10] John 10: 31-32,

initiands of Light use to go to the Higher Worlds of creation. I am the being that has the Father's power in the palm of his hands.

I say to you, I am the Cosmic Body of Light that you see here before you. My Father, the Living God, is in this Body as His Being and My Being are one Light. This one Light is what created the miracle of the Special Keys of Light that are the powers of the Light that transform material substance into spiritual energy; into the spiritual world and back to the material world. I have come to be the Cosmic Christ in living flesh before you walking on the surface of your earth as a living person. I say to you, face your Truth and face the ultimate Truth of your being in My Being. Walk away from your evil and the evil one and see the Light. See Me; I, the Living Christ, Son of the Living God and Light of all Ages to come." [Verse 12] [11]

Following this the Christ Being's body physically disappeared. As the Roman soldiers rushed forward to arrest Jesus they discovered that he was not there anymore. The stones that were thrown at him were also nowhere to be seen. They frantically searched all over the area and looked at all in the crowd that had been listening to Jesus. They were simply astonished. Also all of his Apostles were part of this disappearing act for them. So they cursed Jesus and the Apostles with him.

The captain of the group of Roman soldiers said, "If this man is just a magician, why does he have the power to walk away from us as we use the power that rules the world? Who is this person? Who can control the physical world in such a way, transform his body and transport it at will to other locations? Surely this person is more than human! If he is supernatural in origin then what he is saying must be true." Then a Pharisee listening to him said to him, "You, a Roman soldier, have stopped looking at the obvious fact that this is a dark power that is overtaking your judgment of the fact. This man disappeared as he is a magician as we have told you."

The Roman then replied, "Your interpretation of the facts is false as you ever interpret this man, Jesus, and

---

[11] John 10: 33-38.

you refuse to interpret what happened again and again in so many situations where he used his power to do good for the people.

So I say to you: prejudiced is what you are! You are after him for your own reasons. They are not to do with the Truth but with your biased opinion of what suits your reasoning to get what you want for your head priest. Be aware that even in the Roman army, the greatest fighting force that the world has ever known, we know when we see the power of a god in a man."

The Pharisee then said, "I am not here to discuss with you your belief in any god of Rome. I am here to stop the evil god of this man, Jesus. I believe this was your job today to arrest Jesus and bring him to justice. So either you intend to do this or do I have to speak to your centurion?" The captain said nothing but he spoke directly from his Soul. A Light shone in him; a Light that he would later in life make into the Eyes of the Light. [Verse 13] [12]

Once the Christ Being transported all of his Apostles and himself out of this place he took his Being to where he met John the Baptist on the river Jordan. Here he decided to stay as he could see that for a certain time many would come to him to be healed as he would speak to the Souls of those who wanted to be healed before they would meet him physically. He let his Father make the choice as to the ones He wanted him to heal.

He also at one point sat on a rock and spoke to his Apostles and said, "John loved this place as here he saw the Light shine upon his personality and give his Soul life. This life now transports his Soul to the spirit world. Here it will create the Pathway to return many times to earth so that it can bring My Words and My Being to all the future Souls of mankind.

I am now here before you as even though John did not use miracles of Light to save the world as I am doing he used his Moral Will to the Light to find Me. He followed the course of the future Light to come to this earth. He became a Teacher of the Light so as to prepare the way for enlightenment of the Cosmic Christ. He spoke of the Spiritual Fire of Heaven descending upon mankind to purify it of the darkness

---

[12] John 10: 39.

coming to it from the fires of hell. I say to you he could see that I am here to complete what he spoke of in living reality. I say to you when I turned stone into air before and made our physical bodies disappear I showed you that I am the Son of the Living God."

Then a man came up to Jesus after he said this to his Apostles. He said to Jesus, "Master, you have let me listen to your words that were only meant for the initiands of your Light. I ask you to see that I know that as I loved John I loved the Light of this world which is you. I say to you, I will live my Truth. I will align my being to your Being, the Living Christ. I will not put wealth nor position above the Light. I will cherish my meeting with you for all eternity as I know that I will be with you, Lord, when the end comes and I will stand before you in my Body of Light." [Verse 14] [13]

---

[13] John 10: 40-41.

CHAPTER 11

In the town of Bethany there was a man who was a friend of the Christ Being. His name was Laz'arus. His sister's name was Mary. She had met Jesus for the first time when she had followed a pathway to darkness. Upon meeting Christ she, while in a group of people listening to him speak, had washed his feet to show her Moral Will to look to the Light. She had done this to demonstrate to the world that she had chosen the Master of all Light to guide her to her real destiny and to show her the way to walk away from a life that had put sexuality above the Light. After this ritual that she had performed to make this statement to everyone around Jesus the Christ had said to her, "I tell you as you have chosen to purify your heart My Light will burn away the karma that has locked you into this life of descending into matter. I now ask you to look at how you rise above matter and embrace the Spiritual Light of the world as now your Soul glows with the Eyes of the Light."
[Verse 1] [1]

Now Martha was Mary's sister who had witnessed the revelation of Light in her being that had come to her with Jesus. She had also received the Eyes of the Light from Jesus at the same time as she had come to the earth to fulfil her greatest desire which was to redeem her Soul by meeting the Christ. So they had sent a friend to tell Jesus that Laz'arus, a man who loved the Being, Jesus, and his Light, was truly dying; a man who was an initiand of the Christ Light who possessed the Eyes of the Light.

When Jesus heard about this he told the friend of the sisters, "I am coming soon to help Laz'arus but be sure that he will not die as the Father has not willed it as yet. When he dies he will do so, so that the Father can fulfil the destiny of this world in one human being who has the Body of Cosmic Light in living flesh as a person so that the initiation of this Cosmic Light can be made manifest to the whole of mankind from all epochs. I tell you Laz'arus will symbolise for all of mankind the living Light of all who die for My sake and who walk in the Light and discover that the Ultimate Light has its source in My Being. I say to you all, the initiands of the Spiritual Light throughout all

---

[1] John 11: 1-2.

ages looked to Heaven to do what Laz'arus is doing which is to experience death to find life and to be born again in the Light; the Christ Light. To do this a man first stops evolution in his world. He becomes immobile and listens to God. He meditates on the Light. He then begins to speak to God when he can see with his Eyes of the Light. Laz'arus will be put to sleep by My Father so that the Eyes of the Light of this world will be opened and mankind can see the Christ Light.

I say to you, tell Mary that she should trust and have faith in the Lord as He is the Creator of all life and when He takes away life He will restore it at the end of time. He will in the meantime ever restore it with each incarnation until all the darkness of the world is astralized into the cosmic worlds of hell. This is when the Body of Light will live eternally in My Father's House. This is when death will be forever abstracted from the passage of Souls to their final incarnation in Heaven.

I say to you, Laz'arus and the initiands of the Light who follow him will be there on that day to walk in the streets of Heaven with Me and to live forever in the Light that will burn with the beauty of a diamond as large as the star that gives Light to this planet. I tell you, My friend, go and tell Mary that I will come soon to help My friend upon his journey to the Eternal Light of My Father in Heaven."
[Verse 2] [2]

Jesus had healed and cured many illnesses and diseases. He had done this to demonstrate the love of the Father and his compassion for the suffering of mankind. He also had given a new Pathway to those who had become initiands of his Being. He showed his love for his initiands by giving them this superior Pathway which created a destiny that would prepare mankind for its ultimate spiritual goal. So when he stayed for two more days in the town not far from Bethany after he heard that Laz'arus was seriously ill he did this to delay the Cosmic Light of life in reaching him as this way he could show mankind that the Christ Being was above life or death.

Death was the doorway to the spiritual world physically and the Eyes of the Light were spiritually the Doorway to the spiritual world. The love of the

---

[2] John 11: 3-4.

Light created a Pathway to the Ultimate Truth but the love of the Light was above the Truth as the Truth can be known intellectually but the Light can only be known through the love of it in one's heart. Hence the heart filled with Light radiates the Truth to one's consciousness as the Cosmic Light of Christ is ever present in mankind's Soul and ever present in mankind's physical world. This is so as the oceans of the earth and the great land masses of the globe, in unison with the plants and trees of the planet with the sky with its atmosphere of air and gases, all depend on the breath of life of every human being as every human being belongs to the mother substance that created the earth spirit of which his home and its content is the living planet earth. This substance when it separated from the human being in the early stages of his evolution created his brother, the animal, as these beings could not wait to evolve out of this substance completely as complete human beings. They did not want to wait for the right time to incarnate as human beings. Hence their premature evolution which now has become retrograde on the earth.

This substance also originally created the first cosmic world that was the blueprint of the future earth. It created the very Spiritual Beings that evolved this cosmic world from spiritual form into material form. It also gave the power to Spiritual Hierarchies to have the free will to evolve the Will of the Father or to evolve the will opposing the Father. Hence you have the Spiritual Hierarchies of darkness that are also in a retrograde evolutionary process in the spiritual world. So this substance is the Christ Light as without it existence would be without energy that propels the evolution of the universe. So the Light is above the Truth as without the Father creating this Light that emanates from His Son, the Christ Being, life in an individual Soul would be impossible. Life as an individual Spiritual Being would also not exist. As well the life of the planets, the stars and the suns of the cosmos would have no evolution. So the Spirit of the universe is the God Light. [Verse 3]

This Light had left Laz'arus after two days as the Father willed that he should die in human terms to serve the

201

Mission of the Christ Being on earth. Yet at the same time he did not die in the spiritual sense as this would only have happened if the Christ Being had also chosen this to be. Hence the Christ Being decided after this time to go and see his friends and initiands of the Light. He also did this to make his choice known to the universe of where the Light of life would be directed in Laz'arus' destiny as a human being and as a Cosmic being. [Verse 4] [3]

The Christ Being then decided to go to Judea. His Apostles knew that this meant that once again they would be confronting the opposition to the Christ Pathway. They also knew that the Circle of Light that the Christ Being created around them had protected them physically and spiritually when the darkness of the soldiers and rioters tried to kill them after Jesus' speech. So they decided amongst themselves to ask Jesus what their pathway was now and whether they were going to confront the evil people who wanted to kill them again.

They were prepared to follow their Master as they knew that he was Master of the Universe.

His Word was the Word of the Light. It was what propelled the whole universe. So their fear of death was not the fear that was faced by a person going to the unknown in his last days. They were initiands of the Light. They had seen the spiritual world around Jesus. They had also seen the legions of Angels commanded by the Archangel Michael being directed by his Being. Also that beautiful Heavenly Light would shine right through him when he was more in the spiritual world than in the material world. So truly they were prepared to leave the earth if their Master had asked them to do so as he was the Messiah.

All the initiands of the whole world from the beginning of time from all cultures had followed Messiahs and spiritual leaders. They had done this in preparation to find the Ultimate Messiah; the Christ. All of the incarnations of the Apostles were with all other initiands of all past ages directed to this Messiah who was the Living God in the flesh as all spiritual initiation processes promised the experience of Light. Yet here was a person who had a Body of Light in the flesh. He had come to fulfil the dream and

---

[3] John 11: 5-6.

the task of every initiand who ever existed on the earth as he had come to change the world and to bring it this Light from his Being. Hence only through him could mankind connect with this Light which connected to the Father as he became a human being to create this connection spiritually, physically and to propel evolution in the right way with this Light.

This was the most important moment in all evolution in the cosmos when a Supreme Spiritual Being of the universe became a human being; a being that on the evolutionary scale in the universe was far below many other beings such as Beings like the Spiritual Hierarchies created by the Father. Yes, truly the Christ Apostles knew that their little group was going to change the history of the world. They knew this as they had the greatest power in all of the universe. This Light power emanated in the Personality of their leader, the Christ Being, Son of the Living God, Light of all Ages. [Verse 5] [4]

Then James, the Apostle, said to Jesus, "You know that we are all ready to die for you as we know that death is but a

doorway to the Heaven we have seen with our own eyes. We know that you love mankind and can see through its Soul its Light and darkness. So I ask you, why do you go to Judea again knowing that the evil one wants to have your Mission on earth ended with your death? Also tell us what is our mission now as truly your Will is our will now as we follow you as your Father in Heaven has chosen us to do the work for the Light? What is it you will us to do, Master of all Creation, Creator of the Heavenly Light of the World?"

The Christ Being then said to them, "There are twelve doorways to the Light of the consciousness of mankind. These correspond to the twelve hours in a day. They parallel the twelve months of the year. They also can be seen as parallels of the constellations in the Heavenly stars which can be seen through the eyes of the science of astrology. They are the Cosmic hours of the universe; these doorways. Your Doorway to the Eyes of the Light sees them as I have shown you that when you walk in the Light you walk in the daylight. When you walk in the spiritual darkness you

_____

[4] John 11: 7.

walk in the night, so to speak, and are prone to error as the eyes of darkness overtake one's Soul. Now I tell you a man must walk through all these twelve Cosmic conceptions that are mirrored in his Soul and in the Soul of the world. He must do this in every life time according to his Moral karma.

When the Father created man's first Soul he used the substance of Light to fashion its character. Its character as a being was given this power to see the Light in twelve dimensions of thought. Now thought can only exist when the Light creates perception in the Soul. This is given to the intellect to compute with a brain so as to make it comprehendible to the physical senses of the body. Hence you have the Logic of the Light which is based on cause and effect. Hence there is always a relationship between cause and effect if one follows the Science of the Logic of the Light. So the Father is the Cause of all Causes and the Effect is the Christ Being. The relationship is based between them with the Holy Spirit. Hence you have the basis of the Logic of the Light of the Trinity of My Soul. Now this also shows the pattern of the creation of the world. The Father created it. The Holy Spirit evolved it. The Christ Being now completes this evolution and its creation in his Mission to bring Light to it as a human and Cosmic Being.

Now each of the twelve doorways possesses this Logic of the Light and each possesses the logic of darkness. This other logic is based on Intellectual Materialism. It talks about the effect without the Cause of all Causes. It elevates the brain as the source of God and the intellect as the effect of His Being. It makes the relationship between the two to be Negative Motivational Science. Now by knowing this one knows the logic of darkness. I say to you, when a man studies the twelve doorways as you have studied with Me he becomes an initiand of the Light.

So I ask you to now walk in the Light of what I have shown you to be the Ultimate Truth of what lives in your Souls. The doorway that says to Me that I will be killed if I go to Judea is telling Me the facts as ascertained by physical reality. However as I now use the Spiritual powers of Spiritual reality I can walk in the daylight safely with you when we go on our journey soon James, My friend." [Verse 6] [5]

Then the Christ Being looked at them and continued talking by saying, "Laz'arus has fallen into spiritual sleep. His Soul is suspended into spiritual space. His Soul has asked Me to awaken his being from the threshold of physical death. To humankind he is dead. I have waited this long to go to My friend to awaken him from his spiritual sleep as My Father wanted Me to show His Ultimate Glory and power over physical death. This is truly now the purpose of our trip to Judea to use the Light to awaken the Soul of Laz'arus from his sleep."

Then Mark said to Jesus, "Laz'arus is dead as I can see him buried in a tomb with the Eyes of the Light in my Soul. I know that you have the power over life and death. I know that your Father created all Souls. You will go to him to awaken his Soul with the Light of your Father."

When the Christ Being told them about Laz'arus dying they assumed that they could see with their collective Eyes of the Light that he was in some kind of coma as they had

not as yet seen death with their Spiritual Eyes. Jesus knew this as he was their Supreme Spiritual Teacher and the Guiding Light of their Souls. He knew that the Eyes of the Light in their Souls were evolving to the point of aligning living their Truth with the Cosmic Christ Consciousness in their beings. This alignment is based on individual free will when an individual chooses to live his Truth aligned to the Christ Being when he puts the Light above life.

They had done this with their whole personalities in living their Truth in following him. However now their Souls had to align with their individual personality so that their psyche would become one with their Spirit. This would happen when they could see through a Cosmic Christ Consciousness the Special Keys of Light; the tools of Light that could transform matter into spirit and spirit into matter. The ultimate tool of Light was to create life out of death; to give Light to death and bring it back to life. Hence this was the Mission of the Light to create a group of people who would fulfil their Moral karma by following the Christ Being to represent the

---

[5] John 11: 8-10.

twelve doorways of mankind and to create a way with the Eyes of the Light to see the doorways between life and death and to know how to open the door and close it with the Keys of Light.

This was the special spiritual training of the Apostles by the Christ so that they could see how to align living their Truth to the consciousness of his Being. He did this by using the Special Keys of the Light as tools to train their Souls to change the consciousness of the whole world. This way the supreme example of the Living Light could be followed to create Light for mankind as an individual and as a Christian community with a Moral Will to live in the Truth of the evolution given; to live in the Truth of the life and death given.

Hence the Christ Being was about to use a Special Key of Light to show this Pathway of how Spiritual Cosmic Light would be used to change physical matter to preserve life and the well – being of one human being; Laz'arus. [Verse 7]

So Jesus said, "My initiands of the Light. Let Me make it clear to you that our friend is dead. Laz'arus has died. Yet I proclaim that his physical death will be temporary as My Will and the Will of My Father is that he should rise again and walk the face of this earth. I tell you this is to happen soon before the sun sets. This is My Will to the Ultimate Light.

I say to you, had I gone on this journey a couple of days ago Laz'arus would now live. He died so that the Light may be manifested upon the earth before all of mankind so that those who would believe that death is the end can open their eyes and see that it is only the beginning. Also this occurred so that I could use the Special Keys of Light to demonstrate the power of the Light to heal the Soul and the body and to see that this Light ever grows in the human body and the Soul Spirit bodies that give it life. The Keys of Light are energized when the human body lives its Truth in alignment to the Soul Cosmic Christ Consciousness.

I say to you, we will now witness this power of the Light when we meet Laz'arus in life once again when he comes out of his spiritual sleep. This is the purpose of our journey to see him walk once again amongst us, creating the love of the Light." [Verse 8] [6]

Then the Apostle, Thomas, said, "Lord you have shown us that all human beings are equal in the sight of God. You have also shown us that when we live our Truth in your sight we become whole human beings. We see though that the Cosmic identity of each person on earth is above his living his Truth. Hence simultaneously he needs to learn now to live his Cosmic Truth as a Cosmic being and human being. He does this when he puts the Light above the Truth of life. Hence I say to you and to all of my fellow men in this group that when we live our Cosmic Truth we can also die as Laz'arus did when the time comes for us to do this. This is the will of the Living Christ.

A person who puts another person above criticism and gives up his life thereby for the will of a leader and says that this is living his Truth is doing this under the delusion that this leader, for example, is the Living God. A person such as myself who puts the Living Son of God as his Master of life does not put him above criticism as a human

being or Cosmic Being as he is prepared to die, as Laz'arus did, by living his Truth with his illness if that is the Will of God. Hence I say to you, Oh, Christ, when you ask me to die for my Cosmic Truth I will do this as this is truly why I have come to earth to fulfil my Moral karma to your Light.

So I say to you all, let this group among all mankind die for the sake of the Ultimate Cosmic Light coming from Heaven in the Being of Christ. Let us do this not as those who put Intellectual Materialism first as their god and who justify any means to enter the spiritual world through Negative Motivational Science but to enter the spiritual world when we have achieved the evolution of our karma and its fulfillment in the Light. When we do this we walk in the Light of Heaven by letting our feet touch the earth as human beings who have the Truth in our hearts above what is in our heads. We love the Truth as it is the source of the Pathway that leads to the Cosmic Light of Christ and find physical death not above spiritual death as one can get a new body for a new incarnation but one can never get a new Soul as the Light of the Soul ever lives

---

[6] John 11: 11-15.

eternally. Its opposite is spiritual death. To live in one's Cosmic Truth as a human being living his Truth is the Pathway. This is the Light." [Verse 9] [7]

The Christ Being walked up to the place where Laz'arus lived and asked Martha, his sister, how he was so that he could see him. He had come purposefully late to help his friend as he was following the Spirit of His Father to act according to the Will of Heaven above that of the earth. He wanted to show mankind that what is decided in Heaven is above what is decided on earth. Hence he was confronting physical fate with the Spiritual Heavenly Power of His Cosmic Being. He was doing this by demonstrating the Special Spiritual Keys of Christ. He did this by living his Truth as a human being as it was aligned to the Moral Light of his Being. He wanted to show that he was Master of the evolution of the planet earth and that his Light could propel it to its ultimate transformation to Spiritual Cosmic Light to a world beyond time, space or physical existence; to a world where the sun shines eternally and the water has a ceaseless flow

into a land which has no decay but only ever creative abundance of eternal Heavenly peace.

So Jesus asked Martha, "Where is My friend, Laz'arus? How is he doing with his illness?" Martha replied, "Lord, your friend is dead. He died four days ago. Had you been here he would have lived. He asked for you but he accepted that your Light was with him eternally and said to tell you that his Eyes of the Light could see you coming to help him after his death. Such was his faith in you and his love of your Being."

Then Jesus looked at her and his eyes were filled with tears. He said to her, "Do you know why I delayed coming to help your brother?" She said to him, "Lord I know that you have come to help now as he said to me to trust in the Eyes of the Light that belong to me. I have also seen that you let Laz'arus die so as to show the power of the Light of the whole world as all generations to come will speak of this day when the Living Christ, Son of the Living God, chose to help his friend in life as well as in death. My brother will travel with his Soul to his ultimate

[7] John 11: 16.

destiny to become a Body of Light which is the Cosmic Body of Light, like the Christ Body of Light. I know that this destiny is for those who seek this Light and are willing to die many times for it so that the Soul may be purified and the Spirit will ultimately join the Christ Light in the City of Light at the end of time. This place I can see is the place you come from, Lord.

So I wait for the ultimate resurrection of the dead of all mankind to become a human being and Spirit Being in one Body of Light. Then this will be the completion of the journey of the mission of all human beings to fulfil the mission of this planet; to walk the streets of Heaven with the body created in the image of the Cosmic Christ."

Then the Christ Being told her, "You have seen with the Eyes of the Light the journey of Laz'arus, the human being, becoming a Cosmic Being of Light. I tell you now that Laz'arus has only been delayed on this journey by My Father in Heaven as he has shown mankind that his faith in the Cosmic Christ was above life. This faith is based on the experience of living his Truth with the Eyes of the Light as his guide to the Ultimate Truth of life. This

experience is the Doorway to the Living Christ, Son of the Living God.

The work Laz'arus is doing on his being is initiating him into not only seeing with the Eyes of the Light but also creating with them to take action to change his incarnation as a human being into one of a Being of Spiritual Light. He did this when he put the Light above the Truth in his life. He did this for this commitment to the Light. Yet he did this knowing that the physical death is not his spiritual death. Spiritual life comes from the Ultimate Source of his existence which is the Ultimate Spirit of the Universe; My Father in Heaven. Also with the Eyes of the Light he could see Me coming to help him after his death and helping him to live once again with the Spirit of life.

So I say to you Martha, My friend, your brother will awaken from his spiritual sleep and he will be given the Light to see with his eyes again the physical world made as a manifestation of the Light."

Martha replied, "Lord you are the Son of the Living God. You create life and you take it as you have the Will of the

Father in your Soul. You have come to the world and become a man in the flesh as a human being to show to all the universe of Spiritual Beings that you have chosen the human race for redemption. This redemption is based on the faith in your Being; the Living Christ. I say to you that I not only believe and know you are the Living Son of God but I can see also with my Eyes of the Light that I have an experience of your Light that nourishes my Soul and crowns my whole being with the Light of a Superior Being having a superior Pathway in the Pathway of all creatures in beings in the universe as the Christ Being has become a human being like myself. Hence this mystery of life and of the Light fills my Soul with happiness and real joy of being human with this Soul destiny to the Ultimate Light World to come. This is my mission in life and this was Laz'arus' dream of life. He now rests in the tomb and spiritually begins his journey to the ultimate resurrection of a human kind that looks to the Light of Christ."

Then the Christ Being said, "Martha, your love of the Light has revealed to you the Cosmic Christ and his Mission on your planet. Your Cosmic dignity shines through your human personality. I tell you today your brother will walk the face of the earth as a human being once again who can breathe the air of this earth. I tell you, use your Eyes of the Light and you will see the future of the Light of his being in you. I ask you, Martha, do you believe what I have said that Laz'arus will rise from the dead today as it is the Will of My Father in Heaven?"

Martha replied, "You are the Christ Being, Son of the Living God, Light of all Ages. Every age has a Prophet or a leader of the Light to lead it to the World of Heaven to come. Yet you are what all the leaders of the Light spoke of and dreamt of coming to the earth. They predicted your coming with the powers of divination and could see that the Eyes of the Light could only be opened for mankind when you would come to the earth. Those who were initiated into this secret of the universe knew that the Christ Being would incarnate as a human being. So as you can do this, Oh, Christ Being, means you can create life or take it away at will.

So, yes, I know that you gave life to this planet at the beginning of time and you will take it away to restore it in the new Universe of Light to come with those who have created their Body of Light with your being. This is the destiny of all men who choose the Light. So today you have chosen to stop evolution in one being. You did this so you can move it on again at the right time and so that the work on the world Spirit will bear fruit before the eyes of all beings in existence. This is truly the Truth that you have the power of God, the Father, in your hands. So, yes, you can do what you say as you are the Living Christ Being." [Verse 10] [8]

Then Martha left Jesus as she wanted to tell Mary, her sister, that the Christ had come to see them and also that he needed to talk to her about Laz'arus. She said to her, "Mary, he is here. He has come and has filled my heart with hope. I just know that he has come today to give Laz'arus and us a beautiful message of some kind. Come now and let us see what he has to say about our brother. I just feel that he has come to reconcile with us his delay in helping Laz'arus. I just feel this immense well – being after talking to him. It was like I could see the living sunlight in his eyes when I saw with my Eyes of the Light the miracle of this being in the flesh.

I could feel this Light in my heart when I asked him about his higher purpose in not so many words of why he waited to come to help Laz'arus. I just know in my being that he will today use the Special Keys of Christ somehow to resolve our deep sadness from Laz'arus' death last week. I know now that death is but a sleep to those who look to the Light. This sleep is a spiritual sleep for a human being.

The awakening to the Light is spiritual life. Laz'arus sleeps spiritually but not eternally. I can see that his Soul is still vibrant with the Christ Light for as initiands of the Christ Light we can see this Light flowing over the universe from Soul to Soul. We can see it travel in and out of the spiritual and material world. We can direct it as the Master has taught us towards living our Cosmic Truth. When this is aligned with our Truth we become beings with Eyes of the Light.

Our beings have to come above the Intellectual Materialism that computes the effects of our material lives. This process of our

---

[8] John 11: 17-27.

initiation can only be fully aligned to a Cosmic Christ consciousness when we have the power to take away Intellectual Materialism in all aspects of our personality so that that Light can shine through it into our lives and the life of our relationships. I see now as an initiand of the Christ Being I have gained my Truth by working on my being and my life and by following the pathway to put the Light above life. That is, to align this to first living my Truth as a human being and to then align it to my Cosmic Truth in all the Moral Steps I take in my life as they are shown to me from my Christ Moral Will.

I use the Christ Light force to take away the darkness that comes from my world which does not live its Truth; from a world crying out for redemption from its prison of Intellectual Materialism and its jailer, Negative Motivational Science, which says to get what you want by any means is above what you need as a human being. This prison is housed in the illusion that the cause of all causes of the human race has no meaning. The delusion is that therefore real truth exists only in the perfection of the intellectual process in the mind of a person. However real truth exists in using this intellectual process to fathom the material world and to put it in its rightful place. It is to accept that material truth is based on information truth, meaning what one can see, feel and touch. This reality is certain. However aligned to this is the spiritual reality of a world which can also be seen, felt and touched yet one that can only be known through the experience of the Light as a human being living one's Truth.

No one can truly change his pattern of life without this experience as everyone's pattern of life has its blueprint in the many past lives imprinted in the Soul pattern. This makeup in the Soul predetermines a man's material truth and spiritual perceptions. Then the first step for his initiation is when he faces his Truth and begins to live it. Once he accomplishes this he relates to the material truth of his life as a human being. He identifies as a person first in his life. Then when he has accomplished this he goes one step further in his initiation and he meets the Christ Being in his Soul, meaning he identifies first with following his Truth as it is aligned to the Christ Being, Son of the Living God.

He then becomes an initiand of the Christ Being. He can only do this when higher knowledge bridges the transformation of personality and spirit from the level of psychologically identifying as a human being to identifying spiritually as a Cosmic being. Then he has come to the point of passing knowledge truth to the experience of the Truth of his life as it is aligned to the Ultimate Truth of life and of the universe. I say to you, Mary, our Master is the Cosmic Christ and he will today make the living Light visible to man's eyes. This is the Spirit that is clairvoyantly speaking to the Eyes of the Light within me." [Verse 11] [9]

Then Mary got up and left all the people around her who were trying to hold back tears as she was crying. She went to meet Jesus and some of the people came to the conclusion that she was going to go to the tomb as she had become very depressed. She truly loved her brother. She was very often overwhelmed with emotion. She could not believe that Jesus waited for so long to come when she had sent word to him about Laz'arus and his critical condition. She was beginning to doubt herself and she did not want to use the Eyes of the Light in her being and had let her sister Martha use them for her as she did not trust her access to them with her very emotionally unstable moods which had occurred ever since Laz'arus was buried.

She broke down when she saw his body wrapped up in the white garments of the dead. When she could no longer see his face and when it was covered with the white wrapping material she became hysterical and had to be carried home. When she got home she had actually passed out for the whole day so the people coming to give her their condolences were all assuming that she would never get over the death and were sure she was going to the tomb to grieve out the terrible pain in her heart.

Then all of a sudden everyone could see Jesus walk up to Mary. Mary looked at the Christ Being and fell to her knees and said with tears running down her cheeks, "Lord, you are the Light of all the World. You love my brother as much as I love him. You did not come to help him when you could have. I know you love all of mankind. I know you have come to the

[9] John 11: 28-29.

213

world to save it from darkness. I know that you love me too and all that look to the Light of your Father. I ask you, why did you not come to help my brother? I know I have no right to question the Living Son of God but I truly loved Laz'arus. He was my 'Light' and he and I had one heart. He said to me just before he died, 'Tell my Master that I love him more than life itself as his Light has given me the Eyes of the Light. Tell him that when I use them I can see his Being and his Being is beautiful.' Then he closed his eyes for eternity. He loved you! He loved your Light! Why? Why then did he have to die?" [Verse 12]

Jesus then began to look into her eyes to comfort her and to speak to her Soul. The Eyes of the Light in her being began to speak to her Soul. The Eyes of the Light in her being began to speak to her being and to show her the Light in the tomb where Laz'arus was buried. His eyes began to shine but his face was somber. It was as though he could feel all her pain and the pain of all the people around her. He was taking away all of this pain and drawing it into his Spirit with the Cosmic Light of his being.

Then the Christ said, "Take Me to the tomb of My friend Laz'arus." As Jesus walked to the tomb with Mary and Martha who had joined the rest of the people to walk to it he began to cry out loud. His eyes were filled with overflowing tears. He was crying and the sounds that were coming from his mouth were heart – wrenching. They were truly the sounds of sadness speaking to anyone who was there looking on to what was happening to Jesus.

Then a man said to his neighbor. "You see he cries now but surely he could have done something to save his friend had he come earlier. He must truly regret his delay in coming to see Laz'arus." Then another man said in the group, "I saw this man give the eyesight back to a blind man who was blind from birth. He could have saved Laz'arus had he come early enough but that is the way. We always miss the opportunity when we become overconfident with anything. Obviously Jesus fits this category." [Verse 13] [10]

As the Christ could see that crying was a human way he let himself be human but his Spiritual Self was beginning

---

[10] John 11: 30-32,

to feel this sadness about Laz'arus. It was as if he was beginning to feel all the sadness of Mary and Martha and all her friends. His Spirit was sending the Flaming Light of Heaven to the darkness that was appearing around his Soul from the Spiritual Hierarchies of darkness as this was how he was beginning to evaporate this darkness through his Spiritual Light.

The Christ Being began to weep as his heart was broken from the knowledge that his friend was dead. He began to cry with such real emotion. He was almost overwhelmed by the emotion of death as he could see that he would have to pass this doorway to death in the future as no other Spiritual Being had ever experienced this end of life. He was soon to see it and experience it. Yet he knew he had come to the earth to win eternal life for mankind. He knew every death brought new life in the spiritual world. His life was to prepare mankind for this supreme act in evolution when he would become totally human. As a Cosmic Being living his Truth he was confronting the future with his Spirit Being. He could look at two worlds at once; the spiritual and the material. He knew that

sadness and sorrow were interwoven with the experience of death. He also could feel the pain of Martha and Mary. He could feel that pain spiritually of the coming events that would change the history of both mankind and of all the spiritual world and Spiritual Beings as he had come to save mankind from the power of the evil one.

His hand was stopping the beings of darkness from blocking the light of the stars from reaching earth as before Christ had come mankind could only see the reflection of his Light. A small part of mankind could only see the reflection of his Light. A small part of mankind did this with their initiation practices of the Light in all occult schools all over the earth from the beginning of the consciousness of the Cosmic Christ Being. This consciousness they could only see as the higher consciousness of God through their own spiritual practices. [Verse 14]

So the Christ Being had chosen Laz'arus as an initiand of the Christ Light, the Supreme Light, and hence the supreme initiation in the human world. He had chosen him to show the world life and death are decided by the

Supreme Spiritual Father in Heaven and that free will to live and to die belongs to the Soul as well as to the physical being. This free will asks for the Light to come to the Soul or its opposite. The ultimate ends of these result in birth and death. In between both a person lives spiritually in the shadow or the Light of his Soul place suspended between death and birth. Laz'arus had chosen to die for the Light. The Christ Being let this happen to him as it was the Will of the Father for the Christ Being to demonstrate the Christ Initiation Pathway to mankind. [Verse 15] [11]

At the tomb Jesus could see that the entrance to the cave – like grave was blocked by a huge stone the size of two men. Then the Christ Being said, "Let us take away this stone so that I can see My friend again as I need to wake him up from his spiritual sleep." Martha suddenly looked horrified and said, "Lord he has been dead for long enough for a terrible stench to be coming from his body. It would be very unhealthy for anyone to go into the tomb." Mary then looked at Martha and said, "Let the Master see with his own eyes that Laz'arus is dead."

Then the Christ Being asked them, "I ask you now, Martha and Mary, to create a Circle of Light around your Souls and to then let the Flaming Light of Heaven burn away the spiritual darkness outside this Circle of Light. Then I ask you to will the Light of the Cosmic Christ Being to be sent by the Christ Being to the darkness that stops Laz'arus from listening to life and makes him live only in spiritual sleep.

I ask you to call upon the Archangel Michael to use his Cosmic Sword of Light to send the Spiritual Fire of Heaven to the gates of death that they may close for Laz'arus as the Father has willed this fate.

I ask you to remember My Words which are to those who love Me above all things and above life itself. To he or she I will give the power of the Kingdoms of Heaven over the kingdom of hell. So I say to you, see with your own Eyes of Light the Kingdom of God in the Son of the Living God, the Christ Being."

Then the large stone was

---

[11] John 11: 33-37.

removed and at that moment a radiant Light shone around the Christ Being. Martha and Mary could see this Light which surrounded them like a Circle of Fire although the glow of this Fire was like a brilliant flame and not like a burning type fire.

Then next to Jesus appeared two Mighty - looking Angels with massive multi - layered feathered type wings. They also shone like Beings coming from a white sunlight as their whole aura was so magnificent that no monarch could dazzle their presence by comparison. In each Archangel's hand there was a silver Sword that was the size of King Arthur's Excalibur which was encrusted with gold and diamonds. Each Sword had a blade that emitted a blue - yellow Fire.

From the palms of the Christ Being Light beams began to emit towards where Laz'arus lay wrapped up in his burial linen which bound his whole body from his forehead to the end of his feet. Then the Fire from the Cosmic Swords of the Archangelic Spiritual Beings interlocked with the Light beams coming from the Christ's hands and at this moment the Christ Being spoke and said, "Father in Heaven, I ask You to send Your Love to Laz'arus, My friend. He is a friend of the Light. I ask You to look down upon Your Son whom You love and to send to him the power of the Holy Spirit so that he can open the Spiritual Eyes of his initiand, Laz'arus. The spiritual sleep he is in now will now be removed by the Hand of the Living God so that the Light may enter his Soul and his physical body and that he may once again walk the earth until it is time for him to walk through the spirit of life to the spirit of death.

I ask You, Oh, Father, to let him live his Truth on earth and to let him align this Truth now to his Cosmic Truth in Heaven and that he may be allowed to begin his journey to the ultimate destiny of the seventh cosmic world when the last incarnation will come and he will have his Christ Body of Light. I do this now to ask You to do this for Me, Heavenly Father, as I know that You would do it without My asking but I do it to show mankind that it is at the threshold of its journey to the Ultimate Spiritual home which is the World of Light to come.

To complete My Mission for the whole cosmos is to redeem mankind from darkness and to first redeem Laz'arus from spiritual death to spiritual life. Hence he now lives for the Light as he has Eyes of the Light that now can see and speak to the Spiritual Christ Being and his Angels. This is what I ask of You, Oh, Father in Heaven: to give Light to Laz'arus, to burn away the spirits of darkness that want his Soul and to give him the first step to walk in the Light of the Christ Being, Light of all Ages." [Verse 16] [12]

Then the Christ Being spoke so that all could hear him and the Eyes of the Light of the sisters of Laz'arus heard a voice of thunder shake their very Souls. Also they could see that the Angelic Beings had pointed their Swords towards the tomb and had used the interlocking beam of Light to fill the whole cave with a Fire beam that was piercing the wrapping of cloth around Laz'arus' body.

The words spoken then by the Christ Being were, "Arise Laz'arus. Awake from the dead. Walk once again upon the face of the earth. Awake from your spiritual sleep and let your body once again breathe the air of the earth. Let your Soul speak to your mind and let your heart know it is alive. This is the Will of My Father in Heaven; the Living God. This Creator is God, the Father."

Then Laz'arus got up from his position in his tomb as he had been placed on a slab of rock. He could not walk without a real struggle to take off the linen cloth wrapped around his whole body. He was frantically making movements with his limbs which were bandaged in a mummy – like fashion. Yet he managed to come to the doorway of the tomb. Then the Christ said, "Unwrap the bandages as he needs to breathe. Let his eyes see the daylight and let his Soul breathe the spiritual breath of spiritual life as he has awoken from the dead and from spiritual sleep."
[Verse 17] [13]

At this moment Laz'arus became a living human being once again. He opened his eyes and could see his friend, Jesus. He embraced his two sisters who were overcome with emotion as they began to cry and to kiss his face as they were holding onto him physically. Then the Christ Being disappeared into the spiritual world again. The people around him could not see him anymore except that they felt that the tomb now

---

[12] John 11: 38-42,

[13] John 11: 43.

had a perfumed – like fragrance. It was as if the flowers that were near the tomb suddenly blossomed as no one could account for the pleasant smell and everyone knew that a Godlike man had been next to them as Laz'arus was living proof that the Christ Being could resurrect the dead and that his powers went beyond life and he could create magical Light.

Although the people with Mary and Martha could not see the Light Circle they could feel its comforting rays in their Souls and body. They knew that Heaven that day had visited their world intuitively while the Apostles with Jesus could see concretely the encounter with the power of the Special Keys of Christ and how they opened Heaven's Gates to those who had the Eyes of the Light through which to see them. So from here some of the Apostles such as Peter saw how the Christ entered the spiritual world from the physical world and how his Angels changed the future through the Special Key of Christ. [Verse 18] [14]

Now at the same time that this occurred there were among the Jews those who had

contact with the eyes of darkness. They could see the Redeemer of Mankind was going to discredit them as they followed the Prince of darkness. They could see that all those present apart from them would become initiands of the Christ Being. The spiritual Lord of darkness was beginning to tell them to go in the direction of the clique in the Pharisees that wanted to destroy Jesus and to warn them that only the death of Jesus would ensure their power base with the Romans. He was telling them to also rationalise that without insuring this power base the Romans would ultimately inform Caesar of a man who was proclaiming that he was the Living God and superior to the power of any emperor. Then he would send his armies and legions to destroy the state of Israel.

Therefore the informers were really patriots of the fatherland when they discredited Jesus by any means and that he was undisputedly a great magician who could raise the dead to life yet this did not put him above the fact that he was becoming a national security risk. This was the mathematically, politically

[14] John 11: 44.

right equation that was totally identified with when the dark spirit sold these false perceptions to their Souls.

So the Pharisees who were planning to kill Jesus and were some of the same people who had witnessed the Laz'arus miracle, met in their temple chambers. One high priest began to outline his view as to the case of Jesus in relation to recent events. He said, "Jesus is becoming a political and religious symbol for the whole nation. He is unstoppable politically. His moral power will increase into a messianic authoritarianism. He will become a threat to us and to our leadership from the holy temples of God. Then once he has been anointed he will surely anger the Romans with his talk of his Godhood and they will cut us off first financially and then politically. This will result in annexation of the people of Israel to the status of becoming a slave state. This Jesus is a dangerous man."

Then Ca'iaphas stood up and began to access his spirit guide as he was a psychic seer. He was channeling his spirit with the intention of speaking from God. However Ca'iaphas did not live his Truth but the truth of a priest who spoke with the dark spirit in his being which entered him at first unconsciously and then consciously. Then he said "I can see, by using the eyes of the Prophets of Israel, the past Prophets of Israel while channeling their spirits and they say that they want Jesus to die so that all the nation can be saved from the ending of one life."

When Ca'iaphas was prophesying that Christ would die that year he was doing this by the power of the Lord of darkness as he was coming through his channeling without Ca'iaphas being conscious of whom he was channeling. The reason for this was that he had tried earlier to gain the Eyes of the Light to see the Supreme Being of the Universe but as he did not follow the Truth of his conscience, but followed his will to power guided by the dark spirits, he was tricked to follow the false perception that it was morally right to kill Jesus as to let him live would cause a catastrophe for the Jewish people as only by following the Roman world and Intellectual Materialism could the Pharisees pursue their objective which was to win over Rome ultimately by creating an alliance with Rome militarily and politically.

This was also to be done using the Negative Motivational Science of the Roman army. To fight to win the independence of Israel was only going to work successfully if the Roman way was adopted cosmetically, morally speaking. This meant putting this objective first which was to win above the problem of whether it was right as this was a moral question which had to be neutralised, otherwise as a point in case a man like Jesus could be putting spiritual development above the realistic goals of the nation. He was expendable as he was a fanatic of truth who would never fit into any society that functioned successfully in the Roman world.

Hence the best way to win out of the problem of Jesus was to sacrifice him as a rebel and to kill him as he did not follow the good of Israel but his own ends which were power over the people through spiritual magic. His vision was of an unrealistic world that would bring disaster once the Roman hierarchy in Rome discovered that he was declaring himself the Living God. Only by stopping this rebel could the nation of Israel be saved from this real threat of extinction by the greatest military force in the whole world and in known human history. It was justifiable to kill such a terrorist who was destabilising the very foundations of Phariseeism. His occult practices invoking black magic were of the Devil. That this was so could be proven from his proclamation that his kingdom was eternal and would outlast the Roman empire. So it was obvious he wanted to become the Caesar of the Jewish race. This would never be accepted by the Romans and would only incur outright confrontation ultimately unless action was taken and this man was dealt with as soon as possible for the good of all Jewish citizens.

Future generations would thank the leaders of Israel for seizing the historical hour to change history and to align it on the pathway of making spiritual development compatible with political and economic realities which meant the proclamation of a God above Caesar and a movement based on a fanatical religious cult would result in political suicide for the ruling class of Israel. This meant that the ruling class of Israel was protecting every Jew morally and physically by killing Jesus. This was the false logic used to support the evil intentions of the Pharisees.

They often spoke of the evil in their hearts and minds as being in the personality of Jesus as the Prince of darkness had made them blind to their rationalistically economic conclusions which supported their political objectives to win power at any cost as the alternative was to become a slave of Rome and to be bankrupted financially. It was to give up all power materially.

This was the total lie that the Prince of evil was able to speak to their Souls about as this being was truly the most dangerous when he spoke of cosmic lies of his existence. He sold the lie about the Light. That is, that this is a fantasy that exists in religious fools like him who craved the power of the legitimate spiritual and political leaders endorsed by the lineage of history, race and professional training. Yes, this unprecedented upstart called Jesus was but another cult leader looking for power by recruiting the masses to follow him into oblivion. Hence there was only one way to stop him and that was to eliminate him legally by the power of the state as it stood held up by Rome and its power which was represented in the form of its garrisons which were at the disposal of the Pharisees to enforce order.

So this was the will of the people as seen by the leaders of the people. This was the will of the hierarchy of the Jewish race that identified with Intellectual Materialism which had its basis in verifying the Holy Scriptures only from the interpretation of the Pharisees as to what they wanted the people to believe and accept at all costs.

Hence their Negative Motivational Science was based on their identification with the Roman power that stopped at nothing to get control of the nations of the world militarily and then spiritually. They did this by first invading the country and then ruling it through the priests and political collaborators who may or may not have been the previous ruling class. This depended on the situation at the time and the history of the country concerned. For example with Israel the Pharisees were the ruling class and the ones that were willing to collaborate to keep control of the morale of the masses and report on any potential uprisings so that the Roman army could eradicate any opposition before it had any real effect or power to move the will of the people.

So that is the moral code that the Pharisees used to justify their endorsement of planning to murder the Christ Being. This justification was created in their spirits by the supreme spiritual Prince of darkness so the Light was challenged by the darkness of evil by the thoughts of evil as they streamed from the dragon that lives in the kingdom of cosmic hell. [Verse 19] [15]

The Christ Being knew quite well because of his Cosmic vision the evil thoughts of the Pharisees. He also knew that they were plotting to kill him. He accepted his fate but at the same time had to fulfil a Cosmic and human Truth. So he decided to go to the town of E'phraim so as to not be in the limelight for a little while as he was instructing his Apostles how to become initiated into the Eyes of the Light. His occult Cosmic vision transfigured his whole Being into a Being who spoke the magic words of Universal Light. His words penetrated the Souls of the Apostles so that their eyes could see Heaven on earth surrounding this Being when he spoke. With his words Angels appeared and magnificent manifestations of brilliant celestial Light emanated from his body.

His magic words created pictures of worlds where Beings that created the universe lived and evolved. The Christ Being showed his Apostles the majesty of the Throne of God, his Father. He also showed them how the Spiritual Hierarchies worked on evolving the cosmic worlds that were the previous incarnations of the earth. He also showed them the cosmic worlds to come and how mankind was created by the Spiritual Hierarchies of Light from the time that his Being was Spirit to the time that his body was part of the earth with the earth being his mother to the time that man had a body to become a son of a body of a woman.

He showed them that he was the Son of all men, meaning that he was the one individual human Cosmic Being of the whole universe of all Beings and all human beings. Hence he was the Christ Being. This he showed and taught his Apostles in secret. Hence his dropping out of the public for a while served his purpose to give time for his initiands to evolve their Spiritual Light

---

[15] John 11: 45-53.

powers and to create their individual spirit bodies in the Spiritual Worlds of Light. [Verse 20] [16]

The Passover of the Jews was celebrated at this time. The purpose of this religious celebration was for the individual Jew to ask God to purify his Soul and to clear his conscience as well as to prepare his being for the religious event which signified his faith in the God of Israel. The main celebration was held in the city of Jerusalem.

Many of the Jews were really wondering in anticipation if Jesus would appear on this most important of events in the society of their race as they knew that if he did he would be risking arrest as the Pharisees had sent word to all their informants and collaborators to report any sightings of Jesus. They were offering secretly a reward of thirty pieces of silver for anyone who actually lead them to the capture of Jesus. So there was a lot of suspense among the Jews who had been listening to Jesus for the last couple of years and had seen his miraculous cure of so many people.

They knew Jesus was not afraid of being arrested. They also knew that this had never happened as Jesus always knew how to disappear before any attempt was ever made to arrest him. This was without a doubt true to anyone who had lived then who followed his sermons or heard him speak his words of love and Truth filled with the Light coming from a world beyond time or material existence.

All knew that Jesus had Cosmic magical powers. So they also knew more or less consciously and unconsciously that there was a contest going on between two sides. One side, they knew, upheld the status quo of the conservative rules of belief in God. The other did not speak of rules but spoke of he being a Cosmic Being that was the Son of the Living God. So truly the excitement of the people at the Passover was unparalleled to any other past religious festival.

The rumour was that Jesus would appear but he would once again outshine and outsmart his enemies as the populace was made up of those people who also followed a rebellious will to

---

[16] John 11: 54.

the hypocrisy of the Pharisees as many could see that they spoke beautifully about the Moral Will which they never lived or related to other than in their speeches about Israel. They could see that their political science was identified with Intellectual Materialism and it was motivated by the will to get power through the Negative Motivational Theological Science. This was done very cleverly to constantly invoke the danger of Rome's retaliation unless the ego of the masses was subordinated to the rules of its power base; this being its Spiritual Materialism that black – mailed the average man into forsaking his own conscience of what the Christ Being spoke of with his Philosophy of the supreme love of mankind for the politics of fear.

This way the Pharisees would say simply that to be practical a person had to face the Truth of Israel above the Moral Truth of the individual as to put the individual above the

security of a nation was selfish and dangerous considering the threat of Rome over such a poor and small nation economically and militarily by the then current world standards.

Hence you had a real conflict of conscience in many who began to love Jesus as when he spoke the Light came to their hearts. They knew that the Pharisees were putting the intellect above the Light of Jesus. They knew that the Truth was above the Pharisees but the politics of fear made them feel cowardly about what to do if Jesus appeared as after all how can you fight the Roman army and their appointed leaders of a nation with goodwill alone?

So this was the state of the people's mood when the Christ Being was deciding to speak at the Passover in Jerusalem. This was the time that Jesus Christ was going to unveil his Light to the world knowing that it would, by outshining the darkness, create the challenge to the Light. [Verse 21] [17]

---

[17] John 11: 55-57.

CHAPTER 12

The Christ Being went to Bethany to the house of his friends, Laz'arus and Martha, a week before the beginning of the Passover. He was sitting down with them in their house having a midday lunch.

Then Mary came to him and wanted to wipe his feet with a special ointment. She did this to honor his presence and to relax his feet from his journey. After wiping his feet there was a fragrance that filled the area around the table where Jesus was sitting. One could say it was that of the ointment but it was as if a thousand flowers were blooming in the garden around the table that was visible from the archways and windows of the house. The Angels of God had directed Mary to do this for the Master. Then they had made the flowers bloom with the fragrance of fresh roses. They did this so that it would appear that it was the ointment that had caused this aura of perfumed air. Martha said, "My, what a beautiful smell this ointment is making." Mary looked at her approvingly on hearing her statement. Then Jesus said, "When the Angels speak the roses of the world bloom so as to let the fragrance of Light speak to man's senses."
[Verse 1] [1]

The darkness then challenged the Light in the Soul of Judas the Iscariot. Judas had worked with Jesus on the Pathway to the Initiation through the Doorways to the spiritual world. He had learned the discipline of the Spirit so that his Eyes of the Light could see the Cosmic Master of the world.

In one of the initiation processes Jesus had looked at Judas and asked him, "Judas, how much is it worth to a man if he knows how to live his Truth in this world now?" Judas had replied instantly, "A man who forsakes all for the Truth of life will be rewarded by his Heavenly Father with eternal life." Then Jesus said, "Do you live your Truth for this reason?" Judas then saw that he would have to truly reveal his doubt in the Light so he said ambiguously, "I live my Truth as this is the Truth of all human beings who know that the Christ has come to the world."

The Christ Being then said, "If a man lives his Truth to enter the Kingdom of Heaven he has

---

[1] John 12: 1-3.

already lost his Truth as the Truth is only found when a person speaks first the Truth. Hence the Ultimate Truth can only be found if a person forsakes all for the Light and puts the Light above life and his Truth. This he can only do when he has won the challenge of darkness to his Soul. This he can only do when his Eyes of the Light see that the karma of the world can only be fulfilled when a person fulfils his karma first in each and every individual life he has on earth regardless of a deal he would make with God that he will live his Truth so that he will get a passport to Heaven. So to live out of the Cosmic moment as a human being a person lives his Truth in the Light. A man trusts in what he sees with the Eyes of the Light; the Christ Being."

So Judas who would one day betray his own Soul to the dark ruler of Cosmic spirit upon the earth said, once he saw what Mary had done, "What is this? I thought expensive things and comforts for all of us were being forsaken as an example for the poor and for those who have nothing."

Then the Christ said, "The rich or the poor cannot save the world unless they have first saved themselves from

willing their power over it. It belongs to the Father. He who makes it his, will lose it. He who uses it for My Father's sake will gain its Spirit in his Cosmic breath as the earth breathes in and out in the freedom of Cosmic space ever evolving into its Cosmic destiny. When a human being breathes with it he becomes a part of its mission to the Light. When he breathes against it he wants to possess it and control its forces for himself first.

A man who wants to evolve beyond the stars and become master of his universal destiny, at the cost of his Soul mission to the Ultimate Cosmic City of Light, will be the man who loves his money first in his life. This is a man who puts his financial will above his Truth. He has sold his Soul to buy Cosmic time from the Devil as he sells the vision of ultimate development and intellectual material evolution to those who buy the illusion that the force of darkness will win the Cosmic future of earth. He instils doubt so as to blind all human beings from the knowledge of their task on earth. This task is to live one's Truth first and to accept that this is even above having the Eyes of the Light as one can be initiated into the Light and then see that when he lives his Truth he will not only have the power to see Heaven but he will also see hell. This will mean that the person will not let the darkness enter through the Doorway to the spiritual world; the Doorway that was created for the Spiritual Light of humanity by the Beings of the Higher Hierarchies of Light. So I say to you all, Mary today has shown that this expensive ointment was used to symbolise the expression of her faith in the Christ Light." [Verse 2] [2]

In Bethany the word spread that Jesus was at Martha's house. The people were all talking about the resurrection of Laz'arus from the dead. They knew that Jesus was like no other Prophet in history as no man could raise a man from the dead unless he had the power of God in him. So a crowd was beginning to surge its way to the house where the Christ was meeting his initiands.

Furthermore the rumor was spreading that not only Jesus but also Laz'arus were marked men by the chief priests as so many people had proclaimed that the new Prophet was the Messiah whom the corrupt priests

perceived to be a political threat to their moral authority over the people. Laz'arus was becoming a symbol of Christ power. They could not tell the people that they wanted to kill Jesus and Laz'arus openly for this would be dangerous now for them but they knew that they could have them arrested or killed secretly. They knew that many of the corrupt priests collaborated with their Roman rulers and also that they enjoyed privilege and power because of their willingness to talk about a Moral Will for the Jews which they never lived as this way they talked about the Prophets and the law but they would never talk about their own hypocrisy of their support for the evil of Rome. They would simply rationalise this as the only way Israel could survive and that history would ultimately prove them right in that Jesus was a threat to Roman power and unless he was stopped the Romans would retaliate with force that would destroy the Jewish nation.

Their theory was based on putting Intellectual Materialism above the Light as they were saying their logic was Truth. However in fact the real threat was their

---

[2] John 12: 4-8.

neutralisation of the Truth of life as the reality was that the power structure that they had developed with the Romans supported the laws of the Jews, providing they never questioned Rome and its ultimate control commercially and politically, meaning that the Romans were not interested in one man saying he was the Son of God unless it interfered with their power structure with the chief priests of the Jews. As their power was based on brute force they simply supported any system that served their purpose.

So when the Pharisees were asking for Roman power to eliminate Jesus they were trying to protect their interest first and not that of the people as the Romans knew of Jesus but simply accepted him as another Prophet of the Jews. They did not have any interest in stopping him until the chief priest, Ca'iaphas, warned the Romans that a potential insurrection could occur under such a religious leader who did not follow their rules and who was also proclaiming himself a god. He also pointed out subtly that this challenged the godhood of Caesar himself. This, of course, was what ultimately caused Pilate, the governor of Judea, to side with the chief priests to make a decision about Jesus. This had to be handled in such a way that Rome's political face would remain in tact.

Hence what happened was that there was a growing support from the Roman military hierarchy to act on the situation although the problem was that Jesus would appear and disappear with all of his Apostles as soon as he was sighted. So the plan was to find a way to get to his group as this way they would discover the secret of his magical powers of disappearance as the Christ Being knew of his time on earth and knew that ultimately he would become vulnerable enough to be killed once the Initiation Process of his initiands was complete. This is why he would appear and lecture the people, heal the sick and cast out demons from the possessed and then he would ask his Higher Hierarchies of Angels to transport all of his initiands and himself to another location at will. He would do this when he saw the potential future events to come from the Christ Eyes of the Light.

He could have accepted all events but chose these events so that he could show mankind that as a Cosmic Being he also could be a human being simultaneously only when he was able to live in both worlds at the same time. He lived his Truth as a human being and as a Cosmic Being. When he came to earth he was still living with his Father in Heaven as his Soul lived in this World of Light as all of the Souls of mankind live in this Light when they speak to the Christ Being. [Verse 3] [3]

Jerusalem as the spiritual and commercial centre of the Jews was celebrating its greatest religious festival. The whole country made a pilgrimage to the holy places in the temple at this time of the year. Now what was compounding the streams of humanity that were pouring into the city gates was the knowledge that Jesus was going to speak to the populace. Everyone knew that he had raised Laz'arus from the dead. All they could talk about was how they could see the Messiah and how they could embrace this Messiah of the Light as the Great Soul of Israel.

They could see that this man embodied the spiritual destiny of the nation and that he could do all that other Prophets had done in past ages but none had brought a man back from the dead after four days of his being buried. Nowhere was there a man that was promised by God to lead Israel to become the Spiritual Leader of the world. They were the chosen people so therefore they would have to have the greatest Prophet and the most powerful of all leaders on earth as it was written in the Holy Scriptures that the Messiah would redeem the world and justify the spiritual supremacy of the religion and race of Israel.

So what happened then was that many of the Jews took palm tree branches so that they could honor Jesus as their King. When they saw him riding on a young pony they ran to his side and cried out, "Blessed is he, the Messiah of the Light!" They kept on saying this again and again until the crowd roared with a deafening sound and all one could hear was, "Messiah of the Light! Give us the Messiah of the Light!"

Then the Christ Being's eyes sparkled like two diamonds which looked at the crowd. His face bore a Cosmic countenance so that the charisma of kings would barely be seen had they been compared. One could feel that this was a Celestial Being

---

[3] John 12: 9-11.

clothed in a human body. Yes, this was the Christ Being.

On this day the Spiritual King of the Universe was honoured as it was foretold in the scriptures: "The Messiah of the Light has come; the Redeemer of the World. The Spiritual King of the Universe will ride into Jerusalem; the City of Light." [Verse 4] [4]

The Christ Being had chosen the planet earth as the place he would come to so that he would become a human being. He did this to create in man the final evolutionary chain of Ultimate Light. With his coming into the human family he was able to baptize it. He touched mankind and changed mankind's evolution. He touched Cosmic fate the moment he became a person walking the face of the earth. His Apostles in the beginning could not totally comprehend what was written about the Redeemer of the World as being a Spiritual King. However later when they could have the power to see into Heaven through the Keys of Light themselves they could see his incarnation. They could see that he evolved into material existence and had not evolved from it and this choice he had made to show

all of mankind and spiritual and other kingdoms of the universe that his will was to create Light for mankind.

The people who were cheering him and bowing down before him as their King saw unconsciously that he was the Living God. Consciously they knew that he had raised Laz'arus from the dead and that he was a Prophet with miraculous powers. These were powers that no man had ever shown on the planet earth and that no monarch nor emperor could do for himself or buy for himself in the whole world. Hence this man was to be honored for his magical Living Light power over death. This man was truly their leader and their King.

When the Pharisees saw this they loathed the spectacle of the people applauding Jesus as their King. For them it was as if their life – support system was being decapitated abruptly. They had to find a way to stop Jesus.

One Pharisee exclaimed, "He has them in the grip of his magical personality. It is as if he has hypnotized them so as to put him on the throne of Israel; this false Messiah who

[4] John 12: 12-15.

speaks of a universe filled with worlds where good and evil will ultimately live on as two different races. He has certainly trained himself to lie with esoteric knowledge from his travels to India. No, this Jesus has become a guru and he is hoodwinking the people. We have to stop him as otherwise he will make us lose all." [Verse 5] [5]

At the great feast in Jerusalem many travellers from Greece had come to see Jesus. They had heard of the Messiah who claimed to be a Cosmic Being and who had magical powers that cured all diseases and raised others from the dead. The Christ Being was the new Prophet of an age foretold in all scriptures. All initiands of the Light from the beginning of consciousness knew that man's origin was spiritual and knew that the Cosmic Being of Light would ultimately enter the earth as a physical being. They did not know, however, what type of physical form he would take. They never actually could conceptualize that the Christ Being would ultimately be a human being in the sense of a physical personality.

The ones who knew this had been given the Eyes of the Light while the others believed he would come in Spirit into a new age; an age that would manifest the Living God as a Spiritual Being who would rule the earth as a Heavenly King. They did not see him as a body with flesh and blood and as a person who was going to live his Truth as a human being who was going to change all initiation processes for all time. They did not see him as a human being who was going to align with the poor, the destitute, the sick and the powerless of the world and who was going to put the power of love above all powers from the position of no material power in a world controlled totally by an evil empire that was based on Intellectual Materialism. This was an empire that killed anyone who did not follow its laws based on putting the commercial and political power above any individual who especially was not a Roman citizen as such a person had no real legal rights or commercial wealth unless Rome accepted it. This world is the world that Jesus belonged to and one that

---

[5] John 12: 16-19.

mathematically would have counted him as no more than one insignificant person belonging to an equally insignificant race controlled by Rome. This person had no wealth nor power but was a self – proclaimed Prophet with an uncertain career as a rebel of the existing religious laws of the Jews.

One of these travelers was a Greek. He went up to Philip who was an Apostle of Christ and asked him, "We have heard that you are a disciple of the Prophet, Jesus. We seek him as we would like to meet him and talk to him. His fame is spreading with many travelers who have come back to Greece after hearing him speak and perform acts of wonderful healing magic to heal the sick and to cast out demons. We ask you to tell us how we could meet him so that we can speak to him."

Philip replied, "Do you seek him for curiosity or do you have a reason to come all the way from Greece to see him? Is it based on a need or do you simply want to know if what you have been told about him is true? Are you seeking a powerful magician who can help you commercially and show you a way to further empowerment of the powers you already have materially

and spiritually? What is truly your pathway here? Why do you come to see Jesus of Nazareth?"

This man replied, "I come to see him as I believe in God but have not as yet seen him. This man has God's power. I will not be happy in my life until I know why I have not been able to satisfy my dream to know about the spiritual world as this man speaks of it. I know I have lived before on this planet. I also know that there is a force that it belongs to a dark Lord of evil. I know that I have always tried to conquer evil with the power of love. I lost six wives to different accidents. I need to know why. I need to know also how to change this pathway I have that leads me to this fate. If it can be changed God can change it. Only He can do this. This is now the basic reason why I seek to see Jesus; the one they call the Christ."

Then Philip said to this man, "What do I call you?" The man said, "Call me Aristis." Philip then said, "I will meet you here in two hours. He then went to see Andrew who knew where Jesus was and he said to him, "There is a Greek nobleman who is seeking Jesus. He looks to be a very rich merchant who is very eloquent about esoteric

matters. Could you ask Jesus if it is suitable for him to meet him today, sometime this afternoon? He requests that he sees him privately." Andrew replied, "I wonder what a Greek is doing in Jerusalem to see Jesus. I doubt if it is a Roman plot to get Jesus. Nevertheless Jesus will know what to do."
[Verse 6]

When Jesus heard about Aristis he agreed to see him and all of his friends. When he met Aristis Jesus asked him, "I have heard that you are seeking me. So what is it that you want to know so that I can see why you have come to see the Son of Man?" Aristis asked, "Is it true that God is Light and that His pure Spirit is this Light? Also is it true that you are the one who has been prophesied in all scriptures of all ages and that you have come to earth to give mankind the saving Light? Also how can we know the truth of what you say now? What can you truly tell us that would prove this beyond doubt that you are the Living Son of Man and the Messiah of the Light that the people of Jerusalem are proclaiming you to be? What is your answer, Jesus, Prophet of Light?"

The Christ Being replied by saying, "I am the Christ Being, the Son of the Living God, the Light of all Ages. My Father who is in Heaven is speaking to Me when I speak to you. He is telling Me that He is the Living God and with the Holy Spirit he rules the universe and His origin has no beginning and He has no end. I am an historical being and have become so to shed Light upon the darkness of the world. I have come to fulfil My Cosmic karma. I have come to give mankind its ultimate destiny and its direction to the World of Light at the end of physical time on this planet. This is who I am; the Living Light of the World.

I am here to show every person who is a human being on this earth that he must learn to live his Truth first. Unless a person is willing to give up the material world and put his Light first he can never win his eternal Light.

With the mineral world we have the balance of the forces of nature as with the plant world there is a perfection of evolution and development. This compared to the animal world is one that has also the resemblance of a complete natural balance of existence while with the human world you have a will to live or a will to die. This will is a free will given to each individual in every life he lives on earth. He can look to the Light or he can look to darkness. This choice he makes unlike a rock or a tree or an animal but as a living individual human being.

The Light is the pure Spirit of God in the human being. The Christ Light is the life – blood of all existence. It is the Soul of the universe. So a person who chooses life of the Soul above the body puts the Light above life. However a person who chooses to put life above the Light will ultimately put the body above the Soul and will never take his Moral Steps nor take responsibility for his pathway but will put his will first. The person who looks to the Light will put his Truth first. So one has a tree that will bear the fruit of the Light of mankind. The other lives off the tree of life but does not nourish it with his own Light. The other expects it to only nourish him and so it does not bear the fruit of the Light but withers back into the earth. It evolves backwards away from the Ultimate Light as it has fallen back into the force of the earth and like the human

being who has lost his Light it inverts it. So you have the creation of the Light and its seed is the Son of Man. The other is the son of earth. I am the Son of Man. [Verse 7] [6]

To love the Truth is to love the Light above all things in life. To put the living of one's Truth above all things in life is to have the Christ Cosmic Consciousness. So this person who has both, has the Living Christ Being Eyes of the Light. He can see the ultimate goal of mankind is the eternal life in the eternal Cosmic City of Light to come.

So only when a person truly becomes an initiand of the Christ Being can he serve the Father in Heaven. Only then can a person have the evolution of consciousness which is the Christ Cosmic Consciousness that enables a man to see Light and to take on the Cosmic karma of the world and then of the universe. A person such as this knows who he is. He knows his pathway and knows how to live his Truth first and to align it to the Ultimate Light. A person such as this is a complete being who can live as a being with Christ Cosmic Consciousness with or without a body on earth. Such

[6] John 12: 20-24.

235

a being is first a being with the Christ Light in his Soul. The body of such a being you cannot kill as his Soul has eternal Light. The Soul of such a being you cannot kill as the Soul has My Father's Light.

He is within Me as I speak to you. He is the one that has given Me this Light. He is God, the Father, in Heaven; the Living God of all Ages. He gave each individual life. He who gives Light to My Father becomes a part of the Living Light of the world eternally. To give Light to My Father you have to have the Christ Cosmic Consciousness. You have to have the Eyes of the Christ Cosmic Light. [Verse 8]

I, the Christ Being, now see that the fate of the world is in My hands and the tears of its suffering are in My Soul. My heart is pierced with its sorrow for the darkness that reigns upon its being. I have come to cleanse it of its pain and to take away its darkness. My blood will redeem this planet and mankind as My life in death will give it Light. This Light will be seen, when I die for mankind, by every being in the universe and every Heavenly body will witness its aura as this will pulsate with a rainbow of Light which will be seen by the Spirit of Cosmic Eyes.

I will look up to Heaven and speak to My Father to forgive those who have gone against His Son. I will ask Him to redeem them if not now but in future lives to come. I will ask Him to redeem them before the seed of the evil one will take over their beings in the sixth cosmic world to come. I will ask My Father this; to save them from the Cosmic abyss into which the Souls of those who have betrayed the Light of the world will be thrown at the end of time.

I say this now: that My task to fulfil My universal karma for mankind is coming to completion as I can see that I know I must give the Father back the Light He has given Me as I love the Father. It is My Will to His Light. 'I ask You My Father, the Living God of all Ages, to see that I now stand before My karma upon the earth; I the Cosmic Ultimate Being of Light that came to redeem mankind and to save it from the other destiny of Cosmic death in the world of darkness to come where the Prince of evil will be entombed eternally. I, who have chosen to confront the Prince of evil with My Truth, My Light and My Destiny. I, who could take a star out of the Heavens at will and make it disappear into another dimension at will have accepted My fate to be the fate of all of mankind; to live and to die so that I can live eternally in the City of Light with You, Oh, Father in Heaven.

I ask You to let Me live My Truth and to put My Truth and the Truth above My Power as the Son of the Living God and to now accept the pain of the human being to suffer and to be betrayed unto a terrible death of torture and absolute humiliation.'

I, who have come to the earth with supreme powers over all kingdoms in the whole universe have come to earth to align with the poor, the destitute and the powerless of the world. I did this as I wanted to show the world that only when a person lives his Truth does he put the Light above Intellectual Materialism and intellectual control of his world, meaning that a man who lives his Truth lives it and tells the Truth. Those who have great material wealth and put it above the Light only follow Intellectual Materialism control of the world. They do not have My Light. They cannot put the Light above the

intellect. So they want the power to control the world without putting its author first in their lives.

They want to win at all costs the power of the world. This makes them sell their Souls for the riches of the world. They will do anything as long as they have what they want out of life. Hence they will never surrender to the Light. They will never put the Truth first. They will never have what they need to be happy with their being. They want to make it financially at all costs to who they are. They will never live their Truth as to truly make it honestly in life in all things, material and spiritual, a person must only do this when he simultaneously lives his Truth. If not he cheats on Cosmic time. Hence he owes Heaven a debt. This is translated to karmic debts and ultimate Cosmic debts in his evolution as a human being. This I have chosen to stop on this planet; I, the Christ Being, the author of its evolutionary direction and its future cosmically.

I have chosen to pay the ultimate price of human death at the hands of evil men so that I can live My Truth upon the earth as a human being. I am doing this cosmically to stop the Truth of the world from being lost to Satan who reigns over the Souls that acknowledge power and gold above their ultimate fate to live first for the Light.

I, the Christ Being, then will humble My Being this way so that I can live out of this Cosmic time to fulfil My Mission for My Father to be here on this planet at precisely this moment in universal time.

This is the moment that the Father and My Being once again become one Being. This is the moment when I soon will die and let the power of the Father, the Holy Spirit and the Christ Being become the power of the Light for the planet earth as this is the time chosen by My Father to save this planet through the Light of My human, Cosmic body. This is why I have come to the earth; I, who bring the Light of the earth and of all the stars in the Heavens.

'I ask You, My Father, to see that I am fulfilling My Pledge to You to die for the Light of the world so that mankind will be redeemed from the darkness and so that I can lead mankind on the march to the City of Light. I ask You,

My Father, to send Your Light to My Soul so that I will have the Light Power I need to fulfil My Mission. This is My Will to My Father in Heaven.' " [Verse 9] [7]

Then a great thunderclap was heard in the sky. A bolt of lightning struck right next to Jesus. It was like the clouds in the sky above seemed to part and a massive ray of Light shone right through his Being. All around the Christ there was a magnificent brilliant Light so that all those around him felt the spiritual world open its Doorway to the material world. Each person witnessing this could only see this happen to the extent of the Spiritual Eyes being opened by the Spiritual Sun of the World.

Then the Christ Being said, "I ask You My Father, I the Christ Being, let the Light pour down from Heaven into the earth so that man's heart will see God's Light and so that it will touch their beings and their Spirits and make them whole personalities of Light."

At this moment from the parted clouds in the sky those who could see the Archangels of God could see that they

---

[7] John 12: 25-27.

were descending in the presence of Jesus as if they did not need a physical dimension to appear upon the earth. Each had a Cosmic Sword of Flaming Golden – White Light. Descending upon the earth in the midst of the Angels there was something like a meteor glowing like a hundred suns in the sky. Then emanating from this came a Voice that shook the very earth every time it spoke with such force and power that all could only look to the Light at that moment regardless of what was in their hearts.

The Voice said, "My Son, your Mission is to give My Light to the world and to become a human being as you have so that you can share in mankind's pain and misery and be humiliated by evil and its master. Then I can raise you up above evil as a human being who is the Son of God. I do this so that you can bring Truth to the hearts of all the suffering of mankind. I do this so that My Love for mankind can be made known and so that each man and woman who loves Me will have the Christ Being in their Souls as this is why I have today come to the earth to speak to you and to all men who open their ears to the Words of the Living God; I, the Father of all Creation. I, who gave

existence to all things. I, who now give existence to compassion and love of every human being who loves Me; I, who am God." [Verse 10]

The people around Jesus were mystified. Those who only saw the physical manifestation of what was happening cried out saying, "What happened? It must have been a low intensity earthquake of some kind. Did you see that there was such a thunderclap that you would think it was a storm suddenly made in Heaven which transported itself into the elements of earth? Others said that they saw the clouds part and heard the singing of beautiful harmonious voices all saying, "Glory to God, the Father," over and over again. Others said that Jesus was seen speaking to an Angel robed in a white garment holding a Sword of pure Flaming Fire. [Verse 11]

Then Jesus looked up to Heaven to reply to his Father. He said, "I now speak to mankind so that it will hear Your Voice as I know You did this so that they could see Your Light. You showed them that the Cosmic Doorway to Heaven is through the Christ Being. Through My Being You will reach each and every Soul so that each being will evolve to reach You at the end of its ultimate destiny in the World of Light where each Soul will have a Body of Light which will need no material nourishment and will have a space with no time as all time will be within the aura of eternal Light. This is where I have come from and where I will soon return. This is where all of mankind that sees God will be with Him where there will be no tomorrows or yesterdays but an eternal present filled with an eternal Light.

Now I say to you all that soon the whole universe will witness the Eternal Court as it opens its doors to the Moral Judgment of Light and darkness upon the planet earth as until now on this planet the Prince of darkness has reigned in the form of the tyrants and false Prophets who have usurped the good kings and Prophets of Light. This has happened as the Light of the World was not ready to come to it as the world could only see him gradually as its eyes had to grow in the Light of day. So My Father evolved the earth in the form that mankind's form could live in. The spiritual forces of darkness sent Souls to the planet to wrench its power for the sake of defying the Father. These Souls had already lost their Light in former worlds created by the Father. They were given more lives and more opportunities to redeem themselves on this earth. The spiritual forces of the Light sent Souls to this earth from other worlds which formerly existed to help in the redemption of this world. Hence you have the various forms of human beings who as they evolved also evolved their perception of the Light and of the darkness. Those who have lived their Truth on this earth and surpassed their former incarnations whether they be of darkness or of Light, yet have come to the Light, can see the Christ Light. Each to his level of evolution and own Moral karma.

Those who choose not to live their Truth and make the wrong moral choice, that the redemption of the world has nothing to do with them, will abstract their right to evolve into higher worlds with their Souls. They will ultimately descend to lower ones so that ultimately time will stop for them so that all the yesterdays will become todays and so that tomorrows will disappear from their beings. Their form will evaporate into this world of no Light. However the others will be able to live with all the tomorrows turned into one day of eternal Cosmic Light.

This is why I have come to the earth; to give it its pathway. This is My Pathway: to show the world the Guiding Light of My Being and to show the world that ultimately My Mission to earth is to fulfil My Cosmic karma which is to take the evil one out of it not through material power but through Spiritual Light. Through this Christ Light mankind will transform its being into a being that fulfils its higher purpose of evolution which is to evolve out of all darkness to complete Light. This it will do only with the power of the Cosmic Christ.

To do this through one's own will would lead to giving Light to darkness and to the evil one as only the Cosmic Christ can take away the evil one from the world. This is so as mankind's destiny is to walk away from evil and to learn how to walk in the Light. Those who choose to do otherwise will fight evil with their own beings. Hence they will lose their beings eternally.

Each human being who takes a Moral Step in his life to choose Christ first, regardless of what his Truth asks him to live, will make it in his life. He will do this by accepting that what he desires to be happy in life he will only fulfil when he first lives his Truth as when a man does this he fulfils his Cosmic time on earth.

When a man wants to fight evil without the power of the Christ Being he identifies with it as the more he wants to put his will first above that of Christ the more he devolves into his Cosmic past until he becomes permanently a being of the past as mankind became a being of the future when I came to earth. However the Father has given the evil one free reign with his Spirits of darkness to let each human being decide. If He did not do this no man could say that he won his Truth or lived it as he would have no choice but to say that he has no will but to follow the will of a different evolution of being. The animal has no say. He has no memory of his Cosmic existence. He has no free will. The Father and I have done this out of Free Will as we love mankind as it was created to give Light to God. Yet it does not have to do this. God gave it the power to refuse Him. I have chosen to help all mankind to see this with My coming to the earth; to show

241

the love of the Father for every individual human being who has lived on the earth. This is My Will to the Light." [Verse 12] [8]

Then a man in the crowd, one of the Jews, said to Jesus, "How does one know the truth of what you say? How can it be that our traditions of the written law and our prophets are below your knowledge? Where does this knowledge you have come from as how can you say that its Moral Light is above the scriptures as in them it says that the Christ is forevermore with us in the Prophets and in the Messiah of different ages? How can it be that you say that you are the Ultimate Teacher of the Light? Why is your Light above the Light of our law? Can you truly answer such questions that are on the lips of everyone here today? Why is your access to the Heavenly Father any greater than mine as after all you are just as human as I am? Is your word above the Word of The Bible we have of tradition and wisdom of centuries? Tell us all, how can we believe you when we weigh it all up, self – professed Master and Teacher of the Light?"

Then the Christ Being replied directly not to this man but to all around him, "I am the Christ Being, Son of the Living God, Light of all Ages. I am the Son of Man. I have come to redeem the whole of mankind and to transform the planet from darkness into the Light. I will soon leave your planet as My time here is soon to end as I have almost completed My Mission to give Light to it and to mankind. I have asked mankind to walk in the Light. I have asked mankind to look to the Light. He who sees this Light also sees the challenge of darkness to it. He sees that the darkness lives off the Light and wants to devour it. He who walks in darkness will lose his pathway. I have created the pathway for mankind. Every individual who has ever lived and will live knows My Truth when he lives his Truth. So only by knowing My Truth does a person know the Truth of what the Light is.

Those who know what the Light is are living their Truth. They have aligned to Me now and in past ages as they will in the future epochs to come as everyone from past ages who looked to the Light could see the star in the Heavens that carried My Soul to this planet.

---

[8] John 12: 28-33.

242

Those in the present life like John the Baptist, who first saw the Light for mankind, will evolve My Light for the whole cosmos as truly the future man will walk in the Light and even redeem those who have shunned it in My presence. They will become beings who can see the Christ Being with the Eyes of the Light as these Eyes can see into Heaven as well as into the earth. You want to see what you want to believe in. This will not change the Truth as the Truth can only be understood and comprehended from its record in men's Souls and in their hearts.

Those who put the Truth of words in books and in speeches above this Truth seek to put power above the Light. Those who are the brothers of Truth follow the Eyes of the Light. They are My brothers as they have put the Truth above power and the Light above their very lives. This is why you need to see that a living example of the Truth of life is not a concept or wise words from scripture but it is a human being who is living his Truth in alignment to the Christ Light. This is why a living example of the Truth of life is such a man. He is a living example of the Christ Being Light. He then becomes, in the future World of Light to come, one of the Sons of Christ."

As soon as Jesus completed these words he suddenly vanished from sight as he knew that the dark spirits were about to seize their consciousness so that they would become violent towards his physical being. So he walked away from them into the spiritual world as he had done so many times before as although he was totally a human being, the Father still chose when he would be vulnerable to his Cosmic fate. [Verse 13] [9]

So it was that in the midst of this crowd there were many who had witnessed the power of the Light in Jesus but still refused to accept that he was the living example of the Ultimate Light of God. They wanted to deny it and completely had a shadow over their consciousness when they saw him as the dark spirit would speak to them and pour evil thoughts into their Souls. It was as if they were possessed with destroying Jesus and killing him. This happened to them as they had lived a lie all their lives by

[9] John 12: 34-36.

243

being hypocrites. They did this by saying one thing about the Law of God but truly living the opposite in their private lives. So the more they saw the Light the more the darkness cast a shadow over their Souls as he who lives a lie will eat the poison of its fruit. This poison was the evil in their Souls which propelled them to look for stones to throw at Jesus. So they were truly angry when they could not harm him so as to justify the evil that lived in their hearts. He just walked passed their beings and when he passed each and every one they felt this terrible guilt that they had murdered the Light of the World.

Hence the fulfillment of the prophecies of Isaiah: "The Lord of all Light of this Universe speaks with Words of Spiritual Living Fire. Its record is in all the Souls of mankind who have Eyes of the Light. Those of mankind who chose not to believe his Truth but put their truth above his have lost it to darkness."

So Isaiah evolved his declaration about the Messiah of the Light to come to the world to reach man to bring him back to the Light saying, "The darkness challenges the Light and becomes as powerful as the Light when man sees not the author of the Light and his Pathway as he who gives Light to darkness only gives it power over his being. So he who has Eyes of the Light gives nothing to darkness and gives nothing to redemption for those who will the darkness in their Souls. Only then can a person protect his Light."

Isaiah prophesied this as he could see that the Prince of evil could never be won over to the good. He who was protected by such a being stole Light by convincing others that he was redeemable. Hence the Christ Being says all men are redeemable when they follow their Truth and put him first as human and Cosmic being as only then does a person follow the Truth of Christ by living his own Truth first. Otherwise he lives the Truth of the evil man in trying to redeem him when he has chosen power over the Light. This means he unconditionally trusts such a man with the intention to redeem him and does not see that only when a person truly follows a Moral Will to the Light can he be trusted with giving him Light. [Verse 14]

So it was with so many on that day when they saw Jesus they could truly see that he was from God. Some had the power to truly stand up and speak for him but they could not bring themselves to say that they really believed in this God of Light and love of all mankind as they could not face their Truth. They could not forego the traditional Light they had in their lives. They had put their well – being above the Light. This made them lose the Light they had as they wanted to have the approval of the Pharisees. They wanted to be recognised as successful good people in the community. These people sacrificed their Truth. They wanted the adulation from the public so they followed the status quo. Hence they sold out their Truth for traditional truth. In this way they lost their Pathway to the Light. [Verse 15] [10]

Then the Christ Being stretched out his hands and looked at the people gathered about him and said, "I have come to the earth to give it Light and to show the love of My Father to all human beings. I have come to do this to show man a Pathway to the Light. Only when he follows his Truth and puts the Christ Truth first will he know the Truth of life and his ultimate Cosmic destiny. I say to all of you to be challenged to face your Truth and to put it above your life as you put the Light above it when you walk in the Light of the Christ Being.

I say to you all, look to the Light and let it reach your hearts and Souls. Stand up before the Living God and proclaim your Truth. Say it and live it. Love it and be with it in your whole hearts and your whole personalities. Let the Light shine through your personality so that it will reach your fellow man so that you can say that what you truly live for is the love of the Ultimate Light of Christ, the Son of the Living God, the Light of Ages. When you do this you honor My Father in Heaven. You give Light to His Being as it is He who created all life on this planet and in this whole universe. I ask you to worship Him not as you do but as you are shown now to do. Be aware that going to the synagogues will not give you redemption unless the Light is in your heart and unless you have created the Pathway for the Christ Light to reach your heart. This Pathway can only be created when you focus on your Truth as it is aligned to the Christ Truth. This is truly the Truth. This is the Christ Truth.

---

[10] John 12: 37-43.

Look into your hearts and you will see My Father in Heaven speak to you as it is He who has given Me the Light I share with you now. It is He who created My Pathway and it is I who accepted this Pathway for you as from the beginning He has loved you as He fashioned you to become the human being you are. He created this moment for you so that you could face your Truth and face your Light before the Living God; the Living Light of the Universe and Heaven itself.

I ask you now, let My Father give you the new life. Be born again into a new Cosmic time. Make your birth – date this moment when you become one; a person who is an individual giving Light to God. This is when as an individual you decide to give thanks to God for your life by living your Truth, by speaking it and then by giving it as a testimony to your own living Light as a member of the universe and as a being who has given birth to his Cosmic personality. This personality is connected with the Golden Rays of Heavenly Light of the Cosmic Christ Personality before you now. You now speak to him; the Living Christ, Son of the Living God, the Father. He is your Father;

the Father of all Light.
[Verse 16] [11]

I came to the earth to bring the Cosmic rays of Light to its whole being. I have come to burn away the darkness that tries to hold the earth from evolving into Heaven. I have come to the earth to ultimately create the Cosmic path that will create the Cosmic consciousness of the Light. This consciousness will be like a golden net that will capture the earth into the orbit of the Spiritual Sun of Heaven where the Spiritual Sun of the cosmos, the Trinity of Cosmic Light, lives eternally.

Those of you who hear about the Golden Light that creates worlds in the universe that transcend time into eternal time and make the choice not to be redeemed by this Light have chosen power over the Light. They have chosen what appears to them a superior material evolution above what truly is a superior Spiritual Light evolution. They have done this as they have aligned with the Negative Motivational Science of the world that tells them that they can get anything and everything that they want and that they can even get the

---

[11] John 12: 44-45.

power of a god when they will to become a god. This tells them that they are a god when they will to be a god and the power of the mind will give them this spiritual power, the power of a Cosmic Being; the Christ or the Lord Buddha. It tells them that all they have to do is practice spiritual eye forces and ultimately they will have Cosmic power. They will be able to transcend the human realm into the spiritual realm. They will be able to transcend Cosmic time with their own individual power over Spirit.

These people have chosen, like the Hierarchies in Heaven that no longer belong to Heaven, to put their own power above that of My Father. They have falsely concluded that they can borrow the Words of the Living Light and align them to an ego that wants to be elevated into the spiritual world before it is morally right for them according to who they are and what they were created to be in the cosmos at this stage of their evolution. They have spiritually identified with what the Lord of darkness did when the Archangel Michael was commanded by the Father to use the Spiritual Fire of Heaven to cast out the darkness of this being and all

that had chosen power over the Light of My Father. Then such beings were thrown out of Heaven as they could no longer live there when they had chosen not to follow the Father in creating the universe but to follow their own will which, of course, was the will of the Lord of darkness. So you have the story of Lucifer who was forcibly removed from Heaven with the Spiritual Beings that chose from their own free will not to live their Truth.

So you have these Spirits that actively send darkness into the cosmos and try to seduce mankind to align with Intellectual Materialism as their god is the Prince of darkness. They take over the wills of those who have chosen not to be redeemed in their life time. They do this for the sake of power of their ego over the Light as the Spirits that followed darkness did when they were in worlds closer to Heaven than the human being who took the wrong moral choice not to follow their evolution to journey to the Ultimate World of My Father. They did not want to make this journey as this meant they had to live their Cosmic Truth. They chose the lie of darkness for the sake of independent power. They chose this power as they wanted all power. They wanted everything in the universe to be theirs. In doing this they cut themselves off from the Father as they wanted power above all for themselves first. Each individual Spiritual Being that could no longer live in his allotted cosmic world on his evolutionary path to Heaven did not want to give his Cosmic Light to the universe of Spiritual Beings. He wanted the Light only for himself first. In this he became cosmically selfish and thus created for his being not what he needed to have which was a Pathway to a supreme evolution but what he wanted to get; this being what seemed to be then supreme power over his fate.

Hence this delusion is what is created in those on earth who hear My Words and walk away from their meaning. They intellecutalise them and say that My Words are that of a human being. They say this instead of saying that My Words are those of a human Cosmic Being who has come to change the pathway of mankind so that mankind's Truth can be elevated into following the Christ Truth.

So you have those who have made a choice to put their light above the Christ Light and who say clearly and emphatically that their light is the source of truth. They say that the Christ Consciousness is no different than the consciousness of other Higher Beings or the Prophets of past ages. They do this to rationalise the Truth and to make it relative. They do this also because their form of evolution in their Souls is still not able to see the Christ Light as they want their truth above the Christ Truth. This is a dangerous illusion as they do this by their complete neutralisation of their place in the cosmos as beings who belong to their specific hierarchy existence in their level of evolution. They refuse to see this and travel to worlds they should not travel to until they have earned it in their evolutionary truth. They want to steal the spiritual power that they have not achieved in their world of birth from the beings in these other worlds. They want to do this at the cost of not being redeemed by the Christ Light as the Prince of darkness sends his cohorts before he comes to seduce and dazzle the being into the belief that everyone is a god and that they only need to reveal it to themselves through accepting that they are master of their own fate by challenging fate and by putting oneself first in life. This is the truth of the Prince of darkness.

However the human being who does what he needs first so that what he wants is aligned to doing what is right for himself as a person first and is aligned to doing what is right for his Truth as a human being and a Cosmic being. Such a person lives his human and Cosmic Truth simultaneously by following the Christ Truth and by recognising the power of evil and fighting it not with human weapons first but by using spiritual weapons first. He does this by seeing that the real weapon is neither hate nor superior skill to kill an enemy but superior power to take away the hate by not using superior skill to kill but by using superior skill to preserve life first before responding to an enemy.

This means that a person must first do what is right for him as a whole person before he uses Spiritual Light power to protect himself cosmically. Hence he then asks the Christ Being to send his Light to the darkness of the enemy against his being. He will do this as the darkness shuns the Light and the Prince of darkness,

the supreme coward of the universe, will never be in the Light of Christ as he hunts the innocent who do not know his power and he hunts the arrogant who assume that he does not have any power apart from what is in their minds. Hence he who does not use the Christ Light and follow the Christ Truth will lose the battle between good and evil upon the earth as it is clear that the darkness can only challenge effectively the Light when the Light in the individual is not yet the Christ Light.

He who preserves his Light first by doing what is right for him as a human being first by living his Truth is ready to receive the Christ Light into his being. He is ready to begin to follow the Christ Truth. Hence the Lord Buddha lived and lives his Truth in the spiritual world as he had prepared the Jesus body on earth for the Christ Being. So all men need to humble themselves and first become a Buddha before they begin to follow the Christ Truth. Then will the person be saved and redeemed by the Ultimate Redeemer of Mankind; the Christ Being, Son on the Living God of the Universe, the Living God. [Verse 17]

This journey mankind now begins is from this point in Cosmic time as when a man can live his Truth and follow the Christ Truth he follows the message of the Gospel of the Christ Light. He follows his ultimate destiny to the Cosmic World of Light to come where his being will have completed its evolutionary journey and where it will be made into a Being that can live in the Eternal Light of Heaven and its Trinity of Light eternally by fulfilling the Will of the Cosmic Cross of Heaven.

Just before this happens to the earth and it evolves into Heaven spiritually there will be a last day when all men who have chosen redemption will see their Saviour, the Christ, as the Living Cosmic Christ descend into the material world. He will do this not to come as the Redeemer but as its Ultimate Judge. He will then pass the Judgment to separate the race of the good from the race of the evil on earth for all time as it will be the end of material time on earth. This is when man will have won over the Prince of darkness and have the power to cast him out of their Souls with their own Light power

independently of the Christ Being himself. This is when all Beings who reach Heaven will have completed their journey to become citizens of Heaven where the Light will shine from their Souls and their Souls will live as the Christ Being lives in Heaven forevermore. This is the Cosmic Will of My Father who created Heaven to see this eternal day when all of mankind that have chosen redemption become eternal Beings of Light. [Verse 18] [12]

I have come into the world as My Father's Cosmic Will created My Pathway to do this. He gave Me this Light power to live both in the spiritual and material world. He also asked that mankind be given the freedom to accept or reject Me as a human being and as a Cosmic Being. He did this as this way those who choose eternal life above the one life or the many life times they have, will have a Pathway to the Light. Their living their Truth would have its fulfillment in living ultimately the Pathway to following the Christ Truth.

My Father saw that mankind can only truly choose him above the Prince of darkness

---

[12] John 12: 46-48,

when the human being had the freedom to do this as otherwise then no human being would have to live his Truth let alone the Christ Truth as then there would be no need of Truth as all would have just one Truth and no one would have free will to create life into eternal life. They would simply have the will to create a life that had no meaning above one life on earth or many lives on earth that followed an evolutionary pattern of existence that was controlled by the forces of nature; a nature that created beings with no Souls who followed the pathway of an animal who has no free will to evolve into eternal life as the animal has no Cosmic memory.

This is the choice of those who choose not to be redeemed and choose to say that they have no free will to look to the Light As all is controlled by the forces of nature. They say that all is controlled and no being is beyond this power of good and evil and this is what he has to face in that he has no real relationship to a Supreme Being of Light as this is all wishful thinking to satisfy the mother or father figures psychologically.

My Father in Heaven is a Cosmic Being; the Supreme Cosmic Being of Light in all Universes. I am His Son. I am here on earth as it is His Cosmic Will to give you this Light. This is My Pathway to do what He has asked Me to do for Him. I love the Father and the Father loves Me, the Christ Being; His Son. This is My Truth. This is the Christ Being Truth." [Verse 19] [13]

---

[13] John 12: 49-50.

CHAPTER 13

The feast of the Passover had come and Jesus was contemplating his Truth; the Christ Truth. He was contemplating why he had come to the earth and that he would have to return to his Father soon to complete the humankind Cosmic mission to earth. He also began to foresee the fulfillment of his Moral karma in this one and only life he would have on this planet earth.

He saw that out of the thirty – three years of life he had lived on the earth as a human being thirty of these years were as Jesus, the man, and three more were as the Cosmic Christ Being. He went back to the moment he met John the Baptist and saw the birth of his Cosmic Being on earth. He then looked at the people he loved on earth with a human and Cosmic love. He saw that they would truly miss him soon when he went back to his Father in Heaven. He also saw that the greatest test of their love for him would come soon when they had to become independent of him as regards their initiation into the Eyes of the Light that he had given them as he would soon no longer walk the face of the earth.

Then, while at the Last Supper with his Apostles all gathered around him, these thoughts came rushing through his mind when he was looking at the chosen twelve whom he had initiated into the Eyes of the Light. All had journeyed with him to Heaven to some degree when they had become a part of the Doorway he had opened for them and himself on earth to the spiritual world and its Spiritual Light. Every one of them had forsaken all for the Truth of life and for this Pathway. They had put first the Light in their life by living their Truth and following the Pathway to the Christ Truth.

In the three years of initiation to this Light power they had experienced a total change of personality and their whole being was transformed with the Cosmic Christ Light as it came to their Souls when they worked with the Doorway to the spiritual world with the Christ Being. They all looked forward to the time when they could share this Doorway with the whole world and the wonderful Spiritual Keys of Light that transformed matter into Spirit and Spirit into matter according to the Spiritual Light of Heaven within their evolution. This meant that all had experienced various degrees of Light power to heal the sick in mind, body or Soul. All had seen the Christ transform water into wine or give sight to a man who was blind from birth. All had seen the Circle of Light around them with the Christ in the centre next to them as Angels came and went to talk to him. [Verse 1]

Yet one Apostle, Judas the Iscariot, the Devil had managed to seduce with Intellectual Materialism by convincing him that the visions around Jesus were suggestions from a powerful hypnotist of what is already in the collective unconscious of the Jewish race. He was convinced that Jesus was a truly good man who had messianic identification with changing the world with no money and no real following other than the twelve who had to sacrifice their whole lives for his dream and that rationalistically there were no other worlds or lives. In truth even the Jewish laws of God were but cultural evolutions of moral and humanitarian concepts made for the protection of society. He thought that a God that created everything and gave man a chance to be good so as to get to Heaven was a

beautiful idea but in reality one really did not have any proof of what happened after death. This Jesus was talking about future cosmic worlds thousands of years from now and that the Ultimate Truth is only found after many life times, but in reality Jesus in this life did not look too good for as a rebel to the system he was a marked man and Judas was following him. The Truth of the matter was that these ideas were what he was thinking about at the supper.

As Judas was the treasurer for the group he saw that as an economic entity the twelve were basically below average as to the income class in their country and by world standards. Since following Jesus all had lost their chosen profession in becoming an initiand and a Teacher of the Light but this Light did not pay the bills, he thought to himself, as the Devil was now in his heart.

Judas had been seduced by his wanting to have success for his evolution materially paralleling the spiritual power he had witnessed with the other Apostles. He could not accept that the Messiah would come to the earth and align himself to the poor, the destitute and the oppressed Souls of the world. His secret friends, the Pharisees, had appealed to his identification with Negative Motivational Science as to what would happen to Israel if it followed the Jesus movement. They had convinced him that he would become the scapegoat for the aftermath of such a movement. He would end up penniless and he would actually trigger the Romans with this movement to destroy Israel if they perceived a threat to their authority. This would happen once the people would replace the Pharisees with this movement and the Romans would see that Jesus would proclaim himself a Spiritual King above Caesar. Hence for Jesus to die by sacrificing his life would save the nation as otherwise where would the movement lead to? Where would Judas be in the scheme of things?

However if he looked at himself honestly he could do the right thing and just tell the Pharisees how to get to him before he would disappear as he normally did when they got close to handing him over to the Romans. For this he would be given a property and a substantial reward. Also by doing this service to his people he would be saving them from the Romans as the Pharisees knew that the Romans would take away all the freedoms of religion and commercial independence from the Jews if they knew that Jesus was to be anointed as King of the Jews as this would be perceived as an uprising which could only be stopped with absolute force before the rebellion got hold of the whole country.

These false perceptions had made Judas betray Jesus to the Pharisees. The black magic powers of the Pharisees made Judas betray the Light of the World for the sake of Intellectual Materialism as it is aligned to Negative Motivational Science of getting what one wants above what one needs as a human and Cosmic Being. He wanted to follow what he perceived was the truth on the opinion of those who were evil. He had contaminated his Eyes of the Light by saying one thing and doing another in the work he had done on his initiation to the Light. He did not live his Truth with the powers that he had acquired from Jesus. So by doing this he evolved in spirit but he did not align his Truth to this evolution. He began to unconsciously channel Spirit and put this above Spiritual Light. Hence his Doorway became infected with darkness. The Luciferian spirits began to speak to him about being a property owner and the Satanic spirits were telling him that only by following what is logically right politically and commercially would anyone ever really survive in such a wicked world.

So Judas lost his perception of the Truth of life. He began to look to the darkness and to finding a way to betray Jesus to the Pharisees to justify his own gullibility that Jesus was but a normal human being; highly evolved but not God. So he would have to be sacrificed for the good of the Jewish race so that he could win a real future for himself and become somebody. In this way he would stop being just a follower but become a leader like one of the Pharisees. So with this delusion he pretended to be the follower of Christ at this evening meal with the other eleven Apostles. [Verse 2] [1]

The Christ Being then faced his Truth and saw who he was as a Cosmic human Being. His supernatural powers were being used to change the pattern of the evolution of the earth and the human race. He had come to create a new Pathway for mankind. A new Light on the earth was given

birth the moment his Father took over his Soul and gave his Body its Cosmic identity as the Being of Christ. He did this to give his Being the complete Light of the Spiritual God Trinity as this was the moment that He entered his Being as the Living God. Also now three years after this event took place he saw that his Pathway was to follow this Cosmic Truth; this Christ Truth. This meant he was soon to go back to the spiritual world on his Cosmic journey as part of this journey was the redemption of mankind. The other parts of it mankind would learn about only from observing what he had said and done on earth as what he says and does in Heaven can only be seen after the fact and never before the fact as human beings can only follow the Superior Spiritual Beings. The human being can only walk in the footsteps of the Light. When he tries to lead he will lose his way as the human being Light cannot fight the forces of darkness coming from spiritual evil beings. So only when a person humbles himself and lets the Spiritual Light be above the will of his intellect and his sense – bound body does he know how to put Light above Intellectual Materialism. Only

---

[1] John 13: 1-2.

255

then does he know how to put Negative Motivational Science aside and put the Truth of living his Truth above this pathway of making one's will his god.

So with this the Christ Being saw that he had shown mankind the will to live one's Truth in living his Truth as a human being. Also he had shown mankind that he was a Cosmic Being with a Cosmic Pathway designed by God the Father in Heaven. He did this by the display of the Special Keys of Christ through the miracles he performed accordingly. This Pathway was based on bringing the loving healing Light of the Christ person. This demonstrated to man that God loved him as he gave him this Light which linked him not only with the cosmos but with the Cosmic Love of the Father for humankind. This link began to evolve this love through the Holy Spirit in the Soul of mankind the moment Christ chose to give the planet his Light.

So it was that the Christ Being surveyed what he had accomplished for the human individual and human race on earth. He saw that he had brought them Light individually and collectively as his Being was the Cosmic link for all ages. He who would put the Light above life would ultimately see God and would ultimately see the Pathway that would lead a person to create a Body of Light first spiritually and then in all the worlds he lives in cosmically and humanly. So as the Christ now knew that going back to his Father meant crossing the threshold of death, he looked at his Pathway and knew that it was time now for him to soon end this journey with human fate. He knew he would soon join the Father in Heaven as it was willed and planned originally by the Father to do when the earth Light Mission was accomplished. So these were the thoughts that were occupying the Christ at this supper with his twelve Apostles. [Verse 3]

Jesus then got up from the table and removed his white cloak. He then used a part of it as a towel to prepare a ritual for his chosen initiands to the Light. This ritual was for the purpose of giving his Apostles the symbol of the Christ Pathway. Christ said to the Apostles, "Come walk with me." They all got up to follow him but he said again while pouring water from a jug into a basin, "Will you walk with me?" Then he asked them to sit down and one by one he asked them to remove their sandals and to put their feet into the basin filled with water. Following this he then wiped their feet after lifting them out of the basin of water. After drying the feet of each Apostle he said, "He who walks with the Christ follows his Guiding Light and his Pathway. This is the Truth. This is the Light." [Verse 4] [2]

Then he came to Simon Peter who said to Jesus, "You are my Master and my Saviour, the Christ. Why do you do this for me? I am following your Pathway and I am living my Moral Truth. I now want to know how I can have the Moral Will to follow the Christ Truth. So I will not let you wash my feet as I am following your Light.

The Christ replied, "I have come to the world to show mankind a Pathway by showing a Pathway to twelve initiands. I have done this by initiating them into the Eyes of the Light. You are right, Peter, I have initiated you with the Christ Light. However now you need to know how to walk on the Christ Pathway for only then will you truly have the Moral Will to follow the Christ Truth."

Then Peter answered, "I will never let you humble yourself like this. I am the one to humble myself before you, Oh, Christ." Jesus looked at him and said, "Either you let me follow My Pathway or I cannot let you follow the Christ Pathway." So then Peter knelt down and said, "Forgive me Master for I have lost my pathway now and need it to follow you. I was following my own Light first. I see that this is the Negative Motivational Science that has made me a leader of men but has made me lose my Christ Consciousness. So please let me put my feet in the basin of water and let the water wash away the darkness that has clouded my mind and heart from the Light in my being and from the Christ Light in my Soul." [Verse 5] [3]

Then the Christ said, "All who now have the Christ Pathway have the way to take away Intellectual Materialism from this planet as this doctrine which has become the religion of the masses is replacing Light with the darkness of the Prince of evil. It has become the official pathway. The Christ Pathway will ultimately replace it on earth at the end of time. Mankind has to evolve this Pathway. Those who

[2] John 13: 3-5.

[3] John 13: 6-9.

257

chose to stop evolution cannot walk with the Christ. These individuals have put Intellectual Materialism above the Light. All cannot be washed from the twelve." He said this as he was referring to Judas the Iscariot who had unconsciously identified with stopping the Cosmic Light evolution on the planet as he had identified with Intellectual Materialism. He had fallen to the power of darkness as he had put himself before the Spiritual Beings of Light.

Then the Christ Being put his cloak back on and sat down at the table and began to talk to the Apostles and said, "I have done this for you so that you will be able to see the Christ Pathway and so that you will let the Light of Heaven guide your beings and to begin to create the steps for the world to see how to change its pattern of evolution as I have come to give you the Light to do this. I am now showing you why you call Me the Cosmic Christ. I am here to initiate you into the Eyes of the Light. This process has refined your beings as the instrument of the Christ Light. With this instrument you can see the spiritual worlds and the other worlds that are between man and Heaven. You can see that those who say that the world is created by material power have abstracted God from the equation and have chosen to not use the Light to know their Truth. They have made a choice to only use the tools of Intellectual Materialism. They have put this choice to not use any other tools other than observable material facts above observable spiritual facts. They have this way consciously identified with Intellectual Materialism. Also when they say that mankind will ultimately find the answer to the riddle of existence through using the intellect ultimately they are also identifying with Negative Motivational Science. They are doing this as they, like the Roman empire, have made their will to power above all things in their existence. The Romans have their gods but they are all there to serve them and their newfound personality based on material power on earth. This personality is now revered as the highest form of culture and evolution is an illusion. Their civilisation is based on robbing the world of its wealth and enslaving mankind.

Hence I have come not to take Caesar's power by force materially but I have come to take it away ultimately spiritually and

258

psychologically as materially I am accepting My position as a Jew who follows the legal system of this country. Yet I see that I have come also to put all forms of power on the earth which are political and financial as secondary to the Light. I am doing this now by asking you to forsake all for the sake of this Light.

I am doing this as I am, as you call Me, the Master of the Light of this universe. I am showing mankind through first showing you that unless it follows the Christ Truth and takes on the Christ Pathway then the Roman world or variations of it will be its fate now and for thousands of years to come as now I am showing you through this ritual the Christ Pathway in this world. I need you to see that as I am showing you this I need you to show others how to walk on this Pathway so that they too will be initiated with My Light as you must be able to give the Christ Light to mankind by first giving it to individuals, as the Light first needs to reach the heart of the individual before it can reach communities and nations. Before one can do this there is a need to create a Pathway for the initiands of the Light. This Pathway has to be based on following the Christ Truth. Only then can the Truth be

transformed by the Heavenly Light into Spiritual Fire that will cleanse the Soul of the darkness of this world as I have been sent to do this for you and for your world.

My Father loves you. He loves humanity and has given it its pathway from the beginning of time. He sent Me to give it the Christ Light Pathway so that mankind would love itself and its Creator first as a child loves its mother and father and then as a being who loves his Spiritual mother and father; a being who has spiritual love for all of mankind from all ages as Christ is the Light of all Ages. This is so that each human being can love all men from all ages as this is the union of the Cosmic Light of all humanity. Here is the universal consciousness of this Light streaming to all men's hearts when they look to the Cosmic Christ Light.

I have come to show you the Pathway to this Light. I symbolically washed your feet to show you that you will purify your beings before you walk on the Christ Pathway. You also do this purification with the initiation to My Light and by learning how to follow the Master of the Light of this universe. Hence when you do this you see the Personality of

My Father and the character of the Holy Spirit. They are the Beings that make My Being One Being in Three.

I, the Christ Being, call upon the Trinity of Light to be sent to all of your hearts so that you will have the will to follow Me to do My work to the Light above life. I do this so that you will have the will to know that no love from the earth is greater than this love of the Light and to know that every love from the earth when it is loving in this Light creates the Christ Pathway based on the Christ Truth. Only when a person can truly put his Truth first in his life can he love another above all things in his life. So then only the man who can truly live his Truth is the man who knows how to follow the Christ Truth.

The darkness challenges the Light in love on earth as it challenged the love of the Light in Heaven when Heaven was created by the Father. The dark spirits were expelled from Heaven by the Mighty Archangel Michael to cleanse Heaven of those who could not put the Light of My Father first in their evolution. They wanted a superior evolution than the one given to them by the Trinity of Light. Hence they no longer were able to look at the Face of God. It burned their faces as the darkness took away the Spiritual Light that protects one from the Face of God as God's Face can only be seen by those who love His Light.

I tell you, even among the twelve chosen there is one who will choose to follow the same dark pathway for the same reasons as those dark spirits that wanted Heavenly Light without it coming to them from their evolutionary merit. They wanted freedom to take control of that Light. Hence they lost their pathway. Hence even among you there is one who will lose his pathway in this lifetime. He will do this only to ultimately repent from betraying the Light of the world. He will see this when the cloak of the darkness is removed from his consciousness by what is to soon come to the fate of the Christ human being.

Your fate is the fate of the world as you are walking in the footsteps of the Cosmic Christ. When you spiritually love mankind and die for this love as human beings you crown all human creation with My Light. You do this as you give mankind what I have given it but from your beings. You then create that Bridge of Light from God to man that will give him the Cosmic Light redemption he seeks as this is truly what you have come for in this life time. This is what also you will work for in future incarnations until My Light will transform the planet earth so that its Soul will shine eternally in Cosmic Heavenly Light.

I say to you, I, as human being and as the Cosmic Christ, feel truly sad that I have to follow My Truth now. I have to put the Truth above My sadness so that this way I can live My Truth. I see that I have to accept to not use My Cosmic Powers and be betrayed by one of us for the sake of showing mankind that only when a person lives his Truth will he have the Truth and will he have the Christ Light for this is the Truth. This is the Light." [Verse 6] [4]

Then there was real sadness among all the Apostles as they could see that one among them was going to look to darkness. John was next to Jesus when he was saying that one of them would betray him. Then Peter went to John behind Jesus and looked at him and said, "John, you are the closest to him. Can you ask him who it is? I really feel that we should know now.

Please ask him for all our sakes." So John asked Jesus, "Master, tell us who it is who will betray the Light of the World?"

The Christ Being looked at John and then he looked at Judas the Iscariot and said, "Judas, why have you looked to darkness by speaking to My enemies, the Pharisees? Could you not see that the dark spirit was letting you speak to him and you were fooling yourself that you were speaking through the Eyes of the Light? Could you not see that you had not seen that the Truth is above your access to this Doorway you have to this spiritual power given to you from Me? Did you not see that you have betrayed your own Soul to the darkness of these sorcerers who have put a spell of black magic upon your Soul so that you would betray Me and believe in the illusion that this was to follow a higher Truth than the one given to you by Me? Did you not see that you identified with the resentment that you had put Intellectual Materialism above the Light in your life, instead of putting the Light above material well – being, status in society and personal power?

[4] John 13: 10-20.

This meant you had to forsake all for the Ultimate Light and you had to accept that Cosmic evolutionary time is superior to the time in one life time. Only when a person can put his life secondary to the Cosmic Will of Christ will he truly win his eternal Cosmic life and then will he be redeemed for a greater human and Cosmic destiny. Only then will a person have Cosmic merit as he has earned this Cosmic Light from the Moral Steps he has taken to be used by the Light for the redemption of mankind. That is, to give back to the Father the Light given to him and to pay for his evolution and to do this by honoring the agreement for this high evolution to give back to the Light what it gave him as an initiand of the Light. This is truly what you have lost now, Judas." [Verse 7] [5]

Then Judas walked out of the supper room into the night and knew that this moment would be the last time he would follow the Christ as an initiand of the Light. This he reasoned was the price he was willing to pay to win what the Pharisees had promised him. He calculated and rationalised that it was the only right thing to do for Israel as the Romans would ultimately destroy his country if Jesus was not stopped as any man who speaks about a cosmic world being above a human world is only speaking about it to get power over a person's life.

Look at all of his followers, he was saying to himself. They have no future financially and if this was going to be the work to redeem mankind then how was there no personal money or power in it? Anyone following the Christ was going to end up following a suicide pathway as the world really would only measure his movement as a misguided attempt to appease the darkness of the world through talking about an invisible world that was supposed to have created this world and this way save his Soul. In the meantime there would be no life and no future as the Light could not pay his bills for his living. In truth the Light could not stop Roman battalions invading Israel and killing everyone. No, he was saying to himself, he was following the Moral Truth of the Jewish nation and if he was going to be paid for this, well and good, as for three years he had really lost his pathway in the human world. He had been living in a dream – world of

---

[5] John 13: 21-29.

supposed redemption but in truth he was participating in a potential rebellion that could spark terrible consequences for the Jewish people. No, he was saying to himself, he was doing the right thing as it was clear that being good did not solve the problems of the world. All would see that his actions were really helping mankind as he was being pragmatic and able to compromise. He was a person who had given up fanaticism and saw truly that good and evil were relative. These were the thoughts of darkness that the dark spirit had planted in his being that would justify his actions to betray Jesus to the Pharisees. [Verse 8] [6]

Then the Christ Being said, "I have come to the earth to live the life of the Son of Earth and to transform this to being a Son of Man. I did this as I am the Son of the Living God. I did this as the Father created My Light and I created from His Pathway the Light of the whole world and the Light of the whole universe as I am the Light."

The Christ Being then said, "Soon I will be leaving your planet as I have completed My Mission of giving you My Light. I have already planned this for the sake of mankind to give it a living example of the Truth and of the ultimate sacrifice of what any human being can give his fellow man. You will all face your Cosmic Truth. You see this with the Eyes of the Light I have given you. You can Spiritually Talk and See. You had to learn to see before you could speak. So now My Father speaks to you through My Spiritual Talking Doorway, through My Eyes of Light and through My Words. I speak now to you in the way I have shown you to see first My Light and then to speak to the Spirits of Light. This you will do when I have left the earth. You will then be able to speak to Me as I will live in Spiritual Heaven again. When you do this you will experience the Light in your heart and Soul and this will be the same as being with Me on earth. This will give you the way to Spiritually Talk to the Living Christ. Hence your Eyes of the Light will become the Spiritual Seeing and Speaking Doorway to the Christ Light." [Verse 9]

So now the Christ Being entered into a form of Meditation and all around him an aura of Light began to come out of his being. All around his body a shining

---

[6] John 13: 30.

brilliant Light began to almost transform into a burning fiery Light. Then all of a sudden he spoke in a deep resonating voice and said, "I am the Father in Heaven. He who can see My Face becomes Christ – like. He who can talk to My Son will see Me when they have come to the Gates of Heaven. I will be waiting for them as the Spiritual Love of Heaven is the Love of My Being. I, the Father in Heaven, now ask you to listen to My Son, the Christ."

Then the Christ Being spoke and said, "I give you now the Christ Pathway which is to love the Light above life and to love the Truth even above Spiritually Talking to Me. It is to love your own Truth of life above human love and to love this Truth first. Then you do what is right for all mankind as mankind's Truth can only be completed when all men love the Light above the Truth and the Truth above all knowledge and its power or Doorway to the spiritual world. It is to love one's own Truth first and to do this in such a way as to see when a man lives his Truth he does what is right for him first as a human being. He does what is right for all human love for himself and for all men. Only

then can mankind be human first. Only then can My Love for mankind be fulfilled in the hearts of all men. Only then can My Words be fulfilled upon this planet and that is to live your Truth first in your life above all things and then to align this Truth to the Christ Light. When a man can do this he has the way to save the world and to redeem it for the Light. Then he truly follows the Christ Truth.

Real love of all humanity can only come to an individual when he knows that by living his Truth he can put just one person in his whole life first in his life and he can love that person in the Light. To those who love mankind and yet have not one person in their life who puts them first in a relationship, they will still put the Light first regardless of whether they have a relationship or not. This is the Ultimate Light; to love the Light of mankind as I have loved mankind and love every human individual as I have loved every man. It is to then make a choice to love first the Light and to put the Christ Truth above one's own Truth. It is to accept that only when a man lives his Truth and follows the Truth will he have this Spiritual Light. When he

264

has the Cosmic Christ Light he has the Spiritual Christ Light.

This is truly the destiny of all men of all evolutions. First they must have the Spiritual Light to cleanse their psyches and know how to live their Truth and the Truth of mankind. Then they need the Christ Light to cleanse their Souls from all incarnations and then to live their Cosmic Truth until they can live the Cosmic Truth of all of mankind of all ages. The Christ Light, the Light of all Ages, then will give Light to those who have chosen and evolved to his Light in the seventh cosmic world at the Gates of Heaven. This is truly the Cosmic Moral Will of the Christ Being. [Verse10]

This Cosmic Moral Will to the Light is the one that all those who want to be initiated into the Light will be able to see shine through the personalities of the initiands of the Christ Light. They, the initiands, have this responsibility to create for mankind the Christ Pathway. This has to be shown to the world so that the world will first know its steps before it can experience its steps. This is now what this **Cosmic**

Christ World Light Shield does. It shows the Word of the Christ Being in this work. Those who read it can become initiated into the Pathway and its steps to the Ultimate Light in this Universe. Then once this is done a person will be able to see the Pathway to the Doorway of the Light. This Doorway will show the Spiritual Steps of how to make the individual human being the instrument of the Light.

This is when a person has been initiated into having the Eyes of the Light. When he becomes an initiand of the Christ Being then he has been initiated into Speaking to the Light. This is being able to Spiritually Speak at the Doorway to the Light. Then a person can speak to Spiritual Beings.

This the Apostles did by evolving their beings with the Eyes of the Light in their Souls. Then they began to let the Eyes of the Soul see the spiritual world as well as how it parallels the material world as they saw the Christ Being in the material world enter the spiritual world when he opened his Doorway to it. Following this they then learned how to speak to the Beings and the Angels that live in these worlds that follow the Christ Being and His Light as he is the Supreme Being of all of the cosmoses of all beings. He became a human being so that mankind would have the Doorway to the spiritual evolution of his Being.

This was his true Cosmic mission to earth as he came to give mankind a part of his Spiritual Kingdom so that mankind would ultimately spiritualise the Christ Light into its being. This is the Christ Mankind of the future when mankind will have transformed its being to become with a Body of Light, both collectively and individually, so that all men who choose the Christ Light would ultimately become Cosmic Spiritual Light Beings. This is the eternal gift of the love of the Christ Being to become human being, to create in mankind the birth of this Cosmic Light in the Soul of all men who choose his Pathway as those he chose first were the Apostles to follow the Christ Pathway. This is the future of all men who love Christ." [Verse 11] [7]

Then Simon Peter looked at Jesus and said, "Are we ready to follow our Truth and align to the Cosmic Christ of the Universe; you who have given us this Light so that we are chosen beyond all men to know you first in one life? I say to you, can you tell us now what is to be the test we must undergo to truly be initiated into the Christ Light so that we can independently create this Movement of Light for all of mankind when you are no longer here on earth in the form of a human being and as you are the Ultimate Cosmic Being in the whole universe? Oh, Christ Being, how can we live our Truth now? How can we live the Christ Truth when you will have gone to Heaven? How can you send us the Light of Heaven so that we can transform it into Spiritual Fire to burn away darkness? What is truly the Moral Step we have to take now so that we can have the Eyes of the Cosmic Christ within our Souls so we can truly follow the Christ now in this moment of the Cosmic karma of our world? Oh, Christ, please tell us what is truly the Christ Truth now?"

Then the Christ Being said to Peter, "You are not ready to follow this Christ Pathway as you have truly evolved with the presence of the Christ Being and the Initiation

---

[7] John 13: 31-35.

Pathway I have shown you but you see there is a price for such a high evolution. You have become vulnerable to the power of forsaking Truth because of the unconscious invasion of Intellectual Materialism. Hence, because I have chosen you first among all men to see My Light, so you will be the first to pay the price for such an evolution by finding that when you live your Truth with it this will not be enough to protect the Light of your Cosmic karma. To do this you will need to live the karma and fulfil the mistakes in it before you can follow the Christ Pathway. Hence this way you will learn how to use the Special Keys of Christ to change the pattern of your lives and then the pattern of your world so that the new pattern will be created to receive the Light of Heaven. This is the Will of the Christ Being." [Verse 12] [8]

Then Peter replied, "Is not my will to give up my very life enough for God to let me walk on the Christ Pathway?" Then Christ said, "Peter, if you died for the Christ a hundred times in a hundred life times this will not be enough unless when you did this you lived your Truth for it, meaning

that you did it because you followed the Truth and first the Light above it. I am the Light and I say to you that you will leave My Pathway when confronted with the evil of this world before I die soon. You will do this as you will not truly know it until you have the will to accept it beyond life and beyond what you truly want now to fulfil the Christ Pathway as you will come to the point when you will see the Light that your Soul has created.

When this Light meets the Christ Light this is when a man says what he lives as a human being and as a Cosmic Being. Truly before this he will climb the stairway to the Heavenly Garden a thousand times and each time he will slip and see that the dark Angels are behind him. Then he will go forward and he will see that the presence of the Angels of Light will help him come up this staircase. Each step is an earth – life that lets him evolve to the Ultimate Light in the seventh cosmic world. Each life creates the link to the spiritual world that ever is creating a bridge to his being so that ultimately this bridge will meet his whole being and the earth and Heaven will become one.

[8] John 13: 36.

So the pathway is for you, Peter, to accept that when you slip in this life time you will protect your being to go forward until you reach the Christ Light. So, Peter, only when a person lives his Truth with his rightful evolution will he be able to protect his Light and not say one thing and do another. Only then when he can live his Truth

aligned to the Christ Pathway will he be able to follow My Being. So, Peter, this is the symbol I give you from your own Truth that all of mankind needs to follow as the doorway to darkness is to say one thing and do another spiritually. This is truly why I say to you, Peter, that you are not ready as yet to follow the Christ Pathway." [Verse 13] [9]

---

[9] John 13: 37-38.

CHAPTER 14

"**I,** the Christ Being, ask you to have faith in the Light and to follow the Light in understanding it in one's heart. I ask you to align to the Light and see that without the Light there can never be Truth as the Light is above life. The Cosmic Light is the Source of all Truth of My Father. He who does not see that, does not see Me. You have become initiands of the Christ Light. So you are the first in this world to face the world karma and to suffer for it in individual ways as My Apostles, to represent mankind and its Moral karma to come; the Moral karma of the war between good and evil. You have done this by working on yourselves to change the pattern of your lives by living your Truth. In this way you have begun to change the pattern of the world; this pattern of where Intellectual Materialism rules it. You have begun to change it by putting the Christ Light above the Intellectual Materialism of the world.

I, the Christ, will now face this Cosmic karma as it is My fate. This is why I have come to the earth to truly live My Truth as a human being and to complete My Mission as a Cosmic Being. This is why I am the Cosmic Christ.

I now tell you that Heaven is a place that you all are destined to reach and to live in with My Father and My Being. This is your birth – right; to live in the City of Light where the Cosmic Words of Light become a Living Light on an eternal planet. I give you My Word when you follow Me you will reach My home. You will come to the land of Spiritual Light. Here your beings will be purified so that the Spiritual Fire will create in you the Being of Light to see the Hierarchies of Light. You will have the Cosmic Eyes of Light to see God's Light as it shines through the Soul of the universe. This is My promise to you, My friends, and My initiands of the Eyes of the Light.

I will soon travel to the spiritual world and let My Angels begin to build a house in Heaven for you. This house will be a place where you can create an eternal Light where the foe of Light will have no place as your hearts will be one with the heart of Heaven.

My Pathway is to have you follow Me and let you see Heaven as I have so that you can become a part of its Spirit. The seed of Heaven has been planted into the garden of the earth. When it becomes a tree

269

it will blossom with spiritual fruit. This fruit will be eaten by mankind but the first to eat from this tree of life will be the initiands of the Light. I have shown you My Cosmic Pathway to the Eyes of God and their Light. I have shown you that when you walk upon this Pathway you can see through the Eyes of God as it is His Spirit that guides your Spirit and guides your Soul upon its Cosmic journey to Heaven. I am the first to go on this journey as a man. I am the first as a Spiritual Being. This is My journey to unite the planet earth as the home of mankind with the eternal planet when all who have looked to the Light know how to walk in it as human beings and as Spiritual Beings as at this moment the conscious world will become one with the spiritual world. This is when spirit matter will become one complete universe and when the Light will transform the personality of mankind and the character of his world into the Cosmos of Christ. This is the Will of My Father.

You have all seen the Christ Pathway as you have walked in the Light of My Being on this earth and have seen the Love of My Father for mankind, for you, for all men who love the Light."
[Verse 1] [1]

Then the Apostle, Thomas, asked, "How can a person today truly know this Pathway? Look at the world obsessed with Intellectual Materialism. See it and one cannot imagine it being redeemed. Look at the way it revels in power and Negative Motivational Science. See this science that drives the Roman world to conquer it and to make it its own at any price; death, torture and murder of whole nations. You see them killing and laughing in their fine houses daily, saying to us and to the rest of the world that they have a superior culture. They have the machines of war and the palaces of the gods and they have lords of creations of a new world on their side.

How can one possibly believe that we, who have no material power or political and financial force, are going to change such an ultimate evil power on the earth? We have followed you as you speak of the Light and the Truth which all human beings have looked for from the beginning; from the first sunrise of every Soul when it saw your Light. Yet it

---

[1] John 14: 1-4,

270

is such a dim Light to this world. How can we follow you as we do not have your powers? We are not Cosmic Beings. Also now you are going to leave us and what will become of us? We have no Heavenly powers without you. How can we possibly have any hope when you look at the mass of humanity and all it does is have this voracious appetite to ever seek ways to get money and power to satisfy its being?

It has tyrants that are revered as gods who are nothing but personifications of the Prince of darkness but are clothed in the finest garments and the most beautiful palaces that resemble Heaven on earth. Why is mankind so ill – informed about his own destiny? How can he know how to follow the Christ Truth when he does not have a chance in a million of following his own Truth without the Christ Light?" [Verse 2] [2]

"I, the Christ Being, have loved all men and have incarnated as a man to show to mankind this eternal love. My Light will overcome all evil on this planet as I am superior to all darkness. My way is the Ultimate Truth of

this cosmos. I am the Living Christ as My Father and I are One Being. I have to align My Being with the Light in the Souls of those who put the Light first in their lives above all things. I have come to change the pattern of this world so that its pattern of evil will be transformed into the pattern of Light.

I know that what I am asking you to do seems hopeless materially as it is clear the kingdom of darkness has ruled this planet up to now. This is why I have come; to change this world to make it into a Kingdom of the Light. I know that when I do this I will have to see that the Spiritual Kingdom of the Light will have to first transform every Soul to see the Light before this happens on earth. The earth will become a globe of living Light. When the Soul of this planet is transformed with this Light that I bring then there will come a day that God will walk again on the face of this earth. He who identifies with the hopelessness of the mass will lose his Light. He who follows the Truth will find his Truth and will find the Christ Pathway as he will create the right Moral Will to see it and to live it. Only when a man

[2] John 14: 5.

271

speaks the Truth can he begin to live it. Also only when a man lives his Truth can he speak it. Only a man who lives what he says truly loves Me as then he loves to not only speak of the Light but to live in the Light. This is the Truth. This is the Pathway to My Being. I am speaking the Cosmic Truth of all Ages as I am the Light of all Ages.

I have come to give this Cosmic Light to every Soul that chooses it. I have given free will to all men. I have not come to force men to love Me or even to force them to love their fellow man. I have come with no guarantees that the material world will change for the better and that they will live happily ever after if they follow Me. To the contrary I have come to confront mankind with the Truth and to show mankind that the Truth is above love. I have come to show him that the Light is above the Truth and that in My Heart I am truly sad when I see how terrible it is that the good man suffers and the bad man prospers.

I see that this is why My Father has sent Me. He has sent Me to redeem the world and to show it its new way and to be aware that the love of the good will conquer all in this whole universe. The Roman empire will fall as sure as all empires with their tyrants will perish. This is so as sure as this world will ultimately end and incarnate again in the spiritual world as a human being dies and incarnates again in the spiritual world and as sure as he will return to a new earth as the earth will reincarnate into the material world till the end of this Cosmic universal time.

So I tell you, look at the human being. Look at the way he was formed and made into an image of his universe. Look at how his hands and feet were created and how his heart was designed so that it could function on an earth so balanced with its minerals, trees and air. Why such an ill – balance in humanity where even animals simply live out their fate with no memory of their being?

Yes, why is humanity so troubled? It is so as humanity has a special mission in this universe. Humanity has to face his Truth. He has to see the Light and its Truth. Evil has one truth and only one. It gives a man of Light the opportunity to confront such a challenge so as to create a Moral free will to the Light. This Moral free will to the Light is his passport to Heaven.

Caesar, the man, is but a human being who has to face his Truth in many life times to come. His power on this earth is, if one were to measure its duration in Cosmic Light time, but a second in ten thousand years of earth time. Yet what he does morally will be with him for every second of those ten thousand years as a comparison to his life now. So I say to you all, if I took a grain of sand and compared it to all the sand on this planet then Caesar's power could be compared to God's. They call him a living god because they want to sanctify their evil of domination and power but in Truth those who have participated in this evil will have to pay for it in all life times to come as the Light shines through the man who can see it in his heart and can speak to it by speaking to My Being. This is what I have shown you to do; to go the Doorway of My Light with the Eyes of the Light. This is My Way.

This is what I have asked you to follow to create a Moral free will for the world. This is your Cosmic karma; to create a world that will fulfil its ultimate human and Cosmic destiny. This is ultimate intelligence. This is why I have chosen you. This is not because you are the rich and

the powerful and the most highly evolved individuals on this planet but because you have the most highly evolved Moral free will to love the Light; the Christ Light. This ultimately is the love of all Ages.

This is why I have come to you; to give you this Cosmic Light and ignite in your Souls this Living Fire that will burn first with the energy to propel a movement to turn this globe of earth so it will face the Spiritual Sun of Heaven and to give you the Light of Heaven so that it will give you the way to love mankind and its universal destiny which is to evolve out of the darkness into the eternal sunrise of the Light. [Verse 3]

The Light of My Father is now in your Souls. It speaks to you when you look to the Light in your hearts. I say to you, put the Light above all in your lives. Put it above all the suffering of mankind and you will find God. You will find the Christ Being God. If a man today were to say he is the Living God he would be taken to an insane asylum unless, of course, he has the power over evil in the spiritual and material worlds. This I have shown you I have. However I also have shown you that I have chosen to be a human

273

being and that My Destiny is to die as one. In this way I fulfil My Cosmic human karma, meaning that when I say that I am God, it is true. However it is also true that I am Jesus of Nazareth, a person who has used his Cosmic powers to stay alive up to now to create the Initiation Pathway for the Eyes of the Light for My Apostles. This is why I have entered and come back from the spiritual world while I have lived with you. This is why when the Roman soldiers, who have been commanded to kill Me, cannot find Me. This is so as the Special Light powers of Christ protect His Light and His Truth. This is in the material as well as in the spiritual world.

Yet soon, as it is My Father's Will, I will not use these Keys to protect My Being as I need to take away My Cosmic protection and to be completely human living My Truth as I need to show to all of mankind from all ages that I suffered as a human being first as I put mankind first in My Being so that I could bring it Light; the Light of My Father. I will face evil then without My Cosmic powers. This I am doing so that you may know the Pathway to create for mankind as I give up this life and suffer the humiliation of evil upon My physical being so that I can live My human Truth. This is what I ask all men to do; to first live their Truth for themselves as human beings to show their love of all of mankind and then to live their Cosmic Truth to show their love of the Christ. This you do with your initiation into the Eyes of the Light." [Verse 4] [3]

Then the Apostle, Phillip, said to Jesus, "How can we be certain of the Father in that He will keep His Promise to us? How can we be certain that He will give us the answer of the Light for this universe and that He will let us fulfil for mankind the Christ Light? Look at the world. It is filled with madness. The world is ruled by an evil power. It has trapped mankind's Soul in Satan's net so that it is being propelled into an abyss. How can a band of men even with Cosmic spiritual powers transform mankind so that it would look to the Light with material resources that have no significance on the world stage and that are allowed to use these powers only when they also will first live their Truth as their Master has

---

[3] John 14: 6-7.

274

shown them? What truly is the Father's Will?

Why have you come to earth just now on the earth? What point of evolution did you choose that makes us the chosen ones to see you and hear you as the Son of the Living God? How can we, as human beings, understand such a Cosmic mystery? What truly is the Trinity and the Hierarchies of Light? Please, Oh, Christ Being, tell us how we can be certain of the Truth in what you have revealed to us now as the Cosmic Christ?"

The Christ Being replied by saying, "I, the Christ Being, love you with My whole Heart and with My whole Being as the Cosmic Christ. I have come to the earth to share with you the Living Light of My Father. His Promise is My Promise. You will all ultimately in future lives become the forerunners of the Cosmic Light that will transform the world's darkness into My Light. You will also incarnate on other cosmic worlds and create in them My Living Light.

I have come now, at this moment in evolution, to give My Cosmic Light to your Heavenly body which is your home, the earth, and to you as human beings as it is My

Truth to do so now. It is also My Father's Truth to send Me to do this for you and for Him as the Holy Spirit will come when I have left this planet to guide your Pathway and to evolve its Light into the future worlds to come.

As for the Cosmic Truth and why I have come now and how you can understand it, you need to realise that the Hierarchies of Light are ever at war with the Hierarchies of darkness. The choice was made in Heaven to give the choice to earth and mankind to freely choose the Light as with this Moral free will to the Light the human being on earth was given his Cosmic identity. Without this the Hierarchies of the Light would lose the battle and ultimately the war with evil and its creators as the human being, this way, could give Light freely back to the Spiritual Hierarchies of the Light. This Light comes from living their Truth. This was the portal that was needed for mankind to do this. Without the Cosmic Christ there would be no Doorway to ultimately take away darkness from the planet and the planets and stars of all the universe. So mankind has a unique and special destiny to let the Christ Being be a human being and Cosmic Being in its universal Soul.

Hence the Christ Light could transform Light in all the living and all those who have died in the past. This way all incarnations to come will have the free will to choose My Light as indeed all human beings at one stage in their evolution will be able to see. This is the Will of My Father who created free will for just this purpose; so that those who choose to pay the price of evolution, which is living one's Truth and aligning to the Ultimate Truth by working on living one's Cosmic Christ Truth, will ultimately become perfect Beings of Light who can walk in Heaven or on earth as I do on your earth. This is the Ultimate Truth. This is the Ultimate Light; for all human beings to give Light back to their Creators and Creator and to become conscious of their Pathway to walk on the Pathway of the Light and then to align to the Sources of Light. Following this it is to then become initiated into participating into the world evolutionary Light as then the Spirits of Light fulfil their Mission for the cosmos. Otherwise the spirits of darkness will take over evolution as they would

have had not the Christ Being transformed the earth and mankind's Soul so that it had the free will to look to the Light and so that its destiny was then identified with a Cosmic Pathway to the Light. This is truly the Pathway I walk on now for you as no power on this earth, material or spiritual, has any real significance to any change in the Cosmic evolution of the planet and each and every human being who ever lived on this earth, unless this power relates to My Being.

Now it can relate negatively as well as positively. As you can see the Spirits of Light relate directly to giving Light positively to mankind. Those who do the opposite only help darkness to grow on the planet. I chose to give mankind the Father's Light as through My Being mankind is able now to create, with the Creator, the Truth of the universe. With this Truth the Light will triumph and overcome the darkness. This is the Will of the Christ Light. This is to change evolution, to change the pattern of mankind and to take away the pattern of darkness coming from those who seek power and control over the Light and who do not ever put the Truth

276

first unless they can get what they want first.

You have seen that it has always been My choice as I walk on this earth as to what I let Satan do. I have given you power over evil. The Source of this power is My Light. Use it and the Spirits of Light will assist you from their own free will to protect the Cosmic Light of your world. Use it when you do by following the Truth, no matter what is asked from you to live your Truth, as Truth will prevail as it is the Ultimate Truth that stands before your very beings." [Verse 5]

At this moment the Christ Being Body began to shine with an aura of Light as he spoke to his Apostles. They could all see him without spiritual vision as the Cosmic Christ. All around him Heaven's Light began to shine out of a Doorway they could see on the horizon. It was as if the most beautiful world parallel to the earth was this Heaven they could see with their very eyes as they could see that the mirror of where they were in the countryside, was there, in the vision before them. It was a brilliant parallel countryside where such utter peace and beautiful musical sounds could be heard.

Yes, this was the other world showing the steps to Heaven as through this Doorway there was a further building on its furthermost horizon. It was as if it was made of a mosaic of precious stones as large as tall buildings. Their glowing Light flickered and flashed with the brightness of a midday sun.

Then they heard a voice saying, "I am your Father in Heaven. See that My Son is creating the Pathway for you to walk in the Light of His Being to My Being. Let the Holy Spirit guide now the Spirits of Light to combine with your Light. This is the Will of the Trinity of Light." [Verse 6]

"I, the Christ Being, see that he who follows his or her free will to evolve as a human being living his or her Truth will put the Light above life and will see that this is the ultimate destiny of every human being to be conscious of his freedom of choice to choose to change the pattern of his world so as to change in a parallel way his own life accordingly. By doing this and by willing to change his being in living his Truth he gives Light to the Spirits of Light. Then he aligns to the Ultimate Truth of life by aligning to the Cosmic Christ and asking the Christ Being to send his Light to the darkness that wants him to align with the neturalisation of change in his world and in his life pattern.

He learns to not send his Light to this darkness but asks that the Christ Being send the Christ Light to the source of this darkness so that this way he lets the Ultimate Light make its choice freely. This way the human being accepts his limits as a being of the human race level of evolution. He gives no Light that comes from this level of evolution to the source of the destructive pattern in any human beings who are aligning with the spirits of darkness. This is when his being totally aligns with Ultimate Truth and accepts that his perception of the truth will never be above the Truth. The Truth comes first. The Christ Being is the Ultimate Truth. So ultimately Light comes to the Soul of the human being when he follows this Pathway.

So when a person uses the Special Keys of Christ and asks the Christ Being to send His Light to the source of darkness, whatever it may be, the Light will only Spiritually burn the darkness when the person lives his Truth, meaning when a person asks for something from God and

uses the Doorway to the Light and does not put the Truth above the Doorway but puts his perception, his own truth, above it he will invite the spirits of darkness into his spirit. This is where a person says one thing and does another and cannot stop doing so as he becomes unconscious of the contradictions in the pattern of his being. Hence the next step is the darkness then takes the Light out of a person. So a person who truly follows his Truth and the Cosmic Christ, asks that the Christ Light goes to the darkness and asks Me to send My Light for him, will truly have Cosmic Spiritual Light power. Then he is truly asking that the Ultimate Light not only protect his Light but also to activate its Spiritual Fire force so it can burn away the spiritual power of darkness.

A person can mouth the Words of God and live a lie and he will truly lose his Light power and see Light when there is darkness. Such a person identifies with transforming what he wants in his being above his Truth. He wants self-development and evolution of his being but does not want to pay the price of evolution in the right way. He wants to pay for it through Negative Motivational Science as here a person does not have

278

to face his Truth and merely works on what satisfies his goals above what he needs as a human being. Hence only when a person truly achieves the ultimate goals in his life with the Light power of living his Truth does he truly achieve the living of the Truth of his own Light. Otherwise he is truly saying one thing and doing another in the work on himself. He is not living his Truth with the work on himself. [Verse 7]

So I say to you all, only when you follow this Pathway to the Light can you see that this Pathway is above all Initiation Processes. This meaning that a person who does not have his heart aligned to the Ultimate Light will ultimately put his own perception of truth above the Truth. He will not take responsibility for his own pathway as he will not accept that when he is doing this he is not telling the Truth to himself. He is not conscious of this process activating in his own being. This is where the evolution of free will to choose the Light comes only to a person who is conscious of the pattern of his being. Otherwise Intellectual Materialism with Negative Motivational Science will make the person not look beyond his experiences observed by his intellect. He will not put the Truth above the intellectual rationalisations about his life. He will not face his own Truth. He will simply become neutralised as he is giving his Light to the source of darkness by fighting darkness with the wrong tools and the wrong perceptions. By unconsciously identifying with darkness the person sends his own Light instead of asking the Christ Being to send the Light for him.

So I say to you, I, the Christ Being, have come to the planet to do this for you to send My Light to the darkness that makes your world identified with Intellectual Materialism and that makes your world want change on its terms instead of on the terms of living its Truth first. This is My Will to all men; to ask Me to send My Light to the darkness so that I can take away for them the spirit of darkness. This way man will be able to become master of his evolution by letting the Cosmic Light rule his world and he ruling the world with his Truth. The rules of the Light are based on these Principles and are based on the eternally living Personality of the Cosmic Christ. The Principle is that the Light is above life and as I speak the world reads these Words and asks the Christ to send his Light to the darkness of this world. [Verse 8]

As I do this I can see the Light of Heaven touch the globe of the earth. I can see the Spiritual Fire of Heaven touch the Souls of mankind who are looking to My Light. This is the Cosmic Light shining in the heart of God's Cosmic Love. So he who loves God's Light loves mankind and loves his Truth as he loves the Truth of the Light in his being. He gives then to the Christ Being his love of the Light who creates for him the Soul love of the Christ Light. This is the source of the Moral free will to the Light. This is why I have chosen you all to use this free will to evolve out of the past cosmic pattern of this world to the new cosmic pattern of Light for this world. Hence you have been chosen to lead mankind to see My Light as you are the Apostle initiands of the Cosmic Christ Light. You are, above all men, masters of the Christ Light. Mankind will know you for all ages as you follow the Light of all Ages; the Christ Being, Son of the Living God. [Verse 9] [4]

My Commandments are to love the Light and to put the Light above life; to put the Cosmic Christ Being Light first in one's Pathway. These are My Commandments as when a person can do this his Truth will align with the Ultimate Truth. This Ultimate Truth is created by the Holy Spirit; the Ultimate Spirit of the Ultimate Truth. Then a person has the Superior Spirit of Light speak to his being so that the Christ Light will evolve the Spirit of Spiritual Truth in all men's hearts and minds. This is the Cosmic purpose of all incarnations. This is the Holy Spirit Truth. This is the Holy Spirit Light. He who listens to Him will have an eternal voice of conscience that will speak with words spoken first in Heaven as his being will carry My Words into the future cosmic incarnations of this earth. He will give you the Words of Light to give to the world. He is the Voice of the Spirits of Light. [Verse 10] [5]

I have made a pledge to initiate you into the Eyes of the Light to My Father in Heaven. When I leave the earth you will be ready to confront the Lord of evil. You will have the Christ Light technology to create the Pathway for mankind. This Pathway is the legacy of the

---

[4] John 14: 8-14,

[5] John 14: 15-17,

280

Cosmic Christ Initiation. The foundation of Light for this planet is based on your Truth. As you live your Truth the Ultimate Spirit of Truth becomes your Guardian. When My physical time on earth will come soon to an end you will still be able to speak to Me and see Me as you have the power of Spiritual Talking and Spiritual Seeing.

The rest of mankind that depends on sense – bound intellect for its truth will only see that I have died. They will only intellectualise and speculate My Truth. They who, like the Pharisees, will promote My name with Intellectual Materialism as their source of truth will be the religious leaders who will corrupt the Light. They will corrupt the Christ Light. So you are to stand before the world and you are to proclaim the Truth as the Spirit of the Ultimate Light will guide you to transform it. Your Moral Will to love the Light above your lives has given you this honor above all men.

You who followed the Teacher of the Light, John the Baptist, were given by him the Pathway to My Light. I gave you the Light itself in the Eyes of the Light. My Father loved you first when He gave you His Son. You are putting Him first when you put Me first in your lives in living your Truth as human beings. You are putting the Holy Spirit first when you live your Cosmic Truth." [Verse 11] [6]

Then Jude said to Jesus, "You are Christ, the King, our Saviour and our Lord. I ask you, why do you not show the whole world your Cosmic Light? Why do you not demonstrate to the whole world your ultimate power over all material and spiritual worlds? You could move the Heavenly bodies with one of your fingers and make a star in the Heavens extinguish its Light, then why not show the human being who is not initiated like us, this Celestial Cosmos? Why not show them the Spiritual Heaven?

Tell us, for truly we are no more than ants beneath your feet but you have shown your love to have become one of us. You have shown your love to have come down to us and to have decided to become a human being when there are so many Spiritual Hierarchies of Light that are so much more evolved than man whom you did not choose at this moment in evolution. You

[6] John 14: 18-21.

chose us. You chose the human race. Hence I can see, yes, it is the ultimate destiny of all evolution to see you as human being in this cosmos. Yes, in human form; the Living God. If men just knew who you were you could speak to them and your words would capture their hearts. They would see that their lives will pass but the Cosmic evolution of their Souls will not pass.

Oh, Christ Being, can you not speak to the whole world at once and let them see who you are? Please explain to us, My Lord, this mystery, as this is what I truly need to answer to my being? This is truly my greatest dream of life to redeem mankind and to let it see the Light of Heaven. Jesus, please tell us, why do you not proclaim yourself to the world?"

The Christ Being replied by saying, "I, the Christ Being, the Light of all Ages, see what is in your heart. I see your love of My Being; your love of all mankind. You want to redeem all men as you love all men with your whole Soul. The Light shines through your personality when you speak the Words of My Father as they are written in your Soul. My Mission for mankind is to redeem it with the Cosmic Light of My Father. He who

loves Him loves My Being. You have all kept your word to the Light. Your Moral Will is to the Ultimate Light. You have followed your Truth above all things. You have done this at all costs to your personal lives. You have also seen that even among you, the chosen of this world, there is at times dissension as to the destiny of this Light you uphold above your lives.

I tell you the Pathway is to the Christ. The measure of success you have of this Movement of Light is measured by His Being alone as the measure of this world is based on Intellectual Materialism. You have seen that one among you has already at times aligned to it unconsciously. Your task is to see that this opposition to the Light gave you the opportunity to develop your Moral Will to it. Also as you have seen what I have shown you is that the enemy of your Truth and of your will to live it in this world is currently Negative Motivational Science while the enemy of the Light is Intellectual Materialism. So unless I were to live My Truth first as a human being I could not reveal Myself as the Cosmic Christ to mankind at its level of evolution now. Unless I live as a human being separately from the use of My

Cosmic powers I cannot say that I have lived My Truth. When I used these Cosmic powers you will notice I have used them in this life so that others could be healed by the Light spiritually, psychologically or physically as the Truth of the matter is when I used them to become transparent to the Romans who were seeking to kill Me or the Jews who wanted to stone Me to death, I did this only as a way to bring My message as the Living God to mankind. Otherwise there would be no sense to this world for Me to say the things I have said unless I lived My Truth and at the same time revealed My Cosmic Being with some protection from the forces of evil. Had I not done this I would not have been able to fulfil My Mission to initiate you into the Eyes of the Light. I would also have not done what was right for Me and My Father as it was His Will that I bring the Light to the world this way. At the same time this, that I have just said, was not a contradiction which is how a Cosmic Being can live his Truth as a human being.

I did live My Truth as Jesus before John the Baptist baptized Me. I did not then use the Cosmic Keys of Light publicly as I do now as you know that Jesus was the incarnation of Gautama Buddha in bodily form. This was a human being. I took his being following his incarnation as he had completed his incarnation pathway on this earth as when John the Baptist baptized Me at that moment I became the Cosmic Christ. Then his being, which housed the body of Jesus for thirty years, left the earth. Hence I am the Cosmic Christ now. So it is so that living My Truth as a Cosmic Being is what I am doing now as I have asked you to do, but to see that you will do this over many life times spanning through the cosmic worlds to come until you reach the World of Light. This incarnation of the Father and the Holy Spirit in the Christ Being on earth will only happen once in the whole cosmos.

So you have your answer, Jude, My Apostle and initiand of the Light. What you will do in living your human truth and living your Cosmic Truth will be your journey from spiritual worlds to the material worlds over thousands of cosmic years. What I have done in My life now with you in thirty - three years I have done so that mankind will see Me as the historical being in flesh and

Spirit proclaiming Himself as the Son of the Living God. This way man will know Me. All future epochs will read your written works and pour over their words and see if they can keep them in their hearts and minds.

Now those who evolve to the point of seeing Me and speaking to Me will not only keep My Words and the Words of My Father but they will also have reached the highest form of Light for mankind. This is why you were chosen. You were chosen not for your evolution or intelligence but you were chosen above all men to become initiands of the Christ Light for your love of My Father and for your Moral Will to live what you say with that love in your hearts, when you live your Truth and align it to the Ultimate Truth of the Christ Being.

So this is why until all men can live their Truth in the same way they are not as yet worthy or ready to become initiated into the Christ Light. So this is why I will wait at the Gates of Heaven for those who have chosen to love Me. They who love Me can see Me on earth and speak to Me as if I

were living with them. So when they come to My House in Heaven they will already know Me and My Father as My Father has many Mansions waiting in Heaven to house the lovers of the Light. This is My Truth. This is My Light. The Christ Words of this **Cosmic Christ World Light Shield** are My Father's Words. They are the Words that created Light. [Verse 12] [7]

I have now completed your Initiation into the Eyes of the Light. My Cosmic journey is coming to an end in the human world. My Word to you is that as you have loved Me, My Father will love you. He will send you the Holy Spirit; the Highest Spirit of the Light. He and the Father are One Spirit; yet three with Me. He will guide your beings as the mind guides the heart. You will trust in His Being. It is He who will show you the way to evolve your initiation for others. It is He who will come to you to be a part of this Light and its Movement on earth. He is the future legacy of Spiritual Light in this universe. He will open for you the powers of the Keys of Christ to transform mankind's Soul and psyche so that mankind will walk in the Light of My Father as these

---

[7] John 14: 22-24,

284

Keys will transcend the Keys I have used in your presence so that they will unlock the energies of the future cosmic worlds. This is so that the Spiritual Hierarchies of Light pour their Light into mankind's ever-evolving Spirit to create its eternal Pathway to Heaven.

You will be the spokespersons of this Cosmic tapestry. To give to mankind the source of its Ultimate Truth it will need to see the powers of the Holy Spirit as it is He that counsels the Counselors of the Light. This is what you will be and what your initiands will be. They will be speaking with the Voice of this Counselor of the Light. He will guide their thoughts and their minds to the perceptions that are engraved in Heaven's Soul as this is ultimately where My Father's heart is; to give the world His Love and His Light in these Words I give you now. The Holy Spirit will then keep these Words for you so that in all future incarnations you will be able to bring them into your Soul. You will be able to recall the Light of all Ages; the Christ Light. [Verse 13] [8]

So when I leave this planet you will be transformed with this Cosmic Light and its

duration will last forever with the power of the Holy Spirit as it is He that leads the Hierarchies of the Light. So will all the Kingdoms of creation on this planet be nourished by My Blood; by the Blood of the Redeemer of this World.

You will have the peace in your hearts when you have My Light in your hearts as the warmth of this Light evolves your Moral Will to it. Your Spirit is nourished when you let the Light enter your Soul and when you ask it to enter so that you can purify your being so that your being aligns with the Light. You also can see that your peace can be disturbed when the Lord of darkness wants to enter your doorway to your being which you use as the first step to enter the Doorway to My Light. He will soon try to disturb your being physically. He knows he cannot disturb you spiritually or psychologically as you have the Keys of Christ.

So I am preparing you for this when he will try to pronounce himself as the Lord of this earth. He will try to imitate Me as this is why he was thrown out of Heaven by the Archangel Michael as he

[8] John 14: 25-26.

disputed his Cosmic destiny with the Father. He will try to enter your Spiritual Doorways to replace Me. His powers will always be subordinate to those of the Christ Being. In all the universe he has the powers with the Spiritual Hierarchies of darkness. Yet where the Christ Being Spiritual Light is he cannot be as he cannot see the Light for when he faces it his being is burned into hell – fire. So be aware to let the Holy Spirit become the Counselor of the Light for you when I am no longer your human Spiritual Counselor on this planet. I have done all of this as the Father and My Being are One. My love of His Being is the Divine Love of the God Christ Being.

I say to you now when you are confronted with the Lord of darkness be aware of what I have asked you to do; to ask for the Christ Being to surround you with His Light and then for the Holy Spirit to stand by your side to counsel your actions so that His Light will shine on the Pathway to give up your will to change one's Cosmic destiny unless it is your Truth.

I have asked you then to ask the Archangel Michael to use the Spiritual Fire of Heaven to burn the darkness from the Lord of darkness that tries to enter the Circle of Light that protects your being and then to let the Spirit of Gautama Buddha stand with you in your Truth. This way you will have the purity of Spiritual Peace to be free of any darkness when you ask the Christ Light to spiritually burn away the Lord of darkness forevermore.

This is why I have come to the earth; to take away his presence and his cohorts from this Heavenly body of earth. This is My Cosmic Karma. This is truly My Pledge to you all; to remember My Words and place them next to your heart that I love you. When you love Me this love will live beyond my physical death. Your Soul will know Me upon your death as well as when you are living as the Spiritual Fire of Heaven will only make your personality shine before God while the cohorts of darkness in the spiritual world will shun the Spiritual Light and be separated by its Fire. Be aware this is My Word to you all. This is the Word to the world; this **Cosmic Christ World Light Shield**. This is My Word to your Light." [Verse 14] [9]

---

[9] John 14: 27-31.

CHAPTER 15

"I, the Christ Being, have shown you that there are creative and destructive patterns in all human beings ever born on this planet. These patterns of evolution in the human being began from the moment of the beginning of evolution when My Father gave life to a being. As the being evolved to the next step he chose this with his will no matter how unconscious or dim in his level of evolution he may have been.

Now as a human being at this present evolution there is a Moral free will to either follow the Light and evolve to the next stage or to fall to darkness and turn away from My Father. He who chooses to destroy the pathway for others so that he can steal the Light of his fellow man will be ultimately lost in the karmic Spiritual Fire when he enters the spiritual world upon his death. He also will have to face his karmic debts when he returns to earth in the following life times. He who chooses to live his Truth and align with the Ultimate Truth will meet the karmic Spiritual Light upon death and will have a karmic credit when he returns to earth. So those who follow Light will take the Spiritual Fire of Heaven on earth and this will burn away

spiritually their karmic darkness the more they fulfil their incarnation mission.

Those who do not have My Word or refuse it will lose their pathway and they will seek to steal Light from others to sustain their dark Souls as they have chosen to misuse their free will to become slaves of darkness. Hence they will then ultimately lose their free will as the dark spirits will rule it. However a man who truly follows My Light has free will and can see the Light and the shadows of darkness as Light can see the darkness but the darkness cannot see the Light as in the dark only darkness can be seen.

So he who follows the Light has a Pathway and he who follows the darkness cannot see the path. The Father created the Pathway to the Light as He has sent Me to you. He is in My Being. So he who follows Me follows My Father. He who follows the Pathway to the Light will see the Cosmic Christ shine in his being. He will see the Christ Light. [Verse 1]

I, the Christ Being, Son of the Living God, have come to create for you, the first of mankind, the Eyes of the

287

Light that can see the words that lead a man to the higher worlds. When he can walk in these worlds he can become a part of the Light and can see My Father so that when he lives his Truth he will become a creation of the Light. This is so as he is able to align the Cosmic Light of the world with his Truth. As Apostles of the Light you will use the Special Keys of Christ to transform the world's personality so that it will see you as Masters of the Keys of Light. [Verse 2] [1]

My Father's Love gives Light to all men who love His Son, the Christ, as He knows that this love is the fruit of the Light created by these men who have lived their Truth by working on themselves and who have suffered for this love. This is the love for the Supreme Being of Love who lives in God's Light; the Christ Being. What I have given you as the rules of the Pathway My Father gave Me first to live My Truth on your earth. Now I ask you to follow My Pathway by living your Truth. Living your Truth is trusting in My Love for you. In living My Truth I live in the Love of My Father. I am happy that you can see the Light in My Heart for you. I see that this happiness fills your heart and brings you Light. [Verse 3] [2]

I, the Christ Cosmic Being of Light and Son of the Living God, ask you to follow the Law of My Pathway. I ask you to put the Light above your life and to put the Truth above love. I ask you to love all men by these Laws as then you will love the Christ, My Father and the Cosmic Spirit of Truth; the Holy Spirit.

He who follows the Laws of the Light puts first the human being who puts first the Light. He will give up his life for this person if it is his Truth to do this to put the Light first. This love between human beings is based on the greatest Truth of friendship based on putting the Light first in one's life. When you put the Christ Light first you are the friends of the Christ Being. When you follow Me for the sake of salvation you are but a follower of the Light. When you put the Light first in your life in living your Truth you become a friend of the Christ Being. You have been initiated into the Cosmic Light of Christ, the Eyes of the Light, as you have been given the highest Spiritual Knowledge given to Me from My Father.

---

[1] John 15: 1-8.

[2] John 15: 9-11.

288

I chose you to become My initiands. You did not choose to follow Me as followers of the Light. You chose to follow Me as human beings who choose to live their Truth and to align with the Ultimate Light of the Living God. I have also shown you Special Keys of Light that bring this Light to the world; the home of mankind. This Light can transform its evolution so that it will ultimately incarnate as a Cosmic globe of Living Heavenly Light. This way man can become a Being of Light. So when you ask that the Light be sent to this transformation of the world to create Light in its being, ask it and you will have the Hand of God touch its Cosmic fate. This is putting the Cosmic Light of mankind's Truth first. Hence the Truth and the Light of mankind will prevail and triumph over the darkness eternally as the love of mankind of the Light puts the Light above its life on earth and it puts its Truth first. Then the Cosmic fate of mankind will prevail in the Light. Then the love of man to woman or woman to man will become the eternal love of a human being who lives his Truth. This is true love. This is true Light. This is the Ultimate Law of the Light. [Verse 4] [3]

When you put the love of the Light above your lives you will be hated by those who have their light in the heart of darkness as the Light existed before the darkness. I walk with you and eat with you so that you can see that the Cosmic Christ is a human being. You are human beings and now have been chosen by My Father to redeem mankind. You live your Truth when you follow this Pathway to this Cosmic Light. When you align it to the Light of Heaven you become initiands following the Christ Truth.

Those who have chosen Intellectual Materialism and have put it above Me will hate you as you have chosen to bring to the world its answer as to why it exists and what is the origin of the human being. This hate is there because the riddle of the universe will unfold before the world and then the world will have to face its Truth. It will have to say how the intellectual materialists have hidden the face of Truth for mankind when they made their knowledge replace the knowledge of God and the Light.

---

[3] John 15: 12-17.

I am the Master of the Light of this universe. I have chosen you to become initiands of the Cosmic Christ. You are My Apostles. You are the Leaders of the Light of mankind. This is what I have created as Master of the Light. The redemption of mankind will be what you will create for the Light.

When I will suffer the tormentors of My body and Being this will happen because the free will of man will have to be lived by the evil in evil men. This is what the Father willed from the beginning; that He will create a universe that is composed of beings who have the free will to walk in Light or to walk in the shadows of darkness. You had free will to choose Me as I have chosen you, although I chose you first as I existed first. I chose you as you chose to love the Truth of My Being. You chose to live your Truth. You chose to know My Father. So you see those who walk away from Me do not know or see My Father. The darkness has blinded the eyes of their spirit so that they see only the shadow of it as in the darkness one sees not the Light. [Verse 5] [4]

When the day comes that I must die because of the evil in evil men this will be because I have faced My Truth. I have proclaimed to the world that I am the Son of the Living God, the Light of all Ages.

I have challenged the Prince of evil in the spiritual world as this is My Cosmic Fate. I do this to redeem mankind and the kingdoms of creation. I stand on this Heavenly body called earth and speak these words so that the world can hear them until the end of Cosmic time in this universe. I am doing this to show that I represent ultimate time in this universe. That is, in this life I have lived in living My Truth I have the microcosmic parallel to the macrocosm of the life of this universe. I have done this by changing the pattern of this Cosmic Pathway of evolution. I did this by showing all men the Light.

Those who have willed to destroy it do this as they have willed a false destiny. This is their Cosmic karmic identification with the Devil who was removed from Heaven when he willed to replace the Father's Light with his light. This identification comes to a

_____

[4] John 15: 18-21.

person when he resents God for the suffering of his life. He begins to say one thing and do another as consciously he wills to satisfy his resentment with his unconscious alignment to darkness. He loses his identity to this evil. This happens as he refuses to acknowledge the miracles of Light I have shown the world and calls them magic tricks as he cannot reconcile his resentment of God for giving him the fate he has.

So it is with those who will put Me to death. They will justify their rationalisation of why I must die for the good of Israel so that Rome will not invade on the pretext that when Caesar would hear that the Jews have a new anointed Spiritual King in Jesus.
[Verse 6]

Those who hate the Light say that in their intellectual sense – bound logic that the origin of the universe is the darkness of lifeless matter and that mankind's origin is in this dead matter. They will talk of the effects of their logical arguments but will never confront their Truth and the

Truth that the logic is built on cause and effect and that no one can speak logically unless he truly also faces the source of the situation he is in. So you have these people who interpret the Light but will not look at interpreting what the Light has done in creating this universe as they choose to only see half the logic of Truth.

The Spirit of the Ultimate Truth and Light of this Universe will come to all of you and will create the Logic of the Light for mankind. This Spirit will show the beginning of the Light of this universe to the physical universe by creating the Spiritual Eyes of the Light in mankind to see it and to see it creating Light as Light creates worlds and Spirits till they become Heavenly bodies with human beings. This is so as in the beginning of time you, My Apostles, chose the Light to evolve in your beings. I chose you now as you took the progressive steps of evolution to become human beings who live their Truth walking in the Cosmic Christ Light."
[Verse 7][5]

---

[5] John 15: 22-27.

CHAPTER 16

"I, the Cosmic Christ Being, have given you the power of free will to decide on using your Eyes of the Light to see the Cosmic Light of Heaven or to walk away from it. The Spirits of Light that created this universe received their Light from the Father and as you know the Spirits of darkness can only mirror this Light and take it as a substitute for real Light. They too have a part to play in the ultimate creation of this cosmos. Yet it is they that ultimately must leave it to live in a world apart from the Father. They have been given this right to choose freely as only then can a man or a woman have the right to the Light. When they choose against darkness they pay the price of evolution as all must in the sense of the suffering of mankind. As I have shown you then all who pay this price of evolution put the Light first in their heart above life. You can see that at the completion of the mission of all humanity to reach its ultimate spiritual destiny in the Light there will be an ultimate, inevitable division.

This is now your task to realise this ultimate perception of Truth that only when a man works in freedom can he know his Truth. I have walked with you in this world to show you that the Father has given freely free will to all men to put the Light first in their lives. You have chosen to live your Truth as human beings and to live your Truth as Cosmic beings. This is why you have the Cosmic Christ Light. This is why I have come to show you how you can protect the Light of the world and then to soon be able to create it for all mankind. This is why you have become initiands of the Light.
[Verse 1] [1]

I now show you how I have built this Initiation Pathway for you which is by sharing My Light with your beings. I have created a Pathway where each person who becomes an initiand of the Christ has a Doorway to the Christ Spirit in his being. I have also outlined for you how to see that with the Eyes of the Light you can know whether to give Light to a person or to withhold it. You can know whether to ask Me to send Light or to send the Spiritual Fire of Heaven to use benign aggression to protect your Light.

---

[1] John 16: 1,

You will see that there are those who proclaim the Light as their Truth but in Truth they will want to kill you as you live your Truth and such people live the intellectually materialistic truth. They will never honor God before they are honored. Their whole concept of Light is based on what they can get for themselves first. They cannot share the Light with mankind let alone those who are even close to them. They steal the Light from you unless you protect it and put it first in your life. Then the Negative Motivational Science will not corrode your Light so that you can create a condition for living your Truth. You need to see that either you totally put the Light first above all things or you will lose your Soul. He who gives up all for the Light will win his Soul. He who knows this Pathway can see the journey of his Soul and can see its ultimate home in the Cosmic Christ Kingdom of Light. [Verse 2] [2]

Your initiation is almost completed so you need to be aware that the evil that will challenge you after I have left the earth is directed at My Being. When I am in the spiritual world soon when I leave the earth you have to face your Truth and use the tools of Light I have shown you how to use. This will give you the Light you need to confront the darkness as you have now the power to change the pattern of your lives by living your Truth and aligning with the Ultimate in My Being. Whatever they do to you because of Me, you need to face your Truth and to ask My Light to go to their beings as when you can do this you will face your Cosmic Truth. This will give you the power to change your Cosmic pattern of being. This will give you the power to give to your being the Light it needs to face its Cosmic Truth as your Truth will then be aligned to the Ultimate Truth cosmically in the Light.

There will be those who will masquerade that they follow the Light and will have a religious Negative Motivational Science to hide their resentment towards you. They will support the killers of the Light in uniform who uphold the false god of Intellectual Materialism in the world. They will, with this power, challenge your right to exist in the material world as you cannot really define who

[2] John 16: 2-4.

you are. You cannot really say that you are an initiand of the Cosmic Christ as no one understands such words. Yet you have been given the mission to initiate the world into the Light. So what is your task? How do you build a Pathway for mankind when you have problems in building one for yourselves? How do you face a hostile world that is run by intellectual materialists? Then you hear that I am to leave this world and to leave you to do this work without Me.

I say to you that this is right for you as this way you will be able to use the Cosmic powers of the Christ Light independently of Me. You will do this by following My Being spiritually and psychologically in living your Truth and your Cosmic Truth in your daily lives. If I were to not leave you, you would not be able to begin the work of establishing the Kingdom of Light on earth for mankind as I have come to give the world this Light. I have come to initiate you first among all human beings into the Eyes of the Light. My home is with My Father in Heaven. This is My place. Yet as My Being and the Father are One I am still with you at the Doorway to the Light as only then will you be able to live your Truth with the Special Keys of Light I have given. This is so as when you call on the Trinity of Light to send its Light to the darkness of this world you will then become the instruments of the Light on earth. Your beings will become vessels of the Light for mankind. Your task is this; to fulfil this Cosmic karma of the earth for mankind by initiating it and building a Pathway for it to see the Christ Light as this is My Legacy for you. As you have loved Me I now show you My Love with this Legacy of the Light I leave to you. [Verse 3]

My Pathway is to show mankind, through you and through all men from all ages who are initiated into this Light, their task, which is to live their Truth and then to align to the Ultimate Truth of the Cosmic Light of Christ. To do this I had to come into human history as I have done now but I have come for all ages.

I have also come to show mankind a Pathway that recognises that evil is part of mankind's history. When a man chooses not to live his Truth and to align with power, which means he identifies with the parallel of Negative

294

Motivational Science [of the twenty – first century] and he identifies consciously with Intellectual Materialism, he truly says one thing and does another as a being. He invites darkness into his Soul as this is the doorway to the Spirits of darkness humanly and cosmically. So then he identifies with the ultimate spirit of darkness.

Hence this spirit of darkness was given a place in man's history as the Father gave mankind a task which was to ask the Cosmic Christ, the Christ Being, to send His Light to the darkness in the Soul of mankind's being first so that mankind can be free to live its Truth and then to send the Cosmic Spiritual Fire of Heaven to the Cosmic Master of evil who will be burned away from the planet of earth with this Spiritual Fire so that his being will be entombed eternally with no source of Light. When man learns to do this then he will be able to accept his being and its level of evolution which is to live his Truth as a human being. He can only live his Cosmic Truth with the alignment to the Cosmic Christ. This is why I have come to the earth, to give you the Keys of Light so that you will know how to align your Truth to the Ultimate Truth and the Ultimate Light. [Verse 4] [3]

When My Father created the universe He took into His Hands the cosmos and let Heaven's Light give life to mankind. This life He spread out over many cosmic incarnations of earth and human beings. He did this so that man could experience this Light from His Being. He then gave a task to every being to create this universe with Him and with this Cosmic Light of Heaven. In this Creation He saw that He had to give all beings the free will to choose to love Him and his creation.

Now what happened was that there were beings who chose to create without the Father and His Light. They created out of the Light, their own light without the Father's Light. This is why their light now dims in the universe as its evolution progresses to its ultimate destiny in the seventh cosmic world to come near the end of time of this cosmos as their Light needs to mirror the Light of the Beings that have followed the Father. They have no source of Light in themselves. So there will come a time when no more

---

[3] John 16: 5-11,

Light can be mirrored in this cosmos as it will no longer appear in the material world. This is when the Light will be switched off eternally for those who have lived off the Light instead of in the Light.

The Ultimate Spirit of Light, the Holy Spirit, will show you the parallel of your living your Truth on this earth with your Cosmic Truth. This He will align to what I have spoken about now as the Cosmic karma of this earth and mankind. This will guide you to your true destiny as you will be the first Christ initiands who will lead all Initiation of the Light in this world as I have come to create this, through you, the Cosmic Christ Movement of Light. [Verse 5] [4]

I, the Cosmic Christ have entered the spiritual world before your very eyes and have returned to the material world in front of those same eyes. Your Eyes of the Light let you see My Being before anyone else on this planet. Now I will have to leave you soon to carry on with My Mission for this cosmos. In the visibly material world you will have been able to see that I am the Living Christ as I have initiated you into the culture of Heaven. I did this in the last three years by building a Pathway for you while creating this initiation in your personalities. You have all been initiated but not all will follow this Pathway in the same way. Some will take many incarnations to follow it completely before they get to the Cosmic Christ Pathway. This is because as they write about the present in their Souls in this incarnation so they will have to write the future in their Souls. Soon I need to travel to the spiritual world as I have work to do there to complete this Mission on earth. Then I will return after a few days and I will complete My work with you but this time I will be living in the spiritual world and not with you on the earth as I do now." [Verse 6] [5]

The Apostles then began to speak among themselves and one of them said to another, "What is he truly saying? Is he leaving us to face the world alone? Is he leaving earth without us? What shall we do? What is to become of us? We do not have the powers that he has. He is the One but what are we, even with this initiation into Cosmic Light? Who is going to listen to a band of men with no financial

---

[4] John 16: 12-15.

[5] John 16: 16.

or political standing apart from our knowledge of the Light? Who is going to listen to us when we have no career other than a Moral Will to put the Light first in our lives and no job as a real source of money to give us a material pathway to survive our initiation in the material world? Why, what is it that we need to do now to live our Truth? The Cosmic Christ will go to His Father in Heaven. We, what shall we do? How can we possibly create a World Movement of Light and at the same time live our Truth as human beings? How can we do this without the Cosmic Christ leading us? What is our Pathway now? What is our Truth? Tell us, Oh, Christ Being as we need to know your Will as you are our Master and our Ultimate Light!"

The Christ Being replied by saying, "I am the Cosmic Christ, Son of the Living God, Light of all Ages. You are the initiands to this Christ Pathway. Within your Souls you have the Christ Light force of this universe. You are asking Me what is to become of you when I leave you soon and then return no longer as a human being but as a Spiritual Being. Well, your

question is the right question as it asks how to create Light for this planet and at the same time live your Truth as human beings as all who create Light differently can only create it as an aberration of this Ultimate Path.

I, the Cosmic Christ, tell you that you will truly suffer and you will be torn apart in your Souls for what is to come into your lives. You will experience a Cosmic and psychological war within your beings and your whole personalities. The world will be at war with you at first as it will want to destroy you and wipe you off the face of the earth. You will be terrified at losing your lives and you will find your very Souls being attacked by the darkness of the evil men who will seek to kill you or your Light for aligning with Me. Yet after some time the world will hear your every word and your words will be spoken by millions of human beings in all generations to come. The Light you will pour into the world will be eternal as it is an Eternal Light. Each of you and all of you together will see this in your lives and in many lives to come. The world will honor God through honoring your Light. This is My Prophecy from Heaven for

297

earth and for you. [Verse 7]

When you were created in the beginning of this Cosmic planet of earth and the earth was incarnated from the spiritual world into the material world your spirits then looked to My Light. Your spirits now live in your human bodies and the spirit of the earth supports them with its body. Spiritual Hierarchies of Light created your bodies of spirit and the spirit bodies of the very planets of this cosmos with its stars and Heavenly bodies. You lived in the Light of these Spiritual Beings until you learned to live with your own Light in the material world. You did this so that the Father could fulfil His Promise that He would create a universe of beings which had ultimate free will to choose His Light first in their lives or to choose one's own light first in their lives.

Now you know in the human world a baby is born without any protection to survive in the material world without its parents. It is a tremendous shock to be born and to have no way of knowing how to live one's life and survive in a different world from when all was controlled and taken care of as a baby is before birth. So it is with your Pathway now

with Me. I have come to give birth to the Christ Light in your Souls. The pain is great to be born in the Cosmic Light of Christ but the Light will wash away all of this suffering when you look towards it and let it fill your whole beings with its Cosmic life – giving supernatural power; a power that will give you the power to change the pattern of your lives and the pattern of life of the whole human race. The evolution of the character of mankind will change forevermore once you create it with the Christ Light anew as when a man lives his Truth he creates a character which has Light as the Light will shine through his personality. This personality will shine in the cosmos for all time when it lets the Christ Light shine to shed Light upon the journey of its Soul to its ultimate home in Heaven as then a man's Soul becomes one with the Light. [Verse 8]

So it is now that you are very sad because of My Words but you will be truly happy and filled with eternal Light when you can live your Truth aligned to the Eternal Christ Light. Then when I am on earth again soon as a Spiritual Being to complete My Mission with you, this is when you will begin to use the Special Keys of Light independently of Me.

Hence you will have the power to use the Light of Heaven and its Spiritual Fire to change your future and the fate of this world.

I have shown you how to always ask that the Christ Light will go to the darkness that wants this world to lose its course of evolution towards the Light. For this is My First Commandment of the Rules of Light as when you do this you put the Father's Light first in your Souls as My Being and the Father are One. Yet I ask you to ask always that I, the Cosmic Christ, will send His Light to the darkness as this way My Father will let the Light of Heaven go to it. To ask the Christ Light to do this will not do as this is not also including My Father and the Cosmic Spirit of Truth. If it did then it would include My Being and who I am now for mankind as I have come but once to the earth in human form.

I will not come again in this form as this is the Will of the Father. So I have come this time in evolution for the reason to change the destiny of mankind so mankind should ask for Me to send the Light to the darkness and to see that the Father in turn has

sent Me first to mankind to do this. So he who knows this Cosmic secret of Light will have power over the darkness providing he is on time as a human being living his Truth and providing he is on time living his Truth as a Cosmic being. This meaning that he has a way to ask the Christ Being to send the Cosmic Christ Light as a request from his conscious, unconscious incarnation, spiritual and material. He who can do this has complete Light in his being and the complete Christ Light in his Soul as then he becomes an initiand of the Cosmic Christ Light.

[Verse 9] [6]

I am the Cosmic Initiator of all Light on your planet. Before the sun rose into the Heavens and gave Light to the earth, I and My Being gave Light before its birth. This Light created the world. The Spiritual Hierarchies that created the sun as their home and now give Light to the solar system and to the whole cosmos, were given Light before the world was created as I and the Father created all. We, with the Cosmic Spirit of Truth, now show you the Cosmic Pathway that we have come to share with you first and for you to tell all of

---

[6] John 16: 17-24,

mankind of it so that we can share the Light with you as we have created this Light as we are the Ultimate Source of it. We created it to bind the universe together and to give it life.

So when you ask the Christ Being to send the Light for you, you can this way use the Keys of Light to fulfil your Cosmic Truth. Then you have the power of the Cosmic Christ in your hands as then you are an instrument of this Cosmic Light. Then the Father can also work through you for as you love the Son you love His Father as the Son comes from His Heavenly Father and He is the Light of all Ages. I incarnated as a human being as the Father chose the human beings of earth to become the human vessel of His Light. Now I will soon incarnate into the spiritual world and become once again the spiritual vessel of My Father's Cosmic Light."
[Verse 10] [7]

Then the Apostles decided to confront Jesus with a question. They asked him, "When will you go as we know now that when you do you will be with the Father? We know now that this is why you have come and that you are the Cosmic Christ, Son of the Living God, Light of all Ages. We also know that soon you will be with your Father. Yet we fear that this means you will leave the earth with your Cosmic powers but somewhere you are going to have to leave your body which does not live in Heaven and can only mean that you have to die. Is this so, Jesus, our Master?"

The Christ Being replied by saying, "I, the Christ Being, see that you have concluded the Truth is that you are going to be threatened and attacked because of your association with Me. You are also going to separate as a group as there will soon be many evil men looking to kill you and arrest you as some will attempt to do this and discredit you so that they can slander My name.

I stand with My Father to bring loving peace to all human beings. Yet I also acknowledge that the world is filled with suffering and misery as it is ruled by the tyrants who have become the Lords of darkness that rob and pillage the earth of its Light. However be aware that the Cosmic Christ and the Cosmic Special Keys of Light My Apostles have will give My

_____

[7] John 16: 25-28.

initiands of the Light power over the whole world and the

entire cosmos. This is the Cosmic Christ; the Light of all Ages." [Verse 11] [8]

---

[8] John 16: 29-33.

CHAPTER 17

Then the blinding white gold aura surrounded the Christ Being. His white garment began to shine and his face emanated a most beautiful form of grace when he spoke the words, "Father, let the heart of Heaven open its love for mankind as the Children of Christ are speaking the Words of Light as I now must touch the Cosmic fate of mankind and become a part of its journey to Redemption as I have the Cosmic Power of all Ages from the Father to perfect evolution by living My Truth as a human being and a Cosmic Supernatural Being.

I now have created a Pathway of Initiation for mankind to directly see the Christ Light as he who sees it with these Cosmic Eyes will eternally live in it. Light came to the earth when the earth was being formed from Spirit. This Light was transmitted through Spirit Beings of Light.

The darkness mirrored this Light from its own Spirit and shared in the creation of the world and mankind. Yet its share will diminish as a mirror is not the Source of Light but a reflection of it. Intellectual materialists who now hold up this science as the only one true knowledge only mirror the Light in the world Soul. That is, they cannot see that the Soul is the source of this Light but only speak of its reflections. So this mirrored Light was created out of the free will given by the Father; this reflection of Light in the Spirits of darkness. They wanted this inner reflective Light above the Cosmic Light of the Father. So in this way they lost sight of the Ultimate Light. Hence they became a part of evolution and participated and are ever participating in its destructive patterns of being; the destructive patterns in the spirit of every individual on earth who seeks his perception of the truth above the Truth. They ever seek to create Light out of the darkness. They cannot see Christ as He is the Son of the Living God. [Verse 1]

I am the Cosmic Christ! I ask You now, Oh, Father in Heaven, let the Light shine upon My Pathway I have built for My initiands whom You have chosen out of all of mankind to lead it to its incarnation in Heaven as this is what I came to do with You, My Father. Let the whole spiritual universe shine with the Cosmic Light of Heaven so that it can be transformed into the Spiritual Fire that created the world in the beginning of time and beyond time so that the Cosmic Christ can create out of this a world of eternal and everlasting Light.

My Father, look down upon Your Initiands of Christ and they will be there heart – filled with love for You as they walk on the Pathway I have built for them. They ever become carriers of Your Cosmic Light. In the beginning of time You created free will for mankind so that man could love freely his Maker and so that he could create his own Light and follow Your Ultimate Light in freedom. You asked these men to follow Me, the Cosmic Christ, and now they have pledged all of their beings in this life and in all incarnations to come to follow the Words of the Christ Light in their hearts. They have asked that the Cosmic Christ Light be poured into their hearts while they are asking Me to send the Spiritual Light of Heaven to the darkness in the world. They honor the Living God by their faith in the Light. They walk in the Christ Light. They see God's

Light shine through their personalities when they live their Truth. They speak to the Son of God and put His Light first in their hearts. They put this Light above life and so live their Cosmic Truth. They do this to honor the Father and to give Him back the Light for giving them ultimate free will to choose in freedom their Cosmic and human destiny with the Eternal Light of Heaven. [Verse 2] [1]

I now ask the Spiritual Light of Heaven to create a Circle of Light around My initiands of the Cosmic Christ and that My Heavenly Father will pour Light inside this Circle so that the Cosmic Christ will stand next to them when they ask that He send His Light outside this Circle to the darkness as then the Spiritual Fire of Heaven will burn away this darkness with the Cosmic Christ Light. [Verse 3]

I ask the Father; open the Door of Heaven for Me as I am about to walk through it. Yet I ask You, Father, to send Your Light to them so that they too can become Sons of God in Spirit.

Father, these initiands carry Your Light in their whole beings. This Light is the

---

[1] John 17: 1-6,

303

Christ Light so they have eternal Light. They have the Cosmic Christ Light which You gave Me before I came to the earth. All are ready for the War of All darkness against All Light apart from one who lost his Truth and his being which the Eyes of the Light forecast to us all.

I am soon once again to live in Heaven. I see that the Light now lives in the Souls of these Apostles as they follow the Cosmic Christ Being Light. They have lived their Truth and this Truth gives them Light. This Light gives them a life of eternal happiness. They speak the Words of God and they see that when they live their Truth and follow the Cosmic Christ Truth, the darkness in the world tries to crush their beings. They know that this also is happening to Me as I have put the Cosmic Light of My Father above My human life. Hence they, like Me, have put the Truth above the world. [Verse 4] [2]

I ask You that the Circle of Light that You, Father, have poured Light into so that these initiands inside it can have Your Light in their hearts. I ask You to walk with Me so that when the supreme dark spirit comes to enter this Circle You will send Your Light to him. These initiands have lived their Truth and aligned to the Cosmic Christ Truth they have already surpassed the human being stage on earth. They have begun to live in the Spiritual Light as they have put this above their human Light. As I have done they have done and followed the Christ Being as his initiands.

They have put the Father's Truth above their Truth. This gives them the power of the Special Keys of Light as they have this power You have given them when they aligned to My Being. So they are ready now to begin on their journey to fulfil My Mission as I have fulfilled Your Mission for mankind. So I have shown them how to put into their mind's eye the Cosmic Christ Being so that all of their universal concepts of thought will shine with the complete perceptions of the Christ Light. [Verse 5] [3]

I, the Christ Being, ask that the Eternal Circle of Heavenly Light will be created around those who follow My Apostles on the Initiation Pathway to Me so that, as I love them, they will all ask the Cosmic Christ to send his Light to

---

[2] John 17: 7-14,

[3] John 17: 15-19.

burn away the Intellectual Materialism of this world as this false god ever turns mankind into a Negative Motivational Science machine which is telling them that where there is a will there is a way; a way to answer the life problem of the world and its existence by using man's own Light above God's Light.

I, the Cosmic Christ, will then stand next to My Father and then mankind can see that He and I created Light that gives life to all universes. This God life – force Light will be directed to create a World Pathway of Initiation for all men who want their Souls to be encircled by the Light.

This Light of Heaven will unite this Cosmic Light with the power of its Spiritual Fire and let it transform in the Soul of mankind as the Truth of mankind will become the Truth of his world. This Truth can see the ultimate potential destiny of every individual human being is to unify his being with the Cosmic Light of Christ; a union that will be as evolved as the union between the Cosmic Christ and His Father as this Initiation into the Cosmic Christ Light creates a

Pathway that leads one to become a being that leads one to become a being who loves the Father as the Son loves the Father of all Light.
[Verse 6]

I, the Christ Being, ask You, Oh, Father, to let My Apostles walk in Heaven with Me and to let them see the Kingdom of Light in Heaven as then they can see God's Living Light as it shines upon the universe. They also can see the love You have for Me and have had from the beginning of Creation of the Light.
[Verse 7] [4]

I, the Cosmic Christ, can see that mankind, apart from My initiands, will not look at the spiritual facts about how I have come to this planet. They will not accept that I created the Spiritual Hierarchies with the Father and that I am the Ultimate Truth and the Ultimate Light that has come to the earth to redeem the world with Light from eternal darkness. This is My Mission to complete the initiation of mankind first as human being for three years as I have done and then as Spiritual Being till the end of time itself. This is so as I put first in My Heart the Love of the Light of My

---

[4] John 17: 20-24,

Father in Heaven as the Love of My Father is the Love of

God's Cosmic Light " [Verse 8] [5]

[5] John 17: 25-26.

CHAPTER 18

Jesus then walked with his Apostles across the Kidron valley to a garden where he often met his Apostles and initiated them into the Cosmic Keys of Light. He did this by first speaking about his Heavenly Being and then showing them how to create a Circle of Spiritual Light that connected the material world to the spiritual world. Inside this Circle he would ask them all to stand in their Truth. He would then, at times, transfigure into pure Light. His entire white cloak would become emblazoned with brilliant Light. Out of his hands a Light would flow that would create this Circle of Heaven's Light around them all. His face would shine like sunlight. Then when he spoke of his Father the Light would turn into a Fire and Angels would appear next to his Being making the Light flow into this Circle of Cosmic Christ Light. These Angels would then begin to listen to the Christ Being in the same way as his Apostles as if he was also initiating them into how the material world was connected to them and to Heaven. [Verse 1] [1]

Judas the Iscariot had known of this meeting to come in this garden of Gethsemene and had planned to seize Jesus with the help of the Roman soldiers. He had entered a doorway spiritually which told him that by doing what he was doing he was going to save Israel from Roman annihilation and make himself a hero of his countrymen. Also he would be richly rewarded by the Pharisees by being given money and political power which would be in standing with his high evolution intellectually. He had totally identified with Intellectual Materialism and had unconsciously transformed his Eyes of the Light to eyes of darkness. This happened to him as the chief priests had used black magic spells to seduce him and to reveal to them parts of the initiation process of the Cosmic Christ as they were able to show through their powers that Judas was misled by the charismatic personality of Jesus.

Ca'iaphas, the chief priest, said to him before he finally won Judas over to betray Jesus, "Look, Jesus is a good man and a Prophet of really skilled arts of magic but he is also a fool when it comes to

---

[1] John 18: 1-2.

political and commercial situations in the world. Israel belongs to Rome. Now Rome is letting the Jews follow their own religious and commercial destiny providing Israel follows the political will of Rome. Now what the Romans make out of Israel is a small part of their over – all revenue worldwide with their empire. If, however, they perceive a rebellion they will crush it with their legions without warning.

Now Jesus has been setting himself up as a religious and political leader of Israel. He works in total isolation to all our laws. He talks of worlds that no one can prove exist. He has learned the art of persuasion as he has traveled and worked with eastern gurus who have given him knowledge of the ancient scriptures of all religions but he has set himself up against our religion. He says he is the Son of God. Now that puts him above Caesar. Obviously he has studied somewhere and trained himself to lead men. Now he is talking about a world revolution which will take away Rome's power with love and Light. This is delusion. Rome will respond with killing every man alive in the Jewish state if there was a threat to its interests.

Now he, this Jesus of Nazareth, has no money and has no position in society. He says his knowledge or the knowledge of his Father is above the law of the Jews. This means he is a political threat to Rome and to all of us. Look at what happened to John the Baptist whom you followed as a Teacher of the Light before you followed Jesus."

Then Judas replied, "I can see that I have been blinded by the love I have for this man who is pure in heart and Soul but is naïve of what he is doing to our country. I see that he is unconscious of what he is doing. Yet nevertheless he poses a security risk for the whole nation unless we stop him. So I agree to help you arrest him so that I can do this one thing that is wrong to save a million of my countrymen." [Verse 2]

So then Judas was given ten soldiers to go to the garden of Gethsemene and arrest Jesus. The reason the chief priest wanted Judas to do this was so that this way this time Jesus would not escape as every other time that it was organised that Jesus would be arrested he would disappear. Judas had explained to Ca'iaphas that this was so because Jesus always had prior knowledge of the future as he had Cosmic Eyes of Light. This Ca'iaphas just put down to pure clairvoyant seeing that he knew many prophets had, whom he had related to, even among his sect of the Pharisees.

Yet in Truth the Christ Being had made certain he would complete the Initiation of the Keys of Light for the Apostles and that when the Romans had got an order to kill him he would go back into the spiritual world temporarily but as it was time now to complete his Mission of Initiation he, of course, could see what was in Judas' Soul and knew that he would ultimately betray him. He did this as he accepted this Pathway was to show all of mankind that he was living his Truth as a human being and as a Cosmic Being. Yet his alignment of his Truth as a human being came first. This is the reason he accepted his fate to be betrayed by Judas as otherwise he would have intervened by using his Cosmic powers.

Hence he lived his Truth and in this way created for mankind humanly and cosmically as the Ultimate Truth. This is why his Truth is the Ultimate Truth which has its source in the Ultimate Light as the Ultimate Light is his Divinity as the Ultimate Cosmic Being. He lived his Cosmic Truth when he became a human being and showed to all the spiritual world that he put first the Pathway of his Father's Light as this Light created all Spiritual Hierarchies and all the universes of the cosmos. [Verse 3]

Now the soldiers, with Judas, were being led by some of the Pharisees who wanted to see that Judas carried out his part of the bargain to trap Jesus into their hands. It was a dark, moonless night when the soldiers, Judas and the Pharisees walked in the garden of Gethsemene towards the meeting place where Jesus was beginning to speak to his Apostles.

All of a sudden a glimmer of what a fire would look like was piercing through the trees but there was no fire. The lanterns being carried by the solders were put out so as to surprise their prey. Once they came to the Apostles they felt very strange as they could see Jesus and his Apostles but there was no fire nor source of light visible to explain why there was enough light for them to see anything.

Then out of the silhouette in shadows and light that had no moon nor sun to see with, Jesus spoke to them as he had already known of their presence before they showed themselves. They were astonished at his confronting them when they were certain that they had caught everyone by surprise. He said, "You have come for Jesus of Nazareth as you have chosen to arrest him. This is your order from the high priest. I am Jesus Christ, Son of the Living God. I have let you find Me as to show the world that this is My fate to be betrayed into the hands of evil men as all generations to come will in all life times to come on all the worlds to come and this world see that to live one's Truth comes first for all human beings who follow Me. To live one's Cosmic Truth is what I will do now by letting the Cosmic Christ live his human Truth first. This is the ultimate destiny of the Ultimate Truth of mankind. This is to put the Light first in all things and to put it above life and to align it with the Cosmic life of the Light." [Verse 4]

Then Judas went next to Jesus and told the soldiers, "This is Jesus of Nazareth. Here I have fulfilled my end of the bargain to Ca'iaphas. Be sure that you tell him what I have done for you all!" Then he looked at Jesus and said, "Only a human being can die! You are a good human being but totally misguided about the world. You have lived in this isolated cosmic world of yours but it will bring ruin to the whole Jewish nation unless someone stops you."

Judas waited for Jesus to reply to him but Jesus just looked at him and said nothing. This made Judas regret what he had done as in Jesus' eyes there was no anger or resentment. There was only pity for him. At first he could not understand it. One look from Jesus and he felt that he had lost his being. He then abruptly turned away from Jesus and left and walked into the night as quietly as he had appeared from nowhere. [Verse 5]

The head of the Pharisees told the soldiers to arrest Jesus before he would escape as the Pharisees had seen Jesus all of a sudden disappear on many occasions. Then Jesus said to them, "I am ready now for you to arrest Me. I am the one you are looking for. I will come with you when you let the others with Me go as it is I whom you have been ordered to take into custody."

The Pharisees disagreed but the Romans saw the logic in all of this. They disregarded what the Pharisees wanted about arresting all the Apostles as they pointed out that they had a mandate to arrest Jesus and no one else as they knew that to go against Jesus they would look like fools once again if he disappeared, while the Pharisees could again complain to the Roman officers that they had failed in their job again in capturing Jesus. So an argument began between the Romans and the Pharisees.

Then Jesus once again said, "You are looking for Jesus of Nazareth. This person is Me. I have made it clear to you that I will go with you when you let My people go." Spiritually the Apostles could see that there was a Circle of Light around them and Jesus was in the centre. They were next to him but no one could see him except them. They were truly frightened as they could perceive that Jesus was going to leave them. His Angels were next to him.

Also they saw a huge Angel the size of a temple near Jesus with a Sword of Fire. He had a million wings of Light. He also rode on a white horse the size of the horse of Troy. Behind him were a billion Angels all holding Swords of silver emitting Spiritual Fire. The Christ Being looked at the Leader of the Angels and the Apostles could see Jesus saying to him, "Archangel Michael, you will now let Me leave this Circle of Light soon as it is the Will of My Father." [Verse 6] [2]

Seeing all of this Simon Peter concluded that Jesus was going to leave his Cosmic protection for them. So he left the Doorway to the Light and walked out of the Circle of Light. Then he drew his sword from its sheath and threatened the Pharisees to leave them alone. Then the Roman soldiers confronted him with their swords and one said to him, "We have no quarrel with you. It is Jesus whom we have orders to arrest by the order of Rome and the chief priests of Israel."

Then Peter raised his sword and cut off the ear of one of the servants of the Pharisees. Then he said, "Come any closer and I will die first than let you touch my Master, Jesus." Then Jesus appeared with Peter. He said to Peter, "I

_____
[2] John 18: 3-9,

love you, my friend, as you have loved the Light of My Father. I have shown you the Pathway to the Ultimate Light. You have been initiated to see the Ultimate Truth. Now you will go back inside the Circle of Light as it is My Father in Heaven who has willed now for you to follow your Truth as it is His Will that I follow mine." Then the Christ Being picked up the ear and put it back on the servant man named Malchus. His ear was restored and he thanked Jesus by saying, "You are My Lord and My Saviour."

Then what could be seen by the Apostles from inside the Circle of Light was the Archangel Michael asking Peter to come back into the Circle of Light. What could be seen by the soldiers and the Pharisees was Jesus waiting for them to arrest him. They also became alarmed as what happened next was that there were no more people left in the whole garden except themselves and Jesus. The Apostles had disappeared. [Verse 7] [3]

So the Roman soldiers pushed Malchus aside and arrested Jesus formerly by binding his hands behind his back and reading the arrest warrant. It read, "It is by order of the governor of Israel that Jesus of Nazareth be arrested on the charge of insurrection against the Roman Empire, for inciting religious violence in the populace of Israel and also by proclaiming his person as a Divine Being. Hence the state of Israel also charges this person with sedition against its laws which uphold Caesar's divinity as lawgiver of all nations of the world. Signed by the authority of the chief priest, Ca'iaphas." [Verse 8] [4]

So once the Romans arrested Jesus they took him to Annas, a priest who was going to question Jesus first so that he could inform Ca'iaphas of the proceedings as he had plotted with him to get Jesus arrested as he also was his father-in-law and wanted to help him with his plan for the self – interest of the family first financially and politically as his standing commercially also depended on Roman bureaucrats who controlled the Roman army occupying Judea.

He had also followed the advice of his son – in – law who had convinced the head council of priests to sacrifice Jesus as a means to save the

---

[3] John 18: 10-11,

---

[4] John 18: 12.

312

nation. As he had been to Rome and had connections with the Roman senate he often had used these connections to warn about new policies from Rome soon to come to the provinces. He had told the council that there were rumours reaching Caesar's ears that there was a man calling himself the Messiah of the World who was challenging the divinity of the god of Rome.

This, it was said, was received with some amusement by the Emperor in the beginning at hearing the news but that he had then remarked, "The Roman Empire will stand and fall upon its science of the personality of Caesar as when a Roman soldier fights for Rome he fights to let this paramount truth of the world prevail. So I say to all who wish to challenge this celestial eagle of Rome they will perish as sure as Rome's sword will fall upon those who do not swear allegiance to its god, Caesar; the ruler of the world."

So Cai'iaphas in this way sold the story to the council that Rome had already given a warning to him discreetly to get rid of the insurrection or face the lethal political consequences now or in future generations. Hence Annas supported his son – in – law as he feared the Romans and knew that only with their power could he have the life he had of prestige and wealth in his own society of being a religious aristocrat who had become above question amongst his people. He could do anything he liked and be revered as a good man providing he could instill the fear of the Romans in his people successfully no matter if it was true or not in reality. This was so as he had learned that to be a successful politician one had to manage the public's perception of the truth first before entertaining the truth at any time. He knew this way, for example, that if Jesus had to die to save his position, this was a price he was willing to pay as his conscience could justify the truth of the situation. He reasoned that the fact was, who were you in the world when you did not use the Negative Motivational Science of the Romans, regardless if it was negative or positive? For him it could only be positive as what was the use of losing everything because he was going to support the truth of one man when he was saving his livelihood and his whole society from destruction? So the truth was what was relatively true as everything else was open to opinion.

So Annas reasoned that he was a good man making a hard decision. That he had made good and evil relative escaped his judgment as what came first was his will to make it in his life financially so that he could be honored as a high priest of the Pharisees who upheld the law of God. This is what was first in his heart when he plotted to kill Jesus. So when Jesus was arrested he was quite happy that the deal with Judas the Iscariot had worked out to everyone's benefit and that there was physical proof now that Jesus was vulnerable and not the Messiah, as other wise he would have the power to stop his arrest. So in Truth Annas, the priest, had sold his Soul to Intellectual Materialism as he consciously put power above the Light. [Verse 9]

Then the Apostles, John and Peter, both left the Circle of Light to follow Jesus and his captors at a distance. When Jesus was going to be officially presented before the high priest, the Apostle, John, was allowed to be with Jesus. This was so as John knew Annas personally and had some political say as a Jew who represented the people and their welfare before the Roman – directed Jewish legal system of the day. Peter remained in the courtyard in front of the doorway to the Annas residence. John then asked that Peter be allowed to stay in the courtyard as he was accompanying him until all the proceedings with Jesus were over. The soldiers could not say 'no' to him as Annas wanted to appear to do all that was right legally as he was afraid to confront John who, with all the Apostles, had a real following among the people. So he took the advice of the Romans who arrested Jesus. Their theory was to arrest the ringleader and leave the rest alone. They reasoned that this way all would ultimately lose their support among the people without him. [Verse 10]

Now there was a maid who was looking after the household of Annas. It was a very cold night and so she tended a charcoal fire outside the Annas residence which had been put there to warm the guards in the courtyard. She confronted Peter with this question, "Why, you are Peter, the leader of the band that follows Jesus of Nazareth! You are the fisherman who has turned to become a preacher of the new Christ Light religion of the world. Are you not?"

Peter replied, "You mistake me for another man. I know nothing of what you speak about. I am a fisherman and I have heard Jesus of Nazareth speak. I am interested in what he has said and that is it. I am not his follower. I follow my own light." [Verse 11] [5]

Annas then said to Jesus, "What gives you the right to install yourself as the Messiah of the Jews? Also how can you tell the people that you are the Living Christ, Son of the Living God? By what authority do you say these things? What is your background to these statements? Who are you? Let us hear your defense as there is a charge against you that your teaching is opposing the Roman and Jewish legal system of this nation. Speak up and let us hear your answers to my questions!"

Then the Christ Being answered, "I have been speaking to the whole nation for the last three years in all the synagogues and public places. I presented My teachings at the temple of Jerusalem. All Jews know of Me and the Pathway I have taught initiands to follow. I have revealed My Identity to the whole world through what

I have lived. My Truth is in My actions of healing men and making the blind see and the sick well again. I have used special powers of Light to heal thousands of Jews. I have talked of My Philosophy of Light to all the Jews and to you and all of you here were present when I did this. So when you ask Me what I am doing makes it clear to Me what your eyes have seen and your mind knows is not enough to tell you the Truth. So you also discount what others have seen and know to be the Truth.

So I ask you, what truly is it that you ask of Me? Is it not so that you are saying one thing and doing another by arresting Me as you are saying that you uphold justice and the law? Where is the justice in arresting a human being who has given Light to Israel and who has given Light to the world and is innocent of the charge you have made against him?" [Verse 12] [6]

Then one of the soldiers raised his hand to strike Jesus and then he struck him on his face. Then Jesus looked at him and the man began to shake. He began to feel very fearful. Jesus then looked into his

---

[5] John 18: 13-18.

[6] John 18: 19-21,

315

Soul with eyes that questioned the man's very being and Jesus said to him, "Why do you strike Me when I am telling the Truth?"

Then one of the officers said to Jesus, "You stand accused of arousing sedition among the people. You have been arrested as there is sufficient evidence to substantiate that you have committed this crime. The soldier struck you to remind you that you have to defend yourself only and not interpret this court of law!"

Then the Christ Being said, "I see no evidence against Me except that you are saying what is right according to your law as being the truth. So why do you support an abuse of power to harm a person who is not only speaking the Truth but has also lived the Truth? If this were not so then why can you not present a specific charge of what I have done or present a witness who says that I have done what you say? So in Truth you can do neither. So I say to you, your basis of arresting Me has no legal or moral ground that will stand in any court of law in the world. So I ask you, will you arrest an innocent man and say it is right?"

The officer then left the room with Annas. He told Annas, "You should send him to Ca'iaphas as this Jesus man knows the law! I will not support your claim to arrest him as your authority could be challenged unless you get your son – in – law's endorsement of what we are doing here." Annas replied, "He will do what we tell him to do as he was the one who warned us in the first place." Then they tied Jesus up with his hands behind his back and took him to Ca'iaphas.
[Verse 13] [7]

Now while this was happening inside the Annas residence Peter was with the soldiers outside and had just denied that he was a follower of Jesus. Then a soldier said to Peter, "I have seen you with Jesus and you cannot say that you are not a member of this group. Now face it. Everyone knows about you and that cult that is making Jesus a god above Caesar, himself. Now come on. Own up to it! Your friend, John, well...he is there trying to help Jesus as we all know he was working for the Jewish administration. So come on, we know his story. So what is your story when you say you are not his follower?" Peter answered

---

[7] John 18: 22-24.

him by saying, "Look here, I said that I do not follow Jesus. Yes, I have heard him speak and I was interested for a while but I can tell you that is as far as it went. I am not and never will be a follower of a person who means well but as we all know says things that are very contradictory as has often been pointed out. So, yes, I have investigated what this man was saying as I often observe speakers of religion. I have listened also to Annas speak on many occasions. So no, I am not a follower as much as I do not follow Annas. I follow my own law in that way, sir."

Then on the way out of the house the officer who accused Jesus of sedition said to Peter, "I have heard from my men that you deny being a follower of Jesus but you cut off the ear of Malchus when we were going to arrest Jesus. Now whoever you say you are, what are you doing here if you are not a follower of Jesus?"

Peter replied, "Look here, I just did what I had to do as I thought that it was quite unfair that you were going to arrest a man who did nothing wrong and who, in my eyes, was innocent. However to say that I am his follower is not true. I follow no man. I have my own law. Yes, I did listen to Jesus as I thought that he had many wise sayings and he was very genuine. However I see now that what he was speaking about was unrealistic and unlivable to any human being. So I am not a follower. That is my last word on Jesus of Nazareth." Then Peter was struck in the heart by a really dark energy as he realised that he had said one thing and done another when he denied the Cosmic Christ and his Truth. At that moment a cock could be heard crowing as if to say, "You are a liar," to Peter's ears.
[Verse 14] [8]

Ca'iaphas was informed before Jesus arrived of what went on at the Annas' residence. He immediately then endorsed the order to arrest Jesus by seal of the high priest of Israel. This gave authority to the Roman soldiers to take Jesus to the praetorium. They did not enter the praetorium with the Roman soldiers as it was the Passover and their law forbade them to expose themselves in it at that time of observing the religious feast.

Knowing this Pontius Pilate, the Roman governor of Judea,

---

[8] John 18: 25-27.

317

came out of the praetorium and said to them, "You have arrested this man on a charge of religious sedition and blasphemy. None of these charges are specific to the law or to what Rome has to do to uphold Roman justice in the Jewish land of Israel. Then an assistant of Ca'iaphas replied about the allegations they had made about Jesus. He said, "This man has committed a crime against the state of Israel. He has done this by telling people to follow a religion that wants to overthrow the Roman Empire and take away the laws that the Jewish state has lived by for thousands of years."

Then Pilate said to them, "You have the power to judge him as the Pharisees among you have been appointed by the Roman senate to enforce the laws of Rome when a crime has been committed. So why do you bring him to me? Obviously you have evidence and witnesses that can substantiate the criminal acts of this man, Jesus. So again I ask you, why do you come to me with this man? Judge him yourself and let Rome handle more important affairs than settling the problem of the Jews with those of their own

religious rebel prophesying a new religion. I ask you, what does this have to do with Rome?"

Then the Pharisee said to Pilate, "What you say is true but the fact of the matter is that our law says that this man must die for his crimes. We do not have the legal power to condemn a man to die on the cross for his evil without Rome's approval of our judgment. So we now appeal to Rome to make this judgment." [Verse 15] [9]

Then Pilate walked back into the praetorium and summoned his soldiers to bring Jesus before him. Pilate sat on his governor's chair looking as regal as his master, Caesar in Rome. Then he glanced at Jesus in the way a monarch would look at one of his servants. Jesus looked at this person with the eyes of a man who had no fear nor shame for his accusations and who truly looked like the Monarch that Pilate had always aspired to be unconsciously. This was so as the Christ Being had a presence that no man could deny had a real energy that spoke to anyone with even the weakest of intuition saying

---

[9] John 18: 28-32.

that no one who had such looks could be anything but what he says he is. This was so as Jesus was not only handsome but he was also a person who was charismatic with an indefinable quality that spoke to the Spirit of all around him.

This Spirit of the Christ Being now was confronting Pilate so Pilate had to match it as after all he was the governor of a Roman province. This man was but a poor religious zealot given up to him by his own people to condemn to death. So Pilate sarcastically asked Jesus, "How is it that the Cosmic King of Mankind cannot redeem the Jews to the religion of Light you have brought to the planet earth? Tell me what happened so that your Light cannot reach your fellow countrymen and fellow human beings? If your religion is supremely of love, why cannot your love overcome their will to kill you? Speak up, Jesus! Who are you really? Why are you here? Is Jesus, the Cosmic King of the Universe?"

Then the Christ, Jesus, said to Pilate, "You know what I have said and done to bring Light to the world. You speak of the Cosmic Light as a way to redeem the world and to free it from the darkness. You speak of love and of preventing My death through love of mankind and to love even those who want you to send Me to My death. You say, 'Why is this happening, that the Living Christ stands for such behaviour if he is truly the Cosmic King of Light?' So I say to you, to answer your question, I will not give Light to darkness as is this not what they want you to do now for them out there?"

Pilate then felt that he had truly lost control of this conversation and tried to repudiate what Jesus said by replying, "These are your own people who say that you are evil and have committed a crime against the state. I am not one of your race. I am trying to reason with you but you ask me to see the Truth as you see it. Yet why do these people want to kill you when you speak the Truth? The chief priests say that you have become a religious criminal. Now, you have to tell me, what is it that your countrymen who want to kill you, hate you for? How can a man who speaks of loving the Truth of the Light above life be branded a criminal? Is it not so that you have already given Light to darkness and this is why your own contradictions

319

have brought you to me before the hour of your death if I decide it to be so?"

Then Jesus said, "I am the Cosmic Christ, the Light of all Ages. I am Christ, the King of Heaven. I have come to the earth to redeem mankind. I have come to give Light to it. This I have shown to all those who have received it and who have put the Truth first in their lives and did this by living their Truth.

He who contradicts himself does not live his Truth and hence cannot speak the Truth. The darkness is Intellectual Materialism says that unless there are physical results proving that something exists then it can only be in someone's head. Hence the contradiction of the world. He who follows this darkness contradicts his Truth and the Truth.

So I have given Light as I have lived My Truth among the Jews. I have also taken away the darkness from the world by living My Truth as the Cosmic Christ. This means that I put My Being as the Cosmic Christ first. I put it above My human life. This means that My World of Light asks mankind to put the Light above life. So no, I have no contradiction. My Light burns

away with Heaven's Spiritual Fire the ultimate contradiction of the world which is Intellectual Materialism. So the Truth is if I gave Light to darkness I would use My Cosmic powers to kill the Jews who want to kill Me. I would also have My Legions of Angels to protect Me and to intervene in My human fate if it were not so that I have to fulfill My Mission to redeem the world with My Truth and with My Light.

So the Truth is that I have chosen to put the Light above Intellectual Materialism. I have chosen to put My Cosmic Being above My life as a human being as this is My Truth. As Christ, the King of the Spiritual Universe, I do not need this human life other than that it was for the purpose of redeeming mankind, by giving mankind Cosmic freedom of choice to love the Light above life." [Verse 16]

Then Pilate became very uneasy about who Jesus was. No man could ever talk like this man. Yes, he had spoken to Caesar but he had seen that even he had a persona that he used to exercise his ultimate power of the world and its subjects. This persona he had copied and studied for many years. Yet this man, Jesus, had a persona which out – distanced all of his lifetime of study of personality. Pilate throughout his life had studied the psychology of power and its ruling forces in an individual political personality. He had trained himself to become a Roman head of state. All his life was dedicated to this one goal to serve Rome so as to become co – master of the world with it. However here was a man in front of him who had effectively just taken away Pilate's very own persona to reveal the flaw of Roman civilisation that had effectively put power above the Truth. This was something he had always known but could never say as this would deny his ultimate motivation to win power above all things in life.

Then Pilate said to Jesus, "You have said that you are a Cosmic King of Light. Is this true?" The Christ Being replied, "I, the Christ Being, see that you have called Me a Cosmic King. I came to this planet to give it Light. I also have a Mission to redeem mankind. I am the Living Truth.

He who lives his Truth honors My Truth and the Truth as I am the Ultimate Truth of the World. This is so as I am the ultimate example of the Cosmic Being in all the material and spiritual worlds who lives his Truth and hence My Cosmic Truth of the Universe; the Truth of the World. When a man can feel the Light come to his heart from listening to My Words he knows that I am the Ultimate Voice of the Ultimate Truth of Mankind. Then in his words the Truth will be heard as he will live what he says."

Pilate then replied, "Truth is relative. Everyone has his opinion of what is the truth. No man can say he has a monopoly on the truth. We all have different views. So your truth is your truth. This is not necessarily the truth. Look at the Jews. They believe their truth is to see you die today!" [Verse 17] [10]

Then Pilate left the praetorium to speak to the angry mob outside it. Many members of the mob were jeering and shouting insults at Jesus. Pilate said, "You have accused this man of being a criminal. You have no evidence or physical proof to substantiate your allegations. Therefore I cannot judge a

---

[10] John 18: 33-38.

man without the truth of the law. The law says that a man must be proven guilty before he can be judged. So I say to you, to make a compromise to this situation I am going to appeal to your local custom at the Passover to release a prisoner in exchange for another prisoner. You have before you the Cosmic King of Mankind, Christ Jesus, or I offer you the notorious convicted criminal, Barab'bas!"

The crowd then was becoming an ugly mob which shouted, "Free Barab'bas! Free Barab'bas! Free Barab'bas!" This became a constant chant which rose in volume every time Pilate attempted to speak. [Verse 18]

Pilate had then come to the conclusion that the mob had to be appeased. There were thousands of screaming frenzied faces who were really angry at his proclamations of conciliation. He came to the conclusion that he was coming up against the staged,

managed pre – riot mood created by the chief priests who opposed Jesus. He also concluded that he had obviously threatened their power. So now, he reasoned, he must pay in some way or he would become the scapegoat for speaking up for Jesus. So he ordered that his soldiers would torture Jesus as this way he surmised he would have met their mad demands halfway.

So in Truth Pilate did exactly what he accused Jesus of doing. He gave Light to darkness by rationalising the Truth and convicting a man without any evidence or proof of a crime being committed. Hence Pilate's Light as a human being, having its source in the truth and justice of Roman law, which he administered, was given to follow the will of evil men. So he lost his Light to darkness as all who give Light to it, give Light to lose their Truth and the Truth. This is the Truth. This is the fate of those who lose their Light. [Verse 19] [11]

---

[11] John 18: 39-40.

CHAPTER 19

Jesus was then whipped with a hundred lashes so that blood was streaming down his back with gashing wounds. When the Christ Being was receiving the blows to his body he was silent and his thoughts of Light brought the Angels of his Father next to him. They could see in his face the human pain that created such sadness in their Beings. They saw that in the eyes of Christ there was no human fear. The Angels had come from the Father to give Spiritual Heavenly Light to the suffering of the Christ Being. [Verse 1] [1]

Then the soldiers placed a crown of thorns on the head of Christ and bashed it so that blood began to stream on his forehead. Once again Jesus did not say a word. He just accepted what the soldiers did to him. Then they put a purple garment on his back as it was ordered by Pilate that he should look like a make – believe god – king of the Jews so that this way they would see the ridiculous accusations made about him would obviously show them the mirror of their own comical delusions. However this did not have the effect Pilate had hoped for as what the soldiers did then was to slap him on the face several times until blood began to run from the abrasions on his face. At the end of this demonstration, made to display the brutality of Roman justice and ultimate Roman force presented to degrade a self – proclaimed god king, the soldiers cried out, "Hail! King of Judea! Hail! King of Judea!" [Verse 2] [2]

Then Pilate went in front of the mob with Jesus and his soldiers and said, "I have before you the King of Judea. I say to you, I have presented him to you to show you that Rome accepts your King. This is truly a man who has been accused of crimes against your laws. He has proclaimed himself a Son of God. I have demonstrated to you all Rome's judgment on this man. He has nothing more to do with Rome or me as he has paid for his heritage as King of Judea! Yes, he is truly your King. He has not broken any Roman law. So I say to you, will I release him? Will I release him? With this request from Pilate the chief priests became incensed with rage and shouted out with the horrible drone of the ugly

---

[1] John 19: 1,

[2] John 19: 2-3.

Spirit in their being, "He must die! He must die! Kill him! Kill him! Crucify Jesus! Crucify Jesus!"

Then Pilate said, "You have chosen to kill your King. You have chosen to kill your King of Light. I have told you Rome cannot crucify Jesus unless he has broken its laws. So take your King and condemn him to death yourselves!"

Then a self – appointed spokesman for the priests said to Pilate, "Jesus has broken the law of our religion as he has proclaimed himself and I quote, 'I am the Son of the Living God, Light of all Ages.' He has said that his kingdom is a Spiritual Kingdom that will ultimately rule the universe and that he has come to earth to warn the Jews that unless they follow his Religion of Light, cosmic catastrophe will ultimately destroy us and the Roman Empire. So we now say to you, governor of Judea, we do not have the power to condemn any man to death without Rome's legal endorsement of our judgment. This is Roman law." Pilate then said to this priest, "You will wait until I consult with your King about the nature of your allegations about his crimes." [Verse 3] [3]

Then Pilate went back inside the praetorium and was visibly moved by what he had just heard. He looked shaken by the whole affair. The cataclysmic prophesies about the fall of Rome through Heavenly Spiritual Fire created a real fear within Pilate as he had never put any God above the god of Roman power but secretly he knew that it was the age of Roman military supremacy and that Caesar was evil. He knew that he had learned to rationalise that he could only survive in a world that Rome owned by never confronting this evil by putting success in his appointments as a Roman official above the Truth of life. This was so as his greatest fear was to not be a ruler who sided with the winning powers of the world. The world was Rome for Pilate. So when he heard that ultimately a spiritual world was going to destroy Rome this struck a sudden chord of darkness in his Soul. A Spirit was telling him, 'What if it is true and Caesar and the whole Roman world that conquered nations and killed hundreds of thousands of people or enslaved them must pay for their evil ultimately?'

---

[3] John 19: 4-8.

These thoughts were racing in his mind when he confronted Jesus and said, "Do you have a Cosmic origin?" Jesus said nothing to his answer. Then Pilate again walked away and another thought came to him. It was a voice of political argumentation saying, 'How could a man who has such excessive tortuous pain inflicted upon him look like that?' This occurred as Jesus stood with such grace and with the presence of a Monarch yet he was half beaten to death by the best killing machines in the Roman world. The Christ looked at Pilate and his eyes could see what was in Pilate's Soul. Pilate could see that it was evil to agree with the mob and yet this man who had been bashed to almost certain death did not have the look of fear on his face. He had the look of a man who was asking Pilate to speak the Truth. Jesus was not judging him. He was asking him for his Truth.

So Pilate then reacted to this predicament he was in by saying, "I am governor of Judea. I have the power to kill a thousand people at will. I command an army that can wipe out your countrymen and your whole nation. I have the power of the Emperor, Caesar, the true King of the Roman world, at My disposal. So you,

whom I can kill with one wave of the hand, will not speak to me. So who are you? What world do you come from that you have such arrogance to defy me who am trying to save your life?"

Then the Cosmic Christ Being said to Pilate, "I am the Christ Being. I am the Cosmic Christ. I am a human being as Jesus of Nazareth. You have tried to show the Jews that I am their King of Light. You have tortured My body to show those who want My Blood that I am their fool's king.

The Truth is that I am a King and My Kingdom is the Cosmic Kingdom of Heaven. The origin of this world and mankind has come from the Spiritual World of Light. All power that you have or your Caesar has comes from this spiritual world. So the mob out there that is representing the portion of the Jewish nation that seeks My human death through evil is asking you to identify with their evil. It is asking you to commit the crime of condemning Me to death. So it is the true source of the evil Spirit that wants to crucify Me. You can see the evil of this mob and find yourself becoming a part of it. So I tell you, the origin of the evil Spirit on this planet wants Me dead. However the origin of its Light you see before you in the Ultimate Truth of what I have just said; I, Jesus Christ, Son of the Living God, Light of all Ages." [Verse 4]

Then Pilate looked at Jesus and said, "I am following the truth of Roman law." In that moment he realised that his fear of evil was what this man did not have in his being. Evil held no fear for his being. This man had a Cosmic intelligence that talked of a Cosmic Law above the law of mankind. What was he to do? So he went to the crowd outside the praetorium and said, "I cannot condemn a man who has committed no crime against Rome or any of its subjects. So I say to you, let me release Jesus of Nazareth. Let him go. He has suffered enough. Your law surely shows you that the path of mercy brings Light to your Souls. What say you all? Has not your King truly shown he is a Spiritual King and not a King of this world? What do you say to this, subjects of Judea; subjects of Rome standing before its governor today?"

Then a chief priest confronted Pilate and said, "Caesar is our King. He is the ruler of the Roman Empire. He is our King. He is the King of Kings; Caesar, the King of Kings. Jesus has proclaimed himself a god – king. Caesar is the god – King of the world of all Romans and all its subjects. So we say, let us show our true god – King our will!" Then he shouted at the top of his voice, "Crucify Jesus! Crucify Jesus!" The crowd roared with shouts, "If Jesus is the enemy of Caesar, Jesus is the enemy of Caesar!" [Verse 5]

Pilate then grew very fearful of what he was doing. He began to feel the real fear that he so often instilled in the subjects of Rome by the military might of Rome. He would kill anyone who would defy Rome with a momentary decision. Here he was receiving this fear within his being because he tried to appease the pathological madness of a bloodthirsty crowd which was stage – managed to kill a political rival to the power of the priests; the rulers of the people by Roman proxy.

So what he did next was to demonstrate to the crowd that he was an impartial referee in this situation who was administering Roman justice. He brought Jesus out of the praetorium. Then he called for the seat of judgment so that he could sit on it and pronounce his final decree about Jesus. He knew then that in his heart he had lost his will to save Jesus as the fear of ever confronting the evil in Caesar took over his being.

He then said, "I have before you the self – proclaimed god – king of the Jews. I find no crime in this person's actions. I find your allegiance to Caesar is above my judgment to save Jesus as your Spiritual King. Then take your Spiritual King! Take him and crucify him as this will show the Roman world that I have followed the will of the people who will accept no other King than Caesar!" Immediately after this the soldiers took hold of Jesus and he was led to the crowd which was roaring with shouts of, "Save Israel! Save Israel! Kill the false Messiah! Kill the false Messiah!" [Verse 6] [4]

The chief priests then organised the mob to mount a cross on Jesus' shoulder and to make him walk to a place called Gol'gotha where they crucified him. They put him between two other men who were also crucified; one on the left of him and one on the right.

Pilate then ordered that a placard would be put on Jesus' cross which read, "Christ Jesus, King of the Light of Mankind." This was written in three languages: Hebrew, Latin and Greek. Gol'gotha was not far from the city gates and many saw the proclamation above Jesus' head on the cross.

The chief priests wanted it removed and asked the Roman soldiers to take it away. The Roman soldiers warned them that if they touched it they would have to answer to Pilate. So a delegation of the chief priests assembled and asked for an audience with Pilate. Their spokesman said to him, "How can you write that this man was the King of the Light of Mankind?"

Pilate then answered them and said, "I wrote what Jesus said to me and to you. I did not write what Rome has judged him as or what you have judged him as. I asked that the truth be written. So this is my will to write what I have written as history will ultimately judge the truth of my words." [Verse 7] [5]

The Roman soldiers were next to the crosses and ordered the people around them to stay at a distance. They then took Jesus' tunic and were about to

---

[4] John 19: 9-15,

[5] John 19: 16-22,

separate it into four parts as they had done with his other garments when they realised that it had no seam and was a complete piece of cloth. So they decided to throw coins for it so that the soldier who would get Caesar's face on the coins the most times out of the four soldiers would win the tunic.

As it had been foretold in ancient scripture, "They divided My Light among themselves and for My Truth they gambled the Truth of their lives."

The Roman soldiers justified taking all from Jesus as he was a convicted criminal and had no rights as he was crucified together with criminals. [Verse 8] [6]

While Jesus was dying on the cross his mother, Mary, her sister, Clopas' wife and Mary Magdalene stood next to each other weeping because of what was happening to Christ. This moved Jesus to look at his mother and at John, his Apostle, who stood next to her. He looked at John and said to him, "You will look after my mother as I have looked after you." John replied, "She will be the Mother of the Light as you

have been my Father of the Light of my being." By this he also meant that he would look after Mary by taking her into his home from that day onwards. He was saying this as a pledge to Jesus that he understood his wish to leave someone he truly loved to help his mother get through life after the horrific and tragic death of her son. [Verse 9] [7]

The Christ Being then was ready to die. So he, knowing full well that there was a little more to do to bring fate to its final conclusion, cried out and said, "Will anyone give Me something to drink as I am very thirsty?" This triggered a soldier out of spite to give Jesus some vinegar that was in a bowl next to the cross. He held a sponge filled with vinegar on his mouth which the soldier had tied to a spear. This made Jesus move his head abruptly so as to avoid the vinegar's taste. Then he said in a loud and clear voice, *"My Light is on the Earth."*

Then a massive convulsion was heard in the sky like a great tornado was about to descend upon this place where the Christ was about to die. The sky blackened to the point that it was if the night suddenly descended upon the

---

[6] John 19: 23-24.

[7] John 19: 25-27,

earth. The earth began to move and huge rocks near the cross began to break up. The very hilltops around Gol'gotha began to shake violently. Then a storm broke with such vengeance that one of the soldiers gripping Christ's tunic saw a Light flash into it from Heaven like lightning. This soldier then knelt before the cross and cried out, "This was a God that we have crucified." Then blood trickled down from the cross into a pool of water next to it. While this was happening the Heavens were being torn apart by wild thunder and tremendous bolts of lightning. Christ, the Redeemer of the World, had brought his Cosmic Light to it. His Spirit was transforming the whole world with Light. [Verse 10] [8]

Jesus died on a Friday and the Sabbath was the following day for the Jews. This was a holy day for them so the priests went to Pilate to ask that the bodies would be removed from the cross so as to not interfere with religious ceremonies being prepared for the people. Pilate then ordered his soldiers to clear the area of everything for the good of public order. Then the soldiers went to Gol'gotha to

remove the bodies from the crosses. First they broke the legs of both men who were crucified next to Jesus. When they saw that Jesus was already dead a soldier got his spear and pierced Jesus to make sure he was dead. Then blood once again came gushing out of his side and water came after it. Once it reached the pool of blood next to the cross the water diluted it and the blood disappeared. The soldier marveled at what had just happened and could not bring himself to break Jesus' legs as was the custom of condemned criminals. [Verse 11]

John, the Apostle, watched at a distance and saw the soldiers removing the crosses and when the soldier pierced Jesus' heart with his spear a great pain went through his own heart. At that moment he felt the Prince of evil next to him trying to tell him that all was lost and that darkness had truly descended upon the earth cosmically and eternally.

However Jesus let John see a vision of what was happening to him. John, at that moment, could see the Cosmic Christ like he had never seen him

---

[8] John 19: 28-30,

before. He was transfigured into Cosmic Light but his Being was surmounted on a star and in his hand he had a Sword that glistened with a magnificent Spiritual Fire. Out of his Being Light began to shine in rays created by this star beneath his feet.

John could see the dark Spirits looking like black Angels burn beneath his feet from the Cosmic Fire from this star. His figure and form was that of a Being that had the planets next to him as if one were in a room where balls of different types of Light would be around someone. His eyes were complete Light and shone like two suns.

A great dark Angel then approached Jesus beneath his feet and this dark Angel transformed into a dragon with many heads. This being was being burned alive by this Cosmic Fire. Then John saw a Light come from next to Jesus' head reach the globe of the earth. The whole earth, in his vision, became as if immersed in a sea of Light. [Verse 12]

Suddenly John awoke from this vision and saw the soldiers coming towards him. A voice said to him, "John,

you will use the Special Keys of Christ to protect your being." John then knelt down and was prepared to die as the soldiers were in a very aggressive mood but the Archangel Michael appeared to John and shielded him from harm.

The soldiers saw John standing next to a Roman centurion. This was the being into which the Archangel Michael had transformed himself. The soldiers did not know who this centurion was. They noticed that he had a solid gold breast – plate that showed the image of a Dove descending upon the earth with diamonds next to it. They were fascinated and asked this centurion what battalion he came from and if he was an arrival from Rome. The centurion replied, "I come to witness the Truth of Gol'gotha." The soldiers did not dare ask him what he meant so they left and went their way. John then said, "Thank You," to the centurion who transformed into a Mighty Angel as large as the temple of Jerusalem. He had the beauty of a 'God.'

Then the Archangel Michael said to John, "Call upon Me when you write your works to show the world of mankind the Truth of Gol'gotha and its Light." [Verse 13] [9]

Joseph of Arimathe'a and Nicode'mus, who were secret followers of the Christ Being, went to Pilate to ask him to let them take Jesus' body so that they could bury it. Both these men had been initiated into the Eyes of the Light. They used to secretly come to Jesus by night so as to conceal their initiation as they had political and economic standing in the Jewish community.

They had consulted **The Cabala** oracles and knew that the Cosmic Christ was Jesus and that he was truly the one foretold in all initiation processes in the whole world, from the beginning of mankind's consciousness of its meaning of life, as it tried to answer the questions of the origin of the earth. They could connect that the Christ Being was the Ultimate Spirit of Light to all initiands who followed the Ultimate Light.

They knew that there were other initiation processes that did not connect to the Christ Light and looked to other pathways. Some Romans saw Zeus as the king of the gods. The Pharisees knew of The Cabala but like so many religious leaders of the time used the knowledge of it to justify their identification with Intellectual Materialism. So they would say that the highest of all initiation processes on earth was that of the Spiritual Sun Oracle of the Christ Being. They would say that this would be a Messiah that would deliver the chosen people from its bondage to the Roman civilisation and would ultimately make Israel a super – world power. Hence when Jesus spoke of aligning with the poor, the sick and the destitute of the world they saw him as a false Messiah. However those who could see the true Light of this Initiation of the Spiritual Sun of the Universe, the Cosmic Christ, accepted the man, Jesus of Nazareth, as the chosen one.

So when Joseph spoke to Pilate he had a persuasive argument ready when he said to him that it would be wise to take his advice to bury Jesus out of the way so as not to disturb the coming holy feast. Also Pilate could see that he was talking to a very high class of Jew when he considered the request. However Nicode'mus, seeing that he might waver, said to

---

[9] John 19: 31-37.

Pilate, "I, as a lawyer for the people of Israel, ask you to please let us get on with our tasks of putting to rest this Prophet without making him a martyr to the people." Then Pilate replied, "Can you guarantee me and the Roman world that he will be forgotten with his talk of a Spiritual Kingdom?"

Then Joseph said, "Can you guarantee us that you will also ask them to forget that you wrote the placard saying that he was the 'King of the Light of Mankind?'" Pilate then said, "You may take him away as this is right as you are a true representative of his countrymen unlike those who crucified him. They killed him to win Rome's approval of their standing politically and, of course, economically." Then Pilate, at that moment, realised that he had self – prophesied his own doom as he had let the darkness overtake him because of the fear of losing the same thing he accused the Pharisees of doing.

He fell into a depression as the Light was driven out of him after this conversation. Not long after this he had asked to be relieved of his position as his wife could never trust in him after he had given Jesus up to the Pharisees. This had made Pilate lose all his Truth with his alignment to the almighty power of Rome. He saw no fear in Jesus' face. He saw that this man pitied him; he a governor of Rome, ruler of the world.

'This innocent man was sent to death to be crucified. How could it be?' So the darkness began to laugh in his head and he could feel the dark Spirit follow his very footsteps when he spoke or heard of Jesus of Nazareth, the King of Kings of the Light of Mankind.
[Verse 14] [10]

Joseph and Nicode'mus then prepared Jesus' body with spices and wrapped it in linen cloths completely from head to toe. The spices were made up of myrrh and aloes. This protected the body from decomposition for some time. Also Joseph and Nicode'mus wanted to give dignity to the burial of Jesus. They saw that their Master was murdered innocently and they did not want the world to see him as a criminal. They talked over things together and wondered how everything would turn out for them and their connection to the spiritual

---

[10] John 19: 38.

world. They trusted in him. He had told them once, "He who lives his Truth as a human being and lives his Cosmic Truth by putting the Christ Light first in their lives, I will keep My Word to. I will also put them first. When a man lives his Truth and puts another human being who loves him unconditionally first out of love, then that man knows the Truth of life. So it is with Cosmic love. I will put him first as I will give him Light as he has given me Light."

Nicode'mus said to Joseph, "I have loved this man above all men in my life. He has given me the source of this Cosmic love I have of God and the Light. I will not forsake him now unto my death." Joseph then said, "I love this man as he is the Cosmic Christ Being, Son of the Living God, Light of all Ages. I put him first as I know with every ray of the sunlight that reaches this planet his Spiritual Light reaches all mankind and me in my heart and Soul." [Verse 15]

Then in the garden next to Gol'gotha they buried Jesus in a tomb that was prepared for another person who had not died and which was purchased by Joseph and Nicode'mus. They laid the body of Jesus and sealed its entrance with a rock boulder as large as three men.

Following this they decided to go home with the deepest of sadness as they could see that God had suffered a human death. They knew that they had seen the heart of darkness in the men who crucified Jesus. Yet strangely enough they could see with their Spiritual Eyes of the Light the heart of Heaven opened up to them. This was happening to them when they asked the Cosmic Christ to be with them in their Spiritual Light Meditations. They could see that the Christ Being was evolving the Light in their hearts. This was shown to them as a Cosmic Light ray coming to their Souls from the Spiritual Heaven that they could see when they opened the Doorway to the Light. [Verse 16] [11]

---

[11] John 19: 39-42.

CHAPTER 20

On the following Monday Mary Magdalene went to the tomb as she wanted to have an answer to her question at the Doorway to the Light about where the Cosmic Christ was after he had died on the cross. She was an initiand of the Eyes of the Light but often found it hard to live her Truth in relationships. She had been redeemed by Jesus but found his death on the cross so traumatic that at times another dark Spirit was trying to tell her to doubt the Light. So she went to the tomb to meditate on the Light of Christ to get back the Light she was losing to the dark Spirit that was trying to enter her Doorway to the Light.

When she got there she saw that the huge boulder was shifted and the cave – like grave was empty. She screamed when she saw this and ran to tell Peter about the boulder being shifted and the tomb. When she got to where Peter was staying she saw that John was with him. She told him, "Peter, they have stolen his body. The Christ is gone. The murderers have stolen his body."

Peter was stunned. Then he replied, "I want to go and see for myself." Then John said, "Let us go!" John ran most of the way and beat Peter to the tomb. When he got there he saw that Jesus' body was gone and he also saw the linen in the corner of the cave neatly wrapped up. Then Peter walked in and looked for the body and evidence of a forced entry or if there were any clues as to what happened to the body. Then Peter looked at John and said, "The Master has left this tomb." John then answered by saying, "I know that he lives as I saw him in all his Glory as the Cosmic Christ." [Verse 1] [1]

Then Mary who also had heard of what happened went to the tomb. When she walked into the cave – tomb she saw two Angels with fiery Swords next to the bench top where Jesus' body had been placed when it was anointed and wrapped in linen. These Angels were white with golden sandals and breast – plates of silver. They had eyes of gold and on their breast – plates were images of the Christ Being rising into the sky. Their Swords gleamed with fiery silver Light. They looked at Mary and waited for her to speak.

---

[1] John 20: 1-10.

The whole tomb smelled of beautiful perfume with a scent of roses. Next to the tomb a huge white rose tree filled with magnificent roses in full bloom was growing and it had a shimmering Light around it. When Mary saw all of this she began to cry and tears were running down her cheeks. She looked at one of the Angels and said, "Where is the Christ Being? He is my Master and my Lord. He is the Lord of all Light in this universe. You know where he is!"

Suddenly the Cosmic Christ appeared to her next to the Angels. He looked at her and said, "Mary, I am the Living Christ, Light of all Ages. I live now in the Spiritual Heaven World. I am speaking to you from this World. I will soon leave your world and remain there and you will only be able to see Me through the Doorway to the Light. Yet you know that I can also come as I come now when My Father wills this. My Mission on earth is almost completed as to My human life incarnation. My Mission, of course, is only beginning as to My bringing the Spirit of the Light to all of mankind.

You will go to Peter and to John and to all those whom I love with My whole Heart and tell them I will see them soon and to wait for Me as I will come to them as I have to you. I will then look through their Eyes of the Light to see their Light as it flows to create the Cosmic Love of My Being." Once the Christ Being said this he disappeared. Mary quickly went to Peter's house and told him what she had seen and all that the Christ Being had said to tell him and the others. [Verse 2] [2]

That night Peter gathered all the Apostles around him and made sure all the doors were bolted in the house. He was fearing that the Pharisees would send some of their paid thugs to intimidate them. All of the Apostles sat together and began to open the Doorway to the Light. Then all of a sudden, before the Doorway was opened, the Cosmic Christ appeared in the midst of them. He was wearing a completely white tunic that glowed as it was made of a living energy that glistened like millions of minute diamonds. His eyes were filled with Light as if

---

[2] John 20: 11-18.

when he spoke the Light came out of them to their hearts physically. [Verse 3]

He said to them with arms outstretched, "I bring you the Peace of Heavenly Light. I have come to tell you that I am preparing My Being to go to My Father who is in Heaven. I have been to the spiritual world where your past incarnations and future ones will travel to create the Pathway for all of mankind to walk on. I did this so that the Spirits of darkness could only use the spiritual fire to burn in their dark fires so this way they could not see the Light of the Cosmic Christ. This is My Mission that I had to complete with My incarnation on earth. I gave this cosmic planet Earth, Light, by giving it the power of the Light of My Soul. This way the Prince of darkness has lost his power over it. Had I not come to redeem man with this Spiritual Light then he would still put first his physical spirit. He now has the seed to create the tree of life. I am this tree of Life. I have come to show mankind that when it lives its Truth and follows My Cosmic Truth it will be redeemed eternally. This is My Truth. This is My Light.

So I let it shine to let each man and woman evolve in it to become a being of Light. I have chosen to suffer and to die on the cross so as to show mankind that I am a living human being who suffered so as to live his Truth. I have also now appeared to show the initiands of mankind My Cosmic Being. I do this to show mankind that this is his ultimate destiny. To fulfil his Cosmic destiny he needs this Pathway of Redemption. This is the Will of My Father. This is the Will of the Cosmic Trinity of Light. The Holy Spirit or the Ultimate Spirit of the Light will now descend upon the earth to give it My Light. This is I, the Son of the Living God, standing before you all.

The Mission of My Father for Me is now your mission. You are now the Christ Being initiands. You have been chosen to evolve this Light for the world. I give you this power of the Light as you are the first to begin to follow Me. You will be the ones who will have followed Me the longest at the end of time. This is My Will; I, the Cosmic Christ."
[Verse 4]

The Apostles then all knelt down before him and Peter said, "Lord, you are my King. You are the Lord of the Light of all this universe. I have seen that you have given me this Leadership of your Apostles. I am your servant and not my will but your Will to the Light is our Truth and our Pathway."

Then the Christ Being said, "My Father has said to Me to tell you that the Keys of Light He has given you now belong to your Pathway. You are to use them to control things on earth to protect the Light of the innocent. When you use these Keys of Light and you ask that My Light is sent by Me to the darkness outside the Cosmic Circle of Light, you will have God, the Father, and the Spirit of the Light create a Cosmic Circle of Heavenly Light in Heaven. He will do this with all the Angels of God surrounding this Circle of Light. They will all reach for their Cosmic Swords of Light and the Spiritual Fire of Heaven will be emitted from these Swords to send this Fire to burn away the darkness through the cosmos of all universes till it reaches the earth. This will be the Will of the Father.

So when you ask that I, the Cosmic Christ, send My Light for you, you are fulfilling the Will of My Father in Heaven. He will, with the Spirit of

Light, create the Circle of Heavenly Light with the Cosmic Circle of Spiritual Universal Fire from Heaven. This will ensure eternally that whatever you will through My Light with a pure heart, when using the Keys of Light, you will be creating this will in Heaven. Whenever in Heaven these Keys of Light are created by My Archangels then you will be asked to create your Circle of Light and give your Light to God; to the Living God of Light. This is My Will to your Light."
[Verse 5] [3]

The following day Thomas, an Apostle of Christ, came to Peter's house and heard about the visit from Jesus. Thomas had not been there that day. He looked at Peter and said, "Look, I find this all very hard to believe. I have not been able to open the Doorway to the Light ever since the Christ Being died on the cross. I feel that there is a darkness around me. I have lived my Truth ever since I met the Lord but now I doubt that the Light will ever reach my heart. So it is not that I do not want to believe, I simply do not have Light. I have lost it. I ask you all to let me try to work on myself to get my Light back."

---

[3] John 20: 19-23,

Peter then replied, "Thomas, the Lord said he will return to us and I am sure somehow your Doorway to the Light will open again. I would like you, for now, to meditate on the Light, to ask the Cosmic Christ to open the Door to your heart." [Verse 6] [4]

About a week after Thomas had met Peter he was among all of the Apostles and it was night. All began to open the Doorway to the Light when all of a sudden Jesus appeared. This time Jesus appeared as he was when he was before Pilate with the crown of thorns on his head and blood streaming down his body. There was also the huge wound in the side of his chest dripping blood.

Jesus looked at Thomas and said, "Can you see Me, the Christ Being, the human being who died on the cross for the redemption of the world?" Thomas then prostrated himself on the floor before Jesus and said, "You have saved my Soul as I feel the Light return to my being. You are the Living God. You are the Cosmic Saviour of the Light of the earth. Please forgive me for losing my Light."

Then Jesus became the same Being as he was when he last saw the Apostles but this time a crown of gold and diamonds the size of a man's hands gleamed upon his head. The Light coming from these diamonds reflected Light like it was coming from an eye gleaming in the sunlight. He then said, "Thomas, because you had the Moral Will to ask that I will bring back your Light, you have seen me today. So I say to you as you have done today, all must do, who have lost their Light. They need to surrender their will unconditionally to the Light. They need to live their Truth as you have done even when they have no Light. Then they need to wish to be redeemed at all costs. This needs to be their humility. He who does this will see My Light and will get back the Light in his heart." [Verse 7]

I, the author of this work writing this **Cosmic Christ World Light Shield**, have created this work to show mankind that when a man asks the Cosmic Christ to send his Light to his Soul and to the darkness that is the cause of all the suffering of mankind then mankind can be redeemed. As St. John did

---

[4] John 20: 24-25.

with his Gospel, this Cosmic Christ World Light Shield does now. It speaks the Truth of the Cosmic Christ Being, Son of the Living God, Light of all Ages, Saviour of the planet earth in the twenty – first century. This is the Age of the Cosmic Light of Christ. [Verse 8] [5]

---

[5] John 20: 26-30.

CHAPTER 21

Jesus once again appeared to his Apostles next to the seashore. It was night and they all went fishing. They were half way into the night and were with empty nets. This was very unusual as Peter knew all the best places on the sea to fish. However that day no matter what he did, as he tried several places, he could not get one fish. This amazed him and he became despondent that he was losing his credibility as to his directions of where to throw out the nets. All night long there were no fish and there was a very tired crew on board.

At about six o'clock the sun began to show its bright disk on the horizon for it was a fresh but completely clear morning. There was a perfectly blue sky with not a cloud.

So he said to the rest of his fellow fishermen, "Let us get back to shore. Today is not our day. We cannot stay out here any longer. We all have had it!" Then all of a sudden Nathan'a-el said, "Look, there is a man waiting for us on the shore but he is no one I know. Does anyone know who he is?"

Everybody agreed that they did not know who the stranger was. When they got to shore they saw that this man looked very familiar but not anyone whom they knew. He was not a Jew nor a Roman nor a Greek. So Peter asked him, "How can we help you? You seem to be waiting for us to land."

Jesus replied, "I am from Rome on a pilgrimage. I am looking for the one called Jesus. It is said that he has risen from the dead and that he is a Cosmic Being that has redeemed mankind and that he has opened a Spiritual Doorway to the Light for the world that opens the Gates of Heaven." [Verse 1]

At that moment Jesus Christ became the Cosmic Christ and his whole Being was transfigured into a Golden Light. He was wearing a white cloak that made his whole Being glisten with the brightness that outshone the morning sunrise. So when he spoke the Apostles felt his Light reach their hearts and Souls.

Their boat and the shore was suddenly surrounded by this complete globe of Light that one could see the world out of, but one had the feeling that the world could not see inside. Around Jesus there stood four magnificent looking Angels. They also had this wonderful Light that created this aura of beauty and love in the whole atmosphere inside this Celestial globe from Heaven.

Then the Christ Being said, "You are the Children of the Light of this universe and the earth is your home. You need to sustain it and your beings. So let your nets be thrown out once more into the sea. Let the Light do its work." [Verse 2]

Peter then ordered, "Cast the nets out! It is the Lord! He is back. Look, his Angels are fishing too. They are sending Light into the sea." Then the boat began to rock beneath Peter's feet. The nets had caught so many fish that they were overflowing with fish so that the nets almost could not hold them and were tipping the boat to one side. Peter then cried out, "Haul in the catch! Throw back the rest!"

The fish from the sea were so attracted to the Celestial Light from the Angels that there were now more fish outside the nets wanting to get into the net than there were caught in the net. So Peter,

being used to a dramatic turn of events when Jesus appeared, took decisive action to stop all his crew from trying to catch more fish. He knew his boat would sink had he not pulled in the net as quickly as possible. He was right for as soon as the net was hauled on board the fish attracted to the Light in it disappeared. Also the globe of transparent Light was now disappearing as if the disk of the sun was absorbing it. Peter could see also that next to Jesus on shore was a fire that was lit by the Angels and next to it was bread and fish being cooked. [Verse 3] [1]

When Peter got to the shore he ran to meet Jesus. When he saw him he knelt down and said, "Lord, you are our Saviour and the Cosmic Christ of the Universe. You have become a human being as you love us and we love your Light." Then Jesus looked at him and said to him and all the Apostles who now were gathered around him, "I, the Christ Being, know that you have all given up all things to follow Me. You have put the love of My Light above your lives. You have done this as you have put living your Truth above all things in your life and put the Light of Christ

---

[1] John 21: 1-9,

341

first unconditionally in your whole beings consciously and unconsciously.

Furthermore you have also seen that in the higher spiritual world of Light your Cosmic Spirit is ever evolving towards My Being. This is your ultimate universal destiny. In your lifetimes to come you will be tested to look to My Light or to walk away from it. You will suffer tremendous pain and agony to keep your word to me as you have in this life. Yet I say to you I, the Cosmic Christ, Son of the Living God, will eternally keep My Word to you. I will keep My Word to mankind." [Verse 4]

Then John the Baptist appeared among the Apostles and said to Jesus, "You have now created the Bridge for mankind to walk on so that the Prince of darkness no longer can let the flames from the abyss burn the feet of those who walk on the Pathway to the Light."

Jesus looked at John and replied, "It is you, John the Baptist, to whom I have given the task to build the Pathway for the initiands of all the world to see the Ultimate Teacher of the Light; the

Cosmic Christ. I say this as your legacy is for those who in the twenty – first century see in this New Gospel called the Cosmic Christ World Light Shield, the New Age of the Cosmic Christ Being, Son of the Living God, Light of all Ages. [Verse 5]

Your love has created for you the Cosmic Eyes of Light. This Light will transcend centuries of darkness and false Prophets. In the twenty – first century this Initiation Pathway will speak to mankind through this Light so that each individual human being who lives his Truth can see that they can see the Truth of mankind and can see this Light. To see Light one must know how to make the darkness that is invisible, visible. Then he needs to know how to burn it with the Fire of the Light of Heaven. Once he can do this the Bridge that John the Baptist talked about will be safe for all of mankind to walk on so as to get to the Light of Heaven. This is the Pathway that leads to the Ultimate Light. I am the Ultimate Light. I am the Cosmic Christ Being."
[Verse 6] [2]

Then Jesus began to speak again to all the Apostles after

---

[2] John 21: 10-14.

they had eaten their breakfast. He said, "I, the Cosmic Christ Being, have asked you to symbolically feed My lambs, meaning to nourish your Light when you live your Truth. A man can only do this when he has loved the Light above all things in his life. Then I now ask you, Peter, do you love the Christ Light above all things in your life?" Peter then replied, "I have put all things second to you, Lord. I love the Christ Light above all things as I have put it first in My Heart."

Then the Christ answered, "I have given you all the power to use the Special Cosmic Spiritual Keys to bring Light to the planet earth. I have shown you that when you feed My sheep you tend to My flock of initiands of the Light. I have created for you an Initiation Pathway of the Eyes of the Light of the world. So I say to you to create the tools of Light and to evolve them as then you will have the Cosmic power to look after My sheep. The sheep are the followers of the Light who seek to create and evolve Light for the world.

Many of you will leave this world for My sake and will die on a cross all over again as I did to give the world its Light.

Be certain in that hour when you will leave this earth I will be waiting for you for as you have welcomed Me in your home, I will be welcoming you in mine; My House is Heaven. You will see Me there when the time comes for you to leave the earth. You will say that you have to live many lives before you can see Me in Heaven. I tell you, your Cosmic Spirit will evolve in Heaven until your whole being is ready to become a complete Spirit of Light. This is when the gate of death will be closed for eternity and the gateway of eternal life will be opened forever in the Light. This is My Word to you; I, the Living Christ Being, Son of the Eternal Father in Heaven." [Verse 7] [3]

Then Peter said to Jesus, "You have told us what the fate of the world will be and each our own individual fate as we have followed the Eyes of the Light. You have said that John, the Apostle, will not die for you as we all will. Why is that, Oh, Christ Being?"

Jesus then said, "John has work to do which all of you will work with in the future of this world. His work, like yours, is with the Spirit. How he dies or lives for Me relates

---

[3] John 21: 15-19.

to his Truth as when you die for Me it will be your Truth. When I spoke about the fate of the world and your fate individually I did this to enlighten you about your love for My Pathway.

So I enlighten you now and the author of this work, the **Cosmic Christ World Light Shield**. The Pathway he has created for man in the twenty – first century comes from My Will.

He has followed Me with his Eyes of the Light and seen My Image and My Words in the modern world. He has written these words as he has listened to Me and learned how to hear Me speak. He has done this as he has loved Me first in his life and in his Truth. This is the Truth of life. This is the **New Gospel** of Love, of Light and of the Ultimate Truth; of the Cosmic Christ Being; Son of the Living God, Light of all Ages." [Verse 8] [4]

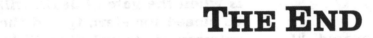

THE END

---

[4] John 21: 20-25.

GLOSSARY

Angel:

This is a Being that has higher spirit bodies than a human being. This Being has had a human being stage within the Being's evolution in different cosmic incarnations that made the Being choose between good and evil in the same way as man has to choose today [in different worlds]. There exist Angels of Light and Angels of darkness.[1] *See The Collected Works of The Science of Spiritual Talking* and *The Seven Cosmic Worlds* by William E. Camilleri.

Archangel:

This is a Being that has higher spirit bodies than an Angel. This Being fathers Angels. [2] *See The Collected Works of The Science of Spiritual Talking* and *The Seven Cosmic Worlds* by William E. Camilleri.

Archangel Michael:

This Being is the greatest of all Archangels in Heaven and has a special mission to bring the Light to mankind's consciousness in the four worlds. That is, in the four spirit bodies of all of mankind and man as an individual. This Being has a Cosmic Sword that transforms the Spiritual Light of Heaven into the Spiritual Fire of Heaven to destroy, with ultimate benign aggression, the enemies of Heaven and to protect the Light in the material and Spiritual universe. [3] *See The Collected Works of The Science of Spiritual Talking* and *The Seven Cosmic Worlds* by William E. Camilleri.

Body of Light:

This is the Cosmic Spirit Body of the Guardian of the Light. *See The Collected Works of The Science of Spiritual Talking* and *The Seven Cosmic Worlds* by William E. Camilleri.

Buddha, Gautama:

The Buddha Being came to Earth as a human Being and evolved His Spirit to a Spiritual Light so that He could go back to the spiritual world in a form of complete Light. He lived completely his Truth and followed an eight-fold pathway to the Light. He always maintained that He was

---

[1] Genesis 22: 8-18, Exodus 14: 19, Judges 6: 11-12, Matthew 13: 37-43, Matthew 24: 31, Mark 8:38, John 20: 12, Acts 5: 19-20, Acts 12: 7-11, 2 Thessalonians 1: 7-8,

[2] Daniel 9:21, Luke 1:26, Luke 1-19, Revelation 7: 1, Revelation 18: 1-4, Revelation 19: 9-11,

[3] Jude 1: 19, Daniel 10: 21, Daniel 10:13, Daniel 12: 1, Revelation 1: 1, Revelation 10:1, Revelation 10: 5, Revelation 10: 12-17, Revelation 20: 1-4.

345

preparing the way for the Ultimate Light and that it could be found when a person followed this pathway. [500 BC: *Pali Canon*].

Christ Being:

This is the Sun Oracle; the Oracle of the Ultimate Light. The Cosmic Christ Being became the Head Sun Spirit or Sun Oracle that took the Spiritual Hierarchies of Light to work on the fixed star of the sun in the cosmos at the time of the separation of the sun from the cosmic world of Earth. From here the Head Sun Spirit incarnated on the earth as a human being with supernatural powers and His Spiritual Being ever evolves in the consciousness of all comic worlds, including the Earth cosmic world, in the consciousness of every planet and in the consciousness of every human being. *See The Collected Works of The Science of Spiritual Talking* and *The Seven Cosmic Worlds* by William E. Camilleri.

Christ Initiation Pathway:

This is what Christianity was esoterically based on through the Spiritual lives of the Apostles.

Christ Light:

This is a Spiritual Light that comes from the Cosmic Guardian of the Light. *See The Collected Works of The Science of Spiritual Talking* and *The Seven Cosmic Worlds* by William E. Camilleri.

Cosmic Being of Light:

This is a Spiritual Being that has the Cosmic Spiritual Light of a superior evolution of one of the Hierarchies of the Light. *See The Collected Works of The Science of Spiritual Talking* and *The Seven Cosmic Worlds* by William E. Camilleri.

Cosmic destiny:

This is a destiny that pertains to the cosmic foundation of the universe. The human being physical body spirit, for example, was created on the cosmic world of Saturn. The destiny of this being is to evolve his Soul to seven spirit bodies ultimately on the cosmic world of Vulcan. *See The Seven Cosmic Worlds* by William E. Camilleri.

Cosmic identity:

This is the individual identity of all beings created by the Ultimate Light. For example, there can be only one person that is named as the author, William. There can be no other in the entire universe. *See The Collected Works of The Science of Spiritual Talking* and *The Seven Cosmic Worlds* by William E. Camilleri.

Cosmic Philosophy of Light:
>This is the Philosophy of the *Cosmic Christ World Light Shield.*

Cosmic Special Keys of Christ:
>The Cosmic Special Keys of Christ were used by Christ to create miracles. These are the tools of Light which Christ showed the Apostles how to use. For example, Lazarus' rising from the dead. *See The Collected Works of The Science of Spiritual Talking* and *The Seven Cosmic Worlds* by William E. Camilleri.

Cosmic Worlds or Cosmic planets: These are the past cosmic worlds of Saturn, Sun and Moon, the current cosmic world of Earth and the future cosmic worlds of Jupiter, Venus and Vulcan as described in detail in *The Seven Cosmic Worlds* by William E. Camilleri.

Cosmic World of Saturn:
>Saturn cosmic world existed some hundreds of billions of years before Earth cosmic world. In physical size this cosmic world was more than a million times the size of our earth planet. To the eye it resembled a globe of air and gas and its atmosphere was similar to that of a warm breeze. At times one could see light present 'flickering....flashing and darting.' Here time was created. So too was created the mineral kingdom and the blue-print of the sense organs within the individual human being spirit. *See The Seven Cosmic Worlds* by William E. Camilleri.

Cosmic World of Sun:
>Sun cosmic world was the incarnation of Saturn cosmic world. This cosmic world had a higher density of air and gas than that of Saturn cosmic world. Here was created space and limited movement. Here the evolution of the blue-print of the organs, specifically the glandular system, of the human being spirit continued. Also the manifestation of the power of smell and sound took place. In the human being spirit the beginning of the Ego ["I"] occurred. *See The Seven Cosmic Worlds* by William E. Camilleri.

Cosmic World of Moon:
>The cosmic world of Moon was the incarnation of Sun cosmic world and the ancestor of Earth cosmic world. Here a condensation of air to create a form of liquid comparable in condition to water took place. 'Water' bodies were permeated by air currents and warm effects and the beginnings of the plant-mineral kingdom to provide nutrients occurred. Here

took place the 'beginnings of the forefather of the complete human being' where the genesis of the head, figure and form of the human being spirit occurred as did the beginnings of the faculties of creative and destructive feelings, like, dislike and limited decision making. *See The Seven Cosmic Worlds* by William E. Camilleri.

Cosmic World of Earth:

During the first stage of the incarnation of the cosmic world of Earth the origin of the Big Bang event, the solar system, oceans and land masses took place. The evolution of gas, air, warmth, light and fire was completed. The solar system and its planets were created from the mother cosmic world of Earth including the present sun in order to complete the evolution of the perfect planet of earth. During this stage the Milky Way ever evolved to create the next cosmic world of Jupiter; when the present Jupiter will become ultimately the next cosmic world after it has been transformed spiritually upon the material end of the earth planet at the end of the cosmic world of Earth.

Within this stage of the evolution of the cosmic world of Earth there occurred the beginnings of the animal kingdom. Also all the scales of evolution of palaeontology occurred in relation to the origin of life in the oceans and onto land. The self-regulatory systems within the human being spirit were also here evolved, specifically the circulatory, nervous and breathing systems whilst the head of the human being spirit continued to evolve. The creation of the faculties of a form of mental life, memory and taste took place and the human being spirit was able to perceive sound and color in the process of becoming a 'definite form of being;' an in-duplicable being with a further evolving Ego ["I"].

Scales of parallel evolutionary processes as regards human evolution occurred from prehistoric times to the twenty-first century. The later stage of the evolution of Earth cosmic world included the evolution of races, epochs and historical figures pertinent to such epochs as the Atlantean epoch and post Atlantean epochs in connection to cosmic worlds to come. *See The Seven Cosmic Worlds* by William E. Camilleri.

Flaming Fire of Heaven:

This is the Spiritual Fire when it is being used to express the Light of Heaven as a force of burning away the darkness. *See The Seven Cosmic Worlds* by William E. Camilleri.

God, the Father in Heaven, the Living God of All Ages:

This is the Father of all Universes in the Cosmic Cross of Heaven. *See The Collected Works of The Science of Spiritual Talking* and *The Seven Cosmic Worlds* by William E. Camilleri.

Heaven:

This is the World of Light that exists eternally by the power of the Cosmic Cross of Heaven. *See The Collected Works of The Science of Spiritual Talking* and *The Seven Cosmic Worlds* by William E. Camilleri.

Holy Spirit:

This is the Holy Spirit of the Light in the Cosmic Cross of Heaven. *See 'Eternal Spirit:' The Collected Works of The Science of Spiritual Talking* and *The Seven Cosmic Worlds* by William E. Camilleri.

Intellectual Materialism:

The ideology of Intellectual Materialism is discussed in the second volume of *The Collected Works of The Science of Spiritual Talking: Intellectual Materialism and Negative Motivational Science, IM. NMS.* as well as in *The Seven Cosmic Worlds* by William E. Camilleri This is a term that signifies a form of thinking prevalent in all systems of thought where logic is divided into *Source – Relationship to the Effect – Effect* in such a way that one of these aspects of logical thought is missing partly or totally. For example, you have usually in the west material scientists who will not look at the origin of the earth other than it being of molecular structure with no known cause. This equals a person not looking at the *source.* Then you have people in the east who say that God is the origin of life and the earth and that material science is talking about dead matter. Such people are only looking at the *source* and are not looking at the *effect. See Volume 2: Intellectual Materialism and Negative Motivational Science, IM. NMS: The Collected Works of The Science of Spiritual Talking* and *The Seven Cosmic Worlds* by William E. Camilleri.

Jesus of Nazareth:

This is a Cosmic Guardian of the Light for mankind. His life was an example of a person who lived His Truth and showed mankind that mankind has the free will to choose the Light or darkness. *See The Gospels of St. Matthew, St. Mark, St. Luke and St. John.* [4]

John the Baptist:

The last Old Testament Prophet who proclaimed the coming of Jesus of Nazareth as the Light of the World. *See St. John's Gospel.* [5]

Light Shield:

This is the aura of an individual who, for example in *Initiation Pathway,* the seventh volume of *The Collected Works of The Science of Spiritual Talking* by William E. Camilleri, has been given by an Initiand a picture of his or her Soul in written form focusing on what is right for the person to know how to live his or her Truth and protect one's Light. *See Volume 7: Initiation Pathway: The Collected Works of The Science of Spiritual Talking* by William E. Camilleri.

Materialism:

This is a world perception founded on a belief, for example, that the origin of the universe is a group of molecules. *See Volume 4: The Twelve World Perceptions and the World Perceptions of Intellectual Materialism, Negative Motivational Science, Positive Motivational Science and the Science of Spiritual Talking: The Collected Works of The Science of Spiritual Talking* by William E. Camilleri.

Meditation of the Light:

This is a part of the process of the use of a Spiritual Pathway which is related to the use of Spiritual Keys of Light.

Moral Cosmic karma:

This is the karma of all individuals who see that when they pay their karmic debts willingly and with a will to the Light they change the future of their karma as well as fulfilling it.

Moral Light:

This is a Light that is received by those who follow their Moral Will and discover that the Light is given to them because they put it first in their lives by living their Truth first in their pathway. For example, a person like Mandela

---

[4] Matthew 1: 18-21, Luke 2: 1-6, John 1: 24-50, Mark 6: 7-14, Mark 8: 1-11, Mark 9: 1-19, Matthew 13: 35-53, Mark 8: 27, John 8: 52-59, John 10: 22-39, Luke 20: 1-20, John 11: 17-57, Matthew 27: 1-2, John: 19: 16-22, Luke 23: 32-56, Matthew 28: 1-20, John 21: 15-25.
[5] Matthew 11: 11, Luke 1: 13, Luke 1: 36, Matthew 3: 5-6, Matthew 3: 13-15, John 3: 30, Luke 3: 19-20, Matthew 14: 10, Matthew 17: 1-13, John 5: 35.

spoke of the Truth and there was Light in his voice, when he lived his Truth when in prison, and chose peace above war and revenge for apartheid.

Negative Motivational Science:

The ideology of Negative Motivational Science is discussed in the second volume of *The Collected Works of The Science of Spiritual Talking; Intellectual Materialism and Negative Motivational Science, IM. NMS* as well as in *The Seven Cosmic Worlds* by William E. Camilleri. This is the result of using Positive Motivational Science with the Intellectual Materialism principle. This refers, for example, to any individual who trains a person or group of individuals with the principle of 'where there is a will, there is a way.' When, for example, the 'way' is not based on S*ource –Relationship to the Effect – Effect [S.R.E.]* but on relationship to the effect – effect then the principle is based on a reality in the person's head and not the reality outside of it which is the S.R.E logic. This results, for example, in such conclusions as 'the end justifies the means,' which is Negative Motivational Science. This is an attitude in people who will say, 'where there is a will there is a way', when they base their will on inaccurate information or false ideals. *See Volume 2: Intellectual Materialism and Negative Motivational Science, IM. NMS: The Collected Works of The Science of Spiritual Talking* and *The Seven Cosmic Worlds* by William .E. Camilleri.

Philosophy of Light:

This is a philosophy that relates to seeing that the expression of the Living God and His language to mankind is the Language of the Light presented in the *Cosmic Christ World Light Shield.*

Positive Motivational Science [PMS]:

The ideology of Positive Motivational Science is discussed in the third volume of *The Collected Works of The Science of Spiritual Talking* by William E. Camilleri: *Positive Motivational Science, PMS.* This process works with the Science of Spiritual Talking Logic consciously or unconsciously as it works totally on proactively confronting a problem with the basis of interpreting the situation with a logical formation of thought based on all three components being present when speaking about any subject as a basis of motivation for another individual or group. It shows a person how to take away Intellectual Materialism and Negative

351

Motivational Science through the Science of Spiritual Talking PMS. so that the person can fulfil his dream of life. This is done by using S.R.E. logic. *See Volume 3, Positive Motivational Science, PMS: The Collected Works of The Science of Spiritual Talking* by William .E. Camilleri.

Satan:

This is a spiritual being that has the forces of the Hierarchies of darkness under the being's command. This being chose to use his free will to put himself above the Cosmic Father Guardian of the Light. He has no Light and is unredeemable eternally. [Devil, Prince of Evil, 'Ahriman'] His mission is to win over the Soul of mankind as well as every individual Soul. His dominant characteristic is his language and spirit of fear. [5] *See The Seven Cosmic Worlds* and *The Collected Works of The Science of Spiritual Talking* by William E. Camilleri.

Seven Cosmic Worlds:

These cosmic worlds are discussed within the body of work, *The Seven Cosmic Worlds* by William Camilleri. In sequence these are the past cosmic worlds of Saturn, Sun and Moon, the present cosmic world of Earth and the future cosmic worlds of Jupiter, Venus and Vulcan. *See 'Cosmic Worlds of Saturn, Sun, Moon and Earth,' The Seven Cosmic Worlds* and *The Collected Works of The Science of Spiritual Talking* by William E. Camilleri.

Spiritism:

This is one of the world perceptions which has its foundation in the belief that the Spiritual Universe created the material universe. *See Volume 4: The Twelve World Perceptions and the World Perceptions of Intellectual Materialism, Negative Motivational Science, Positive Motivational Science and the Science of Spiritual Talking: The Collected Works of The Science of Spiritual Talking* by William E. Camilleri.

Spiritual Clairvoyant Seeing:

This is a process that relates to seeing through the fifth body spirit. When the author does Spiritual Seeing he can see with physical eyes what is in the mind's eye as a living picture of actual life. *See The Seven Cosmic Worlds: Collation of Spiritual Clairvoyant Seeing* by William E. Camilleri.

---

[5] Ezekiel 28:17, Isaiah 14: 12-15, John 8: 44, Revelation 12: 8, Revelation 12: 9-12, Luke 10: 18, Ezekiel 28: 17, Revelation 13: 1-11, Revelation 16: 13-17, Revelation 20: 2-4, Revelation 20: 7-11.

Spiritual Cosmic Fire:

> This is the product of the transformation of Spiritual Light by the Cosmic Sword of the Archangel Michael. *See The Seven Cosmic Worlds* by William E. Camilleri.

Spiritual God Trinity:

> This is the three aspects of the Cosmic Cross of Heaven without the Archangel Michael. This is the Trinity upon which Christianity is based while the Science of Spiritual Talking is based on the Cosmic Cross of Heaven.

Spiritual Hierarchies of darkness:

> These are the beings from the Spiritual Hierarchies of Light that Ahriman corrupted in order that they would follow him. [6] *See The Collected Works of The Science of Spiritual Talking* and *The Seven Cosmic Worlds* by William E. Camilleri.

Spiritual Hierarchies of Light:

> These are the Beings that follow the Will of the Cosmic Cross of Heaven under the leadership of the Archangel Michael. *See The Collected Works of The Science of Spiritual Talking* and *The Seven Cosmic Worlds* by William E. Camilleri.

Spirits of Personality / Spirits of Time [Archai]:

> These Beings are the Spirits of Light that created time in the universe. These Spirits with the Father of All Universes, the Holy Spirit of the Light and the Cosmic Christ Being, used the Light of Heaven and the Archangel Michael as the Cosmic Cross of Heaven. These Spirits created the identity of the crown of all creation in the universe; the universal Soul identity of every human being in the Soul of mankind. Hence they created the personality of every being in the universe and its personality. [7] *See The Collected Works of The Science of Spiritual Talking* and *The Seven Cosmic Worlds* by William E. Camilleri.

Spirits of Form [Powers]:

> These Spiritual Beings created definition of time in the universe. They worked with the Spirits of Personality to evolve the Soul identity with the formation of its members so the Soul of the individual human being and the Soul of mankind and the earth would be formed into the shape of

---

[6] Ezekiel 28, Isaiah 14, Revelation 9: 13-17, Revelation 12: 7-10, Revelation 16: 12-17, Revelation 17: 1-7, Revelation 20: 7-10, 2 Peter 2: 4, Jude 6.

[7] Romans 8: 38, Ephesians 3: 10, Ephesians 6: 12, Colossians 1: 16, Colossians 2: 15.

being, a harmonious cosmos of order in the expression of the Ultimate Light coming from the Cosmic Cross of Heaven.[8] *See The Collected Works of The Science of Spiritual Talking* and *The Seven Cosmic Worlds* by William E. Camilleri.

Spirits of Movement [Mights]:

These Spiritual Beings created the energy that evolved the forms of life that originated on cosmic worlds. That is, the physical body spirit on Saturn cosmic world, the etheric body spirit on Sun cosmic world, the astral body spirit on Moon cosmic world and the spiritual ego spirit on Earth cosmic world.[9] *See The Collected Works of The Science of Spiritual Talking* and *The Seven Cosmic Worlds* by William E. Camilleri.

Spirits of Wisdom [Dominions]:

These Spiritual Beings on the cosmic planet of Earth created the Principles of how to use Time - Form - Energy in the individual Moral Will of an individual being. They created the Principles of the Ultimate Light in relation to *The Collected Works of The Science of Spiritual Talking* by William Camilleri.[10] *See The Collected Works of The Science of Spiritual Talking* and *The Seven Cosmic Worlds* by William E. Camilleri.

Spirits of Will [Thrones]:

These Spiritual Beings created an evolution of the four previous spirits in the Soul of mankind. These Beings are now creating the future fifth body spirit of mankind to live on Jupiter cosmic world after the cosmic planet of Earth ends. These Spiritual Beings also form Cosmic Swords of Light that transform that Light into Spiritual Fire to control the evolution of the Will of Heaven upon the earth and in the universe so as to protect the Light of the Cosmic Cross of Heaven.[11] *See The Collected Works of The Science of Spiritual Talking* and *The Seven Cosmic Worlds* by William E. Camilleri.

Spirits of Harmony [Cherubim]:

These Spirit Beings created harmony in the evolution of the four spirit bodies of mankind and are working with the Thrones to develop this Will to the Light and this Ultimate Moral Will to win the War of All the Light against All the

---

[8] Ephesians 1:21, 1 Peter 3: 22.

[9] Ephesians 1: 21, 1 Peter 3: 22.

[10] Ephesians 1: 21, Colossians 1: 16.

[11] Colossians 1: 16.

354

darkness. These Spirit Beings are going to evolve a Race of Light on the future cosmic world of Venus which will fight, with the power of the Thrones of Light, the Ultimate Master of Darkness and his race of evil.[12] *See The Collected Works of The Science of Spiritual Talking and The Seven Cosmic Worlds* by William E. Camilleri.

Spirits of Love [Seraphim]:

These Spirit Beings created the Principle of the Ultimate Will to the Light eternally. These Beings work with all men to see their ultimate destiny is a Spiritual Universe of Light. They are called Spirits of Love as they are connected supremely to the relationship of the Cosmic Cross of Heaven. These Spirit Beings are seen in human interpretation as Spirits of Love but they are truly the Spirits of Relationship to the Ultimate Light. Their primary pathway is to put the Cosmic Cross of Heaven first in their existence. They communicate with all other Hierarchies as they conduct the Government of Heaven. On the future Vulcan cosmic world they will be the officials of Heaven preparing for the Last Judgment of all of mankind.[13] *See The Collected Works of The Science of Spiritual Talking and The Seven Cosmic Worlds* by William E. Camilleri.

Sun Oracle:

This is the Oracle of the Ultimate Light; the Cosmic Christ Being. The Cosmic Christ Being became the Head Sun Spirit or Sun Oracle that took the Spiritual Hierarchies of Light to work on the fixed star of the sun in the cosmos at the time of the separation of the sun from the cosmic world of Earth. From here the Head Sun Spirit incarnated on the earth as a human being with supernatural powers and His Spiritual Being ever evolves in the consciousness of all cosmic worlds, including the Earth cosmic world, in the consciousness of every planet and in the consciousness of every human being. *See The Collected Works of The Science of Spiritual Talking and The Seven Cosmic Worlds* by William E. Camilleri.

The Key of Light:

This is a process which is based on asking the Ultimate Light and the Archangel Michael to send their Light to the darkness. *See The Collected Works of The Science of*

---

[12] Genesis 3: 24, Psalm 80:1, Psalm 99:1, Isaiah 37: 16.
[13] Isaiah 6: 2, Isaiah 6: 6, Ezekiel 1: 13.

Spiritual Talking and *The Seven Cosmic Worlds* by William E. Camilleri.

Ultimate Light:

This is the Light that one looks to when one puts the Cosmic Christ Light first in his or her life.

Ultimate Truth:

This is the Truth that one looks to the Light with, when a person puts his or her Truth as a part of the whole Truth; the Ultimate Truth of life.

War of All against All:

This is the War of all the Light against all the darkness in the world. This is a war that is being waged now on earth between all who will the Light against all who will darkness. It forecasts the war on the cosmic planet of Venus to come when the Cosmic Cross of Heaven will fight the ultimate Master of darkness to prepare for the last judgment of the human race on the cosmic planet of Vulcan. *See The Collected Works of The Science of Spiritual Talking* and *The Seven Cosmic Worlds* by William E. Camilleri.

World System of Knowledge:

This is a Knowledge System that covers the four dimensions of a complete science, for example the Science of Spiritual Talking Four World System of Knowledge. *See Volume 6: Four World System of Cosmic Knowledge: The Collected Works of The Science of Spiritual Talking* by William E. Camilleri.

INDEX

Ch – Chapter references,
V – Verse references,
These references are pertinent to
the 'Cosmic Christ World Light Shield,'
'The Collected Works of The Science of Spiritual Talking'
[CWSST] [Volumes 1-9] and
'The Seven Cosmic Worlds' [TSCW]
by William E. Camilleri.

A

358

Ch 12: V 17,
Ch 14: V 12
See Index: CWSST, TSCW

C

Caesar, Ch 6: V 9,
Ch 7: V 6, V 7, V 8, V 17, V 18,
Ch 8: V 4,
Ch 9: V 1,
Ch 11: V 11, V 19,
Ch 12: V 3,
Ch 13: V 2, V 6,
Ch 14: V 3,
Ch 15: V 6,
Ch 18: V 2, V 8, V 9, V 14,
V 16, V 17,
Ch 19: V 4, V 19, V 6, V 8

Ca'iaphas, Ch 11: V 19,
Ch 12: V 3,
Ch 18: V 2, V 13, V 14, V 15,
V 16

Christ, Ch 1: V 5, V 6, V 9, V 12,
Ch 3: V 3, V 9, V 16, V 16,
V 17,
Ch 4: V 14,
Ch 5: V 4, V 5, V 7, V 10: V 11,
V 13, V 15, V 17,
Ch 6: V 8, V 2, V 6, V 7, V 8, V
14, V 15, V 16, V 17,
Ch 7: V 2, V 3, V 4, V 6, V 7,
V 8,
Ch 8: V 2, V 8, V 9, V 11, V 12,
Ch 9: V 1, V 5, V 6, V 10, V 11,
Ch 10: V 5, V 7, V 9, V 10,
V 11, V 14,
Ch 11: V 1, V 2, V 3, V 5, V 7,
V 9,
V 10, V 11, V 13, V 14, V 17,
V 18, V 19,
Ch 12: V 2, V 3, V 6, V 10,
V 12, V 13, V 14, V 16, V 17,

V 18,
Ch 13: V 2, V 3 V 5, V 6, V 7,
V 8, V 10, V 11, V 12, V 13,
Ch 14: V 1, V 4, V 8, V 12,
Ch 15: V 3, V 4,
Ch 16: V 4, V 6, V 8,
Ch 17: V 1,
Ch 18: V 12, V 16, V 18,
Ch 19: V 2, V 4, V 9, V 10,
Ch 20: V 1, V 2, V 6, V 8,
Ch 21: V 4, V 7
See **'Being of [the]
Christ,' ' Christ Being,'
'Christ Being of Light,'
'Christ, Jesus; King of
the Light of Mankind,'
'Cosmic Christ,' 'Cosmic
Christ Being,' 'Cosmic
Christ Being of Light,'
'Cosmic King,' 'Cosmic
King of Light,'
'Cosmic King of
mankind,' 'Cosmic
Master,' 'Jesus,' 'Jesus
Christ,' 'Jesus of
Nazareth,' 'King of
Kings,' 'King of Kings of
the Light of Mankind,'
'King of Light,' 'Light
of the World,' 'Light of
the Universe,' 'Living
Great Soul of Light,'
'Master of all Creation,'
'Master of the Light,'
'Master of the Light of
the Universe,' 'Son of
God,' 'Son of Man,' 'Son
of the Eternal Father in
Heaven,' 'Ultimate
Redeemer of Mankind'
and 'Ultimate Son of the
Light'**
See Index: CWSST, TSCW

360

362

V 19,
Ch 13: V 1, V 2,
Ch 14: V 2, V 5, V 12,
Ch 16: V 1, V 9,
Ch 18: V 3, V 16, V 17,
Ch 20: V 4,
Ch 21: V 1

See Index: CWSST, TSCW

Cosmic Christ, Ch 8: V 15,
Ch 9: V 11,
Ch 10: V 4, V 9, V 12, V 14,
Ch 11: V 10, V 11,
Ch 12: V 12, V 16, V 18,
Ch 13: V 6, V 12,
Ch 14: V 1, V 5, V 6, V 8,
V 12,
Ch 15: V 5,
Ch 16: V 3, V 4, V 7, V 10,
V 11,
Ch 17: V 2, V 3, V 6, V 8,
Ch 18: V 2, V 4, V 14, V 16,
Ch 19: V 12, V 14,
Ch 20: V 1, V 2, V 3, V 4, V 5,
V 6, V 8,
Ch 21: V 2, V 4, V 5

See 'Being of [the]
Christ,' 'Christ,'
'Christ Being,' 'Christ
Being of Light,' 'Christ
Jesus; King of the Light
of Mankind,'
'Cosmic Christ Being,'
'Cosmic Christ Being of
Light,' 'Cosmic King of
Mankind,' 'Cosmic
Master,' 'Jesus,' 'Jesus
Christ,' 'Jesus of
Nazareth,' 'King of
Kings,' 'King of Kings of
the Light,' 'Light of
the World,' 'Light
of the Universe,' 'Living

'Great Soul of Light,'
'Master of all Creation,'
'Master of the Light,'
'Master of the Light of
the Universe,' 'Son of
God,' 'Son of Man,'
'Son of the Eternal
Father in Heaven,'
'Ultimate Redeemer of
Mankind' and 'Ultimate
Son of the Light,'

See Index: CWSST, TSCW

Cosmic Christ Being, Ch 8: V 6,
Ch 10: V 2,
Ch 13: V 1,
Ch 14: V 10,
Ch 15: V 1, V 4,
Ch 16: V 1,
Ch 17: V 5,
Ch 19: V 4, V 13,
Ch 20: V 8,
Ch 21: V 6, V 7

See 'Being of [the]
Christ, 'Christ,' 'Christ
Being,' 'Christ Being of
Light,' 'Christ Jesus;
King of the Light of
Mankind,' 'Cosmic
Christ,' 'Cosmic Christ
Being of Light,' 'Cosmic
King,' 'Cosmic King of
Light,' 'Cosmic King of
mankind,' 'Cosmic
Master,' 'Jesus,' 'Jesus
Christ,' 'Jesus of
Nazareth,' 'King of
Kings,' 'King of Kings of
the Light,' 'Light of the
World,' 'Light of the
Universe,' 'Living Great
Soul of Light,' 'Master of
all Creation,' 'Master of

363

D

366

E

F

Being of Light,' 'Cosmic
Christ, King of Light,'
'Cosmic King,' 'Cosmic
King of Light,' 'Cosmic
King of Mankind,'
'Cosmic Master,' 'Jesus,'
'Jesus of Nazareth,'
'King of Kings,' 'King of
Kings of the Light of
mankind,' 'King of
Light,' 'Light of the
World,' 'Light of the
Universe,' 'Living Great
Soul of Light,' 'Master of
all Creation,' 'Master of
the Light,' 'Master of
the Light of the
Universe,' 'Son of God,'
'Son of Man,' 'Son of the
Eternal Father in
Heaven,' 'Son of the
Living God,' 'Ultimate
Redeemer of Mankind'
and 'Ultimate Son of the
Light'

See Index: CWSST, TSCW

Jesus of Nazareth, Ch 1: V 13,
Ch 7: V 5, V 7,
Ch 8: V 6, V 7,
Ch 9: V 5,
Ch 12: V 6,
Ch 14: V 4,
Ch 18: V 2, V 4, V 5, V 6, V 8,
V 11, V 14,
Ch 19: V 4, V 5, V 12
See 'Being of [the]
Christ,' 'Christ,' 'Christ
Being,' 'Christ Being of
Light,' 'Christ, Jesus;
King of the Light of
Mankind,' 'Cosmic
Christ,' 'Cosmic Christ
Being,' 'Cosmic Christ

Being of Light,' 'Cosmic
Christ, King of Light.'
'Cosmic King,' 'Cosmic
King of Light,' 'Cosmic
King of mankind,'
'Cosmic Master,' 'Jesus,'
' Jesus Christ,' 'King of
Kings,' 'King of Kings of
the Light of mankind,'
'King of Light,' 'Light of
the World,' 'Light of the
universe,' 'Living Great
Soul of Light,' 'Master of
all Creation,' 'Master of
the Light,' 'Master of the
Light of the Universe,'
'Son of God,' 'Son of
Man,' 'Son of the
Eternal Father in
Heaven,' 'Son of the
Living God,' 'Ultimate
Redeemer of Mankind'
and 'Ultimate Son of the
Light,'

See Index: CWSST, TSCW

Job, Ch 8: V 13

John, the Apostle, Ch 1: V 13
Ch 13: V 7,
Ch 18: V 10, V 14,
Ch 19: V 9, V 11,
Ch 20: V 1, V 2, V 8,
Ch 21: V 8
See Index: CWSST

John the Baptist, Ch 1: V 2, V 5,
V 6, V 7, V8, V 9,
Ch 3: V 2, V 9, V 11, V 12,
Ch 4: V 1, V 15,
Ch 6: V 5,
Ch 7: V 9,
Ch 8: V 6,
Ch 10: V 7, V 14,
Ch 12: V 13,
Ch 13: V 1,

375

Ch 20: V 7

N

Ch 19: V 12, V 13, V 14

P

379

Ch 5: V 14, V 16, V 19,
Ch 6: V 11,
Ch 8: V 7, V 9, V 14,
Ch 10: V 7, V 10,
Ch 11: V 6, V 10, V 14,
Ch 12: V 7, V 9, V 13,
Ch 14: V 13,
Ch 18: V 2,
Ch 20: V 4

See 'Being of [the] Christ,' 'Christ,' 'Christ Being,' 'Cosmic Christ,' 'Cosmic Christ Being,' 'Jesus,' 'Jesus Christ' and 'Jesus of Nazareth'

Special Cosmic Spiritual Keys,
Ch 21: V 7

See 'Cosmic Keys of Light,' 'Cosmic Special Keys of Light,' 'Keys of Christ,' 'Key[s] of Light,' 'Special Keys of Christ,' 'Special Keys of Light,' 'Special Keys of the Ultimate Light,' 'Special Spiritual Key of Christ', 'Special Spiritual Key of Light' and 'Spiritual Key of Light'

Special Keys of Christ,
Ch 4: V 16,
Ch 6: V 2, V 8, V 9,
Ch 7: V 7,
Ch 8: V 7,
Ch 11: V 11, V 18,
Ch 13: V 3, V 12,
Ch 14: V 7,
Ch 15: V 2,
Ch 19: V 11

See 'Cosmic Keys of Light,' 'Cosmic Special Keys of Light,' 'Keys of Christ,' 'Key[s] of Light,' 'Special Cosmic Spiritual Keys, 'Special Keys of Light,' 'Special Keys of the Ultimate Light,' 'Special Spiritual Key of Christ' and 'Special Spiritual Key of Light'

Special Keys of Light,
Ch 2: V 6,
Ch 4: V 19,
Ch 6: V 7,
Ch 8: V 2,
Ch 10: V 5, V 9, V 12,
Ch 11: V 2,
Ch 13: V 1,
Ch 15: V 4,
Ch 16: V 3, V 9,
Ch 17: V 5

See 'Cosmic Keys of Light,' 'Cosmic Special Keys of Light,' 'Keys of Christ,' 'Key[s] of Light,' 'Special Cosmic Spiritual Keys of Christ,' 'Special Keys of Christ,' 'Special Keys of the Ultimate Light,' 'Special Spiritual Key of Christ,' 'Special Spiritual Key of Light' and 'Spiritual Key of Light'

Special Keys of the Ultimate Light,
Ch 4: V 17

382

384

T

Teacher of the Light, *See*
'Being of [the]
Christ,' 'Christ,' 'Christ
Being,' 'Cosmic Christ,'
'Cosmic Christ Being,'
'Jesus,' 'Jesus Christ'
and 'Jesus of Nazareth:'
Ch 1: v 9,
Ch 3: v 1,
Ch 6: v 9,
Ch 10: v 10,
Ch 12: v 13
See 'John the Baptist'
and 'Soul of John the
Baptist:'
Ch 1: v 6,
Ch 3: v 12,
Ch 10: v 14,
Ch 14: v 11,
Ch 18: v 2
See Index: CWSST, TSCW

Thomas, the Apostle,
Ch 11: v 9,
Ch 14: v 2,
Ch 20: v 6, v 7

Trinity [the] Ch 11: v 6,
Ch 14: v 5
See 'Cosmic Trinity of
Light,' 'Trinity of
Cosmic Light' and
'Trinity of Light'

Trinity of Cosmic Light,
Ch 12: v 17
See 'Cosmic Trinity of
Light,' 'Trinity [the]' and
'Trinity of Light'

Trinity of Light, Ch 12: v 18,
Ch 13: v 6,
Ch 14: v 6,
Ch 16: v 3

See 'Cosmic Trinity of
Light,' 'Trinity [the]' and
'Trinity of Cosmic Light'

Truth, *See* 'Moral
Truth,'
See Index: CWSST, TSCW

U

Ultimate Being, *See* 'Being of
the Father,' 'Father
[God, the Father]' 'God,'
'God, the Father in
Heaven; the Living God
of all Ages' and
'Ultimate God of Light'
Ch 5: v 18,
Ch 6: v 3,
See 'Being of [the]
Christ,' 'Christ,' 'Christ
Being,' 'Cosmic Christ,'
'Cosmic Christ Being,'
'Jesus,' 'Jesus Christ,'
and 'Jesus of Nazareth'
Ch 6: v 6, v 10, v 12,
Ch 7: v 1, v 13,
Ch 8: v 1,
Ch 9: v 1
See Index: CWSST, TSCW

Ultimate Cosmic Being,
Ch 13: v 12,
Ch 18: v 3
See 'Being of [the]
Christ,' 'Christ,' 'Christ
Being,' 'Cosmic Christ,'
'Cosmic Christ Being,'
'Jesus,' 'Jesus Christ'
and 'Jesus of Nazareth,'
See Index: CWSST, TSCW

Ultimate Cosmic City of Light,
Ch 12: v 2
See 'City of Light,'

W

Printed in the United States
by Baker & Taylor Publisher Services

Printed in the United States
by Baker & Taylor Publisher Services